PAUL BLANSHARD ON VATICAN II

PAUL BLANSHARD ON VATICAN II

By PAUL BLANSHARD

BEACON PRESS ❧ BOSTON

BY PAUL BLANSHARD

An Outline of the British Labor Movement
What's the Matter With New York? (with Norman Thomas)
Investigating City Government
Democracy and Empire in the Caribbean
American Freedom and Catholic Power
Communism, Democracy and Catholic Power
The Right to Read
The Irish and Catholic Power
God and Man in Washington
Freedom and Catholic Power in Spain and Portugal
Religion and the Schools: The Great Controversy
Paul Blanshard on Vatican II

Published simultaneously in Canada by Saunders of Toronto, Ltd.

Beacon Press books are published under the auspices
of the Unitarian Universalist Association

Printed in the United States of America

Magazine articles partially derived from this book have been copyrighted by *Encounter*, *The Catholic World*, *The Register-Leader* of the Unitarian Universalist Association, *The Humanist*, and *The Congress Bi-Weekly of the American Jewish Congress.*

First published as a Beacon paperback in 1967

FOR BEATRICE
AND FOR EIGHT GRANDCHILDREN AND
THEIR GENERATION ❧ JUDY, PETER,
NANCY, CLEMENCY, LUKE,
BAILEY, STEPHEN, ALEXANDER

CONTENTS

PREFACE

THIS book tries to do two things: report on the Vatican Council of 1962–1965 and appraise it in the light of traditional American democratic values. In order to carry out the second purpose I have selected for extended discussion and evaluation those issues arising in the Council which, it seems to me, have the greatest importance for Western society. What did the Council *mean* for our future? The answer to that question seemed to me just as important as the simpler question: What happened at the Council?

The public was flooded with good reports about the events at the Council; it was not inundated with over-all critical appraisals of their significance. To carry out the larger function of criticism I have included a great deal of material about the Council's effect on America, including many quotations of fact and opinion in the American Catholic press. In many ways I consider the events in the development of American Catholicism during the Council years more important than the specific events in St. Peter's, although what happened in America could not have happened without the impetus of Council developments. And for me the pre-Council work of Pope John is an organic part of Council events.

Since I want to examine seriously those issues and policies of Vatican II that affect American life, particularly those basic and controversial policies of clerical power that many are reluctant to discuss, I am as much interested in what the Council did *not* do as in its positive accomplishments. It accomplished great things, but it also dodged, evaded, and bypassed several vital issues. The analysis of this process of evasion must be considered a necessary part of the narrative.

Most of the material in this study comes directly from the Vatican Council itself, since I attended very faithfully the second and fourth sessions in Rome, collected all the relevant documents from all sessions, and took full advantage of press conferences and innumerable interviews. But I have chosen not to quote many individuals by name apart from their public utterances. A book like this has to be either personal or impersonal. The impersonal method seems to me better. A drama critic is often more effective if he never meets the actors whose performance he criticizes, and in one sense I conceived of my role in Rome from 1963 to 1965 as a critic without portfolio. I was pleased to make friends with scores of bishops and theologians and to hear their views, but it would not be fair to quote them in conversational fragments.

I cannot, however, refrain from one brief personal comment. I suppose no other American has written so many pages critical of Catholic policy. Certainly no other American writer of my time has been the target of more brickbats in the American Catholic press. When I went to Rome I could not help but wonder what kind of reception I would receive. I must say that no writer was ever treated with more genuine consideration. For me there was complete friendliness, complete interchange of fact and argument, and the greatest possible generosity in supplying me with every pertinent document. The door was open and no intellectual holds were barred.

I came away from the Council feeling that these men were Christian gentlemen of a high order whose sincerity I could not doubt. Although I marveled that they continued to accept certain presuppositions that seemed to me outdated, I rejoiced that the Church they represented could no longer be described as a monolithic glacier of reactionary thought. They had opened the door to the modern world—and to me.

I am often asked: Have you changed your opinion about the Catholic Church? The answer is "Yes," but only to the extent that the Catholic Church has changed. I am as hostile as I ever was to the autocracy of its central power structure and to many of the family and church-state policies that flow from that clerical autocracy. But I am delighted that during the Council years the Church has begun to break out from its medieval cocoon and that it is showing signs of a willingness ultimately to fly with the wings of true intellectual freedom. It is still feudal but no longer frozen. As Pope Paul has put it: "The summoning of the Council has dislodged us from the torpor of ordinary life." The Roman Catholic Church can never again be quite the same after Vatican II.

PAUL BLANSHARD

Rome, and Thetford Center, Vermont

CALENDAR OF DATES

October 9, 1958–Death of Pius XII
October 28, 1958–Election of John XXIII
January 5, 1959–Announcement by Pope John of coming Council
May 15, 1961–Pope John's encyclical *Mater et Magistra*
October 11, 1962–Opening of first session
December 8, 1962–Closing of first session
April 11, 1963–Pope John's encyclical *Pacem in Terris*
June 3, 1963–Death of Pope John
June 21, 1963–Election of Pope Paul VI
September 29, 1963–Opening of second session
November 22, 1963–Death of President Kennedy
December 4, 1963–Closing of second session
January 4–6, 1964–Pope Paul's journey to the Holy Land
September 14, 1964–Opening of third session
November 21, 1964–Closing of third session
December 2–5, 1964–Pope Paul's journey to India
September 14, 1965–Opening of fourth session
October 4, 1965–Pope Paul's address at United Nations
December 8, 1965–Closing of the Council

CONSTITUTIONS, DECREES, AND DECLARATIONS OF VATICAN II

Dogmatic Constitution on the Church
Pastoral Constitution on the Church in the Modern World
Constitution on the Sacred Liturgy
Decree on Ecumenism
Declaration on Religious Freedom
Dogmatic Constitution on Divine Revelation
Decree on the Bishops' Pastoral Office
Decree on Priestly Formation
Decree on the Renewal of the Religious Life
Decree on the Apostolate of the Laity
Decree on Eastern Catholic Churches
Decree on the Ministry and Life of Priests
Decree on the Church's Missionary Activity
Declaration on Christian Education
Declaration on Non-Christian Religions
Decree on the Instruments of Social Communication

CHAPTER ONE ❧ WHAT WAS THIS COUNCIL?

PHYSICALLY Vatican II was a great ecclesiastical circus, a very solemn and holy circus without clowns but with plenty of side shows. The center ring was in the basilica of St. Peter's, the largest and most majestic of the world's churches. The side shows were in countless lecture halls and committee rooms around the Vatican Palace and along the Via della Conciliazione in Rome, just outside the walled, 108-acre state called Vatican City.

It was probably the greatest religious conference of all time. Certainly it was the most colorful, and the color was in the costumes and the faces as well as the vast, gaudy aula—the central hall—of St. Peter's. Nothing quite like it had ever been seen before, even in the long history of twenty previous Church Councils, stretching back to Nicaea in 325 A.D.[1] Those past Councils were all comparatively small, turned inward, little concerned with the affairs of the world, lacking the enormous centripetal pull of a world audience provided by television, radio and wire sources.

At Vatican II the bishops gathered on a lighted stage on which every leading figure cast a towering shadow. Here were all races and almost all nations—sixty-three Negro bishops from the Latin Church alone, and ultimately two Negro cardinals. Black faces and brown faces and Mongolian faces mingled with the great throng of magenta-and-lace–clad bishops who poured out of the basilica door each noon, streamed down St. Peter's Square past the statues of St. Peter and St. Paul like pastel beetles, and climbed awkwardly into their waiting automobiles. The scarlet silk of the cardinals mingled with the softer shades of the bishops. Here and there walked a full-bearded oriental bishop with tall headdress, or a lean superior of a religious order wrapped in conspicuous black. And behind came a few Protestant observers in drab grey pants.

On those rare open days when the pope appeared in the Council and processions formed, the effect was almost blinding. There were scarlet tunics and Renaissance armor and white ruffs and jewel-encrusted crosses and flashing swords and a sea of white miters—and through it all a white-clad ecclesiastical autocrat carried by uniformed guards on a swaying *sedia gestatoria*, known as His Holiness the Pope, Vicar of Jesus Christ, Successor of St. Peter, Prince of the Apostles, Supreme Pontiff of the Universal Church, Patriarch of the West, Primate of Italy, Archbishop and Metropolitan of the Roman Province, and Sovereign of the Holy See and the State of Vatican City.

Inside St. Peter's during much of the open sessions there was the atmosphere of a football rally. Cheers for *Il Papa* were almost as wild as for a long-passing quarterback. Elegantly upholstered bleachers had been erected down each side of the cathedral nave, with scarlet upholstery for the cardinals' seats and green for the others. At the Altar of the Confession under Bernini's towering cedar columns, which looked strangely voluptuous, were the elevated seat for the pope and the almost equally elevated seats for the presiding cardinals of the day.

The electronic age had entered even this Catholic holy of holies. Excellent loud-speakers had been installed in every section of the bleachers so that even in the barn-like vault of the painted ceiling, every word could be heard. A bishop whose turn to speak had arrived simply stepped down to the microphone in his section and spoke his prepared speech, his voice booming out into the vast aula, magnified a hundredfold. Even his voting was electrified. He wrote his decision on a ballot with a magnetic pencil, and computers did the counting with reasonable swiftness.

Altogether there were nearly 2,600 of these bishops, abbots, and heads of religious orders present at any favorable time—a typical attendance figure was about 2,300 out of the world's 2,883 Catholic bishops. Sickness and old age kept many away, and behind the Iron Curtain there were many more whose absence represented virtual internment. Besides the bishops, abbots, and heads of religious orders—all of whom were voting delegates at the Council—there were hundreds of camp followers, some of them more important in the Council results than the bishops themselves. There was the Council "brain trust," the more than 400 nonvoting *periti* or experts who often told the pedestrian bishops what to think and why. There were hundreds of helpers and assistants and auxiliaries, in addition to the non-Catholic observers, the permanent staff members of the Roman Curia, and countless Swiss Guards, Papal Guards, gendarmes, Chamberlains of the Sword and Cloak—down to the gardeners, the keepers of the three Vatican cemeteries, and the cleaning squads for the vast Vatican Palace with its 1,400 rooms.

In spite of its lofty moral purpose, this whole assembly was stratified in terms of rank, the rank of an ecclesiastical imperialism still functioning in the middle of the twentieth century in rigidly defined classes. Everywhere this class stratification was evident. Everywhere clerically produced inequality triumphed over the outward professions of humility and brotherhood. The pope was considered too high even to participate in the Council's deliberations, and he was treated throughout like a divine emperor. The approximately one hundred cardinals, entering the basilica through their own doors with their swishing scarlet silk, were set aside from all ordinary bishops not only by their red plush seats but also by their superior rights in debate. An ordinary bishop could file his speech and wait for weeks to be heard; a cardinal could send in his speech at the last minute and speak at the head of the day's calendar.

The Council never pretended to be a democratic assembly or even a truly representative assembly, although a large part of the public persisted in regarding it as such. Not a single bishop in the vast assembly had been chosen or ratified by the people of his domain. Every one had been appointed by the pope and was transferable by the pope.[2] In the whole assembly there was not a single voting layman or voting woman, or even a voting priest acting simply as a priest. Only in the small group of the heads of religious orders was there any semblance of representation; these men had been chosen in part by democratic process by the members of their orders, although even in this case voting rights were not extended to all members.

The Catholic liberals were just as frank about this undemocratic character of the Council as the non-Catholic critics. "Actually," said the Catholic historian Henry Daniel-Rops, "an Ecumenical Council is not the parliament of the Church; it is not a meeting of elected representatives who have received a mandate from the people . . . there is nothing democratic about the delegation of the bishops' power. An ecumenical council is emphatically not a constituent assembly."[3] John Cogley and Father Gregory Baum put it even more frankly in *America* and *Commonweal*. Cogley, one of the important liberal Catholic laymen at the Council, said after observing its activities that "his [the layman's] part in the actual day-to-day business has been more that of a Hollywood extra than of a supporting actor. . . . You do not kid yourself: this is a clerical affair—the great gulf remains fixed. . . . The style of thought in Rome is invincibly clerical."[4] And Gregory Baum, one of the leading *periti* at the Council, criticized the secrecy of the whole decision-making process by saying: "This whole secretive world is frightening. That the Church of the Lord in some of its governmental forms should have remained in this pre-democratic pattern of monarchical life causes the most painful anguish and depression." Father Baum wrote this caustic criticism of Council procedure more than two years after the opening of the Council, and after he had attended three sessions.

It is quite reasonable to describe the Second Vatican Council as a purely colonial assembly, an advisory assembly, operating within an imperial system, utterly without power to change the Roman Catholic Church except by the consent of the pope. In spite of the enthusiastic descriptions of the Council as the beginning of a "revolution," the Vatican itself never pretended that the Council was anything more than an advisory assembly called for the primary purpose of promoting the interests of that clerical establishment which monopolizes all power within the Catholic system of government. The alleged 590,000,000 Catholic people of the world were deeply interested in this assembly but they had no power in it.[5]

One glance at the power structure of the Church will reveal why no Council operating under present canon law could be anything else but advisory and subordinate. Every ecumenical council, governed under Canons 222–229, must be called by the pope, who presides at every session either personally or through a representative and confirms every decree of every council before it becomes valid. When the pope dies, the council dies. Although the council is given "supreme power over the entire Church," that power is always and specifically dependent on the pope, and "there is no appeal from the pope to the council."

The real working power structure of the Church, described in Canons 242–264, is the Roman Curia with its 12 Congregations, 3 Tribunals, and 6 Offices. Contrary to many journalistic descriptions, it is not the civil service of the Church but a gigantic interlocking network of papal power, an extension of the pope's authority and not of any council's authority. It is not based on any merit system and gives no tenure of office to anybody. It is officially designed only to "assist the Pope in administering the affairs of the Church." In times past it has often gathered unto itself so much power that it has made the pope a *de facto* prisoner of his own bureaucracy. Because of the problems of language and location, the Roman Curia is an Italian machine. Its members speak Italian in their day-to-day activity and operate with an essentially Italian point of view. Of course there are cardinals and bishops from many nations in the various Congregations, Tribunals, and Offices, but the Italian cardinals, sitting on many bodies simultaneously and living permanently in Rome, rule the whole amalgam with the skill and aplomb of an American interlocking directorate.

Nevertheless, in spite of its tremendous power, the Roman

Curia was on the defensive at Vatican II because of several special factors. There was Pope John—and we will discuss his surprising spirit in the next chapter. There was the natural cohesive force of some 2,500 bishops from all parts of the world who possessed a special professional desire for more power and who learned to know each other and to develop new techniques of cooperation. Out of their collective thinking came a new realization of episcopal power and a new appreciation of the failure of the Church's central bureaucracy to provide either justice or efficiency.

In technical organization Vatican II could not be considered an efficient assembly, either from the democratic point of view or the authoritarian point of view. Its method of organization almost invited a perpetual filibuster by the reactionary members of the Roman Curia, and these members were adroit enough to take full advantage of the opportunity. The original agenda was manipulated in order to concentrate on ecclesiastical platitudes while the most important subjects were delayed. A whole week in the second session was dedicated to a discussion of the proposition that holiness is a good thing. The regular 3-hour morning sessions were cut to about two working hours by a repetition of the Mass and special prayers. Speeches, written out in Latin, had to be submitted well in advance, and this destroyed all spontaneity. There was no way by which an individual bishop could stand up and say, "I move so and so," and thus force a vote on the merits of his motion. He could not accomplish this purpose even when the great majority of the assembly might agree with him.

Officially, however, the Church's preparatory work was tremendous and impressive. Over a period of three years the original Preparatory Commission, with about 1,000 aides, collected from bishops and other religious leaders throughout the world literally thousands of suggestions. They sent out to the Fathers 119 booklets on agenda subjects. If there was a fearful imbalance of power in the whole arrangement, that was because of the imbalance in Rome. The original preparatory commissions, although they numbered 871 individuals from 70 countries, were virtually all headed by Italian Curia officials who were systematically conservative in their outlook toward change.

The discussion on the original 69 leading items of the agenda meandered like a stream in broken fields, disappearing underground and coming to the surface again. The original 69 topics were boiled down to 17 and later to 13, but the agenda that emerged was not designed primarily for action. The first session adjourned without a single action on a single item, with many surviving schemata* buried somewhere in a consulting commission or reposing on a desk in the Holy Office or in the Pope's chambers. Subjects doubled back on themselves in such a way that at one time three or more subjects were on a single daily calendar. Even by the end of the second session only two documents had been promulgated. Two of the most important items on the agenda for the non-Catholic world, religious liberty and the Church's attitude toward the Jews, were not even on the Council's original agenda. They were pushed into the forefront of the debate by outside pressure.

The discussions in the aula, the great hall of St. Peter's, were often ineffably boring and repetitive, but this was not always the fault of the bishops themselves. To some extent the monotony was a by-product of the determination of two popes finally to permit a considerable amount of free speech to some 2,500 bishops. A discussion by 2,500 bishops of almost any subject in an unfamiliar language might have ended in some repetition, confusion, and monotony. It did.

Two special factors worked to impair the efficiency of Vatican II as a working assembly. It was essentially a congress of old men, and it operated in a dead language, Latin. Both of these factors are the outgrowth of long-established traditions in the Church. In a sense they are defects of the Church itself rather than defects of the Council. The defect of the outdated seniority system is much the most important of the two, and at the present

* The Greek word *schema*, plural *schemata*, was used in the Council to describe each major draft document.

time there does not seem to be any reasonable prospect of its elimination.

All Catholic bishops are appointed for life, and the average bishop is made a bishop only ten years before he dies, about the time when the average American business man expects to retire. Every bishop has a strong economic motive to hang on to his position even after retirement age. There is at present no compulsory retirement system and no world-wide social security system for retired prelates.

During the discussion of compulsory retirement for aged bishops at the second session, Cardinal Ruffini, aged 75, protested:

> It is wrong to insist on resignation for ailing and aging bishops. Some sick men with great virtue do more good for the Church than some healthier young men. The Pope is the bishop of the Universal Church and yet no one dreams of suggesting that he resign. Leo XIII died at the age of 93 and John XXIII was about 80—[he was actually 77]—when he became pope. Pope John recounted once that when Leo XIII, already at an advanced age, was urging resignation on an elderly bishop, the latter looked at him quietly and said: "Holy Father, we are both old."

Even in the United States, where Catholic bishops seem more vigorous than their European counterparts, and where there is no need to fear an old age of complete destitution, the age level is much too high by standards of private industry or public service. In 1965, according to the *National Catholic Reporter*, 45 of the 141 acting diocesan heads in the United States were 70 or older, while all the cardinals were past 70 except the newly appointed Cardinal Shehan. Cincinnati, Louisville, Indianapolis, San Antonio, Denver, Omaha, and Kansas City had archbishops well past 70 and Portland, Oregon, had an archbishop of 87.[6]

In Rome the situation is much worse. "I know 19 cardinals near Rome who are past 80," said one official of the Holy Office to me mournfully. At the beginning of the first session, the four most important functionaries were the Pope, almost 81, the Secretary of State, 79, Cardinal Bea, 81, and Cardinal Ottaviani, the head of the Holy Office, 72 and half blind. Paul himself was almost 66 when elected, and several of the 27 new cardinals he appointed in 1965 were in their 70's and 80's. Eighty of the bishops who gathered at the first session died by the middle of the second session. During that session there was a special birthday celebration for a bishop of 101, who died shortly afterwards.

The Church handles its problem of aging clerics not only with marked inefficiency but also with considerable cruelty. In the debates on the organization of the Church, one bishop, protesting against the financial neglect of retired bishops, said: "Some bishops who have resigned have had to live in very wretched conditions and have been reduced to living like Lazarus, feeding on the crumbs from the Master's table. Aged parents have a right to stay in their home and their children have an obligation to support them." This protest evoked a warm response from the bishops.

One way to improve the situation would be to have compulsory retirement for old bishops. Cardinal Suenens of Belgium—he was only 59 at the time—declared in supporting obligatory retirement in the second session that "the accelerated rhythm of modern life calls for youthful vigor and young mind and heart. Old age puts a gap between the bishop and the world. . . . The text should make it clear that the obligation [of retirement] extends to all bishops, with the exception of the Roman Pontiff whose office is perpetual in view of the very welfare of the Church." No one, even the exceptionally courageous Cardinal Suenens, dared to touch the problem of senility of popes. At present the Vatican has no machinery for compelling the resignation of a pope, and no place to put a retired pope with dignity.

The impediment of a dead language was also a built-in obstacle at Vatican II, something that the Fathers felt was impossible to overcome, especially after Pope John had committed himself in an astonishingly reactionary encyclical to the continuing glories of Latin. What the Council needed was a simultaneous translation system similar to the one in use at the United Nations, and Cardinal Cushing proposed the adoption of such a system. It was even said that he offered to foot the entire expense. But top Council officials, inspired by the Curia, refused. For them Latin was more than a language tool. It had become a symbol of the past and of their own authority, almost consecrated by centuries of Church history.

Although the Council's adoption of the vernacular for part of the Church's liturgy constituted a welcome breakthrough of the Latin monopoly, the concession did not help the Council itself. The Italian bishops could express themselves fairly well in their heavily accented Italian Latin, but in many cases even the Latin scholars from other nations could not understand them. Each national group tended to have its own way of speaking Latin and, in turn, each one tended to consider the Latin of other nations defective. Although all seminarians who train in Rome are compelled to take all their subjects in Latin, this special training fits very few priests to speak the language fluently or to understand it when spoken rapidly. Cardinal Cushing delighted the bishops with his frankness when he stormed out of the Council declaring that he could not understand the mumbo-jumbo, and that he might as well go home. "I had never heard a lecture in Latin," he declared, "and it was all Greek to me." He quipped that, in view of the incomprehensible Latin, he felt like a member of "the Church of silence." The American bishops were particularly handicapped by the dead-language rule, and even Cardinal Spellman, who had studied in Rome for many years, confessed that he could understand only about half of the Latin spoken.

Into this great concourse came the American bishops, looking a little bewildered, not too sure of themselves, not united on anything, very Irish in their background. Their specialties in the past had been devout Irish obedience to Italian power in Rome, coupled with Irish-American mastery of the working institutions of the Church in the United States. In general, they had accepted Roman dominance as divine, with far more docility than their Italian confreres. Upon arrival they were somewhat shocked to witness a mild, incipient rebellion against such dominance among the German, Dutch, and French bishops. During the first session they lined up rather hesitantly with the Establishment. Cardinals Spellman and McIntyre even opposed the idea of the vernacular in the Mass. Later on, however, the American bishops blossomed forth in the true American spirit, emerging as the leading champions of religious liberty, racial justice, and fair play for Jews.

The American bishops did not seem to realize that they represented the foremost Catholic nation in the world. They had been subjected for so long to inflated European and Latin American clerical statistics that they took them seriously. Brazil and Italy are rated in baptismal figures, in that order, as the first two Catholic countries in the world, with the United States in third place.[7] But it is almost certain that there are more practising Catholics in the United States than in either of these countries, and there is certainly a great deal more Catholic money. The United States with less than 10 per cent of the world's Catholic population supplies almost one-half of all Catholic seminary students. Although American Catholic generosity supplies more than half of all the current contributed revenues of the Vatican, American Catholics have never tried seriously to call the tune. Until 1908 the Church in the United States was a mission church, and it is still afflicted with some of the old mission servility although it is now America's largest church, with almost one-quarter of the population. The cocksure leaders of the Curial old guard took full advantage of that servility in the first session. They looked down their ecclesiastical noses at the new arrivals from America, and made their remarks in the aula on the assumption that they themselves were the supreme masters of clerical knowledge, instructing the foreign fledglings in the true doctrines of the faith.

Then, in the second session, the American mood changed. Some of the American bishops had looked around them at the Catholicism of Italy and decided that American Catholics, in comparative terms, had no reason to be apologetic. American anger, goaded by many patronizing speeches from Italian bishops, burst forth in a Council speech by Bishop Stephen Leven of San

Antonio, given in the name of several American bishops. "Some of the Fathers have taken occasion to preach to us as if we were against Peter and his successors," said Bishop Leven in a press conference repeat of his speech. "For full eight weeks we have been getting lectured, especially about the dangers of association with non-Catholics. . . . It is not our people who miss Mass on Sunday, refuse the sacraments, and vote the Communist ticket!"

In statistical terms the American bishops were outnumbered by the Italians in about the ratio of 240 to 440, but this statistical figure understates the real Italian preponderance. At the Council the Italian bishops out-talked the bishops of any other single country by a prodigious margin. The Italians have captured and held for many years almost all of the upper working posts in the Roman Curia. American bishops are recognized on paper. Few of them can live in Rome and share the real day-to-day exercise of power.

On the whole the American bishops did not present to the world at Vatican II a picture of great intelligence. Why should they? American Catholic bishops are ordinarily educated in the dogmatic rut of the seminary system. Surviving years of obedient service as minor priests in the Establishment, they are finally elevated to the episcopacy after a careful combing of their records to eliminate any priests with anti-papal tendencies. They are chosen primarily for their administrative ability and their docility, not their intelligence. In the Catholic system, great preaching ability and profound scholarship are not requirements for appointment or promotion. Ceremony takes precedence over sermons in Catholic ritual, and neither is as important for episcopal promotion as institutional loyalty.

The American bishops at Vatican II were saved from vacuity by their *periti*, or theological experts. Many of these were brilliant scholars who far outshone the bishops in fame and knowledge. Behind the scenes, the bishops were usually wise enough to let superior wisdom dictate the words chosen and even the policies endorsed. Among these *periti* the Jesuits, as usual, played a leading part. The Society of Jesus is the largest religious order in the world and by far the most influential in the West. It tends to serve as the episcopal brain trust, and it is unquestionably the first religious order in American Catholic education.

The striking thing about the performance of the Jesuits at Vatican II was that the American members took a position quite contrary to that taken by their European confreres at Vatican I in 1870. Then it was European Jesuit maneuvering that had made possible the greatest blunder in all Church history, the declaration of the dogma of papal infallibility by Pius IX. Because of their nineteenth-century policies Lord Acton, the greatest of the English-speaking Catholic historians, had said of the Jesuits that they "existed in order to sustain the credit of the Popes. . . . It is the combination of an eager sense of duty, zeal for sacrifice, and love of virtue, with the deadly taint of a conscience perverted by authority, which makes them so odious to touch and so curious to study."[8]

At Vatican II the American Jesuits followed a different tendency. They stood out as pioneers in the attempt to give the Church a new progressive look. They asked that their Church face boldly its new responsibilities in the modern world. But they are still intensely loyal to the system of centralized power.

Will American Jesuit liberalism continue? It is too soon to say. When analyzed, the Jesuit program is seen to be essentially cautious, favorable to those elementary principles of liberty and progress which are already taken for granted by nearly all Americans, and considered necessary for the continuing accommodation of their Church to the American environment. But they still follow the Supreme Pontiff on such basically reactionary policies as opposition to contraception and the right of divorce. They are leading advocates in the United States of Catholic access to educational funds in the public treasury. Their welcome liberalism must also be accepted with a special caution because of the recent election as Superior General of the order of a Spanish priest, Father Peter Arrupe. Father Arrupe, at the fourth session of the Council, delivered a speech which can only be described as partaking of the paranoiac spirit of the John Birch Society. American Jesuit leaders were so embarrassed by it that they repudiated it in public. The London *Tablet* said of Arrupe's speech that it "can have served only to encourage the lunatic fringe on the right while disappointing, if not actually scandalizing, everyone else." But Father Arrupe, for the time being at least, was unmoved. He told Madrid's Catholic daily *Ya:* "I am strictly opposed to any criticism of the Church. If reforms should be made, this will be done by the duly constituted authority."[9]

Among the American cardinals, Cardinal McIntyre was the most consistent reactionary, followed closely by Cardinal Spellman. The late Cardinal Meyer of Chicago—whose death meant a real loss to his Church and his nation—seemed to stand squarely in the middle of the road. Cardinal Ritter was a little to his left, while the new Baltimore cardinal, Lawrence Shehan, gave the picture of a friendly compromiser. On the extreme left came Cardinal Cushing of Boston, who surprised the world by emerging as one of the most outspoken and progressive prelates in the whole concourse.

Cushing's mood may have had something to do with a very special factor that had a profound effect on the whole American position at the Council. He was the religious superior of John F. Kennedy. In the eyes of European Catholics the elevation of Kennedy to the American presidency had been an enormously impressive event. It seemed to prove that the vigorous new nation of the West, led by a vigorous member of the younger generation, was on the way to becoming a Catholic nation. This triumphalism by implication was widely accepted in Europe. The shining image of the young Kennedy reflected glory on American Catholicism and his tragic death during the second session was both an American disaster and a Catholic disaster. The masses of Europe and America, both Catholic and non-Catholic, were drawn together in overwhelming grief. In that common grief the fact was overlooked that the brilliant young President had been elected largely by non-Catholic voters precisely because he renounced several of the most favored of policies of his own Church.

CHAPTER TWO ❧ JOHN AND THE BEGINNING

THE short, dumpy little man who fathered Vatican II was what the biologists call a sport; he varied abruptly from type. Before he became pope there had been little that was exceptional or distinguished in the career of Angelo Giuseppe Roncalli. When, to the surprise of most of the experts, he was chosen for the papal throne in October 1958 on the eleventh ballot by fifty-one of his fellow Cardinals, he was regarded as a stop-gap compromise. He was within one month of his seventy-seventh birthday. Robert Louis Stevenson might have predicted that he would be an extraordinarily ordinary Pope. Cardinal Suenens, in praising him after his death, said he was "surprisingly natural."

That, I think, was the key to John's success. He had climbed slowly up through the Vatican diplomatic bureaucracy for fifty-four years without losing his warmth and naturalness as a human being. That such a man could emerge from such a process without becoming a routine clerical bureaucrat was miracle enough in itself. It was a double miracle when a man who had been chosen as a middle-of-the-road compromise turned out to be a pioneer of considerable independence and courage.

The whole career of John is an essential part of the story of Vatican II, and the Johannine years between 1959, when he first announced the Council, and 1962, when he opened the first session, form a part of the Council pattern. It was John and the image of John that made the Council possible, and even after his death in 1963 it was the memory of his spirit which inspired the Council Fathers to press on toward that *aggiornamento* he had desired.

The portrait of John XXIII that emerged in the American

press was considerably oversimplified. After he was elected, the cartoonists seized upon his stocky figure, his huge Roman nose, and his twinkling eyes. Genial rotundity became his identifying trade-mark. He was the world's grandfather, wise and kindly, and at that particular troubled moment in history the world certainly needed a grandfather. The sharp contrast between his geniality and the aloof patrician qualities of Pius XII made John seem especially warmhearted.

Actually John did very little to decrease the prodigious triumphalism of the Papacy. He increased the entourage of his papal court and made no substantial reduction in the fearful pomp surrounding each Roman pontiff. The ring-kissing and the kneeling, the *flabelli* (processional fans), and the *sedia gestatoria* continued as before. But John took it all very easily and informally, and made the gaudy papal exhibitionism seem human and natural. He surmounted formality. He is reputed to have said that his up-and-down journeys on the shoulders of his scarlet-clad aides, carrying his *sedia gestatoria*, made him seasick. But he kept his *sedia* anyway and made the cardinals go through all the ceremony of obediences, involving both foot-kissing and hand-kissing.

Pius XII had insisted that all the gardeners in the Vatican gardens absent themselves during his punctually arranged daily walks. John reversed the orders and walked whenever he wanted to in the presence of all the Vatican gardeners. Pius XII had continued the ancient rule of separate eating, which implies that no one is good enough to eat with a pope. John immediately invited a number of guests of both low and high station to eat with him. He dashed about Rome in his black Mercedes, visiting prisoners and lowly priests and, in general, creating a great sensation, with plenty of resulting traffic jams in a city that already had the worst traffic jams in the world.[1]

No one will ever know how much of the resultant image of John that emerged from all this papal publicity was real. Some of it was, no doubt, the kind of sycophantic, institutional publicity that transformed Queen Victoria from a crotchety old imperialist into a genial materfamilias. Probably most of the Johannine image-product was reasonably accurate. John's journals reflect the mind of a man not profound but faithful to his Church to the point of naïveté. And even when we grant that few official personalities ever record the whole truth in their journals, John's own writings seem to dovetail quite consistently with the record of the man himself. Although he became a genial man of the world in handling friend and foe, he was a Catholic fundamentalist in his religious ideas, little troubled by philosophical doubts.

Educated narrowly within the Catholic system from his entrance into a seminary at the age of eleven, he had never traveled far beyond the Mediterranean basin. He learned Greek, Latin, and church history very well; the rest of his education was sketchy, fearfully sketchy. He came from peasant stock in a village near Bergamo, an intensely devout area, and grew up in simple peasant surroundings with five brothers and four sisters. The simplicity of this peasant background never entirely deserted him, and from the very beginning he said that he had always wanted to grow up to be a priest, preferably a priest in his native region. He was never to realize that ambition, although he did serve as a chaplain-priest for a short time in the Italian army during World War I.

Like Pius XII before him and Paul VI after him, John came to power not through the priesthood as such but through the diplomatic wing of his Church. Perhaps the best thing in his background was his absence from Rome for almost his entire career. He was never sucked into the whirlpool of intrigue surrounding the Roman Curia. He was called a "pastoral" Pope at the time of his election largely because at that particular moment his Church needed to stress its nonpolitical character. But, like Pius XII and Paul VI, he was never primarily a pastor. He had never served as the head priest of any large church. He started his climb to the papal throne by becoming secretary to the bishop of Bergamo immediately after ordination and was later called to Rome to help reorganize the Italian Society for the Propagation of the Faith. Then in 1925, at the age of forty-four, he began his long service in the Vatican diplomatic corps, serving for twenty years in Bulgaria, Turkey, and Greece. Almost everybody liked him. Finally, in 1944, he was appointed postwar nuncio to France for eight years. There almost everybody continued to like him. He ended his prepapal career with five years of service as Patriarch and Cardinal of Venice.

In all those years he was friendly, cautious, and orthodox. After becoming Pope he jokingly referred to the fact that at one time in his young manhood the Holy Office had opened a dossier on him because there had been some suspicion of possible heresy. The extent of his "sin" was that he was a friend of the famous heretic Ernesto Buonaiuti, the liberal priest-philosopher of Rome who had been defrocked by the Holy Office for his modernism. Roncalli, although he liked Buonaiuti very much, never followed his famous liberal friend one step along the road to modernism. He rejected "such a ferment and agitation of brains and tongues." The only book he ever wrote was a very long and very dull history of the activities of St. Charles Borromeo, a history which accumulated dust in the archives of the diocese until its author became Pope. Borromeo was humane and efficient in an age of clerical corruption, but he was also an archenemy of Protestantism and an architect of the reactionary dogmas of the Council of Trent that formalized the antifreedom edicts of the era of confessional absolutism. That Borromeo was John's particular hero, both before and after John's assent to the throne, reveals a great deal about the Pope's doctrinal convictions. From the beginning, Roncalli was steeped in the conservative ideas of the Counter Reformation and even after he became John XXIII, he never lost his admiration for his particular counter-reformation hero. In his *Journal of a Soul* he referred to Protestants as those "poor unfortunates outside of the Church," and declared that Catholics must work "for their conversion."

Throughout his whole early career his motto was peace and obedience. "He was not at all easy going," said the London *Tablet*, "either in doctrine or morals." He leaned slightly toward liberalism in social reform but never aggressively. In Venice he ardently supported the Christian Democratic Party. One of the first things he did as Pope was to hand down through the Holy Office the final death sentence to the worker-priest movement in France. His hostility to this movement was especially significant because he had seen it grow in Paris. Later this worker-priest movement was revived in France, but it was utterly different from its original form.

John gained temporary fame as a liberal while serving as Patriarch of Venice in 1957 when he issued a special greeting to a convention of Pietro Nenni's Italian Socialist Party, although Nenni was at that time—and still is—an atheist who calls himself a Marxist. Before this incident, however, Roncalli, in August 1956, had delivered a philippic against wavering Christian Democrats who felt that "in order to bring about social justice, help the poor and enforce the tax laws it is absolutely necessary to associate with those who deny God and suppress human liberties." In those days he repeatedly denounced any political opening to the left.

These two phases of John's early activity are typical of him before he ascended the papal throne. His career was a balanced and dutiful career. The cardinals who elected him pope in 1958 had a right to expect a balanced and dutiful supreme pontiff. In his first activities they seemed to be reassured. In his first selection of twenty-three Cardinals, eleven were Italians, several in their late seventies and only two were Americans. There was nothing particularly unusual in his selections unless the underestimation of the role of the United States could be considered unusual.

In his first address after election John included among those we "bless with an effusive heart" . . . "those laymen who, under the guidance of the bishops, fight in the pacific ranks of Catholic Action."[2] In opening his heart to "those who are separated from this Apostolic Sea," he was careful to point out that "we ardently desire their return to the house of the common Father. . . . In such manner there shall be one sheepfold and one shepherd."

Perhaps that first speech, prepared in the rush of the day after his election, did not wholly reflect the attitudes of the new Pope, but his coronation homily, coming a week later, could not be dismissed as casual, and it did not sound like the expression of a liberal monarch. In it his welcome to separated brethren was quite equivocal: "Into this fold of Jesus Christ no one can enter if he is not under the guidance of the sovereign Pontiff, and men can securely reach salvation only when they are united with Him, since the Roman Pontiff is the vicar of Christ and represents his person on this earth."[3] All this is extremely conventional Catholic doctrine but in the light of John's later reputation as the greatest ecumenist of modern times, the language seems strange.

In July 1962, shortly before the opening of the first session of the Council, John issued a letter to women religious that contained scarcely a glimmer of twentieth-century realism. It advocated Pauline obedience, the "constant sacrifice of your 'ego,'" and the "annihilation of self." It deplored the "search for small comforts" by nuns and suggested that the thorns of poverty "must be loved in order that they may become roses in heaven." It exalted the contemplative life over "the heresy of action." It was evident that Catholic liberals who were looking for some emancipation of women religious under the new pope would have to look elsewhere.

Probably John was never a conscious theological reactionary; in fact, he seemed to have little interest in formal theological controversy. He took orthodox theology for granted as fundamentally true. His institutional conservatism was emphasized several times during 1959 and 1960, even after he had announced that he would convene Vatican II. In 1959 he appointed Cardinal Ottaviani, the worst reactionary in the Curia, as Secretary of the Holy Office. On June 29, 1959, he issued his *Ad Petri Cathedram*, an "appeal to separated Christians to reunite with the Church." This time his language was even more ecclesiastically egocentric than it had been in his coronation address.

Early in 1960 John called together the first synod of the clergy of the diocese of Rome to meet since 1461. Robert Neville, former member of the *Time-Life* Bureau in Rome, in *The World of the Vatican*, a book that deserves much more attention than it has received, has described that synod. Carlo Falconi has included a pungent summary of the events of the synod in his work, *Pope John and the Ecumenical Council.* John, instead of giving the clergy of Rome any real opportunity to discuss and revise their own very strict diocesan rules in an open assembly, imposed upon them through a preparatory commission a new constitution of 770 articles, corrected by himself, regulating their conduct down to the last motor scooter and the last bathing suit. Every priest and brother was forbidden to drive an automobile or a motor scooter without previous written permission from his religious superiors. A priest living alone was forbidden the right to have a television set. A priest could stand up at a bar for a short beer but must not sit down to drink it. Priests were forbidden to join Rotary clubs. American seminarians in Rome could not even attend the Olympic Games of 1960 freely. They were allowed to see several of the events after securing permission, but boxing and wrestling matches were forbidden as were all swimming events in which women participated.

These were trivial and traditional restrictions, relatively unimportant in themselves, but in considering the character of John they have importance because of the method of their imposition. Rome was the Pope's own diocese and in that diocese John saw no need for any liberal updating of the undemocratic processes of his own Church. In this, his "little Council," called after he had announced in June 1959 the big Council and hailed as one of his objectives the genuine renewal of his Church, he clung to the old absolutist traditions that in Canons 356–362 give the priests in a synod no authority whatever against their bishops. Under these canons, the Bishop "is the sole legislator in the synod"; if the vote is 99 to 1 against him, his 1 vote "represents" the will of the synod. Incidentally, the rules of John's synod were so absurdly strict that it has been impossible to enforce them against Rome's priests and seminarians. They are being widely disregarded.

In his own synod John even went beyond canon law and ignored the requirements that the subjects to be acted upon in such a synod be freely discussed. After the preparatory commission of this synod had done its work, the 700 priests, rectors, teachers, and others meeting in the Hall of Benedictions held three sessions, celebrated a Mass, listened to an irrelevant sermon by the Pope, and sat quietly while the final diocesan canons were read to them in complicated Latin. If this was a dress rehearsal for the main Council, it did not presage anything remotely resembling free speech.

Of a piece with this adherence to ecclesiastical tradition was John's Apostolic Constitution about Latin, issued in June 1962. It strengthened and reinforced the rule that all Catholic priests, even those priests of the non-Roman Eastern rites who are partly Byzantine in orientation, who had never accepted the Latin tradition, must master Latin and "show themselves submissive to the will of the Apostolic See on this point." "Since in our times the use of Latin is contested in many places," said the Constitution, "the ancient and uninterrupted use of Latin [shall] be maintained."

More important than this set of rigid commandments for Latin was John's 1961 encyclical, *Aeterna dei Sapientia*, a hymn of praise to St. Leo I, a pope in the fifth century.[4] John, on the fifteen hundredth anniversary of Leo I's death, hailed him as "The Doctor of the Unity of the Church," and directly related his eulogy to the "unity" sought by Vatican II. Leo I was a stalwart enemy of Manichean and other heresies of those days and a champion of the Council of Chalcedon against the "robber" Council of Ephesus. He was one of history's most ardent advocates of unalloyed papal primacy.

John, in this 1961 encyclical, which was issued more than two years after his decision to hold a Council, was quite frank in underscoring the conventional lesson for those interested in Christian unity:

> It is indispensable, however, to the unity of the Faith, that there be union among the teachers of the divine truths, that is, the harmony of bishops among themselves in communion and submission to the Roman Pontiff. . . . We decided to convene the Second Vatican Ecumenical Council. We did so, confident that the impressive gathering of the Catholic hierarchy would not only strengthen the bonds of unity in faith,

> worship and government, which are the prerogatives of the true Church, but would also attract the attention of numberless believers in Christ and would invite them to gather about "the great pastor of the sheep" Who entrusted their perennial custody to Peter and his successors.

It is apparent that in John's mind at that particular moment the only hope of ecumenism was in reabsorption into the Roman fold.

John's conventional expressions of traditionally narrow concepts received very little attention in the American press. The two things that did receive attention, quite deservedly, were John's two great encyclicals, *Mater et Magistra*, issued on May 15, 1961, before the Council had begun, and *Pacem in Terris*, issued on April 11, 1963, shortly before John's death.[5] *Mater et Magistra*, reviewing the whole field of Catholic social doctrine from Leo XIII down to current issues, accomplished one important purpose: It placed the Catholic Church on the side of social reform and foreign aid to underdeveloped countries. Equally important, it rambled over the whole field of poverty and social discontent without indulging in the usual tirade against Communism. While it horrified the editors of the *National Review*, it so delighted the Italian Communists that they had portions of it reprinted in a pamphlet with the hammer and sickle on the cover, thus giving the impression to many semiliterate Italians that John XXIII had endorsed the Communist ideal.

John, of course, never endorsed either the Communist ideal or Communist methods. But he did squarely place his Church on record as favoring what the English translators called "socialization," although that word does not represent John's meaning with entire accuracy. It was such a revolutionary thing for a Pope to say warmly favorable things about the welfare state that American liberals were enthusiastic. The *New York Times* recognized the importance of the occasion by publishing the entire 25,000-word encyclical in four closely packed pages, and Hubert Humphrey inserted the text in the *Congressional Record*. *Mater et Magistra* was of historic importance in the development of Western thought because the leader of the largest Christian church had stopped repeating stale anti-Communist clichés and recognized the whole world's moral responsibility for destroying poverty. The significant new emphasis in John's massive and somewhat turgid epic was a flat endorsement of the idea that rich nations had an obligation to help poor nations.

The encyclical was progressive enough to make the pugnacious editor of the right-wing *National Review*, William F. Buckley, himself a Catholic, describe it as "a venture in triviality," and it was conservative enough so that the *Michigan Catholic* could rightly say: "Socialization and socialism in *Mater et Magistra* are not synonymous terms and let us not make that mistake."

Actually, in endorsing socialization, John XXIII had defined it in very cautious terms as "the progressive multiplication of relations in society, with different forms of life and activity, and juridical institutionalization." This ambiguous jumble of polysyllables, sounding like an American sociology textbook, was seized upon by both rightists and leftists as confirmation of their own aspirations. Reinhold Niebuhr hailed the encyclical for endorsing "the whole philosophy of the welfare state," while the *Chicago Tribune* plucked out sufficient conditional statements from the encyclical to use the subhead "O.K.'s Private Property."

The *Chicago Tribune* was nominally correct, but Niebuhr more clearly reflected the encyclical's total spirit. The encyclical really was a mighty forward step in the social thinking of a church that had often used its influence in the past to bolster the most reactionary forces in Europe, Asia and the Americas. It signalized the turning of the Church's energies to the things of this world in a new spirit of cooperation with European liberals and moderate socialists.

The Jesuit magazine *America* rebuked those "otherwise good and loyal Catholics" who are "making such fools of themselves these days" by attacking John's encyclical. And it added: "That goes especially for those Catholics who by their simplicity and lopsided approach to the awful menace of communism—typified at its worst by membership in the John Birch Society—are de-emphasizing *Mater et Magistra* and thus endangering the cause that is dearer than life to all of us."[6]

Few commentators noticed that in tracing the evolution of Catholic social thought from Leo to himself, John skillfully passed over several things in the Church's record that did not accord with the theory of a constant forward movement in that evolution. *Mater et Magistra* used those portions of Leo's *Rerum Novarum* which represented him as vigorously pro labor, omitting the basic Catholic paternalism that led him to endorse labor organizations only with the proviso that "the foundations of the organization" must be laid in religion. Leo XIII had in mind the development of great Catholic trade unions to defeat the rising power of European socialist trade unions. John did not pursue that thought vigorously because, on the whole, the confessional trade unions of Europe have not been successful in their organization campaigns, and the Vatican is reluctant to tie itself to a movement that appears to be going downhill.

John's endorsement of foreign aid for the underprivileged was quite unequivocal, and it must have shocked the membership of the John Birch Society, an organization that admitted in its early stages that its membership was predominantly Catholic. The Pope said:

> The solidarity which binds all men and makes them members of the same family imposes upon political communities enjoying abundance of material goods not to remain indifferent to those communities whose citizens suffer from poverty, misery, and hunger, and who lack even the elementary rights of the human person. This is the more so since, given the growing interdependence among the people of the earth, it is not possible to preserve lasting peace if glaring economic and social inequality among them persists.

After such a paragraph it would have seemed logical for John to note that the greatest single obstacle in the way of a decent way of life for the underprivileged nations of Latin America and Asia is the too-rapid growth of population, and the rejection of birth control. Instead, while recognizing the seriousness of the population explosion, he launched into an attack on those who advocate contraception, claiming that

> the relationship between the population increase on the one hand and the economic development and availability of food supplies on the other, does not seem—at least for the moment and in the near future—to create a difficulty. . . . Hence the real solution of the problem is not to be found in expedients that offend against the moral order established by God and which injure the very origin of human life, but in a renewed scientific and technical effort on the part of man to deepen and extend his dominion over nature.

The most striking paragraph in *Mater et Magistra* was one which escaped critical comment in the American press. John, although he used several laudatory phrases about freedom and the personal initiative of individual citizens, specifically reasserted the right of the hierarchy of his Church to dictate *both* the moral and political conduct of Catholic laymen. While conceding that Catholics should be animated by "a spirit of understanding and disinterestedness" in cooperating with non-Catholics for good purposes, he said:

> It is clear, however, that when the hierarchy has made a decision on the point at issue, Catholics are bound to obey their directives because the Church has the right and obligation not merely to guard ethical and religious principles but also to intervene authoritatively in the temporal sphere when it is a matter of judging the application of these principles to concrete cases.

John's second great encyclical—his eighth in sequence—*Pacem in Terris*, was issued between sessions of the Council.[7] It created an even greater stir than *Mater et Magistra* because it seemed to go further in the direction of world government and also in the direction of a compromise with Communism. By the time it was issued, in April, 1963, it was accepted by many as the valedictory of a great pope, since John was already mortally ill, and he died two months later. Because of its timing and its authorship, *Pacem in Terris* became virtually a Council document.

The encyclical began with a precautionary routine sentence: "Peace on earth, which men of every era have most eagerly yearned for, can be firmly established only if the order laid down by God is dutifully observed," but the concessions to modern secular movements for world order and peace attracted far more attention. If the platitudes were very general they were also quite realistic and meaningful. Especially attractive to a world living in terror of nuclear war was John's paragraph:

> And one must bear in mind that, even though the monstrous power of modern weapons acts as a deterrent, it is to be feared that the mere continuance of nuclear tests, undertaken with war in mind, will have fatal consequences for life on earth. Justice, right reason and humanity, therefore, urgently demand that the arms race should cease; that the stockpiles which exist in various countries should be reduced equally and simultaneously by the parties concerned; that nuclear weapons should be banned; and that a general agreement should eventually be reached about progressive disarmament and an effective method of control.

This came with special force from the leader of a church whose journals, particularly in the United States, had often approached a pro-war stand in the struggle against the Communist nations. In fact, the principles laid down by John XXIII in *Pacem in Terris*, although they were for the most part familiar repetitions of liberal thought, were probably more important for the future of mankind than anything that happened at the Vatican Council itself. John's peace appeal made possible the peace policy of Vatican II.

The encyclical did not stop with a plea for disarmament; it went further and attacked the superstitions of racial injustice by saying that: "It is not true that some human beings are by nature superior and others inferior. All men are equal in their natural dignity." And it included a strong exhortation in behalf of the

United Nations, suggesting that "the public authority of the world community must tackle and solve problems of an economic, social, political or cultural character which are posed by the universal common good." Altogether, *Pacem in Terris* was probably the most forward-looking encyclical written by any pope, and the reception which it received throughout the world was enthusiastic and enduring.

John felt obliged to sound a conventional warning against identifying social and political movements with the "false philosophical teachings regarding the nature, origin and destiny of the universe," but he immediately softened this oblique rebuke to the Communists by suggesting that movements questionable in themselves might "contain elements that are positive and deserving of approval. It can happen, then, that a drawing nearer together or a meeting for the attainment of some practical end, which was formerly deemed inopportune or unproductive might now or in the future be considered opportune and useful."

The Communists of Italy immediately interpreted this last paragraph as an invitation for Catholics to welcome the opening to the left in national politics. They contended that "a drawing nearer together" meant an alliance between Christian Democrats and Nenni Socialists, engineered primarily by Pietro Nenni of the Socialists. And some of them even contended that a vote for a Communist could not be considered inappropriate in the spirit of such a statement. In the election of 1963, trading on this assumption, the Communists jumped their proportion of the national poll about 3 per cent to 25 per cent of the total, while the Christian Democrats lost nearly 5 per cent.

John's sins appeared to be magnified in the eyes of Christian Democratic conservatives by the fact that he, rather conspicuously and in the presence of a whole group of jealous journalists in the very month preceding the issuance of *Pacem in Terris*, had summoned into his private chambers for an unprecedented private interview Alexei Adzhubei, son-in-law of Nikita Khrushchev, with his wife Rada. He had talked to these exponents of Communism and atheism for at least fifteen minutes. The rumor was that

John had sent a sealed envelope to Khrushchev expressing willingness to receive the Russian leader if he came to Rome.

Some conservative Catholics in Italy thought that many of the 500,000 new votes for Communism came partly from the popular reaction to the statement by Rada Adzhubei that the Pope had workingman's hands like her father's. Cardinal Siri, of Genoa, leading conservative, was later quoted as saying that John "has done things in four years which the Church will need forty to remedy."

Some American Catholics were also badly shaken by the implications of John's alleged acceptance of Communists. "The crackpots in our ranks," said the Jesuit magazine *America*,

> think that the Pope sold out to the Communists. More sensible critics fear that his great desire for peace led him into the idealist trap of denying inconvenient realities. These people, we think, misunderstand what the Pope was trying to do. He did not speak as a statesman, like President Kennedy or Premier Khrushchev, responsible for conducting the foreign policy of a major military and political power. John XXIII spoke as the head of a universal Church and addressed himself to both sides at one and the same time.[8]

This was true so far as it went, but John XXIII by virtue of his official position was not only a powerful political figure in Italy but also the moral leader of a bloc of non-Italian Catholic political parties in Europe, promoted and sometimes even financed by the Vatican. These parties had attempted to serve as the spearhead of the opposition to Communists and Communism. When their leader spoke such gentle words to leftists, those words were bound to have a marked effect on political developments in Europe.

The sentiments expressed by John in *Pacem in Terris* were more apt than original, more humane than Roman Catholic. Humanity welcomed the peace-on-earth emphasis without necessarily accepting the suggestion that peace on earth had any necessary or even natural connection with Catholicism. There was a satirical tone in the comment of *La Nazione* of Florence on the public fuss over *Pacem in Terris*.

It is still a little staggering to discover that the United Nations, conceived by a couple of Protestant Christians, Roosevelt and Churchill, on board the *Potomac* in one of humanity's darkest hours, rests upon principles that the Catholic Church is today preaching so movingly—the liberty of man from every form of tyranny, peace and the repudiation of war and the acceptance of the principle of arbitration, assistance to under-developed peoples, solidarity and cooperation between nations in all fields. So the message of the *Potomac*, the four freedoms of Roosevelt, the San Francisco Charter and all the institutions that have grown out of it, were just fore-runners of the pronouncement of John XXIII, and anticipations of the principles of the Catholic Church put into action before the Encyclical of Holy Thursday 1963 set them out and expounded them so eloquently.[9]

An equally satirical comment could have been written about the origin of the economic principles in John's earlier encyclical, *Mater et Magistra*. Most of these concepts had appeared long before in political platforms of the New Deal and the Fair Deal, or in the pronouncements of the social democratic parties of Europe. Many Christian leaders throughout the world are willing to confess their indebtedness to the pioneering work of non-Christian secularists in the field of moral reform. At an Anglican Congress in Toronto, held between the first and second sessions of Vatican II, an English canon announced that Christian concern for social justice "owes not a little, under God, to the stimulus of Marx"; he even suggested that Christians should thank God for Sigmund Freud!

When John died in June, 1963, and was given one of the most impressive funerals in the history of man, all these sniping criticisms were forgotten. He had already become a legend before his death, and the legend proceeded to grow thereafter. He became the symbol of a mighty man who was also supremely humble and supremely human, a man who cut through the artificialities of power and asserted the supreme value of the warm heart.

But it is relevant, amidst all the deserved admiration for John the human being, to ask how much John the father of Vatican II intended to make his Council an opening to the *ecclesiastical* left. Did he really have any conception of Christian unity as non-Catholics understand that term? The primary answers must be postponed to a later chapter, but certain preliminary observations can be made here.

On the whole the evidence seems quite convincing that John, in spite of his sincere personal sympathies for Orthodox and Protestant Christians, at no time ever departed in his thought from the standard Catholic doctrine that the only acceptable kind of Christian unity was return to Rome. One can comb all his encyclicals without finding any assurance in them that this ancient and arrogant concept of Christian unity was compromised in any way. Many words can be found expressing sympathy, good will and brotherhood for non-Catholic Christians of East and West, as well as some suggestions of regret for past bitterness. But nothing more.

Indeed, it is apparent that the notion of making Vatican II into a great forward step toward Christian unity was quite incidental to John's purpose. Perhaps it was entirely accidental. He first conceived of the Council as a Council for the renewal and strengthening of his own Church with very little significance for non-Catholics. The story has been frequently told that in an interview he opened a window in his study and said that his purpose in calling the Council was to allow the winds of the world to blow through the Church. It is interesting, but its significance is doubtful. He himself did not apply that analogy to the Council. Otherwise how was it possible to explain the fact that he planned to have its sessions secret right up to the moment of the Council's beginning? The activities and deliberations of the body were made public only after the sessions had begun and then only in response to tremendous pressure from the Fathers themselves and from world media of information. The narrowness of John's conception of the scope of the Council was dramatically demonstrated on the day of its opening when he told a Catholic Action mass meeting that "there is hope that it [the Council] may finish before Christmas." No one who thought of the Council as a serious negotiating or planning agency for world Christian unity could have predicted so short a session. There was not a single subject on the original agenda of the Council providing for direct conversations with non-Catholic Christians and, as we shall see later, there were many, many items reinforcing the differences between Rome and the schismatic or separated brethren of Orthodoxy and Protestantism.

Pope John in his journals has described as "entirely my own idea" the notion of a Council, and at first the idea seemed to surprise even the author. In his opening allocution at the first session of the Council, in describing the manner of his announcement to seventeen cardinals on January 25, 1959, John said: "It was completely unexpected, like a flash of heavenly light, shedding sweetness in eyes and hearts." (This may be considered slightly inaccurate history since John had already discussed the idea with his Secretary of State.) In his short speech of announcement he did not even give a hint of any program for bringing Protestants or Orthodox back to his Church. He stressed the decadence of current society, its materialism and the need for renewing doctrine, discipline, and Catholic solidarity. "Separated communities" were mentioned only in passing.

Then an official communiqué about the speech mentioned the proposed meeting as constituting "an invitation to the separated communities to seek for unity." It went beyond John's actual words. The world responded with such a roar of approval that, from that time forward, the "ecumenical" or Catholic-universal Council became the ecumenical or world-Universal Council, aiming to bring all Christian peoples together. Never has there been a clearer, though unconscious, demonstration of the alleged thesis of William James and John Dewey that truth is what works. The call for Christian unity worked, at least for publicity purposes, and the editors of the world, weary with stale denominational quarrels, made sure that it kept on working. They were so zealous in wanting it to work that, consciously or unconsciously, they weighted their news columns in favor of the most optimistic interpretation of Council developments.

John's very limited concepts about Christian unity were quite clearly exposed to view in the following year on June 5, 1960, on the day after he named ten commissions for the forthcoming Council. In an address on that day he spoke of "that fervor of our separated brothers . . . of drawing closer to the center of religious unity, 'the one, holy, catholic and apostolic Church.' This increased phenomenon of the turning of souls toward Rome as toward a center of religious unity is part of that other phenomenon of the formerly infidel regions that are now visited by the flame of the Gospel." He spoke of "the return of the churches of the Orient to the embrace of the one, holy, catholic and apostolic church." Then he said: "Oh, what a marvelous event this would be, and what flowering of human and heavenly charity would there be in setting in motion the joining of the separated brothers of the East and the West in the single Flock of Christ, the eternal Shepherd! This should represent one of the most precious fruits of the forthcoming Second Vatican Council."[10]

It is evident that after one and one-half years John had come to a realization of the great importance of Christian unity as a public aim of the Council, but it is also evident that he had never once swerved from the traditional and narrow view of the Roman Curia that this must come about only through reunion with Rome.

CHAPTER THREE ☙ PAUL, THE INSTITUTIONAL MAN

THE man who succeeded John XXIII, Paul VI, became a more important factor in shaping the destiny of Vatican II than John himself. The first session belonged to John; the last three sessions belonged to Paul.

The possessive verb essentially describes Paul's role. He made the great majority of the hard decisions in the Council years, and it will be his primary responsibility to see that the Council's proposals are embodied in effective programs in the future. Since, under the Vatican system of power, his decisions can outweigh those of all the other bishops combined, his character and outlook must be primary objects of scrutiny in any appraisal of the Council itself. He did not choose to overrule the great body of bishops in many matters, but the fact that he could overrule them made the Council Paul's Council even more than it was the bishops' Council. Paul began the Council years as one of many Italian cardinals; he took full advantage of his supreme authority throughout the last three sessions and at the end of the Council he was the most conspicuous and powerful religious figure of the century.

Paul, when writing to his diocesan constituents as a cardinal, had once spoken of John's "enchanting goodness," and had gone on to say that John's words "flow simple and noble almost without interruption. . . . The lines of his thought and action unfold, simple and direct, as though the obstacles and anxieties of our time had no power to trouble him."

There may have been a great deal of hidden envy in that tribute. Paul himself has on the surface no enchanting goodness, nor any natural unfolding of simple nobility. His is not an outgoing personality. The adjective "aloof" is the one most often applied to him, although he is probably not more naturally aloof than Pius XII was. When, as the young Giovanni Battista Montini, he first announced his desire to become a priest, the doubt of the local authorities was not about his devoutness or his intellect. They wondered whether he was not too ingrown to be a good priest, too introspective and aloof. He was not then, nor has he ever been, what Americans call a good mixer. As Pope he soon mastered the conventional, openhanded gestures of friendly piety necessary for every picture-book pontiff in papal ceremonies, but his heart never seemed to go out to the people with the natural warmth of Pope John.

Paul VI is a complicated, subtle, and indirect man, full of dignity and anxiety, sagacious rather than profound, an institutionalized person rather than a natural one. Pope John is said to have referred to him as "His Eminence Prince Hamlet," but Hamlet stands for something more fiery and independent. Could anyone expect fiery independence from a man who lived for so many years in the Vatican Palace, working anxiously and faithfully under the shadow of two imperious popes? In a sense he was the product of Rome and its Curia as John was not. Also, John looked like everybody's grandfather while Paul looked like everybody's senior schoolmaster, a rather stern schoolmaster who seemed to be looking from his deep-set eyes under bushy eyebrows for evidence of sin among his pupils. At first photographers could not uncover a natural smile, although the smile finally arrived after several months of practice.

Paul had been attached to the central headquarters of the Vatican for nearly thirty years, with seventeen years of direct service under two popes, two years under Pius XI and fifteen years under Pius XII, a term of service which made him outwardly into a completely docile instrument of papal will. Practising that docility, he had risen from holding a clerkship under Pius XI to being Secretary of State for Ordinary Affairs under Pius XII. During all those fifteen years under the later Pius, Montini refused to sit down in the papal presence, even when pressed to do so, even during the long interviews that occurred almost daily. He even stood each time he received a telephone call from Pius XII.[1]

His early experience was almost wholly papal and Roman. Unlike Pius XII, he had never had any foreign assignment except a brief stint in 1923 in Poland as attaché to the apostolic nunciature in Warsaw, a stint that was interrupted by that same physical frailty which kept him out of war. He had worked without interruption in the central Vatican Secretariat of State for twenty-nine years, from 1925 to 1954, when he was named Archbishop of Milan. Then, for publicity purposes, he was suddenly described as "pastoral," perhaps because he had supervision of many pastors in his new assignment. He had never been pastor even of a village church. He visited his diocesan churches with great vigor and became a successful archbishop.

From the very beginning, his encyclicals as pope were cautiously conservative, and this cautious conservatism continued through the four sessions of the Council into 1966. The *Christian Century* summed up very well the reaction of American liberal non-Catholics to the new pope when it commented on his first encyclical, *Ecclesiam Suam* in 1964: "It is the product of a man who has not made up his mind, who hangs in intellectual suspension between transition and progress, ecclesiastical democracy and papal autocracy, unifying charity and divisive dogma. Consequently he offers in his first pastoral letter a kind of encyclical supermarket in which everyone can find what he wants if he has the patience to look for it."[2] The *Christian Century* editor might have added in mitigation of Paul's ambiguities that most modern papal encyclicals tend to speak with double meanings because of the papacy's desire not to rock the boat. Double-talk is a traditionally fine art in papal history. But Paul's double-talk seemed to be more than ordinarily ambiguous. He opened the window, as *Time*'s editors remarked, but kept "checking the thermometer lest any cold drafts seep in. . . . the nuggets of assertion and advice in his own writings often seem like spiritual rafts bobbing half-hidden in a holy sea of howevers."[3]

Later on in his reign, several liberal Catholic journals were much more severe in their judgments. *Commonweal* said in April 1964 after the second session of the Council had ended, that "there is not much evidence that Pope Paul is vigorously pursuing the implications of Pope John's initiatives. On the contrary, the few things Pope Paul has said seem to lend credence to the reports of a repudiation of his predecessor's attitudes and explorations."[4] By the end of the third session even Xavier Rynne, who had tended to optimism in appraising Paul when he first ascended the papal throne, was blaming the dismal collapse of that session on "the character of Pope Paul."

Paul waited for fourteen months to issue his first encyclical, a longer waiting period than that of any recent pope, and then he produced a pronouncement that was so balanced that *Time* said the key word seemed to be "but." At that particular moment Paul could easily have given the liberals more encouragement, especially since they had shown such great power at the first session of the Council. Instead he gave them "dangerous ambivalences." The phrase is that of the editor of the *Christian Century* who had been very hopeful about the potential ecumenism of Vatican II. Equally friendly and hopeful had been another American Protestant leader, Henry P. Van Dusen, former President of Union Theological Seminary. Speaking of the "millions of non-Catholics who have rejoiced at the manifest liberation and revivification of world-wide Roman Catholicism during the 'Johannine era,' " Van Dusen bluntly declared in September 1964 that the new pope's first encyclical "stirs non-Catholics with dismay. . . . in each ambivalence, the final and decisive alternative is negative."[5]

During the first session of the Council, which Montini had attended as cardinal and archbishop of Milan, he had been quite voluble, making three major speeches on the Council floor and writing both a pastoral letter and weekly letters for his diocesan newspaper, *L'Italia*. Always he spoke in glowing terms of Pope John. His letters reflected the views of an intelligent follower, not of an intellectual pioneer. He was just progressive enough in his commitments to keep both sides guessing as to his real feelings about the great conservative-liberal battle that was taking place at that time. Whenever possible he substituted questions for dogmatic answers; balancing judgments for firm opinions. Typical of his outlook was a paragraph from his second letter to his diocese: "There begins a solemn dialogue, new and exalted, between the Church and the modern world. Will there be understanding? Response? Let us think and pray."

In such prepapal utterances Montini was on entirely safe ground in saying, "It will therefore be a Council of positive rather than punitive reforms; of exhortations rather than of anathemas." He chose a balanced position by saying: "The present structure of the Church certainly needs overhauling but it cannot be substantially changed."[6] At the same time he admitted that the present movement "might lead" to a "greater and more organic internationalization of the Church's central government," and apparently he saw nothing inappropriate in this so long as the absolute authority of the Church was maintained. He affirmed that authority in no uncertain language.

His choice of words about separate communities of Christians was equally skillful. "Let us hope," he said, "that the Council will loosen the fetters of past memories." He landed on the safe side by declaring: "May we all long for our Lord to grant our prayer for the reuniting of Christians around Peter and the apostles in communion with him." This could mean only one thing, the return of Protestants and Orthodox to Rome. Several years earlier, before the pressure for a change of birth control regulations had become as intense as it is today, he had committed himself unmistakably in a pastoral letter to his Milan people against "the vicious practice of avoiding conception unlawfully."

About the same time, in 1960, he revealed an equally balanced set of views concerning the economic order. He favored a "tempered gradualism in [economic] reform." He warned against "selfish riches" and mentioned "the need for a more equable distribution of economic goods," even "a proper share in a company's profits," and, perhaps, "a share in its management." At the same time he paid tribute to "private initiative in the economic order" and reminded his hearers that the Church "will light the way for men of good will."

A review of all his published prepapal utterances reveals Paul as a fairly able preacher, much more skillful with precarious words than John, doctrinally cautious, but slightly left of center in social matters. If that slightly left-of-center position is seen to be the most politically feasible position for a candidate for pope, the remark is not necessarily invidious. Paul had been cautious throughout all his life in his major commitments. His eleventh-hour sagacity before becoming pope was not an eleventh-hour invention.

Catholic liberals at the Council were profoundly worried about their new pope's Italian policies. Paul aroused new anxieties between the third and fourth sessions of the Council by reactivating the notorious Civic Committees of Italy, originally organized in 1947 for the elections of 1948 and 1949. At that time the Vatican had plunged into Italian partisan politics as an avowed enemy of the left. These Committees, in spite of their noble purposes, used methods in fighting the left that were not unlike those of the rightist forces in the McCarthy era in the United States. They made anti-Communism a fanatical religion under the leadership of McCarthy's Italian counterpart, Dr. Luigi Gedda. Happily, Paul, although a collaborator with Gedda, had never been a fascist. His record vis-à-vis Mussolini had been that of a critic rather than a friend.

Certainly Paul's caution both before he ascended the papal throne and afterwards was not because of any lack of understanding. All observers agree that the present pope is a very intelligent man. His caution is part of his intelligence—and his comprehension of Catholic history. Having come up through the Vatican diplomatic bureaucracy and surely having witnessed the fatal effect of even a single blunder on the career of a bureaucrat, he learned to practise caution from long experience. Monsieur Jean Guitton, an important French lay auditor at the Council, compared John and Paul in a 1963 interview by saying:

> John XXIII when he encountered serious difficulties raised himself above them by an act of supernatural faith; he surmounted them, he rose right above them, and so made them disappear. Paul VI, on the other hand, swoops on the difficulty like an eagle—he has the green-blue eyes of an eagle—he

> sees right through it, he feels it. . . . Paul VI likes to go to the heart of the matter, and cause the solution to emerge from the core of the problem.[7]

Most people respect eagles but do not like them very much. This was to be Paul's fate, at least in his first years as pope.

In one respect Monsieur Guitton overvalued his idol. Far from going to the heart of most of the important matters before the Council and finding a solution, Paul chose to evade many a problem and smother controversial issues with ecclesiastical irrelevancies. When he was chosen pope, the *New York Times* headline read: "New Pope's Views as Cardinal Strongly Liberal." The gracious judgment was a little premature. The adverb could be questioned. Paul could more properly be called slightly or ambiguously liberal.

On the credit side of Montini's nine-year period of service in Milan was the initiation or approval of various ecumenical activities with the Protestants and Orthodox in that city.[8] As archbishop, Montini definitely veered away from any bitter condemnation of Protestantism, particularly from a pastoral letter attacking Milan Protestantism that had been written two years before he took the Milan post. He helped organize and he approved the first regular meetings between Catholic priests and Protestant pastors in Italy, and Italian Protestants rated him more intelligently "ecumenical" than John in respect to the amenities of Catholic-Protestant relationship in their country.

On the debit side of Montini's Milan record was the suppression of an independent liberal Catholic fortnightly, *Adesso*, which the Holy Office killed in 1962, apparently with Montini's full approval. In this incident Montini turned loose upon the *Adesso* liberals the full conventional sarcasm of authority, saying that "some people with ludicrous temerity speak of 'humble disobedience' to the hierarchy as a right and as a brilliant discovery of the spiritual life." For Paul, it seemed that "What is missing is a sincere and loyal 'sense of the Church.' " Enzo Forcella said in the *New Republic* of this incident: "I had the opportunity of reading the letters that the future Pope Paul VI sent to the editor of that journal (*Adesso*). They have the harsh, imperious note of the superior writing to his inferiors and, in addition, carried the veiled threat of spiritual sanctions. Here the tone is more that of Paul III, instigator of the 'Holy Roman Inquisition' than that of John XXIII."[9] The *Adesso* editors, protesting their right to "make use of those gifts of God, intelligence and freedom," decided that they had no alternative but to shut down their paper.

Montini demonstrated a different kind of spirit in 1962 when he took an unusual step as archbishop and appealed directly to Dictator Franco of Spain to grant clemency to certain Spanish students who had been protesting against the dictator's policies. This earned him some Spanish hostility when his name came up for election as pope in 1963.

After such a record as archbishop many journalists called Montini an enigma when he was elected pope, and one year later many of these same journalists were still puzzled by the conduct of the man. On his first anniversary as pope, Robert C. Doty of *The New York Times* said that his "personality, his character and the orientation of his policies [are] still wrapped in enigma and contradiction." Mr. Doty indicated that one of the sources of the difficulty in assessing Paul was contained in a statement he himself had made that he hoped to emulate his three predecessors, "Pius XI for his strong will, Pius XII for his knowledge and wisdom, and John XXIII for his limitless goodness." Unfortunately, these three popes represented so many diverging and even contradictory attitudes toward the world that no pope who attempted to imitate all of them could be anything else but a bundle of contradictions. Paul attempted to hide the contradictions in clichés, as, for example, when he summarized the relationship between church and state by saying: "The Church's mission is to carry the sacred into the relationship with the profane in such a way that the sacred is communicated without being contaminated, and the profane is sanctified without being falsified."

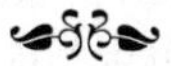

Giovanni Battista Enrico Antonio Maria Montini was born to middle-class parents in Concesio, near Brescia, in northern Italy, on September 26, 1897. His father was a fairly well-to-do lawyer and journalist, a devout Catholic, and a supporter of the founder of Christian democracy in Italy, Don Luigi Sturzo, who was ultimately removed as a political leader by Pius XI when the pope decided to compromise with Mussolini. The older Montini was a crusading member of the Italian parliament for three terms as a representative of Sturzo's Christian democracy. The future pope must have learned much about the techniques of influencing public opinion from his journalist father. As a child young Montini was so frail that for several years he had private schooling. His training was entirely within the Catholic system, in a Jesuit high school in Brescia and at the Gregorian Institute in Rome, with later study in Catholic canon law at the Ecclesiastical Academy in Rome.

Can the product of such narrow training be called an educated man? It is a question that goes to the very heart of the criticism leveled against Catholic seminary training by some of the liberals at the Vatican Council, especially by liberal Catholic journals in the United States. But no Catholic, of course, would directly question the educational qualifications of a pope. Paul had the training which was fairly typical of Catholic bishops throughout the world, a narrow training with heavy emphasis upon languages, philosophy, and Christian tradition. He is a reasonably gifted linguist who speaks enough words in eight modern tongues to greet public audiences in their own languages. His verbal equipment includes some heavily accented English and a somewhat better understanding of written English. He has some claim to knowledge of the United States, since he visited America twice for brief intervals in 1951 and 1960. He received an honorary degree at Notre Dame and made a short motor trip with twenty-four hour stops in such cities as New York, Chicago, Detroit, Boston, Philadelphia, Washington, and Baltimore.

After becoming pope he demonstrated not only great interest in world affairs but great skill in promoting his image as a salesman of brotherhood and world peace. His unprecedented visits to Israel and India in 1964 and to the United Nations in 1965 were well handled and constructive in their total effect. If the statements issued during these visits revealed no great intellectual originality, they at least served to remind the world of its desperate need for peace. On the peace front Paul carried on in the legitimate succession to John XXIII, and most nations, recognizing the need of moral leadership in behalf of peace, welcomed him warmly as a peace advocate.

Oddly enough, the one thing in Paul's past that recommended him most to the liberals at the Council was the fact that for a time in 1954 he seemed to be estranged from his father-image, Pius XII. The inner circle of the Roman Curia apparently thought that his assignment to Milan, even to so large and important a diocese with almost four million nominal Catholics, could be considered a demotion. It was rumored that he had been kicked upstairs for demonstrating real independence. Wild statements about the reasons for his alleged demotion crept into some sections of the Italian press. No one yet knows what were the motives that led Pius XII to move out his most faithful servant from the immediate papal household and then, after making him archbishop of Milan, to delay the granting of a red hat. If Montini had not had to wait for his cardinal's hat until John became pope, he might well have been elected Roman Pontiff himself in 1958 instead of John. (A pope does not need to be a cardinal or even a bishop to secure election, but for many centuries this double qualification has been considered necessary.)

As it was, Paul became the first of the fifty-two cardinals appointed by John when he became pope. After John's death it was evident that Montini was a heavily favored candidate to succeed him. Widely and favorably known among the foreign cardinals who had participated in the long drawn-out choice of John, he possessed the basic qualifications considered necessary for a pope. He was Italian; he was archbishop of an important city; he was an experienced member of the inner bureaucracy; and he was sixty-five, an appropriate age for a papal candidate.

His personal life had been lived entirely free from scandal. He was pro-Council in his record without any extremist connotations. In the first session of the Council he had carefully refused to identify himself with either liberals or conservatives. These qualifications scored for him a fairly quick election as John's successor in June 1963 on the sixth ballot. The election scarcely came as a surprise, since Montini had been rated as most likely to succeed by many journalists.

The Council liberals would probably have preferred a non-Italian pope, and faint gestures were made inside the papal conclave in that direction but without any real hope of success. It was said that two reasonably young and vigorous cardinals outside of Italy, Leo Joseph Suenens of Belgium and Franziskus Koenig of Austria, had some following in the conclave. It was also said that the conservatives, under the leadership of the redoubtable old warhorse Ottaviani had agreed among themselves to support another Italian cardinal, Ildebrando Antoniutti, a rather colorless Curia stalwart who had served as nuncio to Franco's Spain for nine years. Ottoviani himself was considered too partisan to have any chance of election, and his partial blindness helped to eliminate him. The voluble archconservative, Cardinal Ruffini of Palermo, the Barry Goldwater of the Council, would have been a possibility only if the right wing had captured the whole Church.

The choice of a pope by an elaborate ceremony is called an "election." It is a pity that there is not a better English word. The choice of Paul at this important moment in Church history, perhaps the most important moment in *all* Church history, might be more properly described as a selective appointment. The selection, accomplished in the sealed Sistine Chapel with the traditional flourishes of pomp and ceremony familiar to the world, was made by eighty cardinals, most of them of advanced age and previously chosen for their loyalty to the whole system.

All the outward precautions were taken to make sure that the voting was honest and accurately counted, but the final precaution could not be taken. These cardinals did not necessarily represent the will of their Church because no attempt had been made to make the process of selection truly democratic or truly representative. They were aged routinists, samples of a tradition-bound bureaucracy, with only a few scattered individuals who deserved the description "liberal." Of the cardinals only seven were below sixty, and eighteen were past eighty. Twenty-nine were Italian, but this figure was not an index of Latin strength in the College of Cardinals. The Italians, Latin Americans, Spaniards, and French together dominated the scene. The United States had only five votes.

It was rumored—Rome was full of such rumors—that Cardinal Spellman played a key role in convincing other conservatives that Montini was acceptable as a successor to John, in spite of the fact that Spain's Franco had appealed to his six Spanish cardinals to vote against the Milan archbishop. It was said that Spellman had a long private talk with Montini shortly before the conclave and apparently came away feeling satisfied that he would not be too abrupt or progressive in carrying out the Johannine program. It was said also that all five of the American cardinals voted for the winner. It was universally conceded that the drive for a non-Italian pope was only a token drive—there is no immediate prospect of the selection of any non-Italian to the papal throne for many, many years.

In the coronation on June 3, 1963, the Council liberals found no cause for rejoicing. The ceremony itself was as barbarically imperialistic as ever, including the "obediences" of the cardinals who were obliged to kneel and kiss the pope's hand. The ceremony ended when Cardinal Ottaviani placed the crown on Paul's head and intoned in Latin; "Receive the tiara adorned with three crowns and know that thou art the Father of Princes and Ruler of Kings, the Vicar on Earth of Our Saviour Jesus Christ, to Whom is honor and glory through the ages."

Paul's coronation homily contained little that was controversial except two passages, one on the Virgin Mary and one on the separated brethren. Paul implored "the help of the most gracious God, through the intercession, first of all, of the Virgin Mother of God." This seemed conventional enough but it was also a trifle controversial coming after the Council discussion of ways to soften the impact of Mariology on Protestantism (see Chapter 9). Then, in describing the appeal of the Council to the separated brethren, Paul expressed hope that the Church might "adapt its forms to the needs of the times, and so present the Church to the Christian brothers, separated from its perfect unity, in a way to make attractive, easy and joyous to them, the sincere recomposition in truth and charity, of the mystic body of the sole Catholic Church." Protestants and Orthodox were slightly puzzled by that word "recomposition." Certainly there was no hint in such language of any negotiations with Protestants on a basis of equality.

Paul dispelled some of these misgivings when he opened the second session on September 29, 1963. To those of us who were packed into the great aula for several hours, sweating in the overheated and badly organized crowd, the impression made by the new pope was mixed. He spoke with power and conviction, his voice ringing out almost with the firmness of youth, although it had a slightly displeasing metallic note in it. His professions of warmhearted good will for everybody concerned would have produced more assent if he had reduced the medieval and servile elegance of the whole proceeding. Although he walked part of the way down the central aisle, there was nothing else about his ceremonial conduct that day to symbolize humility or equality. He was accoutered to the papal limit of elegance, with *sedia gestatoria*, great flabelli, satin-cushioned prayer desk, and brocaded robe.

He might have excused the aged cardinals from the ceremony of obediences—it was the third time since his election they had been obliged to perform this ceremony—but they walked across the great central space of the aula, climbed the steps to the papal throne, bowed deeply, and kissed the pope's right hand in obeisance. After the cardinals came two archbishops and two bishops, representing all the bishops, who knelt and kissed the pope's right knee; the procession ended with two abbots and two general superiors of monastic orders who acknowledged their lowly status by genuflecting and kissing the pope's right foot.

Paul's opening speech on that day was, on the whole, cautiously orthodox, with hopeful sorties into the twentieth century. He appealed to separated brethren in a manner which was much more than an invitation to return. But, in spite of his very cordial expressions, the meaning of the invitation was somewhat ambiguous. Speaking of the "representatives of the Christian denominations separated from the Catholic Church," Paul said:

> Our voice trembles and Our heart beats the faster both because of the inexpressible consolation and reasonable hope that their presence stirs up within Us, as well as because of the deep sadness We feel at their prolonged separation.
>
> If we are in any way to blame for that separation, we humbly beg God's forgiveness and ask pardon too of our brethren who feel themselves to have been injured by us. For our part, we willingly forgive the injuries which the Catholic Church has suffered, and forget the grief endured during the long series of dissensions and separations. May the heavenly Father deign to hear our prayers and grant us true brotherly peace. . . .
>
> Our manner of speaking toward them is friendly, completely sincere and loyal. We lay no snares. We are not motivated by temporal interests. We owe our faith—which we believe to be divine—the most candid and firm attachment.
>
> But at the same time We are convinced that this does not constitute an obstacle to the desired understanding with Our separated brethren, precisely because it is the truth of the Lord and therefore the principle of union, not of distinction and separation. At any rate, we do not wish to make of our Faith an occasion for polemics.[10]

That last sentence could be accepted by the world joyously. Men were tired of religious polemics. The great American newspapers and television networks played up the new pope's conciliatory words. The world wanted religious peace.

If all that Pope Paul said and did during the Council had matched this passage in his opening speech, the world's judgment of him would have been almost unanimously cordial. As it was, he seemed to move downward from that peak of broadmindedness. His abrupt dismissal of the Council's majority views on two occasions at the end of the third session in 1964, when religious liberty and Jewish relations were being debated, made him, for a few days at least, the most unpopular pope of recent times. When he was carried down the central aisle of St. Peters on his *sedia gestatoria* on the final day of that third session, a spectator could almost feel the waves of cold anger that came from the bishops in the flanking rows of seats as he passed them by. Here was a man who had talked cooperation with all the bishops and with all faiths in public and then had quietly, perhaps only temporarily, surrendered to the pressure of a few. Long before this sour denouement the real Paul had become visible through the surrounding mists of adulation. In celebrating the reactionary Council of Trent during the second session the new pope seemed to put his seal of approval on what Lord Acton had described long ago as "the stamp of an intolerant age" which "perpetuated by its decrees the spirit of an austere immorality." "Let's face it," said one archbishop to a reporter for *Time*, "he's weak."

It would be more accurate to say that Paul, by the end of the third session, had revealed himself as primarily an institutional strategist bent on retaining centralized Roman power when the world crisis and the crisis within Christianity needed a pioneer reformer with both courage and vision. If, in Emerson's words, an institution is the lengthened shadow of a man, Paul had reversed the process. He had become the lengthened shadow of an institution.

In the final session Paul had the sagacity to correct his own image by several reasonably progressive moves, but it was then too late to alter his fundamental reputation. Although by that time his leadership had become reasonably productive, he had given the impression that his motives were personal and ecclesiastical, not human or universal. Like other popes, he had fallen a victim to the institutional narcissism of his Church. When a critical choice confronted him he seemed to think in terms of the fate of the particular institution that he served. He finally promulgated near-orthodox doctrine in the most fundamental controversies of his age, the controversies about birth control, mixed marriage, a celibate clergy, and papal supremacy. (We shall describe Paul's role in these controversies in the chapters that are to follow.)

In spite of Paul's weakness and vacillation in dealing with crucial issues at the Council itself, he staged a sharp recovery in reputation outside the Council in 1965 and 1966 by acting as a self-appointed leader in the movement for world peace. He scored a triumph of showmanship for himself and his Church. Some hostile critics believe that he deliberately sought to demote the Council's prestige by his 1965 visit to the U.N. at the height of the Council sessions. He certainly shifted the world's attention from the Council to himself, but it is not necessary to deduce anything venal from this papal strategy. Paul is a shrewd political strategist who possesses a genuine ambition to become the world's peacemaker. No one doubts the sincerity of that ambition or the worthiness of its object. It may be that history will give him his greatest accolade for shifting the emphasis of his Church from a negative anti-Communism to a positive commitment to world government.

CHAPTER FOUR ❧ COLLEGIALITY TO INFALLIBILITY

"THE Very Roman Catholic Church" was the heading over an editorial published at the beginning of the first session of Vatican II in the London *Tablet*, the most intellectual of the English Catholic journals. The heading sums up very well the crucial underlying issue of papal authority as it came to the Council.

For at least seventeen centuries the Catholic Church has been "very Roman." With the exception of the period of exile during the Avignon Papacy, about seventy years in the fourteenth century, the Church's capital has always been in Rome. Its bureaucracy has been centered in Rome both geographically and intellectually, and its pattern of government has imitated the pattern of the Holy Roman Empire.

During all those seventeen centuries the officialdom of the Church worked steadily to strengthen the central Roman authority, and this process of centralization was increasingly focused on the personal power of one man, the pope. His ascendancy over other bishops was gradually established during the first four centuries of Christianity, then his primacy was read back retroactively into questionable fragments of scripture and tradition until it became a "divine" dogma, and finally the capstone of papal infallibility was added to the whole mixture in the First Vatican Council of 1870.

In this long process the Papacy went far beyond the Roman Empire itself in autocratic centralization. Even today no monarch of the world is treated with half the official deference accorded to "the servant of the servants of God." The pope is *sui generis*, and his claim to a special exalted status has been frozen into Church dogma at the level of divine revelation.

God, it is claimed, has established a personal, absolute government over His only Church through a specific command delivered by Jesus Christ to Peter and to the other apostles, and recorded in the sixteenth chapter of Matthew. This pledge and command, as it appears in the English version of the Catholic Vulgate, reads:

> And I say unto thee: That thou art Peter; and upon this rock I will build my church, and the gates of hell shall not prevail against it.
>
> And I will give to thee the keys of the kingdom of heaven. And whatsoever thou shalt bind upon earth, it shall be bound also in heaven: and whatsoever thou shalt loose on earth, it shall be loosed also in heaven.

This ambiguous "rock" passage, not repeated elsewhere in the Gospels and disputed by many of the world's greatest biblical scholars, is now used by the Church to "prove" that Jesus established a chain of clerical command for his church after naming Peter the first pope.[1] Attached to this elementary belief is the supplementary and equally important belief that all the popes since Peter have inherited the divine and exclusive sanction for the personal type of autocratic government represented by the Papacy.

Although it is impossible within the scope of this book to analyze the mountains of controversial literature centering on the "rock" passage and the dogmas derived from it, it can be said without fear of successful contradiction that (1) Peter probably went to Rome at some time during his life but there is no evidence that he was ever a pope there; (2) Jesus never manifested any intention to establish a particular autocratic form of government for his church; and (3) the dogma of papal infallibility is wholly without respectable support both in scripture and in the earliest Church traditions. Many scholars, both Catholic and non-Catholic, share some or all of these conclusions; some of their works are listed in the Notes.[2]

None of the fundamental Catholic assertions of papal authority were directly attacked at Vatican II. Both papal primacy and papal infallibility were blandly accepted as established truths, as self-evident as the sunrise and as indisputable as the Ten

Commandments. All the discussions on papal authority and the Church's form of government began where most non-Catholic criticism leaves off. There was no frontal attack in St. Peter's on the weakest and most extreme of papal claims, the dogma of papal infallibility. In this respect the bishops of 1962–1965 showed much less courage than the bishops of 1870.

Nevertheless there was a strong tangential attack on the operations of the Roman papal machine, and the battle in this area consumed more time and created more headlines than any other struggle during the Council years. The Council had not been in session for a week until it became clear that, although papal authority could not be directly attacked by any faithful bishop because it had become a divine dogma, the implications and applications of such authority could be challenged indirectly. The ostensible target of any criticism was not the Church itself, or even the pope. The critics preferred to aim their barbs at the most vulnerable part of the Roman apparatus, the ruling congregations and offices that make up the pope's cabinet and bureaucracy in the Roman Curia. The weapon of reform chosen for attack was the concept of the collegiality of bishops.

This battle against the abuses of power of the central bureaucracy of the Church was only one manifestation or symbol of the larger struggle. The deeper issue was the issue of decentralizing and slightly democratizing the gigantic, pope-centered power structure in Rome. But no one ever used the word "democracy" on the aula floor in connection with the liberalization of the central machinery of the Church; the word appeared very rarely even in the press conferences. None of the bishops wanted to say forthrightly that the whole papal complex of power was as outdated as feudalism and should be superseded by a self-governing church of the Catholic people.

Pope John and the members of the Roman Curia were caught by surprise when the challenge to centralized Roman authority initially cropped up, in the first session. The agenda had been arranged by appointed commissions to avoid as much as possible any direct challenge to the power structure. The first topic considered, the liturgy, was about as far away from the dangerous shoals of controversy as it could be. The Roman Curia leaders, who had never wanted a Council in the first place, seemed to believe that if the bishops talked long enough about minor things such as the language of the Mass and slight revisions in the liturgy the larger critical movements against papal absolutism might evaporate. They were surprised when virtually every topic seemed to lead ultimately to the question of authority. The heavy guns of the liberal opposition began firing point blank during the final week of the first session when the schema on the Church came up for discussion. This was the schema that outlined the basis for Church authority and ultimately became the Dogmatic Constitution on the Church.

As the debate on authority developed in the four sessions, three primary concepts were involved, the collegiality of bishops, the primacy of the pope, and the infallibility of the pope. In addition to these three primary concepts a fourth was brought up briefly, lay participation in the Church. The introduction of this concept seemed at first almost accidental and apologetic. There was little momentum behind it at first, since the few laymen present at the Council as observers had no power except advisory power and they seemed to have no great inclination to assert their rights against the hierarchy. However, the existence of the Catholic laymen seemed to require some official recognition, and that recognition was finally given in modified form in a decree, on the Apostolate of the Laity.

In the whole discussion of the issues of power and authority in the Church, the favorite verbal device for the advocates of reform was the phrase "collegiality of bishops." The phrase meant that bishops have a claim to share in the government of the Church together with the head bishop of them all, the pope, because the power of bishops had come from the original "college" of the apostles. The phrase did not imply directly any demotion of the pope himself or any challenge to his supreme authority.

The advocates of a new declaration on the collegiality of bishops claimed that their program was actually unfinished business for Vatican II because the issue of bishops' authority had been on the agenda at Vatican I when that Council was interrupted by the arrival of victorious Italian troops in Rome in 1870.[3] This military disaster, they argued, should not be allowed to prevent the completion of a new definition of episcopal authority. In 1870 the pope, Pius IX, had attained the full measure of his ambition. Now, respectfully, the bishops of Vatican II asked for a modest share in the completed scheme.

By collegiality they could mean several things. The word was batted about during Vatican II with considerable dexterity as well as ambiguity. Bishop Mansilla of Spain was quite in order during the debates in October 1963 when he said that the term "collegiality" is equivocal and ambiguous and that Church tradition supplies no apodictical (meaning certain) arguments for its juridical existence.[4] In the Council discussions it meant some kind of sharing of authority by the bishops with the pope, an interlocking of power with the Supreme Pontiff. The real question, of course, was how much sharing? And where did this bishops' authority come from, from the pope, from Christ, from vague tradition, from the Bible, or from a previous council? And what were its limits? How far could such collegial authority range?

Almost everybody at the Council agreed that there were two lines of authority in the Church, one stretching from Christ through Peter to the pope, the other stretching from Christ to the apostles as a group, then to the bishops as a group, or at least to the bishops individually. The serious questions in the discussion arose when someone tried to disentangle and distinguish between these lines of bishops' power and papal power. There was no disposition anywhere to deny supreme papal authority officially but there was, especially among the liberals, a rather confused determination to limit absolute papal power indirectly by creating a clearer, parallel and slightly competing line of bishops' authority. Above all, the liberals wanted to define bishops' power more clearly so that it could be used as a weapon against the Roman Curia.

Bound up in this situation was the claim of the Council itself to power. If the Council had been an ordinary legislative body with some kind of power over the whole Curial system of the Church, it is probable that a majority would have voted quite promptly for the demotion of the Holy Office and the downgrading of many other offices and congregations functioning in Rome. Lacking that authority, the bishops attacked the issue tangentially by trying to find in Catholic history the precedents that would make the collegiality of bishops seem not only traditional but also superior to the authority of the Curia. Thus the movement for the collegiality of bishops served as a kind of test of liberal power.

Although the full debate on the Church, which included the problem of bishops' functions, started in the first session, it did not break out in full battle until the second session, and finally reached a burst of acrimony (and voting) in September 1964 in the third session. The original drafts on the subject were met with a cross-fire of criticism on the Council floor. Between the first and second sessions, 372 suggested amendments were sent in for the schema on the Church. No one knows how many of these amendments were accepted, since the facts about such matters are not always made public. But everybody knew that collegiality was the hottest subject under discussion and that proposals about its application were pouring in.

Pope Paul introduced collegiality obliquely shortly before the second session started in a speech to the Roman Curia on September 21, 1963. His address was even more striking than usual in its ambiguity. It meant one thing to *Osservatore Romano* and another thing to the newspapers more friendly to the liberals. Paul praised the Curia for loyalty and achievement, asserted that "no hesitation regarding the principal wishes of the Pope will ever come from the Curia, and that the Curia will never be suspected of any differences of judgment or feeling with regard to the judgments and feelings of the Pope." Having expressed this monstrous overoptimism, Paul went on to open the door slightly to the idea of collegiality by saying that the Curia would not oppose "some representatives of the episcopacy" becoming "associated" with the Pope "in the study and responsibility of ecclesiastical government."[5]

What did *that* mean? At least one journalist went wild with hopeful conjecture and interpreted Paul's words as "a partial retreat from, or reinterpretation of, the dogma of infallibility of the Popes," an interpretation sharply corrected three days later by Paul himself. In a general audience he reminded his hearers of his own primacy as the sole heir of St. Peter's throne. Then, a few days later, after he had been borne into the aula on the shoulders of fourteen attendants, he made it quite clear that although he paid lip service to the concept of the power of the bishops and called for a discussion of the collegial issue, it was with the provision that bishops would be "taking for granted the dogmatic declarations of the First Vatican Council regarding the Roman Pontiff." He included also the provision that there should not be "a turning upside down of the Church's present way of life or a breaking with what is essential and worthy of veneration in her tradition."

Again the phrases of exception in Paul's language were so vague and general that the whole pronouncement became substantively meaningless. The Pope's tone, however, meant much to the liberals, and that meaning was primarily negative. It meant, as one Curial official assured me: "Council be careful! Leave the reform of the Roman Curia to me." It meant that no bishop or theologian who wanted advancement under Paul VI could feel secure in taking liberties with papal supremacy. Collegiality if carefully defined continued to be an acceptable idea—had not Paul himself endorsed it in a letter to his constituents while serving as Archbishop of Milan?—but collegiality must be kept in its place.

That slightly subordinate place was allegedly scriptural. The apostles had acted together, so the theory ran. As a group they could be called a college if one cared to use the word "college" very loosely. Perhaps Jesus intended that this group as a group should inherit at least part of the power of his Church. Hence they acquired by usage and apostolic succession some authority in Church government in their own right in conjunction with, but not in opposition to, the authority that passed down to the Church through Peter and his successors, the bishops of Rome.

It was exceedingly difficult to find in the New Testament any real support for anything more than the minimal interpretation of this alleged collegiality of the bishops. Cardinal Ottaviani asked bluntly: "When did the Apostles act collegially?" He got from learned men no very definite answers. In the second session one of Ottaviani's reactionary compatriots, Cardinal Ruffini of Palermo, three times attacked the whole idea of the collegiality of bishops, declaring that it had no biblical authority whatever.

One should be reluctant to agree with Cardinal Ruffini about anything, but a careful examination of the so-called collegiality texts in the New Testament shows nothing more than some loose form of cooperation among the apostles. Their nearest approach to collective action as a college came in sending out early missionaries (Acts 6:22, 23), but even in this passage the apostles acted with the elders and "the whole church." The chief statements attributed to Jesus that refer to alleged collegiality (Matthew 18:18;28:18–20; Mark 16:15; John 14:16; 17:26; 20:21) do not reveal anything beyond a general intention to send out disciples to evangelize the world. There is no evidence of a determination to commit apostles and the church to a rigid form of organization.

There was, of course, much group activity in the early Christian church, including the laying on of hands to authorize missionary representatives to go out, and a certain amount of supervision by Paul and the apostles. But such phenomena scarcely sustain the elaborate scriptural claims about collegiality.

Catholic theologians are on stronger ground when they forget about scripture and argue for collegiality from their own Church's tradition. They can point, for example, to the famous "Collective Statement of the German Episcopate" issued in 1875 when the rumblings of German anger against the dogma of papal infallibility had convinced Pius IX that he must make some concessions if he wanted to hold his German followers. It can be argued that the concessions to bishops' collegiality he made to the Germans in 1875 were the concessions he might have been forced to make at the Vatican Council in 1870 if its course had not been interrupted by the invasion of the Italian army. Astonishingly enough, Pius IX gave unqualified endorsement to the following points in that German bishop's letter:

> The Pope cannot arrogate to himself the episcopal rights, nor substitute his power for that of the bishops; the episcopal jurisdiction has not been absorbed in the papal jurisdiction; the pope was not given the entire fullness of the bishops' powers by the decrees of the Vatican Council; he has not virtually taken the place of each individual bishop; he cannot put himself in the place of a bishop in each single instance, vis-à-vis governments; the bishops have not become instruments of the pope; they are not officials of a foreign sovereign in their relations with their governments.[6]

These rather startling concessions—startling in view of the declaration of papal infallibility in 1870—partly depend for their significance on the interpretation of several of the slightly ambiguous phrases. They did not change the fundamental power of the pope to appoint all the bishops, to remove them from office so long as he did not destroy their status as bishops, or to announce in Rome new dogmas in opposition to the opinions of all bishops. These papal powers were made clear not only in the Constitution *Pastor Aeternus* of 1870 but in the canon law promulgated in the revised code in 1918.[7]

This is all quite confusing, since divine authority seems to flow in two streams through pope and bishops but always with the proviso that one stream, the stream flowing through the bishops, can be diverted at will by papal edict. The confusion is not cleared up even by the Church's greatest theologians. Father Karl Rahner, one of the best of the progressive theologians, has admitted in one sentence of Germanic length that

> . . . it is not easy to understand how it is that a bishop has inalienable rights *iuris divini* which the pope cannot take from him, how it is that he governs his flock in the name of Christ and his own name, and not in the name of the pope, how it is that he is no mere functionary, when nowhere in our ecclesiology are we able to lay down within definable limits which rights the episcopate as a whole, and hence the individual

> bishop, inalienably and irrevocably possesses; when the pope has undoubted right, immediately and in any given case, and without having to observe any judicial process, to intervene directly in any diocese and in any of its affairs, to appoint or to depose any bishop.[8]

In other words, there is a conflict of authority between popes and bishops but nothing specific must be done about it. The incorrigible Maximos IV Saigh, Patriarch of Antioch, proclaimed in November 1963 that something should be done about it. In his defiant French he asked for a "permanent synod" to assist the Holy Father, a synod with rotating, short-term membership and authority even over the Roman Curia. He got nowhere with such a bold proposal, but by this time the sentiment of the fathers was for definite proposals. With the opposition of only a small die-hard minority, they approved in September 1964 a series of propositions looking toward a new collegial organization in the Church.

In spite of the affirmative votes in behalf of some kind of collegiality, Cardinal Ottaviani and his cohorts, during the second and third sessions, tried to persuade the delegates that solemn votes by the Council on the subject were merely "advisory" and that the Theological Commission, of which Ottaviani was head, had a perfect right to proceed as if the collegiality of bishops could be buried by the Curia at will. It was at first feared that Ottaviani had the support of the pope himself in this maneuver, but on this particular issue Pope Paul decided not to defy the majority of the bishops directly.

One reason for his acquiescence was that in November 1963 a real crisis in authority arose in the Council concerning collegiality. More than eight hundred Fathers, including twelve cardinals, annoyed by Curial opposition, signed a petition to the pope asking him in effect to call off the Holy Offices' stalling tactics and recognize the will of the liberal majority on the question of collegiality. The aged but very influential Cardinal Frings of Cologne led the attack on the Holy Office. Cardinals Spellman and McIntyre did not belong to any liberal majority at that point but the most advanced of the European and American cardinals did. The pope ironed things out with some equivocations as usual. He endorsed collegiality but . . .

By the time the Constitution on the Church was finally promulgated toward the end of the third session, the chapter covering collegiality acknowledged papal primacy no less than twenty times. Paul helped to sterilize the collegial concept with a *nota*, printed on a separate sheet of paper, inserted after the debate on the floor had been completed. This nota was considered undebatable because it came from the "Higher Authority." It was read on the floor by the Secretary General of the Council, Archbishop Pericle Felici, who pointed out that the votes of the Council on the whole subject must be received in the light of this "preliminary explanatory note." Although the *nota* was not very different from the expressions of sentiment already accepted by the Fathers, it did underscore Papal supremacy in a very heavy-handed manner. It said: "In all of these it is apparent that we are dealing with a joining of the bishops with their head, and never with an action of the bishops independently of the pope. In that case, lacking the authority of the head the bishops cannot act as a college—as is clear from the very notion of 'college.' This hierarchical communion of all the bishops with the Sovereign Pontiff is certainly a solemn teaching of Tradition."

Some of the Fathers were very much annoyed that, after all the discussion about the authority of bishops, something should be added to documents which had already been worked over so thoroughly by the Council. After years of discussion, the pope, while insisting on remaining anonymous as the silent author in the background of the *nota*, was now adding something to the Council's resolutions that could not be directly attacked. His critics were doubly handicapped in questioning his intervention because they were not sure how much Curial authority and personal authority was represented by the *nota*. Liberals reasoned that if their collegial decisions could be so easily altered by the pope without any formal advance consideration by the Council itself, when the pope was only a few yards away from them in the Vatican Palace, their chances of success in disagreeing with the pope later on were very slim. Although the whole subject of collegiality in the first three sessions ended on this rather sour and indeterminate note, since the pope created no senate of bishops at that time, Pope Paul recognized the necessity of meeting the demand of the bishops by some concrete program.

The pope finally announced a partial surrender to the wishes of the majority at the beginning of the fourth session on September 14, 1965. Although his partial surrender was welcome, the bishops were still skeptical. There was no applause for his announcement in St. Peter's, although the bishops applauded Paul heartily a moment later when he announced his trip to the United Nations in New York. By this time the bishops were wary of any purely verbal concession and their wariness was quite justified.

When the September 14 announcement was analyzed carefully, the paragraph about collegial reform was seen to be full of conditional features. A new organization was to be called an Episcopal Synod, not an Episcopal Senate. Synods are organizations subordinate to bishops over which bishops have virtually absolute control. This particular synod was to be subordinate to the Bishop of Rome. The new organization could be called into being only by the pope, not by any action of the bishops alone. It was to have no legislative powers unless the pope conferred some legalistic or legislative powers by special pronouncement. There was no indication that it would have any regular sessions since it was to be convened only "according to the needs of the Church, by the Roman Pontiff, for consultation and collaboration when for the general good of the Church this will seem opportune to Us." Even the monarchic "Us" instead of "us" was significant.

In order to save the pride of the die-hards of the Curia who had opposed the whole thing, Pope Paul added: "In a special way it can be of use in the day-to-day work of the Roman Curia to which We owe so much gratitude for its effective help. Just as the bishops in their dioceses, so We too always need the Curia for carrying out Our apostolic responsibilities." This made it possible for the beleaguered conservatives to argue that even the new Synod would, in practice, be subordinate to the Curia.

There was one very hopeful feature in the whole plan. The greater part of the bishops in the Episcopal Synod were to be chosen by the National Episcopal Conferences. This move away from centralized Roman dictation was hopeful. But, lest any student should believe that the reform constituted a thorough democratization of the Church, he should be reminded that every bishop is chosen by the pope and is removable by the pope at will, that there is no place in the new scheme for any representation by the great masses of the Catholic people, and that even priests as priests are totally disfranchised in the entire set-up.

The bishops were somewhat surprised and very much relieved on the next day, September 15, 1965, when the Pope actually walked into the aula without his *sedia gestatoria* and promptly implemented the new plan with a *Motu proprio*, read by Archbishop Felici, describing how the new Synod was to be set up.[8] Judging from the description, the new Synod would have somewhere between 100 and 200 members; no country would have more than 4 members; the Pope could add his own personal appointees up to 15 per cent of the total; the Synod would have a permanent General Secretary and assistants; the cardinals in charge of the Roman Curia offices would sit in as full members. It was estimated that with about 52 episcopal conferences functioning in various nations in the world, the combined system of appointment and election of prelates by conferences could bring the Synod up to about 120 members, perhaps to 150.

The new Synod would still be lopsided and merely advisory. Italy would still have enormously disproportionate power, since it would have the same number of regular bishops as the United States and in addition the heads of offices of the Curia, who have been traditionally Italian. Even the bishops elected by episcopal conferences could be disapproved by the pope if he saw any signs of rebellion against his authority. The progressives, making the best of a disappointing gift, agreed that much would depend on the choice of a General Secretary for this new agency. The first meeting of this new Synod has already been set for 1967, but the pope has not announced its scope or purpose.

Wildly overoptimistic descriptions of the new scheme immediately appeared in the press. Many commentators seemed to forget that the new instrument was only advisory to the pope, with no independent powers of its own. Also the new Synod will be structurally temporary, not permanent, since all participants in it will lose their membership as soon as any given session ends.

Some of the overoptimism about the new Synod was, no doubt, a matter of clerical pride. The progressives had fought so long and so hard for genuine reform in the power structure of their Church that they did not want to admit the inadequacy of the reform they had secured. They did not want to go home and say that the mountain had labored and brought forth a mouse.

So, on September 20, 1965, they warmly applauded a fulsome letter of thanks to Pope Paul for the "beautiful and promising novelty" of collegiality which he had given them, neglecting to point out that his "gift" was minimal and that it left them and the Catholic people without any representative institution possessing definite powers. The conservative Italian press accepted the reform without apprehension because it was hedged about with so many restrictions. The Communist journal *L'Unita* was more blunt. "A more restrictive measure of collegiality," it said, "could not be given." It described the "conquest of the innovators" as "emptied from within to the greatest possible extent." About ten days after the announcement of the new machinery of consultation, Cardinal Marella, in a press conference, when asked whether a new Synod might actually develop democratic powers and elect a pope, replied that such a development might come "possibly in the year 3,001."[9]

Nevertheless, the bishops had a new instrument of power. It was feeble and its status was equivocal, but it represented a breakthrough in the long centuries of abject subjection to the pope. Its existence was recognized not only in the schema on the Church but also in the Decree on the Pastoral Office of Bishops. Whether it amounted to anything would depend upon the sincerity and progressiveness of each succeeding pope.

The Council's new gospel of collegiality meant absolutely nothing to the hundreds of thousands of priests throughout the world. They were not permitted to share in that collegiality and they were given no new bill of rights in the schema on the Church or in the schemata that discussed bishops, liturgy, or priestly formation. They were described as "co-workers with their bishops" and consecrated "through the ministry of the bishop"; bishops were told to "gladly listen" to their priests. It was even stated that some new form of priestly group action might be encouraged in the shape of a "senate of priests representing the presbytery." But this reform must wait for postconciliar action by the Commission on Canon Law, and in the meantime priests are told to "sincerely look upon the bishop as their Father and reverently obey him."

No suggestion was advanced in the final texts on the Church or on priestly training that the power of bishops over priests should be modified in any way. At present priests can be jurisdictionally removed at will by their bishops and shipped off to a mountain monastery—or a Chicago slum—for repentance. Although the bishop does not have the uninhibited power to discharge his priests from the priesthood out of hand, the power to transfer them out of any position is tantamount to the power to destroy them as priests. This jurisdictional power over priests is still possessed by the bishops, and the priests have no machinery of self-determinism to challenge that power.

When priests sit in local diocesan synods, they are wholly subject to the veto power of their bishop over that assembly. If the bishop votes one way and 99 per cent of the priests vote the other way, the will of the bishop determines the outcome. All priests are appointed and assigned by bishops, not by congregations of the faithful. There was not a single parish priest as such present with voting rights at Vatican II, although a number of pastors were brought in as observers and some were permitted to say a few words to the assembled bishops.

This neglect of the priests did not pass entirely unnoticed. The bishops were somewhat startled during the third session when

112 of their number from Brazil and elsewhere denounced the original statement on priests as too paternalistic and pointed out that it "urges on priests things we dare not impose on ourselves." This criticism touched a sensitive spot, since the bishops of the Church are not all pledged to poverty. Their way of life, in spite of relatively low cash salaries, is often considered most luxurious by their poverty-stricken priests.

The new machinery for collegiality also meant nothing to the laymen of the Church. They were not included in its beneficence, a result that can scarcely be considered surprising, because there were no voting laymen in the Council to demand any new rights. Most of the few laymen who lived around the edges of the Council as correspondents, observers, or advisors seemed to have no will to demand anything for themselves in the power struggle. The representatives of Catholic lay organizations were flaccid, genial, and obedient in their expressions of gratitude for being allowed to sit on uncushioned seats at the edge of the arena and let the pope and the bishops run the Church. They were especially grateful for being called "the people of God" in one flowery schema, although that schema gave them no power whatever.

The word "laity" comes from the Greek word *laos*, meaning people. The hierarchy did not concede anything special in the nature of power by calling the laity the people of God. In the Council there was not a single lay delegate with power to vote, nor was there any layman who possessed the right to speak without a special grant of privilege coming from the appropriate clerical authorities. As Bishop Ernest Primeau of New Hampshire, one of the more effective progressives among the American bishops, remarked in the debate on the role of laymen, the impression now given to the world is that the function of the Catholic layman is to "believe, pray, obey and pay." Even Pope John did not seem to realize the necessity for bringing laymen in on the ground floor of the Council. He appointed a preparatory commission on the role of laymen without a single representative of the laymen themselves.

When the appropriate commissions brought forth the first

draft of the schema on the laity, in the second session, one good thing could be said for it. For the first time in the history of the Church the higher clerics had deigned to discuss laymen formally. Even Michael Novak, lay author and correspondent at the Council, who had been a leading critic of conservative policy, was grateful for that much attention to laymen, and declared: "The Church will never be the same again." But he added: "Even so, it may be doubted if many of the Fathers really grasped how clerical the Church is, how preoccupied it is with ecclesiastical matters, how great a chasm yawns between it and the world of men."[10]

A typical view of the function of the laity was expressed by Cardinal Ruffini of Palermo, the most persistent vocalist of the right wing. "More than ever," he said, "the hierarchy and the clergy are sorely in need of the assistance of the laity. Nevertheless, this does not authorize us to speak of a 'mission' of the laity. The laity does not share in the mission conferred by Christ on the Apostles." Then he went on to argue against anything that might lead to a weakening of the position of the hierarchy. Cardinal Bacci of the Roman Curia backed up Ruffini with similar reasoning, opposing the use of the phrase "universal priesthood" on the ground that the priesthood of the laity is not all-embracing.

The chasm between the lay and clerical points of view became more and more apparent as the debates proceeded. One bishop declared that the proposed words treating laymen handled them like little altar boys at the base of a clerical pyramid. They were treated like servants of the Church who had no participation in power. The lay auditors, of course, could not introduce any statement about the laity nor could they debate any statement on the floor or vote on it. There were ten of these lay auditors in Rome by the time the second session began—later increased to 12. Their presence, as one Jesuit commentator said, "was mostly symbolic and decorative." For the most part they were carefully chosen, cautious Catholic organization leaders who seemed to be a trifle surprised on arriving in Rome to find any discontent about lay status among the bishops.

The debates on laymen were almost wholly in platitudes.

There were plenty of exhortations for "cooperation" between clerics and laymen but few suggestions for definite grants of power to laymen. There was an almost feudal attitude of paternalism apparent in the addresses. "It is the hope of the Council Commission on the Lay Apostolate," said Archbishop William E. Cousins, a member of the Commission, "that the laity will accept the invitation to become part of the life of the Church."[11] There was no hint that the laity could invite the clergy to enter *their* Church. "There are many who interpret the great attention given by the Vatican Council to the laity as a kind of democratization of the Church," said Bishop deCastro Mayer of Brazil. "But this is wrong. The Church will never abandon its divinely established monarchical structure . . . the laity, mindful that they are the sheep in the Kingdom of God, will remain docile and will allow themselves to be guided by their legitimate shepherds."[12]

It is not surprising that some of the new and vigorous liberal laymen of the Church who were present at the Council as correspondents rebelled against this patronizing attitude. A group of laymen that included both Michael Novak and Robert Kaiser of *Time*, describing themselves simply as men "who under Providence, find themselves in the city of Rome," issued an appeal to the Council that was distributed in mimeographed form to the delegates and the press. The actual demands of these laymen were very mild. They did not ask for themselves any membership rights that stockholders possess in an ordinary corporation; but their rhetoric was sharp and it made an impression on the bishops as well as the press. "The present structure of the Church," they said, "under the accretion of the centuries, does not seem to reveal the light of the Gospels. In the minds of many, the Church is not the people of God but an ecclesiastical society of clerics and those who obey them."

Then the laymen asked:

> Are there safeguards for the layman against the misuses of ecclesiastical authority, misuses which through human frailty sometimes occur and which deprive him of rights proper to him by nature or by baptism, and prevent him from

seeking just restitution when wrong has been done him or his name? . . . do not the judicial proceedings of ecclesiastical curias, Roman and local, content themselves with moral standards formulated in 1588 and not fundamentally amended in the revisions of 1908 and 1917?[13]

The Catholic laymen were not advocating outright rebellion against clerical authority. Michael Novak, who may be taken as fairly typical of the new liberals who wish to stay in the Church, declared: "Laymen must seize initiative, express the faith that is in them, argue with their clergy about what seems good for the Church in their environment. But once a decision is made, laymen must also obey their shepherds. It is necessary to learn how to be a lion, and how to be a lamb—and when to be which."[14]

If these few lay critics behaved like lions at Vatican II, they were not entirely alone. Some of the bishops partially agreed with them as to needed reforms. Archbishop Eugene D'Souza of India suggested that laymen could well replace some clerics in the Vatican's diplomatic corps and in the Curia itself, a suggestion that undoubtedly left some of the aged Curia cardinals gasping a little. D'Souza's language was even better than his suggestions. Attacking the idea that a layman should do nothing without his bishop, he said that this concept meant "untold abuses and repressions of initiative. The people of God is not a totalitarian state where everything is run from the top." Bishop Stephen Leven of San Antonio, making a brisk speech that violated all precedent by actually introducing some English, championed the idea of "lay senates" to help bishops.

While this debate was going on in Rome, a parallel debate on Catholic laymen was developing in American Catholic journals, and some very frank words were being written. James O'Gara, in *Commonweal*, headed one of his editorials "Structures, Not Rhetoric." He contended that it was still "wildly exaggerated" to call this "The Age of the Laity," and he held up the Vatican Council itself as "the classic example" of the lay problem because it was set up without any machinery to allow the layman to express his views. True, some machinery of a sort was set up after the Council started, but "the point is that something is wrong when such after-the-fact corrections have to be made." O'Gara's chief indictment read:

> Modern man may be sharply different from his medieval forebears—or even from his grandfather. He may have a university education, he may be the master of politics, of sociology, of economics. Politicians may appeal to him and advertisers court him. When it comes to the Church, though, his role is unlikely to be much different from that of his unlettered ancestors. Unless he lives in an unusual parish or diocese, it is likely to be that of passive onlooker—active in the sense that he lives the life of grace, of course, attends Mass, receives the sacraments, but passive in the sense that he himself plays no more active role than that.[15]

Many other lay critics were much less polite. One of them, writing a letter in *Commonweal*, declared: "The position of the layman in the Church is analogous to that of the Negro in American society."

The conservative elements in American Catholicism did not take this attack on Church machinery with composure. The arch-conservative *American Ecclesiastical Review*, published at the Catholic University of America, still in a technical sense the most authoritative Catholic journal in America, conducted a campaign against "dangerous ideas" infecting laymen. In a 1962 article on "The Bishop and the Layman," Father Donald Dietz, praising the attitude of Pius XII, declared that "the three dangers that preoccupy the Holy Father are three lay dangers. For the bishop as teacher there is the danger of 'lay theology'; for the bishop as priest there is the danger of an exaggerated lay priesthood; finally for the bishop as ruler there is the danger of a lay autonomy in natural law, in the moral aspects of social and political problems." He reminded his readers—and his views undoubtedly represented the views of the masters of Catholic University at that time—that the pope and the bishops "have care over all problems in the social and political fields inasmuch as they are moral problems."[16]

In terms of past pronouncements Father Dietz undoubtedly had the better of the argument. Pius XII, to whom he referred, had quite expressly condemned "emancipation of the laity" in an important address in 1951 to the World Congress of the Lay Apostolate. At the same time he had opposed any tendency to bring the world's lay groups together into an international federation. Pius advocated lay political action for Catholic goals but was obviously frightened by any thought of a "lay international" that might challenge the Pope and the Roman Curia in fundamental matters of political policy.

In canonizing Pius X in 1954, Pius XII was even more specific in condemning any attempt to share the teaching function of the Church with the laity. Even today lay professors in Catholic seminaries are very unusual. When the Pontifical Gregorian University of Rome, the chief theological seminary for the elite of the American priesthood, named its first lay professor in 1965, the event was considered worthy of a special news story. The lay professor was an American psychiatrist with twelve children.

Such eleventh-hour, patronizing moves toward recognition of laymen did not make much impression on those American laymen who had been agitating for something substantial in the way of rights. During the Council they began to use satire very effectively in ridiculing the exclusively clerical control of their own Church. *The National Catholic Reporter*, quoting from Peter Gallagher's *An Emerged Layman's Lexicon*, said more about lay rebellion in the Church in five short sentences than the bishops had said in their various official pronouncements.

The Hierarchy

Pope. Servant of the servants of God.
Cardinal. Servant of the servant of the servants of God.
Bishop. Servant of the servant of the servant of the servants of God.
Priest. Servant of the servant of the servant of the servant of the servants of God.
Layman. Rich man with servant problem.[17]

When the Constitution on the Church and the final version of the Decree on the Apostolate of the Laity were made public, it became clear that the Catholic layman cannot speak of "his" institution when he speaks of the Church. He belongs to that institution in a poetic but not in a plenary sense.

It is not surprising that a Council that had failed so completely to give any shadow of democracy to the Catholic people finally ended its deliberations on the Church by confirming line by line and precept by precept the same infallibility of the pope that had been proclaimed in 1870. In the Dogmatic Constitution on the Church, the Pope and the Council declared (italics added):

> This is the infallibility which the Roman Pontiff, the head of the college of bishops, enjoys in virtue of his office, when, as the supreme shepherd and teacher of all the faithful, who confirms his brethren in their faith (cf. Luke 22:32) by a definitive act he proclaims a doctrine of faith or morals. Therefore his definitions, *of themselves, and not from the consent of the Church, are justly styled irreformable*, for they are pronounced with the assistance of the Holy Spirit, promised to him in blessed Peter. Therefore they need no approval of others, nor do they allow an appeal to any other judgment.

There was no Lord Acton present at Vatican II to pronounce this doctrine a "fraud" in the name of Catholic scholarship, or to charge that bishops submitting their minds to such fancies "solemnly blessed with their lips what their hearts knew to be accursed." Indeed, as the London *Tablet* remarked when the Council was coming to an end: "If a man had to try to compress into one sentence what the Second Vatican Council had done, he could say with most confidence that it has further enhanced and reinforced the already great authority of the Pope."[18]

CHAPTER FIVE ☙ RELIGIOUS LIBERTY, EXTERNAL

FOR American Catholics the most explosive subject at Vatican II was religious liberty, which at the beginning was not even listed as a subject. Even in the second session, it was buried inconspicuously in a chapter in the schema on ecumenism, but finally it was given the dignity of a chapter by itself. Passing through six versions and 120 speeches in the aula, it became for the American bishops the big subject, the one best cause around which they could rally with all the power and enthusiasm they possessed. As an independent declaration it was finally promulgated in 1965.

The French, even the Germans, did not seem deeply concerned about this subject. Did they not have reasonable religious liberty already? Why worry about *that* when there were so many other things to worry about? The Spanish, the Italians, and many of the Latin Americans did not care to open a subject that might cause trouble for hierarchies already occupying privileged positions in many nations. In any case, the leaders of the Curia did not relish any extended discussion of the subject. Why disturb the Church's present policy? Many of the European and Latin American bishops seemed to think of religious liberty almost entirely in terms of freedom from Communist domination.

Not so the Americans. As the London *Tablet* remarked: "What collegiality is to the French and ecumenism is to the Germans and social justice to the Latin Americans, religious liberty is to the Americans, the schema that really matters." One reason why religious liberty mattered so much to the Americans was that for several generations American Catholicism has labored under the accusation that the Church tends to stand for religious liberty only when it suits the Church and that when Church authorities gain enough power in a country they then deny to other cults the very freedom they have claimed for themselves while in a minority. Quite bluntly in the second session Bishop Emile Josef DeSmedt of Bruges, Belgium, admitted that there was some merit in this criticism and contended that if a Church was going to change its image, a really consistent pronouncement on religious liberty was needed.

In addition to this reason about consistency there was another more conventional reason. The American bishops, raised in a climate of freedom, breathing the atmosphere of liberty, knew that their Church had grown in a century and a half from the smallest to the largest Church in the nation. When Bishop DeSmedt spoke out for religious liberty, they could well add: And for us it works!

Bishop DeSmedt opened the religious liberty subject for general debate in November 1963 with a detailed *relatio*—an introductory explanation—that must have seemed to most of the American bishops utterly conventional, just the kind of endorsement of freedom that American Catholics had become accustomed to. There are four reasons, DeSmedt argued, why the Council should proclaim man's right to religious liberty: the truth of the claim; its utility as a defense against atheistic materialism; the recognition that men must live together in peace; and the advancement of ecumenism.[1] It was under this last item that he pointed out how many non-Catholics had the impression that the Catholic Church demands religious liberty in countries where Catholics are in the minority, but denies or limits it after attaining a majority. He flatly opposed any kind of external coercion to force any religion upon any human being. Previously in a Council speech DeSmedt opposed the substitution of the phrase "religious tolerance" for "religious liberty." He wanted liberty to be considered as an affirmative virtue.

DeSmedt's personal attitude won immediate and warm response from non-Catholics throughout the world. The Protestant Federation of Italy commented in a news release: "Before all else one needs to underline the pastoral warmth, the spiritual firmness, the courageous and noble insistence with which the principle of religious liberty was affirmed which, until now, has had more opposers than sustainers in Catholicism."

This was during the second session. From the days of the first session the American bishops had carefully nursed the idea of a religious liberty pronouncement. The idea had been sponsored by the Secretariat for Promoting Christian Unity and warmly favored by its head, Cardinal Bea. But, during the second session, religious liberty had been unceremoniously dumped from the chapter on ecumenism and indefinitely postponed.

In the third session the United States forces came back forewarned and ready to fight. The American Jesuit Father John Courtney Murray played a key role in the fight. Although not a delegate, he was a very important *peritus* whose writings on religious liberty had won a wide audience in the United States.[2] This tall, scholarly theologian from Woodstock College in Maryland had been so outspoken about the need of complete *external* religious liberty in the past that, for a time, a Vatican censorship had been imposed on his writings. To use his own words, he had been "disinvited" to the first session of the Council, presumably because the leaders of the Curia did not welcome his presence. But when the American bishops saw which way the wind was blowing at the first session even Cardinal Spellman, ordinarily the last person in the world to ask for liberal assistance, decided to reverse his usual attitudes. Ultimately he was responsible for bringing Murray to Rome as an expert, and in the end Murray wrote the most important parts of the religious liberty declaration.

The principles of religious liberty advocated in all the drafts on the subject must have seemed very elementary to most of the American bishops and theologians. The texts had strong anti-Communist implications but they skated around the evils of Catholic totalitarianism. They did not mention by name those Catholic countries where the Church had shared in the suppression of religious liberty for non-Catholics. Thus, while asserting splendid principles of freedom, they helped to save the faces of those conservatives in the Church who had been inconsistent in their loyalty to freedom. Such conservative leaders as Cardinal Spellman, for example, had been extraordinarily friendly to Franco's Spain and over the years had made many excuses for a Spanish church that practised much discrimination against Protestants.

For most of the American bishops, however, the suppression of religious liberty in such countries as Spain and Colombia had long been a source of acute embarrassment. They knew that their Church could not consistently accept the benefits of American democratic freedom if it reversed its position on religious liberty in predominantly Catholic countries. Consequently, the passage of a broad and general statement on religious liberty became for most of the American bishops an emotional and logical necessity. And to their credit they fought a good fight, demonstrating tenacity and near unanimity. When the statement was finally adopted, although it was full of inconsistencies and weaknesses, it was a distinctly American achievement.

Unhappily, the American bishops soon discovered that even the eloquence of Bishop DeSmedt made no impression on the conservative leaders of the Curia. Some opposition views were expressed in the aula that seemed to come right out of the Inquisition. Perhaps some of the opponents were influenced by the precarious political situation in Italy at that time. They feared that any further softening of Catholic policy and doctrine might be seized upon by the Communists. As Milton Bracker, writing in *The New York Times*, said: "Many, and probably most, of the Italians refuse to concede that the basic principle of freedom of conscience, as enunciated by Pope John XXIII in his last encyclical, *Pacem in Terris*, does not constitute an invitation to Italians, or at least 'permission' for them, to become Communists."[3]

The heaviest opposition, however, was not primarily political; it was theological and very self-righteous. Cardinal Ottaviani, head of the Holy Office, conceded that the Church had always taught the principle that "no one must be forced into religion," and he cited Tertullian to prove it, leaving out the Inquisition. But he scoffed at the notion that every person therefore had the right to follow his own individual conscience. A Catholic's obligation is to follow the divine conscience, not his own personal judgment, he argued. "The principle," he declared, "which says each one has the right to follow his own conscience must suppose that the conscience is not contrary to the divine law."[4] It is a "very serious matter," he contended, that every kind of religion should have the liberty to propagate itself. This would "evidently result in harm for those nations in which the Catholic religion is the one generally held by the people." It might even cause them to be "rent asunder."

Ottaviani did not mention the problem of Protestants, Greek Orthodox, or Muslims in nations that might be torn asunder by Catholic proselytism, nor did he appeal to the ecumenical spirit of Pope John. His speech in the second session, delivered on September 23, 1963, fell back on all the old institutional clichés of exclusive truth. "The rights of the true religion," he argued, "are based not only on merely natural rights but also—and to a much greater degree—on the rights which flow from revelation."

This line of reasoning was supported in the second, third, and fourth sessions by several of the Spanish, Latin American, Italian, and Irish bishops. Cardinal Ruffini of Palermo, the most talkative of all the cardinals, offered the standard argument in the third session: the Catholic faith, being the only true faith, was entitled to support from government while other faiths were entitled merely to tolerance. He contended that although no one should be forced to profess any particular faith, God and the state should see to it that the true Church is always favored. He repeated this line of reasoning in the last session in opposition to Cardinals Spellman and Cushing, declaring that "The State has the obligation as a State to worship God." He was joined in this view by Cardinal de Arriba y Castro of Spain, who said that free worship "will ruin the Catholic Church if it is put in effect in those States where Catholicism is the leading religion . . . only the Catholic Church has the right to preach the Gospel."[5]

This was familiar territory to Spanish bishops, since they had used these arguments for years to justify a certain amount of discrimination against Protestants in Spanish churches under the 1953 concordat between the Vatican and the Franco regime. This concordat established two grades of "religious liberty" in Spain, real religious liberty for Catholics, and conditional religious liberty for the "private" exercise of faith by non-Catholics. The result is that even today, when police pressures have been relaxed and Spain is moving toward a more democratic concept in government, no Protestant Church for Spaniards in Spain is permitted to look like a Church, with a steeple or large external cross, and no Protestant clergyman is permitted to carry a recognized professional card. Such a card, in the Spanish syndicate system, brings many economic privileges with it.[6]

This was also very familiar territory for the bishops from Colombia, although some friendly meetings between Catholic and Protestant leaders had occurred there. The Colombian government still requires all students in all public schools to receive instruction in the Roman Catholic faith, under an agreement with the Vatican that excludes all evangelical activity from a large part of the country.[7]

It was perfectly evident as the debate proceeded that when the conservatives advocated religious liberty they were thinking primarily of freedom *for* their Church, particularly for their Church in Communist countries, while the progressives, including many of the American Catholic bishops, were thinking of freedom for all faiths, even freedom for unbelievers. Concerning Communist policy, conservatives and progressives were united; they were bitterly opposed to it, and Pope Paul had expressed that opposition before the Council opened its fourth session at the Catacomb of Domitilla, just outside Rome, by comparing the suffering of Catholics under atheistic regimes to the suffering of ancient Christians in the catacombs.

The American bishops, embarrassed by the inconsistencies of Spanish Catholic policy, would have liked to forget the Spanish and Colombian aspects of religious liberty. But the Spanish leaders at Vatican II would not permit this. The Archbishop of Madrid, Casimiro Morcillo Gonzalez, made a public statement in the summer of 1965 that could not be ignored:

> In Spain Catholic unity is the principal çohesive element of nationality. To break it would be like breaking contact with Spanish history, literature and culture. It would mean . . . opening the door to foreign influence and sedition . . . the separated brothers must abstain from proselytizing and from all attempts to evangelize Spain, which is a country already deeply evangelized . . . the state must keep on being Catholic in religion and Catholic in education.[8]

A similar line was followed in the second session by Spain's newest cardinal, Jose Bueno y Monreal of Seville, who condemned any attempt to proselytize in a country where Christianity "had been in practice for centuries." *The New York Times*, in a sharp editorial on "Spain and the Vatican," declared: "In Rome Protestants are 'separated brethren'; in Spain they are damned souls who are still agitating for the right of public worship."[9]

By the time the third session began, the American bishops realized that they would have to bear the brunt of the battle to make the Declaration on Religious Liberty a reality. Cushing of Boston and Meyer of Chicago made the best American appeals. Cushing had brushed up his despised Latin until it sounded quite acceptable in spite of that traditional South Boston longshoreman's accent, and he was heard with special attention because it was his first speech at the Council. The Church, he declared, must "show herself to the entire modern world as the champion of liberty, of human liberty and of civil liberty, specifically in the matter of religion," and he deplored the fact that "the doctrine of the Church on religious liberty in modern civil society has not yet been declared clearly and un-ambiguously." Then he proceeded to lay down in two propositions what he considered the only consistent policy. First, he pointed out that "throughout her history the Catholic Church has ever insisted upon her own freedom in civil society and before public powers."[10] And then he added, "that same freedom in civil society which the Church has ever insisted upon for herself and her members she now in this our age also champions for other churches and their members, indeed for every human person." As a clincher he quoted Pope

John's general endorsement of liberty in *Pacem in Terris*. He sat down to the reverberation of loud applause.

Although Cardinal Cushing did not commit himself to all the phraseology in the proposed declaration on religious liberty, he did endorse the general principle, and he stated reasons that were acceptable in the entire democratic world. One pleasant and somewhat surprising concurrence came from Cardinal Silva Henriquez of Chile, who spoke in the name of fifty-eight Latin American Fathers, serving to remind the Council that not all Latin American bishops follow the Spanish line. Paying the usual respects to the necessity of freedom *for* the Church, he stressed the need of endorsing a wider religious liberty in order to win back the unchurched masses of Latin America. The situation, he argued, called for something like the United Nations' recent document on religious liberty, basing the claim squarely on "the recognized dignity of the human person."[11] But, being a representative of many Latin American bishops, both progressive and traditionalist, he felt it necessary to end with an attack upon proselytism, claiming that true religious liberty would put a brake upon proselytizing Catholics to another faith.

After the heated discussion of religious liberty in the second session it was evident that the overwhelming majority of the Council favored some kind of a declaration. But there was wide disagreement on details. When the proposal was sent back for further changes, a flood of proposed amendments came in. Still the American bishops were confident that when the proposal was returned in the final days of the third session, they would score a quick and final triumph. What was their consternation when, about a week before the end of the third session, rumors began to circulate that all was not well with the Declaration on Religious Liberty. Someone was threatening it, blocking it, delaying it, possibly even killing it. Who would dare to do that at the last moment? Naturally enough, the Curia was suspected. But what of Pope Paul? By this time, after his conduct on collegiality and other controversial matters, a great many of the bishops had ceased to rely on him.

The progressives' worst fears were realized on Thursday, November 19, 1964, which came to be known as Black Thursday. Though it had been promised on the previous Tuesday that a vote would be taken on religious liberty on the 19th it was found that some 200 die-hard prelates, mostly Italians but including 25 or more Spanish leaders, had resorted to a technicality calling for further delay. Their real object, of course, was the total defeat of the religious liberty declaration because, in their opinion, it went too far; it endorsed liberty as a human right for everybody whereas they wanted nothing better than "tolerance" of the errors of non-Catholic faiths. In a special petition to the leaders of the Council these prelates claimed that since the religious text had been heavily revised, the rules called for further examination of the refurbished text before voting.

Since there was no time for such fresh examination before the end of the session, the petition really argued for delaying action on the matter for another year. The argument for delay had some legal substance but no moral substance whatever, since the whole question of religious liberty had been considered for at least a year and the overwhelming majority of the Council members wanted to vote on it immediately. But suddenly, on that Black Thursday, Cardinal Tisserant, who was president of the board of Council presidents, broke into the proceedings and announced that since "several Fathers are of the opinion that not enough time has been allowed for the examination of the text on religious liberty," the Council would not proceed to the vote as previously announced.

There followed something as close to a riot as august bishops were capable of. No one pulled anyone else's beard or threw a gavel at an episcopal head, but the total effect was just as striking. The fact that the trickery of the conservatives had been perpetrated with some slight show of parliamentary legality—there really *had* been enough revisions of the liberty declaration to bring the final form under cover of the requirement for longer consideration—did not help matters much. The real offense was the arbitrary flouting of the will of the majority without an opportunity to vote and by a process that was secret in the planning and humiliating in the result. The strategy of the conservatives was sprung upon the Council majority, evidently with the approval of the Pope, like a trap. The bishops had been treated like wayward children while the whole world was looking on.

When the postponement had been announced, cardinals and bishops swarmed down to the floor of the aula in full view of the television world, gesticulating like baseball fans when an umpire has indulged in a fantastically incorrect decision. The late Cardinal Meyer of Chicago, usually serene, took the lead along with Cardinals Ritter of St. Louis and Leger of Quebec. Somebody said: "Where is there a sheet of paper? Let's get up a petition to the pope. Surely he would not approve all of this." In a few minutes, right on the floor while other speeches were in progress, some 500 prelates signed a petition "with reverence"—but obviously without any reverence at all—calling on the pope to intervene in order that "a vote on the declaration of religious liberty be taken before the end of this session of the Council, lest the confidence of the world, both Christian and non-Christian, be lost."

Here was an opportunity for Pope Paul to be realistic in meeting the demand of world opinion. European and particularly American newspapers played up what they called the November crisis with front page headlines. "1,000 Bishops Balk at Moves to Drop a Vote on Liberty," read the headline on the front page of *The New York Times*. "U.S. Bishops 'Revolution' For Liberty" was the corresponding headline in the *New York Herald Tribune*. Some European papers were just as sensational. The reaction among the Protestant observers was also vehement. One of them said, according to Robert Doty in *The New York Times:* "We have seen the naked face of what we have always feared in Rome." Dr. Douglas Horton, former dean of Harvard Divinity School, and one of the most friendly observers at the Council, declared: "I would say that the Protestant reaction is 'Do we want to be tied to a church like that.' "[12]

Part of the revulsion was caused by the fact that the sidetracking of the religious liberty declaration did not come singly; it came as part of a package of three arbitrary acts in the closing days of the third session, all traceable in the last analysis to the caution and conservatism of Pope Paul. One of the other papal acts that had annoyed the liberals was the insertion by the Pope of nineteen changes, some of them anti-Protestant, in the schema on ecumenism. The other had been the announcement on Wednesday that he would name the Virgin Mary "Mother of the Church." The Council Fathers had studied and discussed the whole question of the status of the Virgin Mary for three years and had voted against doing what Paul now arbitrarily did on his own authority (see Chapter 9).

On Black Thursday the bishops, puzzled and angry, blew off some of their steam by applauding Bishop DeSmedt of Belgium to the echo when, a few minutes after the great crisis, he read his *relatio* defending the religious liberty declaration that had just been sidetracked. They broke into his discourse five times with applause while the presiding moderator of the day, Cardinal Doepfner of Munich, pleaded vainly for silence. The liberal bishops had hoped for a change in the Pope's view, but they were plunged into angry despair again on Friday when Pope Paul refused to budge in his support of the small conservative minority of the Council that had temporarily captured a narrow majority among the Council Presidents. It was reported that among these Council Presidents the conservatives had outvoted the liberals by only one vote and, since the Council Presidents nominally controlled the agenda, this small margin in a commission of higher prelates determined the issue in spite of the will of the great majority of the Fathers in the Council itself. In blocking immediate approval Pope Paul held that he was only supporting the rules of the Council as they had been written. The religious liberty issue could go over until the next session for "further study."

In the United States the journalistic reaction was strongly against the Pope in the liberal Catholic press as well as in the secular press. In fact, Black Thursday was a turning point in American press coverage of the Council. From that day forward

American readers of the secular press received a more realistic description of what was actually going on at Vatican II.

The uproar over the sidetracking of the Declaration on Religious Liberty at the end of the third session was so great that it obscured a number of important facts. It obscured, for example, the fact that Bishop DeSmedt in his *relatio* made tremendous and unjustified concessions to the conservatives, evidently to get the chapter squeezed through the conservative doctrinal committees. He whitewashed the antiliberty teachings of Pius IX in the encyclical of that pope, *Quanta Cura*, and in his *Syllabus of Errors*.[13] In these famous reactionary epistles Pius IX had justified his own teachings in opposition to religious liberty because of the alleged false ideology of the rationalists who were opposing him at that time. In effect he repudiated religious liberty based on unbelief, thus making liberty conditional on some kind of faith. That Bishop DeSmedt was embarrassed in trying to reconcile modern religious liberty with the principles advocated by Pius IX was indicated in his closing remarks when he said: "It is evident that certain quotations from the popes, because of a difference of words, can be put in opposition to our schema. But I beseech you, Venerable Fathers, not to force the text to speak outside of its historical and doctrinal context, not, in other words, to make the fish swim out of water."

The trouble with this charitable attitude toward all past declarations against religious liberty by the popes is that the fish allegedly trying to swim "out of water" are actually words supposed to be absolutely authoritative, some would say infallible, expressed by past popes. Leo XIII denounced democracy as mob rule in an encyclical long after the decree on infallibility, and Pius X, who reigned in the twentieth century, issued his *Pascendi* in 1908 and his antimodernist oath in 1910. Pity the poor progressives at Vatican II! In order to get their religious liberty statement adopted they were saddled with the necessity of reconciling their own relatively advanced ideas with the Church's reactionary teachings about liberty in the past.

The published record of antiliberty statements by the Church, confirmed even in recent years, is overwhelmingly on the side of the conservatives. As James Hastings Nichols has said: "Roman Catholicism, ideally and in principle, condemns civil and religious liberty."[14] If this did not apply to the majority of the bishops at Vatican II—and I think it did not—there were many antiliberty ghosts in the Catholic closet to haunt those liberals who contended that religious liberty and Catholicism were consistent with one another.

Nominally the most authoritative American Catholic theologian at the Council was Monsignor Francis J. Connell, who had served as Dean of the School of Sacred Theology at the Catholic University of America for many years and, during all the sessions of Vatican II, served as a member of the American bishops' press panel. Connell, in his famous treatise on *Freedom of Worship: the Catholic Position*, had declared that "the mere fact that a person sincerely believes a certain religion to be true gives him no genuine *right* to accept that religion in opposition to God's command that all must embrace the one true religion."[15] Although Connell had added that "This does not mean that they [Catholics] may punish or persecute those who do not accept the Catholic faith," he said that "they are justified in repressing written or spoken attacks on Catholicism, the use of the press or the mails to weaken the allegiance of Catholics toward their Church, and similar anti-Catholic efforts." Connell still held firmly to these opinions at Vatican II.

Although Connell's reasoning seemed outdated in the irenic atmosphere of Vatican II, the debate on the sixth version of the Declaration on Religious Liberty, which began during the first week of the final session, still produced many comments on that subject that would have been quite acceptable to Torquemada. "Truth and falsehood cannot be given equal treatment," said the incorrigible Ottaviani, rising to oppose the Declaration on theological grounds. He charged that the texts chosen from the scripture to support the liberal view had been chosen "unilaterally" with partisanship, omitting the solemn fact that Christ threatened damnation for those who rejected the faith. Other speakers were equally emphatic. There is no liberty against objective truth, said Cardinal Cooray of Ceylon, and only the Catholic faith is objectively true. "If all men are given the right to a public profession of any religion, it will be an insult to the Catholic Church," said the Archbishop of Portugal's colony, Mozambique. "That would be the equivalent of proclaiming to the world that the Catholic Church is only one among many." The prelate from Mozambique regarded this last alternative with unmixed horror.

One Spanish bishop, condemning the "modern itch for all kinds of liberty," said flatly: "Two principles are in conflict in the Declaration [on Religious Liberty], the principle of the Natural Law calling for religious liberty and the principle of Divine Law which demands the protection of truth. The Divine Law must prevail or else we have humanism." "Entire tradition," said Bishop Carli of Segni, "teaches that non-Catholics do not have the right to propagate error and that therefore they can only be tolerated." The aged Irish Cardinal, Michael Browne of the Roman Curia, climaxed his speech in the religious liberty debate of the final session by declaring that: "The spreading of another religion in a Catholic state is a violation of public morality and harms the right which Catholics enjoy not to have their faith endangered."[16]

But the tides at Vatican II were running against such narrow-mindedness. This was partly because the American bishops and their *periti*, representing the richest section of world Catholicism, were there to demonstrate that religious liberty worked. The star of the American delegation was John Courtney Murray, whose chief function was to give the pedestrian bishops the right words with which to change some ancient doctrines without admitting that they were being changed. He built verbal bridges to the modern world very effectively, and the American bishops crossed over on them joyously, delighted that they could be good American democrats and Catholic scholars at the same time. Murray argued that certain teachings of past leaders of Catholicism were not applicable at the present time in their original sense, since they had been designed to meet certain historic situations, and those situations had changed. Doctrine, he alleged, could "develop," a polite way of saying that it could change without any necessary admission that it had changed.

This adroit formula for changing a "changeless" Church was frequently used at Vatican II by theologians who were bound by their Church's veneration for tradition, but it was not always accepted as worthy of honest men even by Jesuit leaders whose institutional past is commonly associated with such linguistic manipulation. In another connection, Father John C. Ford, S.J., of the Catholic University of America declared after the end of the Council: "I do not consider it theologically legitimate, or even decent and honest, to contradict a doctrine and then disguise the contradiction under the rubric: growth and evolution."[17]

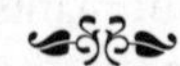

When, after three years of struggle in committee and in St. Peter's, the debate on the Declaration on Religious Liberty was finally concluded, there emerged a statement which was epoch-making only in the sense that it was the first formal declaration of its kind by the Catholic Church. Catholicism after centuries of delay had finally caught up at least in part to the United Nations, to Western Protestantism, to Western democracies, and to the social democratic parties of Europe in advocating what had been written into the American Constitution more than 175 years before.

Bishop DeSmedt, in introducing the Declaration in the last session, pointed out rather ruefully that 100 governments throughout the world had, in effect, beaten the Church to it in proclaiming religious liberty in their Constitutions. At least 50 of these had written such provisions into their Constitutions in the preceding eighteen years. He might have added that the World Council of Churches had produced in Geneva a seven-point statement on religious liberty that was better phrased and less ambiguous than the Declaration produced by Vatican II.[18] One bishop, speaking in the aula, Bishop Jean Rupp of Monaco, actually suggested that the Council could save time and effort by adopting the seven

Protestant-Orthodox points en bloc, but this idea was rejected as beneath the dignity of the "one true Church."

The final statement on religious liberty was an important achievement. It will make the struggle for religious liberty throughout the world easier. From now on every libertarian can cite an official Catholic pronouncement endorsing the principle of liberty.

The text itself, however, was a rhetorical nightmare looking as if the first parts had been written in the majestic prose of Father John Courtney Murray and other parts pieced together by some assistants in the Holy Office. The final brief section resembled the prose of professional diplomats in the Vatican's Secretariat of State. One could almost see the transitions from the progressive to the conservative viewpoints. Nevertheless, the affirmative vote for the Declaration was a glorious victory in the history of an institution that had fathered the Inquisition. If it was conditional, ambiguous, and inadequate, its sponsors could fall back on Tennyson's vision of a world where "Freedom slowly broadens down from precedent to precedent."

Perhaps the best paragraphs in the Declaration read:

> This Vatican Council declares that the human person has a right to religious freedom. This freedom means that all men are to be immune from coercion on the part of individuals or of social groups and of any human power, in such wise that no one is to be forced to act in a manner contrary to his own beliefs, whether privately or publicly, whether alone or in association with others, within due limits.
>
> The Council further declares that the right to religious freedom has its foundation in the very dignity of the human person as this dignity is known through the revealed word of God and by reason itself. This right of the human person to religious freedom is to be recognized in the constitutional law whereby society is governed and thus it is to become a civil right.

The question was naturally raised: What did the Declaration mean by saying that both private and public religious activity should be permitted within due limits? What limits? Apparently the phrase was intended to mean—and the meaning was spelled out in various ways—that civil religious liberty should always be granted within the exigencies of public order. At one point the statement was made that "the practice of religion in society should be immune from coercive interference by the state, except when it either disturbs the peace or flouts public morality or infringes the right of others." Such exceptions are pretty broad, and either a Communist or a fascist regime, if it cared to act in bad faith, could quite easily manufacture a pretext to outlaw a hostile religious sect on the ground of its opposition to public morality or its tendency to disturb the peace.

But everyone must recognize that some limitations are necessary on all kinds of liberty. There is, in fact, no such thing as absolute liberty of conduct in an interdependent world. Even the United States does not guarantee absolute religious liberty to practise suttee, preach polygamy, or exhibit poisonous snakes in a pulpit. Vatican II was quite normal in saying there must be some "due limits" to religious liberty.

It was natural that the Council should condemn, as it did, the kind of limits set by dictatorships in Communist countries. The Council reminded the world that there are cruel persecutions of the Church in such countries "even if the right to worship God is recognized in the Constitution."

The Declaration was not quite so clear in attempting to apply the new philosophy of religious liberty to Catholic countries where the Church had long been established. Its most significant paragraphs on this theme read:

> If, in view of peculiar circumstances obtaining among peoples, special civil recognition is given to one religious community in the constitutional order of society, it is at the same time imperative that the right of all citizens and religious communities to religious freedom should be recognized and made effective in practise.
>
> Finally, government is to see to it that the equality of citi-

zens before the law, which is itself an element of the common good, is never violated, whether openly or covertly, for religious reasons. Nor is there to be discrimination among citizens.

The phrase "special civil recognition" could mean the kind of special preference given to Catholicism in such countries as Spain, Portugal, Colombia, and Italy, under concordats between the Vatican and the respective Catholic regimes. Thus the Declaration indirectly approved the idea of an established Church provided opposition faiths were given some freedom. Probably out of deference to Spanish Church leaders, one sentence was inserted in the final draft saying that "Everyone ought at all times to refrain from . . . a kind of persuasion that would be dishonorable or unworthy, especially when dealing with poor or uneducated people." This is the kind of admonition that Spanish Catholic leaders have been using for years against "evangelical propaganda" among the uneducated people of their parishes. Such words could be used to justify some kind of continuing suppression. However, the tone of the whole Declaration on Religious Liberty was so progressive that it will serve as a kind of potential charter of future freedom for Protestants in all Catholic countries. Protestant attorneys can now appeal to the best and the most specific sentences in the Declaration to affirm their claims.

At the final session of the Council the conservatives forced the addition to the Declaration of several sentences recognizing Catholicism as the one true faith whose claims are superior to all other faiths. The final Declaration said that "this one true religion exists in the Catholic and Apostolic Church. . . . Religious freedom, in turn, which men demand as necessary to fulfill their duty to worship God, has to do with immunity from coercion in civil society. Therefore, it leaves untouched traditional Catholic Doctrine on the moral duty of men and societies toward the true religion and toward the one Church of Christ."

How much did this last-minute insertion of conventional reactionary dogma really mean? Probably a great deal. Conventional Catholic theologians can now cite chapter and verse to back up their claims that the Church's structure of authority is still the same. In a public analysis shortly after the issuance of the Declaration, the National Catholic Welfare Conference of the United States, the official organ of American Catholic bishops, carefully pointed out that the Council does not teach "that Catholics may freely accept or reject the teachings of the Church. There is in the Church a *magisterium* established by Jesus Christ himself, and in certain circumstances, guaranteed by the charism of infallibility."[19] Several months after the Council had ended, the standard Catholic diocesan papers of the United States were still teaching that the old exclusive dogmas of the Church in the field of religious liberty held good. Here, for example, is the answer of Father Raymond J. Neufeld to an important question on the meaning of the Religious Liberty Declaration, as published in the Brooklyn *Tablet* of February 3, 1966:

> *Q.* With the declaration on religious liberty coming from the ecumenical council, has the Church changed her teaching on the principle that "outside the Church there is no salvation?"
>
> *A.* No. The Council's Declaration on Religious Freedom states that "the human person has the right to religious freedom. This freedom means that all men are to be immune from coercion on the part of individuals or of social groups and of any human power, in such wise that no one is to be forced to act in a manner contrary to his own beliefs, whether privately or publicly, whether alone or in association with others. . . ."
>
> Though this declaration rules out force and coercion in a person's beliefs and religious practices, it leaves untouched the traditional Catholic doctrine on the moral duty of men and societies towards the true religion and towards the one Church of Christ. According to their human dignity, men are bound by moral obligation to seek the truth, especially religious truth. Once it is found, they are bound to adhere to it and order their whole lives in accord with the demands of truth.

So, the old principle holds—anyone who knows that the Catholic Church is the one true Church and willingly remains outside of it, cannot save his soul.

The Church teaches that one who is not nominally and actually baptized a Catholic may, in some instances, be saved; but that his salvation is nevertheless, through the Catholic Church.

Buried in the middle of the Declaration was a paragraph that received almost no attention in the press. It sought to justify tax subsidies to sectarian schools as "true freedom." It read: "Government . . . must acknowledge the right of parents to make a genuinely free choice of schools and of other means of education, and the use of this freedom of choice is not to be made a reason for imposing unjust burdens on parents, whether directly or indirectly."

Did "unjust burdens" mean tuition for parochial schools? The discussions in the press conferences clearly indicated that it did. Cardinal Spellman, speaking with great vehemence on the subject, had scored a success (see Chapter 15). Both the Declaration on religious liberty and the schema on education argued for educational subsidies by trying to bring them under the umbrella of religious freedom. The phrase "unjust burdens" was strengthened in the final draft by the addition of the significant words "directly or indirectly."

Cardinal William Conway of Armagh, Primate of Ireland, wanted to be even more specific about linking freedom with tax support for Catholic schools. He argued that it would be contrary to religious freedom to withhold tax grants to schools because they provided religious instruction. This doctrine, of course, is the exact opposite of the theory of religious liberty and nonestablishment expressed by the United States Supreme Court in its recent decisions in the fields of prayer and Bible-reading. The Court has consistently held that the establishment of religion in a school takes it out of the tax-supported category. The Council reasserted the familiar Catholic claim that the Church, being the chief guardian of the education of all Catholics, is entitled to subsidies for its educational enterprises.

Without the intervention of Pope Paul in September 1965 on behalf of the liberals, it is quite possible that the Declaration would have been postponed indefinitely. During the week before the final vote, the conservative attack was stepped up until an appearance of very strong opposition was created. The opponents seemed almost as plentiful as the advocates. Many Italian and Spanish prelates warned that the adoption of this dreadful measure would lead to indifferentism, laicism, and the eventual collapse of the Church in Catholic countries. This gave the coordinating committees of the Council, dominated by conservative cardinals, an excuse to attempt the final sidetracking of the whole pronouncement on religious liberty. An emergency meeting was called for Monday night September 20, the night before it seemed likely that a final vote would come. It was reported that the committees considering the whole proposal voted either 15 to 9 or 16 to 9 to postpone the vote on the flimsy ground that there would be so much opposition that the Church would be embarrassed before the world by the "rebellion" in episcopal ranks. It was an ominous fact that after two years of debate about a principle considered elementary and basic in Western society a majority of the most powerful leaders of the Church wanted to postpone any commitment on the subject.

Then Pope Paul performed one of the few courageous acts of his Council career. He overruled the dilatory commission and forced a vote on the religious liberty draft. The unusual decisiveness of his conduct at that moment may have been traceable to the immediate situation. He was about to take off for New York for a public appearance at the United Nations and the Yankee Stadium. It was doubly advisable that he appear there as the representative of a Church that stood for religious liberty. It was also supremely ironical that, in the end, the Council progressives who had a clear majority on their side had to fall back on the autocratic primacy of Pope Paul to secure a vote.

The next morning after Paul's decision, the Cardinal Moderator for the day, Cardinal Agagianian, simply interrupted the proceedings and railroaded the Declaration on Religious Liberty to a vote. Apparently the procedure that he adopted was without precedent, and even the progressives admitted this. He called for a standing vote on the closing of the discussion, even though there were more than 100 bishops waiting to speak on the issue. When this closure motion was adopted by an overwhelming majority, Agagianian called for a written vote on the Declaration itself. The margin of victory, 1,997 to 224, surprised even the progressives. Some of them had predicted only the day before that the conservatives might poll 500 votes. The Pope had spoken, and only 224 die-hards had cared to defy him at such a moment.

One reason for this wide margin of victory was that the endorsement of the "one true Church" meaning of the proposal was written into the adopting motion. The Fathers were asked to vote on the proposition: "Whether the text on Religious Liberty is acceptable as a basis for the definitive Declaration which will come after further amendment *in the light of the Catholic Doctrine on the true religion* and the amendments proposed by the Fathers in discussion, which will be subsequently approved according to the norms of Council procedure" (italics added). The "Catholic Doctrine on the true religion" emphasizes the fact that no other religion has an *objective* right to spread its error. When the more sophisticated progressives read that phrase, they knew that their battle was not ended, even with the adoption of the Declaration.

Theological experts in the press conference held immediately after the passage of the Declaration admitted that it might take "years" for the principle of religious liberty in a Catholic-dominated state to seep down into the various dioceses. The Declaration itself had no teeth. Everything would depend on how strict the hierarchy wanted to be in enforcing it. Certainly the Spanish hierarchy had no great inclination to enforce it. Even in the United States the conservative diocesan press, representing the overwhelming majority of Catholic subscribers, published very cautious appraisals of the new Declaration. The Declaration, according to Paul H. Hallett, chief editorial columnist of *The Regis-*

ter, "implicitly affirms the right in a predominantly Catholic nation of the people to make a social and not a merely private profession of faith, to demand that all legislation have a Christian inspiration, and that the religious patrimony of the people be defended against every assault."[20]

In the chorus of rather indiscriminate praise for the new Declaration in the American press, the sober analysis of the *Christian Science Monitor* stood out. "While this makes a tremendous step forward for the Catholic Church on this issue," the editor said, "the Declaration with its reservations is still a far cry from the advanced religious liberty found in the United States. It allows, for example, for a continuation of a state church. The concordat whereby a sovereign state grants the Catholic Church special privileges is considered entirely proper. The provision that no one should be forced to act or be prevented from acting according to his conscience, except where his action would infringe public morality, public order, or the rights of others, leaves the door open for possible continued religious harassment and persecution."[21]

CHAPTER SIX ❧ RELIGIOUS LIBERTY, INTERNAL

In spite of the passing of the Declaration on Religious Liberty, the final battle left many of the combatants in a state of doubt. The Declaration covered only the external relations of the Church. The original title of the schema, as suggested by Cardinal Urbani, had been "Civil Liberty in Matters of Religion." Many of the journalistic reports of the debates had given the world the impression that the Council was debating the whole territory of religious freedom. Actually, the final Declaration was completely silent about the great system of internal censorship within the Catholic Church.

For most Americans this internal censorship within Catholicism was far more meaningful than any external impairment of religious liberty. There is complete external religious liberty in the United States, so secure that the concept is rarely called into question by anybody. The Communist countries and Spain, where religious liberty is restricted, seem far removed from the American experience. As Father John B. Sheerin, editor of the *Catholic World*, has put it: "To defend religious liberty in America is about as daring and progressive as to defend motherhood."

But the censorship of the Catholic Church has always been one of the chief obstacles to ecumenism and one of the barriers separating Catholics, particularly priests and nuns, from the rest of the American intellectual community. Under Canon 1399 every Catholic is forbidden to read any book or magazine directly attacking Catholic doctrine unless he receives special permission from a competent clerical authority. Although permission is usually secured quite easily, the fact of the prohibition is there. In the twentieth century a purple curtain is erected between every Catholic and the books he wishes to read in the field of religion. It would be difficult to discover a more unqualified and inexcusable denial of religious liberty.

Neither this prohibition nor the prohibition of contraception nor the prohibition of mixed marriage—all very important restrictions on the liberty of the person in the name of religion—were brought into the Declaration on Religious Liberty. These omissions made the ultimate meaning of the Declaration quite unclear. Did the dignity of the human person, which was so warmly praised in such commendable language, include the dignity of members of the Catholic Church who might want to read freely in the literature of other religions or even of atheism? Father John Courtney Murray readily admitted that the Declaration was designed to give atheists equal religious liberty in principle with believers, but he also declared that he recognized the right of the Catholic Church to ordain censorship for its own members, only disagreeing with certain abuses in censorship, such as the abuses practised by the Holy Office, now known as the Congregation for the Doctrine of the Faith.

Father Murray later made it clear that he wanted the "narrowly limited" conception of religious freedom in the Declaration extended to other aspects of the modern world. He declared that "the text itself was flung into a pool whose shores are wide as the universal Church. The ripples will run far."

The Declaration, while asserting the rights of Catholic citizens to financial support for Catholic schools, did not choose to assert any right of Catholic parents in the field of education against their Church. Even Canon 1374 was not criticized, although the Jesuit magazine *America* had suggested that it should be eliminated as a questionable restriction on freedom.[1] (Canon 1374 is the rule that forbids any Catholic child to attend a mixed or public school without special permission of his bishop.)

The net effect of these omissions about the liberties of Catholics from coercion by their own clergy was to leave the Catholic layman about where he had been in respect to clerical authority.

It was evident that many of those who voted for the Declaration still thought of religious liberty as primarily (1) freedom for the Church to operate, and (2) the absence of personal anti-Catholic coercion by any force outside the Church. The coercive effect of Church rules on Catholics themselves, rules against birth-control, against mixed marriage, against attendance at public schools, and against the reading of any books opposing Catholic doctrine, were somehow maneuvered into the background out of the range of religious liberty as defined in the Declaration. The excuse for this maneuvering was that all these details were not necessary or germane to a broad statement of principle about the liberty of man in society. It is difficult to escape the conclusion that the real reason for the omission was the fear that any thoroughgoing attempt to make religious liberty real within the Church risked defeat by the conservatives.

This silence about religious liberty inside the Church during the debate on the Declaration on Religious Liberty was not, however, typical of the whole Council. In fact one of the most striking features of Vatican II was the battle against internal censorship by the Holy Office, which broke out in the second session during the discussion on the function of bishops. This Council attack on the Holy Office came to a climax on November 8, 1963, rather unexpectedly. For many years fear and hatred of the Holy Office had been widespread, especially among younger Catholic scholars, and they had been looking for a champion against the Office and its head, Cardinal Ottaviani.

Finally, on that November day in 1963, a champion was found. He was, on the whole, a rather surprising champion. Not young or professionally aggressive or noted as a left-wing leader, although he belonged to the more liberal segment of the Council, he was a member of several congregations in the Roman Curia and of the Commission for the Revision of Canon Law. He was the seventy-six-year-old Joseph Cardinal Frings of Cologne, who spoke out quite abruptly. The methods of the Holy Office, he said, "are a cause of scandal to the world. No one should be judged and condemned without having been heard, without knowing what he is being accused of, and without having the opportunity to amend what he can reasonably be reproved with." The procedural methods of the Holy Office, he declared, are "a source of harm to the faithful" and out of harmony with modern times.

The bishops did not even wait for Frings to finish before they burst into applause; it was the first time during the Council that applause had actually interrupted a speaker. When he sat down he received an ovation in spite of the rule against such demonstrations. Apparently this was what hundreds of prelates, even high-ranking bishops, had been thinking for years about the Holy Office, and at last a Cardinal had spoken their thoughts for them.

Naturally enough, Ottaviani was deeply hurt. Had he not spent thirty-five years of his life in the confines of this Office protecting the faith against all these modern heretics? He replied rather contemptuously and emotionally that the attack on his Office was based on ignorance and that, in any case, such comments are a "reflection on the Vicar of Christ" since the pope himself, as everybody knows, is the prefect of the Holy Office and the Office speaks for him as the successor of St. Peter.

Technically, this view of the Holy Office as the voice of the pope is correct. The Office, located in a grim old palace of brown masonry just to the left of the Bernini Colonnade of St. Peter's, is the most powerful of the institutional power structures in Catholic Christendom. Created in the thirteenth century by Pope Innocent III as a kind of spiritual F.B.I. and Un-Catholic Activities Committee, it operated the Inquisition and struck terror into the hearts of all dissenters for centuries. In fact, its official name was the Holy Office of the Inquisition until 1908. It still operates—or operated until 1966—the doctrinal censorship system of the Church, banning books for heresy, displacing liberal professors from Catholic seminaries, controlling all ultimate questions concerning mixed marriage, and recommending excommunication for the wilfully dissident. It is supposed to be the Vatican center of faith. In practice it is the Vatican center of intellectual terror.

Every priest everywhere in the world who picks up a pen to record his thoughts for an audience must pause and ask himself:

What will the Holy Office say about this? If the Holy Office says that he has departed from the faith and that he is promoting un-Catholic concepts, no power on earth, except that of the pope, can save him. He may be banished to a mountain monastery in the midst of a brilliant public career with no public or private explanation of the reasons, and his would-be book may be quietly suppressed without the public's even knowing that it has been suppressed. This penalty has been meted out to some of the most noted thinkers of modern Catholicism, and only the exposure on the floor of Vatican II brought this story of suppression to the outside world.

In spite of Ottaviani's claim to papal sanction, recent popes have had very little to do with the working decisions of the Holy Office. The Pope is the institution's Prefect, but this means almost nothing in daily decisions. He never attends a meeting; he signs almost every document put before him for signature; and in some cases a disciplinary warning may be issued without his even knowing about it. The executive authority of the Office, nominally in the hands of some eleven cardinals who are primarily residents of Rome, is exercised by the Secretary, and the Secretary during the whole Council was the redoubtable conservative, Cardinal Ottaviani.

Although the procedure of the Holy Office is not modelled after a drum-head court-martial, it denies—or did deny until certain changes in 1966—ordinary civil rights to rebellious priests and Catholic authors. Under Ottaviani's leadership methodical consideration was given to hundreds of cases in the field of heresy, mixed marriage, and doctrinal deviation. Usually these cases were quite thoroughly considered by the regular staff, numbering about twenty-five, with careful reports by appropriate committees and often with long discussions among the cardinals. Bishop Dino Luigi Romoli, who had served on the staff of the Office for eight years, declared that before condemning a published work the Office "makes vast, accurate, and intensive investigation, by consulting with highly qualified experts from various linguistic and national groups to be incontestably objective and secure in its judgment. At times such investigations take several years, so great is the delicacy with which the Holy Office treats this matter."[2]

Very few theologians and bishops at the Council appeared to agree with the adjective "delicacy" as applied to Holy Office procedures. The more common descriptive adjectives were "heavy-handed" and "stupid." No one seemed to object to the fact that preliminary discussions in the Holy Office were kept secret from the outside world, since it would be unfair in many cases to a would-be victim if charges against him were made public before they were even adjudicated. But very strenuous objections were raised against the practice of the Office in condemning books and magazine articles without warning and without adequate opportunity for the author himself to defend his views.

After Cardinal Fring's attack on the Office, a quiet and dignified American priest, Monsignor Henry Cosgrove, who had served on the Office staff as a qualificator for many years, appeared before the American press panel to explain and defend the procedures of the Office. Although his style was persuasive, his explanations fell flat. Someone, he contended, had to protect the faith. The men who ran the Holy Office were dedicated to the task of protecting a sacred institution in a troubled world. Their decisions, perhaps, were not always perfect, but somehow the faith had to be preserved and the world redeemed from confusion.

Monsignor Cosgrove's description of Holy Office procedure in handling charges of personal misconduct was more satisfactory than his description of procedures in handling books. The accused man might—usually did—get some kind of a hearing; the accused book often was not considered worthy of such treatment. Cardinal Ottaviani passionately declared that no case was ever decided by his Office without studying "the evidence." In the case of a man there might be a necessity for personal examination and confrontation; in the case of a book Ottaviani apparently thought that the book was enough. It could be "studied" by the Holy Office panel without any troublesome challenge from any lawyer for the defense or from the author himself. Authors are sensitive human beings and their reasons for arriving at certain views may be quite irrelevant. This procedure saved the officials of the Holy Office from that searching cross-examination of their own views that might have raised the embarrassing question: Who is the real heretic here?

Ottaviani's defense seemed to convince no one except the already convinced. Granted that a great institution must have some protective machinery against heresy, should that machinery not be as scrupulously fair as the machinery, let us say, of a civil court? The very rules of the Holy Office, as many bishops and theologians at the Council testified, were themselves secret. As John Cogley wrote shortly after the Frings-Ottaviani fracas, "the Holy Office's procedures, judged by the standards of jurisprudence maintained in the Western World, are grossly primitive."[3]

Non-Catholics at the Council looked on with unalloyed joy as the exposé of the Holy Office gained in momentum. This was the kind of criticism of Catholic censorship that they had been waiting to hear. They gave great credit to the Jesuits for the exposure, since the Jesuit magazine *America* had published just before the beginning of the second session a list of procedural practices of the Holy Office which "have come under particular criticism," condemning the "essentially negative" attitudes of the Office and particularly the "practice of anonymous denunciations on which the Holy Office so often seems to rely." Father Robert Graham, S.J., associate editor of the magazine, charged that "The Holy Office operates under a secrecy almost as severe as that of the confessional, and it never publishes its own rules, which it changes without promulgation." Then he proceeded to list the following procedural shortcomings of the Holy Office, which "have come under particular criticism":

> Books or articles are judged without the author's being heard in his own defense. Teachers are ordered to be removed from their posts without having any specific charge made against them, much less being given a chance to defend themselves.
>
> Notice of the condemnation of a book is sometimes made public before the author himself is informed.

> The reputation of authors is not adequately safe-guarded. Little effort is made to differentiate between a writer with a distinguished record of service to the Church and another who is a declared enemy of the faith. Calumnious accusations against authors are not punished when their falsehood is discovered.
>
> Even the bishop whose imprimatur has been granted to the edition condemned or ordered to be withdrawn from sale, is not consulted or informed.
>
> Grounds for the condemnation are not given, except perhaps in an unofficial and allusive form, without a shred of canonical force, in the *Osservatore Romano*. In disputed areas, such as modern philosophy, which require specialized knowledge, the decision is taken without consulting experts in the field as to the exact meaning of the writing under examination.[4]

Serious criticism of the Holy Office came also from outside the ranks of Catholicism, even from observers at the Council. One of the observers who had experienced Holy Office restrictions, Dr. Frederick C. Grant, Episcopal scholar and author of *Rome and Reunion*, wrote in this work:

> In Rome, in 1963, I tried to call upon and pay my respects to an eminent New Testament scholar at the Gregorian University. I was unable to do so, as he was being "inhibited"; he could eat in the refectory, I gathered, read in the library, write in his room, but not receive guests, talk with students, or teach classes. The inhibition resulted from his reading of works by Rudolf Bultmann—one of whose early books I had translated and urged students to read, over many years. Such tyranny may be explained from the dogmatic and legalistic point of view, but not from that of free scholarship. It would be unthinkable in a Protestant or Anglican seminary or university. It smacks of the Inquisition.[5]

And Dr. Grant added: "It will be a long time before the silencing of Teilhard de Chardin is forgotten."

Rudolf Bultmann, of course, is a "dangerous" theologian from the orthodox Catholic point of view, and also from the point of view of many Protestant thinkers. His extensive writings allegedly demythologizing the orthodox interpretations of the New Testament have made him a very controversial figure throughout the ecclesiastical world. But the question involved in such censorship is not whether Bultmann is correct but whether adult Catholic scholars should be allowed to read him and then discuss his ideas with adult non-Catholic scholars. Should a Catholic theologian, under protection of the oath of obedience, be treated like a child?

The questions raised by Dr. Grant are of special importance because they reveal that the censorship system of the Holy Office cannot be treated in isolation. It is part of a gigantic system of control which affects all branches of Catholic education. It goes back to the description of seminary policy contained in the Council's Decree on Priestly Formation: "The whole seminary program permeated with a cultivation of reverence and silence." The reverence is understandable; the silence too often means the denial of intellectual freedom. Dr. Grant's experience is of special importance because the Gregorian University is the institution in Rome where most of the American seminarians are trained for the priesthood. When it stands for intellectual suppression, its policy has direct relevance to the future of American Catholicism.

In general, the Gregorian has been a bulwark of conservatism, attempting to protect its students from currents of modern scientific thought by restrictive rules that can only be described as medieval. During the Council sessions it refused to allow the Lutheran biblical scholar Oscar Cullman, an observer at the Council and a friend of Pope Paul, to give a biblical lecture at the institution. The papal Biblical Institute joined in the refusal. Cullman is far nearer to the Catholic position than Bultmann, and his exclusion from the Gregorian and the Biblical Institute provoked wide criticism. He finally delivered his lecture to 1,000 people at a French Church in Rome in the presence of Cardinal Tisserant, a striking proof that the power of the Holy Office was cracking.

For many years the spirit of the Holy Office has dominated the seminary life in Rome, where the elite of the Catholic world come for final priestly training. American students find that their intellectual life during the seminary years is almost hermetically sealed. They must dress in the cassocks prescribed for Europe. They may not, ordinarily, return to the United States during their four-year course. They may not attend theaters or even witness soccer games without special permission. They are forbidden to attend lectures by non-Catholics or read books attacking the Catholic position. In 1960, after much agitation, they were allowed to attend some of the Olympic Games in Rome but their attendance was sharply restricted even after Pope John had greeted the athletes. When one of these students was asked recently what he did for amusement he replied: "We walk around the roof and wonder if it would not be better to jump off." Occasionally the students are allowed to attend a concert or the private showing of a film.

The students of the North American College were permitted to attend American press conferences during the second session and they crowded eagerly into the small hall where these conferences were held. But soon it became apparent that many novel and dangerous concepts concerning Catholic doctrine were being expressed by skeptical-minded correspondents from both Catholic and non-Catholic journals. Permission to attend the conferences was thereupon withdrawn.

Under canon law the Holy Office is absolutely within its rights in imposing censorship upon Catholic professors and Catholic institutions, either directly or through other Church bodies. It is the official voice of the Church in censoring books and booksellers. Indeed, its censorship powers extend to the whole Catholic world everywhere, lay and clerical.

Catholic canon law still bristles with detailed instructions and rules for internal censorship, with more than twenty canons being devoted to book censorship and kindred forms of intellectual supervision.[6] The ban includes not only all books that defend heresy or ridicule Catholic dogma but also all non-Catholic Bibles. Nominally the Office still operates the Church's *Index* of forbidden books although it has fallen into disuse and was virtually shelved by Pope Paul early in 1966. No systematic effort was made at Vatican II to abolish this *Index*, but it was denounced and ridiculed several times during the debates. One official of the Holy Office admitted that if the 4,000 to 5,000 books on the *Index* could be reconsidered in the light of present knowledge, at least 90 per cent of them would not be included.

This sense of embarrassed regret about the *Index* was quite general at the Council, and it is even more general among Catholics in the United States today. Very few American Catholics have ever seen the work. One reason for the scarcity of the volume in the United States is that the Holy Office has added almost no books in the English language in recent years. The *Index* has become virtually a continental and an Irish affair, and, in view of strong reactions against it, Pope Paul may soon abolish it officially. Nominally, it still carries many famous names on its condemned list, from Voltaire and Paine to Gibbon and Kant, including all the works of some ninety-seven authors. No American writers have been banned in recent years. Only four recent European writers have been singled out recently for specific condemnation, Jean-Paul Sartre, Simone de Beauvoir, André Gide, and Alberto Moravia. In each case the ban has increased their sales and added to their prestige.

In the Council debates, the clinching argument against both the *Index* and the Holy Office was that some of the Church's greatest recent theologians had suffered from its arbitrary rulings. These included Father Yves Congar and Father Karl Rahner, who had both suffered warnings and suppressions, only to surmount them and become two of the most influential thinkers at the Council. Most famous among the Holy Office victims had been the French Jesuit Teilhard de Chardin, who died in 1955 at the age of 74. He suffered a posthumous condemnation by the Holy Office in a *Monitum* issued just before the Council began, declaring that he was ignorant of "the traditional framework of philosophy and theology." Earlier Teilhard had been banished to Africa and Asia for years while some of his most important writings were being suppressed. In death he won sweet revenge, becoming a world best seller among Catholic authors.

The general censorship of the Church over literature is by no means confined to the Holy Office itself. Under canon law every bishop in the world is authorized, even urged, to become a little Holy Office in himself, criticizing, praising, and if necessary banning any literature that will be injurious to his flock. Several times during the Council the exercise of such episcopal censorship in Rome itself embarrassed the Council liberals and advertised to the world the narrowmindedness of certain Catholic practises. The Vicariate of Rome, headed by the aged Cardinal Micara, suddenly decided in 1963, during the second session, that two books in English were doing harm to the faithful in Rome and should not be promoted or displayed in Catholic bookstores in the city. They were *Pope, Council and World* by Robert Blair Kaiser of *Time*, one of the best books produced about the Council, and another excellent work, *Letters from Vatican City* by Xavier Rynne. Both books had been caustic in exposing the shortcomings of the Curia. Rome bookstores, it was said, received a special letter from the Vicariate declaring these two books unfit for "doctrinal reasons." For several hours all was confusion concerning the "suggestion" from Cardinal Micara. Some Catholic bookstores were suddenly "out" of the books, but some of the largest stores ignored the "suggestion" altogether. Within a day the Kaiser and Rynne books were back in the stores, and the advertising had helped their sales. It was evident that Cardinal Micara's zeal had been considered bad public relations by the "Higher Authority."

During the Council in 1963, another "heretical" book was ordered out of all Catholic bookstores in Rome, *The Priestly State; Marriage or Celibacy?* by a French Dominican priest, Pierre Hermand, who had left his religious order to say that he thought priests should be given the option to marry. In Rome such partial suppression is an old story. In 1954 Cardinal Micara had ordered all Catholic bookstores in Rome to remove from their shelves Giovanni Papini's successful novel *The Devil* because Papini contended that hell is not eternal and that an all-merciful God would some day shorten its duration by pardoning the Devil himself.

Very few bishops in the United States would be foolish

enough to undertake such specific censorship of specific books. Past experience has proved that any public denunciation of a work critical of Catholic policy only serves to advertise it. Censorship of universities, however, is another matter and one that is very common in the United States. It is far-reaching in its effects. During the Council the Catholic University of America in Washington, the most official of the Church's American educational institutions, demonstrated how a university may practice its censorial powers unwisely.

In February 1963, while Pope John was still alive, several lectures at the University by four distinguished Catholic scholars, all priests, were suddenly cancelled after the four men had been sponsored for a Lenten lecture series by the graduate student council at the University. The four men were Hans Kung, Godfrey Diekman, the late Gustave Weigel, and John Courtney Murray. In announcing the ban the University Rector, Monsignor William J. McDonald, said: "The Catholic University is under the jurisdiction of all the bishops of the United States. Because of this unique status it takes no official position on those issues and policies still unresolved by the Council."[7] This explanation was wholly specious since the University had been using its own magazine, the *American Ecclesiastical Review*, throughout the Council sessions to attack the whole position of Catholic liberals in the most specific and caustic language.

The reaction throughout the American lay Catholic world to this censorship was angry and wholesome. Great audiences appeared to greet the banned speakers at other institutions. From within the University faculty came some protests, although most of the professors were intimidated into silence. The University's best known historian, Monsignor John Tracy Ellis, joined the chorus of criticism. One priest dared to put his finger on the probable source of much of the censorship policy, the power of the reactionary Apostolic Delegate to the United States, Archbishop Egidio Vagnozzi. As one bold priest put it in a statement quoted in *Harper's Magazine:* Vagnozzi "stands astride all access to Rome, preferments come through him, so also do censures, penalties, and blacklists." Since American bishops own the Catholic University, they could have stepped in at any moment and reversed the ban. All but a few of them chose to remain silent.

Archbishop Vagnozzi, a papal appointee who could easily have been transferred to another post if Pope Paul had disagreed with him, continued after the Council to be just as reactionary as before. Early in 1966, speaking at the dedication of a Catholic seminary in Florida, he described the purpose of Catholic universities as the creation of "a purely Catholic cultural environment," and said: "When there is definite teaching by the Church concerning any matter, no Catholic is free to teach differently. In like manner, it cannot be tolerated that, in a Catholic university . . . anything be taught contrary to the definitive Catholic tenets. There is here no question of infringing upon a healthy academic freedom, but of preventing an unhealthy license and ultimate chaos."[8]

One difficulty about such internal censorship in the Church is that it is almost impossible to discover exactly which authority is responsible for blocking a lecture, suppressing a book, or cancelling a theatrical performance. Ordinarily, no prelate wishes to be identified in the public eye as an opponent of free speech. This was especially apparent in 1964 when, for the first time in its 15-year history, a whole series of television programs on the Catholic Hour was cancelled because the discussions threatened to treat frankly some of the marriage problems discussed at the Council, particularly the problem of birth control. The pressure for the ban was attributed to Cardinal Spellman's chancery office but nobody could get any official confirmation of this claim. Of the proposed speakers, two were to be well-known Catholic liberals who had expressed some sympathy with the notion that Catholic birth-control prohibitions should be changed. The ostensible reason for the cancellation, as issued by the National Council of Catholic Men, was that "the whole question of Christian marriage should not be discussed while it was still before the Vatican Council . . . the Holy Father has indicated a discussion of this matter should not get out of hand." The executive director of the National

Council of Catholic Men, after the cancellation of the series, admitted that he had never had any direct contact with the prelates who killed the program.

The question naturally arises how much the new Declaration on Religious Liberty will affect the workings of the internal censorship system in the Church, particularly in the United States. Probably the spirit of that Declaration will help the progressives a great deal because the bishops of the United States have now been put on record in favor of the principle of freedom of conscience, a principle that was questioned in the textbooks before the Council was convened. Father Murray, admitting that in the Declaration itself "the principle of freedom was narrowly limited," rightly contended that: "Some of the conciliar Fathers–not least those opposed to the Declaration–perceived that a certain indivisibility attaches to the notion of freedom." But the censorship arrangements based on canon law will not be changed unless the pope decides to go beyond the Council's Declaration and attack internal censorship directly.

Thus far, one of the most serious forms of intellectual censorship in the Catholic system remains untouched. This is the literary censorship that requires every priest writing on any subject, or any layman writing on Catholic doctrine, to secure from his diocesan censor the official *Nihil Obstat* (nothing objectionable) and from his bishop the *Imprimatur* (let it be printed). This rule of canon law was not disturbed by any moves at the Council.

This preventive censorship kills far more books than are killed by the Holy Office. Catholic liberals in the United States have been fighting against it for years but they have been successful only to the extent that incidental blunders in the system have been exposed. Occasionally books have been freed for circulation that would have otherwise been suppressed. The system itself is still in existence, firmly entrenched among the powers of local bishops. Every diocese must have its censor; every censor must be subject to a bishop; and both must be subject to those very stern canon laws that condemn deviations from standard doctrine.

Ostensibly the system is designed "to protect the reader," but in practice it intimidates the progressive priest. If he goes outside the censorship system to publish a book, his future is in doubt. He constantly feels over his shoulder the intruding gaze of the diocesan censor who will ultimately tell him whether there is anything in his book contrary to Catholic teaching. He knows the name of the official censor but not the name or qualifications of the critical reader who may be delegated to sift his words. Usually he knows that even if he submits his work to non-Catholic publishers, these publishers commonly submit to Catholic authorities any manuscripts touching upon Catholic themes. Under this system, many a critical work about Catholic policy, written by competent theologians and priests, is never published.

This system even affects non-Catholic translators in the literary world. Elizabeth Bartelme, writing in *Commonweal* in 1965, pointed out that: "In many dioceses a translation from a foreign language, unless the translator is a Catholic, will not be given an Imprimatur. The translation may be accurate, beautiful and completely in accord with the original, but unless the translator professes the faith, his translation cannot be published with permission."[9]

Fortunately for the reputation of Catholicism, the internal censorship rules of the Church broke down during Vatican II. Critical appraisals of the Council itself by Catholics were not considered "doctrinal." One of the reasons for the breakdown was the sheer volume of literature on the Council produced by Catholics and non-Catholics. Altogether more than 3,000 books on the Council had been produced in all languages by the beginning of the fourth session. It would have been impossible for the Holy Office to catch up with such a flood of literature even if it wanted to, and most of the bishops realized that censorship of any of these books would be strategically unwise. In Washington the Bureau of Information of the National Catholic Welfare Conference decided to be exceptionally broadminded about bibliographies. It listed in its Selected Bibliography on the Council some caustic books attacking the Church, including at least one summary by an ex-priest and another very critical attack on Pope

Paul by a priest who was soon forced out of the Church. Critical articles and books about the Council by Catholic writers blossomed all over the landscape, and their authors were not even called upon the ecclesiastical carpet.

Tight clerical control of the Catholic press is probably a more important element in Catholic internal censorship than the supervisory machinery for censoring books. During the Council, Catholic press censorship began at the top with the Vatican's unofficial daily newspaper, *Osservatore Romano*. In practice *Osservatore* is the voice of the Vatican's Secretary of State, who controls the journal, subject to the pope. Throughout the Council it served as a kind of pompous, papal house organ, as openly conservative as it dared to be, shading the news against the progressives and omitting or playing down some of the most important facts of the sessions. It sought to create the impression that, on the whole, the Vatican's policies were the best of all possible policies in a serene and obedient world. During the first session, *Osservatore* doctored the news shamelessly, but this doctoring did not pay off. As soon as foreign correspondents discovered the inferior character of *Osservatore*'s coverage, they ceased to pay any attention to its biased interpretations.

At first the public relations machinery of the Council was a joke, a very bad joke. Although there were plenty of skilled stenographers reporting every word of the Latin speeches in the basilica—the third session alone produced fifty miles of recorded tape—the texts of the speeches were not made public and, at first, even the names of the speakers were suppressed. A Vatican cleric, after each session, passed out one-page leaflets in seven languages summarizing the morning's "proceedings." There were no names attached to the sentiments expressed, and often the texts, having been made up the night before, did not accurately report anybody's words.

This ostrich-like attitude toward the world's press had been traditional at the Vatican. I had seen some of its effects when I served as a correspondent in Rome during the Holy Year of 1950. For the leaders of the Curia the Church does not need publicity; it simply *is*. Let the world come to it! Behind this attitude of lofty condescension there is a feeling of unease about the total effect of contact with the modern world and its dangerous views. The Curia leaders had not wanted a Council in the first place. Let the press break through the cassock curtain if it could!

At the Council this attitude soon broke down under the determined pressure of some nine hundred correspondents of the world's news media who swarmed over St. Peter's Square and the surrounding buildings like hungry mosquitoes. Italian newspapers were soon printing in their afternoon editions the "secrets" of the morning sessions of the Council, and Paris journals were carrying the names of every speaker, properly attached to his sentiments. In *The New Yorker* the hybrid journalist-priest, Xavier Rynne, was soon telling the Fathers themselves, and the wide world, a connected and factual story of innermost events, often more accurate than the bishops could secure on their own initiative. (On one cold morning in 1963 at Redemptorist headquarters in Rome I had an hour-long interview with the alleged kernel of the Xavier Rynne complex, a Redemptorist priest named Francis X. Murphy, who flatly denied with twinkling eyes that he was Xavier Rynne. But he did finally admit that he might have had more to do with the Xavier Rynne product than a casual observer.)

All this had changed by the opening of the second session. Officials of the Council had finally been persuaded that the Church's public image must be an image of free discussion, not suppression or secrecy. They began to realize that, given a friendly world press, the Church had much to gain by publicity, even critical publicity. Although correspondents were never permitted to attend the main working sessions in St. Peter's, they were granted something better, press conferences daily in their own languages at which they were free to ask the most penetrating questions and expect honest replies.

At the beginning of the Council the American Catholic press was almost as obedient as *Osservatore Romano*. At first American

Catholic editors seemed rather bewildered by the startling new events of the Council. Dominated by Irish-American bishops, the regular diocesan press of the United States had for many years been more Roman than the Romans, more papal than most of the European Catholic journals. This was particularly true of the two chief American diocesan chains, *The Register* of Denver and *Our Sunday Visitor*. These papers, of course, could not be officially opposed to Pope John but they could be discreetly pro-Ottaviani in many of their articles and editorials. During the first session they were quite consistently conservative and chastised those Catholic liberals who were "besmirching" the good name of the Church. When the American bishops began to shift toward a real *aggiorniamento*, these journals shifted slightly toward the left also. But they continued throughout the whole Council to feature vacuous encomiums of the Church's power structure and to play down the seriousness of the revolt against the authority of the Roman Curia.

This diocesan press is the greatest single obstacle in the United States to the attainment of internal religious liberty. It controls the denominational flow of information to the American Catholic people. It has a kind of built-in censorship because most of the diocesan papers are either owned by the bishops and subsidized directly by the dioceses, or by some other church agency. There is no parallel to it in the American Protestant world. Its partisanship during the early part of the Council became so apparent that it evoked a number of sharp exposures by non-Catholic journals. Most of the Catholic diocesan papers, said *Newsweek*, "play the same game of houseorgans subservient to the aims of ecclesiastical authority. Whether in the tight society presided over by Cardinal James Francis McIntyre of Los Angeles, or within the subtler confines of Cardinal Francis Spellman's New York, clerical news management is so pervasive that honest reporting of the Church and its institutions is often neither welcome nor possible."[10]

One reason for the "clerical news management" is that these diocesan papers are all served by one news agency owned by the Church, the news service of the National Catholic Welfare Conference. The men who operate this service are honorable men but they are hostages to their Church in a double sense: they are professionals on the Catholic payroll, and the journals they serve are owned by officials of the Church. Monsignor S. J. Adamo, writing in *America* of August 14, 1965, has well described the limitations of such ownership:

> Have not the bishops kept the diocesan editors like pedigreed dogs, pampered but made to heel? Is their growling and barking (once some of them snapped their leashes) so dangerous as to justify alarm? I think not. . . .
>
> Most bishops felt, nevertheless, it was wiser and safer to keep the diocesan weeklies at heel. They recoiled at criticism, for they considered that disloyalty; and they periodically interrupted the free flow of information, for they considered certain items of news imprudent at best and scandalous at worst. Furthermore, through their control of the National Catholic Welfare Conference News Service, the bishops could exercise news management at the source, and did. Repeatedly, NC News Service has been requested by Church leaders to ignore this, soften that, cover up some other news story. As a result, diocesan newspapers, which depend on NC, have been embarrassed over and over again by the appearance of dramatic religious news stories first in the secular press. (Actually there is no valid reason why the NCWC should own a news service; this is the root of the problem of freedom of information.)

One factor in breaking the hold of this controlled diocesan press in the United States has been the rise of a number of liberal Catholic organs whose editors have dared to challenge episcopal policies directly. The most important of these new organs, born during the Council period, was the *National Catholic Reporter* of Kansas City. Another newcomer, edited by a Catholic, was California's *Ramparts*, extremely militant in its style and content. For many years the liberal Catholic weekly *Commonweal*, edited by Catholic laymen, had been virtually the only independent voice in American Catholicism criticizing the policies of the higher clergy. The new *National Catholic Reporter*, also edited by laymen, went *Commonweal* one better by opening its pages to astonishingly frank discussions of such subjects as celibacy, the sequestration of nuns, the veneration of doubtful relics, and the stupidities of such leading Catholic reactionaries as Cardinal McIntyre of Los Angeles. The *Reporter* was especially outspoken on matters of racial justice. With writers like John Leo and James Johnson, operating under the editorship of Robert Hoyt, this journal began to scoop the standard Catholic newspapers so often with sharp and informed comment that many bishops became alarmed over its successes. It featured the writings and activities of such liberal theologians as Hans Kung and John Courtney Murray.

The conservatives in the American Church counter-attacked briskly. "There is a coterie of Catholic writers," proclaimed Archbishop Joseph P. Hurley of St. Augustine in a general attack upon the American Catholic liberal press, "publishing their articles in a few Catholic papers, who specialize in vilifying priests. . . . I catch again the fleeting glimpse of the Communist face or hear again the characteristic intonation of the Communist voice in a few of our Catholic papers."[11] (St. Augustine was the city that would not allow Negroes to swim in the Atlantic ocean.) Even the new Baltimore Cardinal, Lawrence Shehan, a mildly progressive leader, attacked the "shocking irreverence" and "false intellectualism" of those sections of the Catholic press daring to criticize indulgences and the Church's teaching on the sacraments.

As a result of such criticisms and because of the enormous, concentrated power of the bishops, the future of the liberal Catholic newspapers in the United States is somewhat uncertain. Can they survive after the Council? Is their financial support sufficient to carry them over the inevitable lag in interest that is bound to follow the Council? John G. Deedy, Jr., writing in *Commonweal* before the last session, expressed some despair, particularly about the continuation of competent liberals in the regular diocesan papers. The best laymen, he pointed out, are already leaving those controlled papers that they too often regard simply as house organs designed to preserve the Establishment. The task of house-organ journalism is not an attractive occupation for adult minds. According to Mr. Deedy: "It is reasonably safe to say now that the anxiety and authority to report fully and with uninhibited honesty [about the early sessions of the Council] were momentary phenomena. . . . Windows that were thrown open during the Johannine period have slipped back into place. The Catholic press is once more its cautious, colorless, docile, predictable self."[12]

"I keep up with about thirty of the most prominent Catholic papers," wrote John Leo, liberal contributor to both *Commonweal* and the *National Catholic Reporter*, ". . . and it is my experience to find that only two or three of them have any editorial comment to make when the issue at hand is at all sticky." Usually the diocesan editors wait for the final word from the episcopal residence before committing themselves on anything controversial, and then their opinions are echoes of the opinion of their owners. Most of the editors, of course, are priests to begin with, many of them religious-order priests, and their professional futures are doubly controlled by their bishops and the heads of their orders.

Only time can tell whether Mr. Deedy's gloomy prediction is justified. But one thing is certain. During a portion of the years of the Council much of the American Catholic press was redeemed from what Mr. Deedy calls the "lusterless clericalism" of the episcopal house organs by the courage and capacity of a few dedicated Catholic liberals. In view of their courageous contribution, it is doubtful if American Catholic journalism can ever again return to the complete servility which characterized the pre-Council years.

It was natural that the new American liberal counter-attack on Church censorship in the Catholic press should center upon Cardinal McIntyre of Los Angeles, because he was the most aggressive champion of censorship, the most reactionary of American cardinals at the Council, and a czar in his own right in the huge Archdiocese of Southern California. Some of the seminaries in his jurisdiction even went so far as to ban *America*, *Commonweal*, and *Time* from the seminary libraries. Edward R. F. Sheehan, writing in the *Saturday Evening Post*, reported that in one seminary under McIntyre's jurisdiction the students secretly mimeographed the highlights of *America* and *Commonweal* and distributed them for 75 cents a semester.[13] When the famous Catholic liberal, Archbishop Thomas Roberts of Bombay, received several invitations to speak in southern California, Cardinal McIntyre's chancery office informed the doughty archbishop that he would not be welcome.

McIntyre's completely imperial control of the Archdiocese of Los Angeles should serve to remind the student of Catholic institutions that the whole censorship system is one complete system, with tentacles in every portion of the world-wide institution. The editor of a Catholic paper, the head of a Catholic seminary, the monsignor who wants to become a bishop, the bishop who wants to become a cardinal, the priest who wants to stay in his parish a few more years before retiring on a miniscule pension—all these men are under orders from above in an intricate system of authority that does not permit any intervention of democratic power by the Catholic people at any point in the process. Technically every priest may appeal to his bishop or even write a personal letter to the Pope. Long experience has proved the futility of this latter remedy. As Mr. Leo has put it: "The simple fact is that personal rights the secular world has taken for granted for generations are violated regularly in the antique operations of the Church."

Because Cardinal McIntyre is a cardinal and also a racial and economic reactionary, he has demonstrated more clearly than any other American bishop the power to ruin the careers of priests within his jurisdiction. His actions have been extreme because he is personally an extremist, but the power he has used in suppressing the liberty of priests in his jurisdiction is wholly authorized, a recognized and legitimate expression of a system of internal censorship of the person within the Catholic community. It represents the ultimate, though indirect, destruction of the liberty of the mind.

McIntyre's most famous case was that of the young Los Angeles priest, Father William H. DuBay, who, after three years of public struggle, was finally suspended from the priesthood early in 1966. DuBay had taken an active, fighting role in the struggle for racial justice in Los Angeles over the objections of his cardinal. He was originally transferred from a suburban Los Angeles parish for publishing in his church bulletin an article with a positive view about racial integration. He was transferred again after preaching a provocative sermon on racial justice. Next he was reprimanded for using unapproved prayers and songs at a children's service. After being suspended from the priesthood and ordered to a monastery, he was reassigned to a parish. When Cardinal McIntyre refused to speak out for California's fair housing law, Father DuBay created a national sensation by cabling Pope Paul asking for the cardinal's removal. For a time he tried to conform by humbly kneeling before the cardinal in the presence of 200 other priests and kissing his ring. But it was of no use. When his rebellious spirit flared up again, he was transferred to a hospital, forbidden to have a car, and told not to discuss the primacy of the human conscience in public. DuBay ended his cycle of revolt by advocating a trade union for priests and publishing a book called *The Human Church* in which he said—just before he was finally suspended: "Can the reform of the Church so ardently desired by all be accomplished without democratic reforms? We can easily criticize Church prelates, complain about the lack of free speech and free assembly, bewail the Church's scandalous inertia to meet social problems and the one-hundred-year gap between the Church and the world. But can such defects be remedied without drastic changes in the Church's political life?"[14]

DuBay's case was extraordinarily spectacular but not extraordinary. At least eight other cases of priestly rebellion had occurred during the same period, and many of them had attracted national attention. Fortunately, public attention had begun to turn not to the eccentricities of individual rebels or individual bishops but to the system itself, which denied basic human liberties to the working force of American Catholicism, the parish priests. In September 1965, 260 American Catholic laymen and women from

26 states sent a personal letter of protest about Cardinal McIntyre's policies to all American bishops, pointing out that under the new Constitution of the Church, adopted at Vatican II, laymen had been directed to make known "their needs and desires" to their bishops. They pointed out that "religious and priests teaching in the schools are not permitted today to teach the principles of Pope John's encyclicals, nor are they allowed, without fear or restraint, to act in accordance with the Church's teachings on social justice and international understanding." Such protests had been punctuated by the appearance of liberal priests and even of nuns on racial and economic picket lines throughout the United States.

John Leo, writing in *Commonweal*, put his finger on one underlying injustice in the present internal censorship system of the Church, the need of more just grievance machinery for priests. Although no bishops pressed for such machinery at the Council with any great zeal, Mr. Leo's indictment of the present system may ultimately force even the reorganized and rechristened Holy Office to modify its machinery. "Despite the fact that under Canon Law a priest has recourse to the Pope," he said, "in practice the time-honored procedure has usually been to refer complaints back to the bishop against whom they are being made. It is still the only legal system in the world where the accused man can become a judge. The result is that a Church which stresses so much the inalienable rights of persons in society recognizes no inalienable rights within its own body."[15]

Although Pope Paul has not revealed any willingness to modify the stern powers of the bishops over their priests, he has decided to yield a little to pressure against the arbitrary acts of the Holy Office by changing that institution's name and by modifying its procedure in several respects. One day before the end of the last session, Paul issued a *motu proprio*, titled *Integrale Servandae*, in which he changed the name of the Holy Office to the Congregation for the Doctrine of the Faith, and reduced its arbitrary powers in several particulars. Accused theologians and writers are in the future to be given some rights of representation and appeal; the rules and regulations of the office may no longer be kept secret; regional conferences of bishops are to be consulted when their subjects are under suspicion; and extra specialists are to be brought in when questions of heresy and conformity are at stake.

This is a beginning. Whether it is more than a beginning will depend on the way in which the new regulations are followed up.

CHAPTER SEVEN ❧ THE JEWS

No one could have foreseen at the beginning of Vatican II that the angriest and most bitter discussions of the whole four-year period would arise over one fragment of one schema which was not even considered worthy of separate treatment at first. The Cinderella subject of Vatican II was the statement about the Church's relation to Jews. Starting as a small segment of the schema on ecumenism in the second session, it attracted so much public discussion and controversy that it was eventually rewritten several times and finally incorporated into a new and important Declaration on the Relation of the Church to Non-Christian Religions, promulgated in October 1965.

The whole discussion began with a thoughtful suggestion by Pope John that perhaps the Council should say something special about the Jews to express Christianity's great indebtedness to them and to establish better relations between the Church and the Jewish people. There can be no doubt about John's simple, heartwarming feeling of sympathy for the Jewish people. When a group of Jewish leaders visited him in 1960, he extended his arms and said: "I am Joseph, your brother."

Pope John's suggestion about a Jewish statement was turned over to Cardinal Bea's Secretariat for Promoting Christian Unity, although it was not, strictly speaking, within the scope of Christian unity endeavors. No one in the Church thought that Judaism could or should be united with Christianity, but everybody agreed that better relations between Catholics and Jews should be fostered and promoted. The Secretariat for Promoting Christian Unity, staffed by eager young progressives, was the logical agency to build a bridge between Catholicism and Judaism.

It was recognized that any friendly move in the direction of the Jews would have to be handled with the utmost care. The current barriers between the Vatican and Israel are substantial. The two powers have never exchanged ambassadors, and the Vatican, next to the Arab nations, has probably been the foremost enemy of Israel policy in taking over a portion of Jerusalem. It has repeatedly asked that Jerusalem be internationalized. For its part, Israel stood almost alone against Spain, in addition to the nations of the Soviet bloc, in the 1950 United Nations dispute over the condemnation of Franco's government. Israel's admission to the U.N. in 1949 was blocked largely by Vatican-inspired political moves in the Assembly, following the issue by Pius XII of a special encyclical, *Redemptoris Nostri*, calling for the internationalization of Jerusalem and the guarantee of all traditional Catholic rights there.[1]

Far more serious than this disagreement over international policy in Israel is the long record of anti-Semitism promoted by Rome over the centuries. Probably most Americans did not realize how long and disgraceful that record of anti-Semitism had been until the whole subject was aired in the world's press during the sessions of the Council. American anti-Semitism—and there is plenty of it surviving—has never been a distinctly Catholic phenomenon. In fact, the Protestant variety has been somewhat more conspicuous because our population was so overwhelmingly Protestant in the beginning and because such fanatical organizations as the Ku Klux Klan have been, through the accident of geography, more Protestant than Catholic. The Klan, promoted chiefly by Southern Protestants, helped to bring American Catholicism and American Judaism a little closer together by coupling them in its denunciations. The shadow of the Pope and the shadow of Shylock were closely associated in the bigotry of the nineteenth century.

In Europe the history of anti-Semitism has been a more distinctly Catholic responsibility, although Luther was definitely anti-Semitic and millions of his later disciples succumbed to Hitler's propaganda. The Catholic Church used the power of the Catholic state to suppress and persecute Jews in many European countries during the long period of church-state union, a period that still exists in modified form throughout a large part of Europe today.

Many of the early Church fathers were as definitely anti-Semitic as Gerald L. K. Smith. St. Chrysostom called a synagogue a "house of vice," "worse than a brothel," "a den of brigands," and "the cavern of devils." Although he was not the first Christian preacher to apply the word "deicide" to the Jewish people, he was the most vociferous in spreading the idea.[2] From his preaching was derived the policy of describing the Jews as "Christ-killers." "However unwittingly," says President Abram L. Sacher of Brandeis University, "Chrysostom, with help from St. Gregory of Nyssa, forged the weapons for the blood-stained centuries that followed. . . . The iron car of history with its cargo of hate went careening through the ages, setting off the medieval Talmud burnings, the enforced baptism and the autos-da fé in public squares, the gabardines and the badges of shame, the compulsory missionary sermons to Jews which Popes decreed and which went unrevoked until 1848."[3]

Anti-Semitism, more or less quiescent from the fourth to the tenth centuries, burst into flame with the First Crusade in the eleventh century, which was climaxed by the slaughter of 10,000 Jews. The Catholic clergy played a very active role in fomenting anti-Semitism in many parts of Europe, and the wildest tales of Jews as drinkers of Christian blood who engaged in ritual murder were circulated as gospel truth, often after Jewish victims had been forced to "confess" their fantastic atrocities by torture.

An American priest, Father Edward H. Flannery, has recently catalogued some of these crimes in his book *The Anguish of the Jews*.[4] In terms of quantity they did not rival Hitler's genocide, but in spirit and motive they came very close to the Hitler performance. At the very beginning of the First Crusade in 1096 the hordes of fanatical nobles and peasants who set out to destroy the Eastern "infidels" turned on the European Jews and, in many places, massacred in mob attacks all Jews who refused baptism. It is estimated that in that first year of the crusades one-fourth to one-third of the Jewish people of Germany and Northern France were slaughtered or committed suicide. The infamous yellow badge imposed on Jews in Hitler's day had many precursors in medieval Europe, a yellow sphere in France, a *Judenhut* in Germany, and a pointed hat in Poland. The Fourth Lateran Council, convoked by Pope Innocent III in 1215, followed the Pope's pronouncement of an anti-Semitic policy: "The Lord made Cain a wanderer and a fugitive over the earth, but set a mark upon him, making his head to shake, lest anyone find him should slay him. Thus the Jews, against whom the blood of Jesus Christ calls out, although they ought not to be killed . . . yet as wanderers must they remain upon the earth, until their countenance be filled with shame and they seek the name of Jesus Christ, the Lord." This Fourth Lateran Council prescribed a special dress for all Jews, partly to prevent any intermarriage with Christians.

This catalogue of old horrors, largely traceable to the Christian Church of the Middle Ages, should not obscure the fact that some anti-Semitism is endemic in the New Testament itself, and some anti-Christianism is endemic in Judaism. All religions tend to promote self-glorification and derogation of competitors, and neither Christianity nor Judaism is an exception. During the 2000-year competition between Christianity and Judaism it has not been fashionable for religious competitors to regard each other with amiable charity. "Ye are of your father the devil," said Jesus to some Jews in John 8:44—or at least Jesus is said to have said these words in a burst of bitterness. His attack was directed chiefly against the clerical leaders of Judaism, not against the Jewish people, but it was, nevertheless, an attack. The Nazis located several anti-Semitic verses in the New Testament and used them most effectively.

On their side, many Jewish leaders, even the most liberal leaders, have been quite candid in outlining certain truths that are distasteful to orthodox Christians. In a 1965 work, *The Jewish People, Faith and Life*, Rabbi Louis I. Newman, one of the most progressive of American rabbis, had this to say about Christianity:

> A certain Saul or Paul of Tarsus, a Hellenized Jew, at first an opponent and later a zealous adherent of the Nazarene, saw

in the story of the life and death of Jesus, as preserved in the Oral Tradition, the opportunity to create a new religion, to be preached among non-Jews in the Roman Empire. He first propounded the idea of the "Dying and Risen God," based upon non-Jewish precedents, and applied it to Jesus as the "Christos," the Greek name for the "Anointed One" or the Messiah . . . the new religion became violently anti-Jewish, and has remained such throughout the centuries to the present time. This does not alter the fact that Judaism was the mother-faith of Christianity, even though the daughter-religion turned against its parent.[5]

Such theological considerations had little to do with the Jewish issue at Vatican II. Pope John wanted to substitute good will for hate in dealing with the Jewish people; he wanted to close the gap of misunderstanding that had existed for so long between Jews and Catholics. For this reason the original statement on the Jews, started in 1961, was incorporated into the chapter on ecumenism and brought to the floor as part of this chapter in the second session. Since it had come from the progressive Secretariat for Promoting Christian Unity, it was phrased in a charitable manner. Cardinal Bea, apprehensive about Arab and Eastern-rite Catholic reaction, tried to head off opposition by explaining that he brought his statement to the Council with the explicit sanction of John XXIII, who had seen and approved the statement about five months before his death.

Bea explained that the statement was not political in any sense, but religious. "There is no question of recognizing the state of Israel on the part of the Holy See," he said; ". . . there is obviously no danger that the Council will get entangled in those difficult questions regarding the relations between the Arab nations and the State of Israel, or regarding so-called Zionism." The aged and winsome cardinal, perhaps the most attractive figure in the whole Council, tried to meet head-on the argument that Jews are "Christ-killers." He said:

> There are those who object: Did not the princes of this people with the people in agreement, condemn and crucify

the innocent Christ, the Lord? Did they not "clamor": "Let his blood be upon us and upon our children"? Did not Christ himself speak most severely about Jews and their punishment?

I reply simply and briefly: It is true that Christ spoke severely, but only with the intention that the people might be converted and might "recognize the time of its visitation." But even as he is dying on the cross he prays: "Father forgive them, for they know not what they do . . ."

The Jews of our time can hardly be accused of the crimes committed against Christ, so far removed are they from those deeds. Actually, even in the time of Christ, the majority of the Chosen People did not cooperate with the leaders of the people in condemning Christ . . . those among them who cried out to Pilate "Crucify him!" formed a very small part of the chosen people. . . . If therefore not even all the Jews in Palestine or in Jerusalem could be accused, how much less the Jews dispersed throughout the Roman Empire? And how much less again those who today, after nineteen centuries, live scattered in the whole world?[6]

Cardinal Bea's attempt to keep the Jewish statement out of politics was fruitless. The Catholic prelates from the Near East and the representatives of the Arab governments immediately raised loud protests. His Beatitude Alberto Gori, the Latin Patriarch of Jerusalem, objected on the ground that the Jews should not be singled out for special treatment while those of other faiths were omitted. This point had some weight, but it was generally recognized that the real reason behind it was the fear of persecution by Arab governments in countries where Catholics comprised a tiny minority. The Coptic Patriarch of Alexandria wanted all discussion of Jews dropped. "To treat the question of Jews is at this time dangerous and there is no reason to do it." Even the ancient Patriarch Maximos IV Saigh, usually an outspoken liberal rebel, thought that Jews should not be singled out for special charity when so many Catholic minorities were living among Moslems. He is an Eastern-rite Catholic who claims the patriarchate of Jerusalem along with those of Antioch and Alexandria. (No one is expected to get all these intricacies of competing jurisdiction unscrambled.) Of course the extremist conservatives at the Council joined with the I'm-afraid-of-the-Arabs groups to oppose any special decency to the Jews. Cardinal Ruffini of Palermo, second only to Ottaviani in conservative energy and ahead of him in lung power, described the proposed statement on the Jews as a "panegyric of Judaism."

As it appeared in the second session, the document on the Jews, sandwiched into the chapter on ecumenism, was brief and reasonably clear in its repudiation of anti-Semitism, even though it was irritatingly patronizing in tone. "The Church of Christ," said the text, "recognizes that the beginnings of her faith and election are found in the Patriarchs and Prophets," and Catholics "cannot forget that she is the continuation of that people with whom God was pleased, in his mercy, to establish the Old Covenant." The document declared that "it is unjust to call them [the Jews] 'deicides,' because it is the sin of all mankind that caused the suffering and death of Jesus Christ." At the end, this preliminary document exhorted: "The common patrimony between the Church and the Synagogue being so great, this Council recommends that there should be a reciprocal esteem and knowledge between Catholics and Jews, while it deplores and condemns the persecutions of the Jews which have taken place in recent times."

Little did the *periti* who had inserted those words "deicides" and "deplores" realize what storms were to be created later on. The whole question of anti-Semitism and the guilt of the Jews for the Crucifixion was so fraught with bitter emotion that shaded syllables became the occasion of bitter disputes. If John XXIII had realized how sensitive Jews, Moslems and Eastern-rite Catholics were about the whole question, he would probably have disposed of the matter in a Vatican White Paper without any arguments on the Council floor.

As it turned out, the most disastrous thing happened—disastrous from the ecumenical point of view. Because of the opposition by conservative die-hards, by the Vatican Secretariat of State, and by Eastern-rite Catholics, the whole statement on the Jews was suddenly postponed in the closing days of the second session. A new statement was ordered, this time to be composed with the "advice" of the Coordinating Commission of the Council, a more reactionary group than the Secretariat for Promoting Christian Unity.

Jewish leaders of the world were dismayed, and they did not hesitate to say so. Was the Catholic Church still anti-Semitic? Would it sacrifice a principle for the sake of its political relationship with Arab powers? No one could tell how much truth there was in the flood of publicity from the Middle East on the subject. Cardinal Bea, obviously disturbed, accepted the delay with as much grace as possible. Liberals in the Council suspected that Arab opposition was being quietly fomented by anti-Semitic conservatives as an excuse for sidetracking the Jewish document, but no one could be sure of this. Several vicious anti-Semitic documents were circulated among Council bishops during the second and fourth sessions, but no one could determine how much fanatical strength they represented.

There were a number of demonstrations in Arab countries, and the usual Moslem protests of horror against even any inferential recognition of the status of the Jewish nation. The Vatican Secretariat of State, headed by the aged Cardinal Cicognani, tried to reduce the whole statement on the Jews to a minor section in the chapter on the Church, and thus avoid reprisals. Cicognani could point to the bitter and irrational reaction against the Jewish statement in Jordan where the heads of Eastern-rite Catholic communities were forced to defend themselves against a drive to seize Catholic schools. In December 1963, a Cairo newspaper, in describing the Pope's coming visit to Israel, had warned that he might be shot—and had then, characteristically, suggested that the assassin would be a Jew! "Who would guarantee for us," the editor asked, "that the Zionists would not kill the Pope during his visit to the Holy Land, whether in Jordan or Israel, and accuse the Arabs instead?"

The revised document on the Jews emerged in the third session as part of a longer statement "On the Relation of the Church to non-Christian Religions." It was finally adopted by a wide margin in the closing session. In its final form it had the reluctant but solid support of the American bishops, including Cardinals Spellman, Meyer, Ritter and Cushing—the reluctance was based solely on the belief of some that the statement should have been stronger. On the fundamentals of the issue the American bishops were as unanimous and concerned as they had been in supporting the Declaration on Religious Liberty, and their support was doubly welcome because there are more Jewish people in the United States today than in any nation in the world.

The revised statement, however, was considerably weaker than the original statement. If this fourth-session statement had been the only document made public, it might have been received quite graciously by world Jewry. As it was, the watering down of certain terms of condemnation made the Church look relatively anti-Semitic—and I do not believe that the Catholic Church is substantially anti-Semitic at the present time. The long wrangle over the wording of the various texts was humiliating to Jews throughout the world. Without courting the role, they had been forced into a position in which they looked like supplicants for justice at the Vatican Council. When the Council hemmed and hawed about the wording of a simple statement that might have been dashed off in a few hours, world Jewry reacted strongly, though not always publicly. The central grievance, of course, was the difference between the first and later drafts of the statements on the Jews.

The Italian Waldensians, the most substantial Protestant group in Italy, analyzed the differences between the first and later drafts with great care, claiming several of "the gravest mutilations of the text." The first "mutilation" was the elimination of the word "deicide." The earlier document had said: "The Jewish people should never be presented as a people rejected of God or accursed or guilty of deicide." The later (and final) text said "The

Jews should not be presented as rejected of God or accursed . . ." In press conferences the staff members of the Secretariat for Promoting Christian Unity, rather apologetically, defended the change of wording on the ground that the word "deicide" had "an odious sound," a statement which few would care to deny. Then the Secretariat proceeded to explain that the use of the offensive word could lead to false theological interpretations.

The second "mutilation" was the excision of the word "condemned" from the phrase "deplored and condemned." The change occurred in the paragraph describing past persecutions and hatred of Jews. About this change the Waldensians said:

> The difference between "deplore and condemn" is too large to argue that condemnation is implicit in deploration. There are in fact various ways to deplore a fact, and the *damnat* served precisely to qualify the *deplorat*, stating precisely its content and intent. All this has disappeared, and it is really difficult, not to say impossible, to understand how a Council could not find the courage to condemn anti-Semitic persecutions, not even after Hitler, being content with a general deploring. But the suppression of the *damnat* is yet more disconcerting if it is remembered that this verb already existed in a document of the Holy Office, which said among other things on March 25, 1928: "The Holy See . . . in disapproving any hate and conflicts between peoples, thus yet more strongly condemns hatred against the people that once was elected by God, that hatred which is commonly called anti-Semitism." Although between 1928 and today the Jews have undergone one of the most monstrous persecutions of all their history, the Second Vatican Council did not deem it necessary to confirm that *damnat* which the Holy Office, 37 years ago, knew well how to use.[7]

When the watered-down text was being discussed in the fourth session, the Chief Rabbi of Rome expressed "a word of true astonishment for the tenacious, medieval enmity shown by some Council Fathers," and added wryly: "The Jewish people, the people of God, does not 'deplore,' but condemns most categorically all forms of persecution, whether aimed against its friends or its enemies."

Liberal Catholics condemned the revised draft as "vague and circumspect," declaring that "the key question of deicide and special Jewish guilt is glossed over in the crudest manner . . . if we are serious about erasing Christian anti-Semitism, we cannot settle for the mild form of lip-service now before the Council."[8] In a press conference at the fourth session Father Thomas Stransky of the Secretariat for Promoting Christian Unity admitted that "we may have committed a faux pas in changing 'condemn' to 'deplore.' " Almost everybody sympathized with Father Stransky and his liberal co-workers, who had been caught in the middle of a controversy which they did not welcome.

All the wrangling over verbiage might have been dismissed as of secondary importance if Pope Paul had not expressed, in April 1965 in a Passion Sunday speech, some sentiments about the Jews that were instantly interpreted–and quite correctly–as evidence of some lingering traces of anti-Semitism in the Pope himself. In discussing the gospel account of the Crucifixion in his homily, Pope Paul said that it is "a grave and sad page because it narrates the conflict, the clash between Jesus and the Hebrew people, a people predestined to await the Messiah, but who, just at the right moment, not only did not recognize Him but fought Him, strove against Him, calumniated Him, and finally killed Him."[9]

Coming after the Council had endorsed a new attitude toward the Jews, opposing any propaganda which would create hatred, this pronouncment by the Pope created consternation among both Jews and liberal Catholics. The highest authority in world Catholicism had revived the old charge of Christ-killing in a public speech. A "Vatican spokesman" in Rome tried to soften the Pope's phrases in a statement to *The New York Times*, which, incidentally, had played a key role in forcing public discussion of this basic issue. According to the "spokesman," the Pope had only been intending to elaborate the point that rejection of Christ was still prevalent today. The explanation fell flat. Critics of Pope Paul were not so much concerned with his official intentions as with the revelation of latent prejudice. The Chief Rabbi of Rome and the President of the Italian Jewish Communities expressed their "painful astonishment" over the fact that Pope Paul had revived "the accusation against the Jewish people of killing Jesus."

In these caustic exchanges some of the facts about the "guilt" of the Jews began to emerge. Joel Carmichael, author of *The Death of Jesus*, writing an article in the *Congress Bi-Weekly* of the American Jewish Congress, described Pope Paul's attitude on the Crucifixion as "fundamentalism," and his words as "a characteristic piece of official self-righteousness." He pointed out that, in spite of all scholarly research to the contrary, in "the view of traditional, magical Christianity as exemplified by Paul VI, the continued existence of the Jews as a collective entity . . . is comprehensible only as another fact of the endless war between God and the Devil, with the Jews, of course, remaining an appendage of 'Father the Devil,' as the Gospel of John has it."[10] Carmichael's analysis at once served to damn Paul VI and to assign him to a large company of the damned—all those Christian fundamentalists both Catholic and non-Catholic, who have carelessly accepted an anti-Jewish account of the Crucifixion without adequate evidence.

Probably most non-Jews in the United States regard the whole charge of deicide against the Jewish people as so absurd that it is not even worth discussing. If Jews of the time of Jesus killed him, so what? Men do not inherit guilt for twenty centuries. There are other more important things to talk about. If this type of non sequitur should become prevalent, would not all Christians be blamed for the savage cruelties of the Crusades? People rocked with laughter when the incomparable Israelite from the Carolinas, Harry Golden, suggested at the end of the Council controversy on the Jews that Jewish organizations should call a Jewish Ecumenical Council of their own "for the purpose of issuing a Jewish Schema [of forgiveness] on the Christians," absolving them of guilt for Torquemada, the Second Crusade, and American quotas in medical schools. Golden solemnly predicted that anti-Semitic practices would doubtless disappear "now that we are no longer guilty of the death of Jesus."

Equally cleansing laughter was created when Arlene and Howard Eisenberg in an article on anti-Semitism in *Look* magazine, published between the third and fourth sessions of the Council, led off their discussion of the subject with the doubtless apocryphal story of the Catholic and Jewish boys who, engaged in a school-yard fist fight, exchanged the following comments during the tussle.

"Hey, what's this all about?"
"You're Jewish, aren't you?"
"Yes, but what's that got to do with it?"
"I'm gonna beat you up because the Jews killed Christ."
"I had nothing to do with that. It happened 2000 years ago."
"I know. But I just found out about it this morning."[11]

Unfortunately, there are some Catholic strongholds in the world where Catholic children have "just found out about it this morning." It is this persistent anti-Semitism in some Catholic schools and the implications about "Christ-killing" in some religious lesson-books that have caused more concern among Jews than any other phenomenon. In Spain, for example, some of the most popular tracts used in the past in the national schools have gone far beyond "Christ-killing" and pictured the Jews as murderers of Catholic children. In one famous textbook story used in the primary schools of Spain a seven-year-old Catholic boy is murdered by leading Jews because "they loathed children who loved the Virgin and the Lord." Quebec, almost as Catholic as Spain, has only recently dropped from its third-grade readers the story of "A Jew's Christmas" in which a Jewish father, a baker, throws his child into a flaming oven because the little boy had gone with friends to a Catholic religious display. The boy miraculously survived his ordeal of fire.[12]

Is there any substance to the ancient belief that the Jewish people of Jesus' time actually killed him? Not if we use the phrase

' accurately. Cardinal Bea, in defending the Jewish
e third session, freely admitted the guilt of "the
anhedrin at Jerusalem" for their share in the killing
strenuously attacked the theory that this implied
Jewish people *as a people* either then or now.
, it should be remembered, was a Roman method of execution. Jews used several other devices. Pilate was not a Jew but a Roman official. The flagellation and crowning with thorns were the deeds of Roman soldiers. The Jewish scholar Jules Isaac, who interviewed Pope John on the subject, has summarized in his *The Teaching of Contempt* his own views and those of many other scholars on the subject.[13] He argues convincingly that the gospel accounts of the Passion were weighted against the Jews because, written long after the event, the Christians at that time wanted and needed to appease the Roman authorities. They renounced all connection with their estranged Jewish brothers and absolved the Romans as much as possible. The soundest historical deduction seems to be that Jesus was crucified by the Romans as a political messianic agitator.

When a revised statement on the Jews emerged early in the fourth session as part of the declaration on non-Christian religions, it was impossible to avoid the conclusion that the Jews had been let down. In spite of the recognition of Judaism as the mother religion of Christianity, Jews were lumped in the statement along with Moslems and Buddhists. The tone adopted toward the Jews was unnecessarily patronizing. After objections had been raised, the statement was changed a little, but the final draft was still objectionable from the Jewish point of view. It was asserted that "by His cross Christ our Peace reconciled Jew and Gentile, making both one in Himself." To Jews this seemed to be an involved way of saying that Judaism no longer had any real excuse for existence.

Although there was no direct, unequivocal call for conversion in the final statement, it was noted that "the Church awaits that day, known to God alone, on which all peoples will address the Lord in a single voice and 'serve him with one accord.' " The word "deicide" was never restored to the document, although American bishops and others fought hard for its restoration. When it came to the delicate question of the guilt of the Jews for the Crucifixion, the text produced an unsatisfactory straddle, declaring that "all" Jews could not be held guilty but refraining from specifically absolving all the Jewish people. The final wording ran: "True, the Jewish authorities and those who followed their lead pressed for the death of Christ; still, what happened in His Passion cannot be charged against all the Jews without distinction, then alive, nor against the Jews of today."

That seemed to be a way of saying that Christ's suffering could be charged against *some* of the Jews of his day. The scriptural reference used in this paragraph was to the famous, and very partisan, passage in John 19 which reads: "When the chief priests therefore and officers saw him, they cried out, saying, Crucify him, crucify him. Pilate saith unto them, Take ye him, and crucify him; for I find no fault in him."

When, after all this, the final statement on the Jews emerged, it contained so much of genuine good will and contrition that if it had been the original statement on the subject it would have been received by the world Jewish community as quite acceptable. The final statement was received by the Jewish community with public politeness partly because Jews recognized the good will behind the imperfect text and partly because they realized the futility of further protest. Their lingering vexation was caused chiefly by the fact that the whole discussion had revealed so many vestiges of archaic prejudice still existing in high places.

The final section of the final document read: "The Church rejects, as foreign to the mind of Christ, any discrimination against men or harassment of them because of their race, color, condition in life, or religion." The statement also said that the Church "deplores the hatred, persecutions and displays of anti-Semitism, directed against Jews at any time and by anyone." If these statements had been made before the rise of Hitler, they would have been welcomed as quite adequate by nearly all Jews. As it was, the final statement was widely regarded as a watered-down compromise, an inferior substitute for an all-out condemnation accompanied by a confession of past shortcomings by the Church in confronting Nazi policies. One-third of the Jews of the world had been murdered before and during World War II under a policy of genocide which had been condoned by millions of "Christians." Old words of contrition were scarcely enough at such a moment.

In the excitement over the Jewish issue, a new tenderness, somewhat condescending, toward Moslems and Buddhists in the final text passed almost unnoticed. In discussing such non-Christian faiths, the text assumed a reasonably civilized attitude of charity, declaring, "The Catholic Church rejects nothing that is true and holy in these religions. She regards with sincere reverence those ways of conduct and of life, those precepts and teachings which, though differing in many aspects from the ones she holds and sets forth, nonetheless often reflect a ray of that Truth which enlightens all men." The statement expressed special "esteem also for the Moslems" since "they adore one God" and "though they do not acknowledge Jesus as God, they revere Him as a prophet," and "they also honor Mary."

When the Jewish statement was voted on in the final session as part of the pronouncement on all non-Christian faiths, the favorable vote was better than 9 to 1. An earlier vote accepting the section that omitted the word "deicide" had been about 7 to 1. No one will ever know how many of the opposition votes on this section came from Eastern-rite Catholic representatives who had the support of the Vatican Secretariat of State in opposing concessions to Jews for purely political reasons, and how many came from the last-ditch liberals who thought that the final version of the Jewish statement had been watered down too much. Probably it is safe to say that not more than one-tenth of the Council fathers revealed any substantial evidence of anti-Semitism. The American fathers and their *periti* came through the whole affair with flying colors. In fact, their attitude presages a new era of good will between Catholics and Jews in the United States. In October the Catholic bishops of the United States created a new ten-man commission to establish formal contacts with the American Jewish community. An able Catholic liberal, Monsignor George Higgins, will have much of the responsibility for making this organization useful.

❧

Meanwhile, something happened off stage that greatly heightened the drama of the battle over the Jewish statement. Between the first and second sessions of the Council Rolf Hochhuth's play *The Deputy* appeared first in Germany and later in Paris, London, and New York, creating a tremendous uproar by its stinging indictment of Catholic anti-Semitism in Germany and particularly of the weakness of Pius XII in facing the Nazis. In literary terms it was not a great play but it spoke with great conviction. It indicted Pius XII as a vacillating and evasive pontiff who failed to use his powers courageously in defying Hitler at a moment when defiance seemed to be a Christian duty. It was not anti-Catholic as such, since its hero was a young Jesuit priest who went to his death in Auschwitz proudly wearing the Jewish Star of David.

The world is not always moved most deeply by great art. There was enough truth in the crudities of *Uncle Tom's Cabin* to blow up the whole slavery system, partly because it was so timely. *The Deputy* was one of the most timely plays in the history of drama. The best critics thought that Hochhuth's characterization of Pius XII was somewhat unfair, but the solemn truth emerged that at the most tragic moment in history he had not spoken out against Hitler's savagery with a voice that might have been heard around the world. His excuse was that at that particular moment his speaking out might have doomed many millions of Catholics who lived under the shadow of Hitler's power. If there is some substance in this excuse—and there is a little—it was not convincing to the Jewish people.

In the uproar over *The Deputy* Pope Paul was caught in a very unfortunate position. One of Pius XII's closest associates throughout much of the period from 1937 to 1954, Paul could have remained silent about *The Deputy*, but he decided otherwise. As Pius XII had adopted him as a protegé, so he now adopted

Pius XII as the hero of a defensive crusade, thus making *The Deputy* a personal and Council issue. Perhaps he should receive credit for this rather uncharacteristic boldness in coming to the rescue of the reputation of his former chief. Paul's defense of Pius XII was one of the last acts he performed as Cardinal Montini of Milan before his elevation to the papal throne in 1963.

His letter of defense of Pius XII, published after he had become pope by the London *Tablet* in its issue of July 6, 1963, and by *Commonweal* in this country on February 28, 1964, "justified" every particular of the old pope's conduct in dealing with the Nazis concerning the Jews:

> History will show how vigilant, persistent, disinterested and courageous that conduct [of Pius XII's] must be judged to have been, when viewed in its true context in the concrete conditions of that time. . . . Hochhuth's play . . . entirely misrepresents him . . . it is not true that Pope Pius XII's conduct was inspired by a calculating political opportunism. . . . Let us suppose that Pius XII had done what Hochhuth blames him for not doing. His action would have led to such reprisals and devastations that Hochhuth himself, the war being over and he now possessed of a better historical, political and moral judgment, would have been able to write another play, far more realistic and far more interesting . . . about the vicar who, through political exhibitionism or psychological myopia, would have been guilty of unleashing on the already tormented world still greater calamities, involving innumerable innocent victims, let alone himself.

Pope Paul's comments summed up the Catholic defense of his former chief about as well as it could be summed up. The defense remains unconvincing for many reasons. It contains the implicit admission that at the most inappropriate moment for silence in all history the head of the Roman Catholic Church did keep silence. If the practical motive had something to be said for it—and that part of the argument can never be conclusively settled—the explanation seemed almost an insult to the Jewish people. What are Christian principles for if they cannot be publicly and firmly enunciated at a moment when 6,000,000 innocent human beings are going to their death? For the Jews no moral obligation could be imagined more compelling than the obligation to speak out at the moment when Pius XII did not speak out.

Coupled with this conviction were several disquieting auxiliary facts. Paul VI, in spite of all the revelations about his former chief, began in 1965 the formal process of making him a saint. This seemed to demonstrate that Paul was not quite aware of the depth of feeling among liberals throughout the world, both Jewish and non-Jewish, about the record of Pius. It was Pius XII, as Pacelli, serving first as Papal Nuncio to Germany and later as Papal Secretary of State under Pius XI, who was largely responsible for the Hitler-Vatican pact of 1933. Out of that pact the Church gained financial and political benefits from Hitler at the very moment when he was rising to power. In fact, it is doubtful that he could have risen to complete power without the implied moral sanction the pact conferred on the Nazi regime.[14]

Another disquieting fact was that *The Deputy*, obviously because of Vatican pressure, was not permitted a performance at a regular theater in Rome; it was harried by the police and ultimately suppressed after being partially presented before 150 spectators in a Rome bookshop. Italian officials, in suppressing the play, invoked the 1929 concordat between Italy and the Vatican that contains special guarantees against any public offense to the Papacy. The Vatican daily, *Osservatore Romano*, in condemning the attempt to produce *The Deputy* in Rome, reminded Italy that the guarantees against papal insults are "an integral part of the Italian Constitution."

The position of the Vatican in world opinion had not been improved when, in November 1964, certain new documents involving Pius XII and the Nazis were published by the British government. One of them was a memorandum of September 12, 1941, by Fritz Menshausen, Counselor of the German Embassy to the Holy See, saying that "in his heart, one is assured time and again, Pius XII stands on the side of the Axis powers."[15]

In the attempt to refute this and other revelations about Pius

XII, the Vatican decided to make public in March 1966 a volume of letters written by Pius XII over the years to German bishops. The letters contained many expressions of anxiety and even despair concerning the troubles in Germany as Hitler rose to power, but there was no specific mention in them of the German detention camps for Jews or of the murder of the Jews. The concern of Pius was for his beloved Church and the members of that Church who were losing their peace and their privileges under Nazi rule. The total effect of the new publication was to confirm the conviction of the Jews that Pius XII had failed to use the full authority of his position in their behalf.

In the noisy quarrel over *The Deputy* and the specific shortcomings of Pius XII, many background facts concerning the Church and fascism were almost ignored. By the time of Auschwitz Europe was reaping the whirlwind for the weakness of Pius XI in facing fascism in Italy in the 1920's. *Then* was the time to speak out against fascism, and Pius XI did not speak except to complain about strictly ecclesiastical matters. He never championed democracy as against fascism, and he jettisoned the only political party of Catholic orientation that might have challenged Mussolini successfully, the Catholic Popular Party of Don Sturzo. Sturzo was forced out of leadership of the Popular Party in July, 1923—I was living in Italy at the time—and two months later Pius XI virtually signed the party's death warrant. Two months after that, Mussolini gave Pius XI his payment by providing Catholic instruction in all Italian state schools. Pius XI entered into the 1929 pact with Mussolini, which was an even more important moral bonus for the Italian dictator than the Vatican-Hitler pact was to be for the German dictator.

One year later, in 1930, Pius XI issued his famous encyclical *Quadragesimo Anno*, now hailed by some Catholic liberals as a platform for social reform but which contained, in addition to some liberal sentiments, one ominous passage which is now almost universally neglected in Catholic seminaries outside of Spain and Portugal.[16] This passage conferred limited but important approval on the fascist trade unions and their policy of "peaceful collaboration of the classes, repression of Socialist organizations." In practice the "repression" led to the murder of democratic trade union leaders. Pius XI could not have been ignorant of the real methods of the fascist unions, since Mussolini had been in power almost a decade when this encyclical appeared. The labor section of *Quadragesimo Anno* was to become the spiritual charter for Franco's labor-suppressing syndicates in Spain, which finally triumphed in 1939 with the blessings of the Vatican and the armed support of Hitler and Mussolini.

During these years of the rise of fascism the personal record of Pope Paul, as Montini, was quite good. He was never a fascist even though he allowed himself to be used as part of an opportunist clerical machine. But the total record of the Vatican during these years has been steadily glossed over. Two famous encyclicals written by Pius XI in 1931 and 1937, *Non Abbiamo Bisogno* and *Mit Brennender Sorge*, are often described in Catholic journals as anti-Nazi and anti-fascist. If they are read carefully, it will be discovered that they merely chided the Nazis and fascists for threatening or destroying Catholic educational and ecclesiastical privileges. The German encyclical, *Mit Brennender Sorge*, was not written until Hitler had closed 20,000 Catholic schools and launched a campaign of persecution against members of Catholic religious orders.

After the appearance of *The Deputy*, there appeared, in 1964, a far more devastating exposure of Catholic guilt in dealing with the Nazis, Guenter Lewy's *The Catholic Church and Nazi Germany*. Lewy presented a carefully documented account of the conduct of the German bishops during the Hitler period. Their conduct, of course, was not entirely unique. In many respects it was no worse than the conduct of German Protestant leaders. Implicit in the rise of Hitler to power in Germany is the weakness of *all* Christianity in facing up to its moral responsibilities.

Lewy's story amplified the case against Pius XII. He had not only served as Papal Nuncio to Germany from 1920 to 1929, and as Secretary of State during the time of the Vatican-Hitler pact, but he had been the Church's chief adviser on German affairs through the generation in which Hitler rose to power. He could not have been ignorant of the full meaning of Hitler's philosophy. He chose to bargain selfishly for ecclesiastical advantage with a leader whose moral monstrosity was already too apparent.

In the process of bargaining Hitler reckoned on the Church's institutional selfishness and won. "They will swallow anything in order to keep their material advantages," said Hitler to Rauschning, jeering at the morality of the German Catholic bishops. "The bishops gladly recognized that the new [Hitler] state promoted Christianity, raised the level of morality and fought the battle against Bolshevism and godlessness with vigor and success," said Bishop Wilhelm Berning in the summary he made to Hitler in 1933. Although the bishops did not like Hitler or his anti-Semitism, they swallowed him along with his anti-Semitism knowingly. In Hitler's 1933 conversation with Bishop Berning, he (according to Lewy) "touched upon the Jewish question, and again stressing the fundamental agreement between National Socialism and Catholicism, pointed out that the Church always had regarded the Jews as parasites and had banished them into the ghetto. He was merely going to do what the Church had done for 1,500 years. Altogether, Hitler affirmed, he was personally convinced of the great power and significance of Christianity and he therefore would not permit the founding of another religion. . . . Being a Catholic himself, he would not tolerate another Kulturkampf, and the rights of the Church would be left intact."

Lewy's judgment is that the Church, in spite of occasional heroic protests by some individuals, actually justified "moderate anti-Semitism" during the rise of the Nazis, and "merely objected to extreme and immoral acts." He declares that "from the time Hitler came to power all the German bishops began declaring their appreciation of the important natural values of race and racial purity. . . . When Hitler started to pursue the purity of the German blood in his own ruthless way, the overwhelming majority of the German Catholics . . . dutifully obeyed his orders and promptly forgot the warning against using extreme and immoral means in defense of one's race given out by their bishops."

Apparently Hitler's clinching argument for Catholic cooperation was his statement at the end of the Berning interview: "We shall keep the confessional schools in order to bring up believers." Hitler also promised to continue the Catholic organizations if they promoted Christian ideas, maintained a "positive relationship" to his state, and eliminated all the residues of liberalism and Marxism.

Lewy's severe judgment of Catholic guilt in dealing with German policy was underscored in 1966 when Saul Friedlander's *Pius XII and the Third Reich* was translated from the French for American publication. The Eugenio Pacelli who emerges from Friedlander's pages is a professional diplomat who has lost his sense of proportion in dealing with human values.

One of the startling facts about Hitler's "cooperation" with the Church is that, in spite of flagrant and deliberate violations of the 1933 Concordat, he never ceased to pay his subsidies to the Church until the very end, and the Church continued to accept those subsidies. In formal terms the Concordat of July 20, 1933, signed by Pacelli for the Vatican and by Papen for Hitler, struck an ignoble bargain. In return for the recognition of religious instruction, "to be taught in accordance with the principles of the Catholic Church," the Church assumed the obligation to stress in such instruction a "patriotic, civic and social consciousness and sense of duty" to the Hitler regime. In return for this promise of allegiance, the Church was given veto power over every Catholic teacher of religion in the schools, and the government guaranteed maintenance of the existing Catholic schools and the right to establish new ones. In return for that favor, the Church promised to exclude priests from active politics; and with this bargain the Catholic Center Party passed into oblivion.

After the war, the German bishops tried vainly to identify German Catholicism with the few Catholic martyrs to Nazi savagery. To this day they are fighting successfully to keep the Hitler-Vatican Concordat alive in order to receive its institutional benefits. Neither Pope John nor Pope Paul renounced this concordat, nor did Pius XI or Pius XII when the most flagrant violations of it were continuing under Hitler. The Church was jubilant when, on March 26, 1957, the concordat was interpreted as still binding on West Germany by the West German Federal Constitutional Court.

The irony of the present situation is that, although a great many educated Catholics agree with the general indictment of their Church's policy vis-à-vis Hitler, the Church cannot completely cleanse itself of old sins by frankly confessing the profound institutional and papal errors. Catholic leaders feel obliged to protect the memory of popes who have served in our time as vicars of Christ. Institutional pride, papal primacy, and papal infallibility are all stirred in to a mixture of shaded history that must be served as an apologia to Catholics of the rising generation.

But the future can be a great deal brighter than the past. The final statement of Vatican II condemning all forms of anti-Semitism was sincerely promulgated as a platform for future conduct. There is no doubt that it will bring new decencies into the relations between Catholics and Jews in the future. The very ventilation of unpleasant truth about present and past abuses constituted an immense gain for tolerance and good will. Catholic textbooks are being revised to purge them of anti-Semitic paragraphs, and Catholic-Jewish meetings of understanding are blossoming throughout the world. If the final utterance of Vatican II on the Jews was inadequate, it still marked a gigantic step forward toward a future of fair play.

CHAPTER EIGHT ❧ HOW MUCH CHRISTIAN UNITY?

MANY people thought that the primary object of Vatican II was to reunite all the churches of Christendom. Certainly by the time the first session was over, the original purpose of Catholic *aggiornamento* had been blended with something larger, a desire for some kind of concert or union or cooperation in the whole Christian world. There was a general agreement, to use a phrase of Cardinal Bea's, that the "sorrowful religious wars" of the past should be deplored and that a new atmosphere of brotherly good will should be developed.

To some extent in the past this general desire for good will has been deliberately uninformed. Based on an ostrich policy in preference to critical realism, it has become traditional in the United States in recent years to regard as bad form any critical examination of the doctrinal underpinning of any faith by any person outside that faith. Liberals vie with each other in looking the other way when one religion starts to criticize another religion, partly because such head-on disputes have turned out to be sterile as well as needlessly bitter. Consequently American "brotherhood" in religious matters is often based on both ignorance and silence concerning vital issues.

In this atmosphere, several phases of the church-union problem received very little public attention during Vatican II. Would a possible union of Christendom carry with it any perils for freedom and democracy? For nonbelievers? For Jews? For the separation of church and state? For relations with the non-Christian continents?

Almost everybody assumed that the concept of church union

was a good thing in itself, not needing any detailed defense. And almost everybody except the church historians neglected the long, meaningful, and depressing history of past efforts in the direction of church union by Protestants, Catholics, and Orthodox. Probably millions of Americans thought that Pope John in 1959 initiated the modern movement for Christian unity when he announced the Council. In fact, this was not true. John's Church has long been the most intransigent opponent of Christian reunion. As we have seen, John himself never formally abandoned the chief traditional demand of his Church—that all Christendom be united in a power structure headed by the pope.

A few Catholic leaders were not only aware of their own Church's intransigence in past unity movements, but they were willing to regret it publicly. Pope Paul himself deplored past shortcomings by declaring: "If any fault for this separation can be laid at our door, we ask pardon for it both from God and from our brothers who may consider themselves to have been offended by us." Many American Protestant leaders were quite willing to forget past Catholic sabotage of unity movements and to express regret for Protestant foot-dragging. Some Catholic leaders joined in the expressions of regret. Bishop John J. Carberry, Catholic bishop of Columbus, who had been appointed head of a subcommission to discuss unity with American Protestant organizations, was repentant when he addressed the 1965 General Assembly of the United Presbyterian Church. Referring to Catholics as latecomers in ecumenical activity, he said: "We now come with joy touched by the spirit of grace, happy to arrive . . . we regret our delay."[1]

The final decree by the Council on ecumenism was promulgated in November 1964. Both the statement and the journalistic treatment thereof were full of those ambiguous, optimistic phrases about cooperation that may mean something or may mean nothing, depending on later events. Opening with a declaration that: "The restoration of unity among all Christians is one of the principal concerns of the Second Vatican Council," it went on to speak of that "remorse over their divisions" felt by "divided Christians," and the need of fairness in dialogue with "our separated brethren." However, the major difficulty, the potential subordination of all Christians to Rome, was ignored.

The Council never even reached a discussion of the most acute immediate problem in Christian reunion, the specific terms of cooperative activity. Such questions were left hanging in a gentle fog of good will. Everybody agreed that the fog was better than a war cloud and enjoyed the new amiable atmosphere of mutual respect and courtesy. Nearly everybody also agreed that the personal good will generated at the Council was genuine. But in the end the most important issues of Christian unity were not discussed, partly because this Council had never been designed as a genuine confrontation of plenary representatives of the people of Christendom, Catholic, Protestant, and Orthodox.

However, the real issues were vigorously discussed in the coffee bars and at some of the press conferences, and this was profitable even if it could also be described as superficial and sentimental. A few skeptics questioned whether the ultimate cause of Christian unity is best served by starting with amiable manners and sentimental good will. It might have been better, they said, to start directly with the basic disagreements even if the initial atmosphere proved to be somewhat quarrelsome. This approach was rejected out of hand in favor of a nonspecific amiability.

Two moves by Pope John helped to create interfaith friendship, the foundation of the Secretariat for Promoting Christian Unity, under the direction of Cardinal Bea, and the cordial invitation to Protestant and Greek Orthodox bodies to send observers to the Council. These two gestures complemented each other. The Protestant and Orthodox observers were treated as honored guests, even when they represented institutions that had been strongly anti-Catholic in the past. The Secretariat for Promoting Christian Unity cultivated and informed the observers and simultaneously spread the message of good will and understanding throughout the world. The observers met with the Secretariat representatives once a week for discussion. The leader of this whole effort is one of the most charming and genuinely spiritual men in the Church, Augustin Cardinal Bea, a Jesuit cardinal of German birth who had been confessor to Pope Pius XII. Somehow he had come up through the Institution without becoming completely institutionalized. His frail, stooped figure—he was born in 1881—became a symbol of Christian cooperation throughout the world. The young priests who worked under him in the Secretariat carried out their tasks with the same spirit. Staff members of the Secretariat including two Americans, Father Thomas Stransky, C.S.P., of Wisconsin and Father John Long, S.J., of New York, specialized in explaining every narrow dogma of their Church in terms that would be most acceptable to non-Catholics. If at times they stretched their liberal interpretations close to the boundary of heresy, this brought only delight to the progressives inside their Church, and to the Protestants. They maintained open and frank discussions with non-Catholics concerning the most controversial differences of doctrine and policy even at a time when the Roman Curia was attempting to commit the Council to contrary types of reaction. The more the Curia discounted their efforts the more popular they became with the liberal majority.

Cardinal Bea himself became an ecumenical hero on both sides of the Atlantic. Since he was a cardinal, even the conservative Catholic University of America did not dare to boycott him as it had boycotted lesser leaders among the liberal Catholics. His speaking tours in the United States became tours of triumph even when his actual statements, upon careful analysis, revealed few concessions to non-Catholic points of view.

❧

One of the difficulties about ecumenism is that the term is so loosely used that participants in the so-called ecumenical dialogue often pass each other like railroad trains on parallel tracks. In the United States during the Council the various meanings of the word descended into absurd confusion. One writer in *The Christian Century* coined twenty-six words in a "glossary of ecumenics" to satirize the confusion. Included were "ecumaniac," "a person who believes that all Churches are better than his own"; "ecumenopause," "a Council's change of life"; and "ecumonotony," "books dealing with the ecumenical movement." In 1965 the Boston *Pilot* told the world about "the Second Ecumenical football game to be played at Boston College . . . between the Buffalo Bills and the Boston Patriots," sponsored by a guild of the licensed beverage industry.

The word "ecumenism" is derived from the Greek word *oikoumene*, meaning the whole inhabited world. Such a definition does not bring us much closer to twentieth-century clarity, and "ecumenism" has come to mean a very special thing in current Christian development. Dr. W. A. Visser't Hooft of the World Council of Churches has said that there are at least seven meanings for the word while Father Ronald Cowley of Georgetown University summed up its present ambivalent position by saying: "For the great mass of Catholics in the world the reality underlying what has come to be known as the ecumenical movement could be attained only through submission to the See of Peter. But for non-Catholic Christians ecumenism already implied an aspiration to Christian union going beyond denominational loyalties."[2] This double meaning of ecumenism during the Council often made it seem that Catholics and non-Catholics were talking a different language.

In spite of verbal confusion, however, the Council's decree on ecumenism actually made a number of important concessions to Protestantism, and later on the Constitution on The Church in the Modern World confirmed the spirit of these concessions by saying: "Our hearts embrace also those brothers and communities not yet living with us in full communion. To them we are linked nonetheless by our profession of the Father and the Son and the Holy Spirit, and by the bond of charity."

The decree on ecumenism, speaking of the movement for "the restoration of unity among all Christians," which is called "ecumenical," conceded that: "Taking part in this movement . . . are those who invoke the Triune God and confess Jesus as Lord and Savior. They join in not merely as individuals but also as members of the corporate groups in which they have heard the gospel, and which each regards as his Church and, indeed, God's." This was a neat compromise wording that allowed Protestants to claim that their churches were really churches but did not quite commit the Council to saying that they were really churches. The wording was adopted after a brief flare-up at the second session over the question of whether non-Catholic churches should still be regarded as simply collections of individual baptized Christians.

In the final wording of the decree on ecumenism it was conceded that all those who are baptized "have a right to be honored by the title of Christian." It was even said that "The Catholic Church accepts them with respect and affection as brothers." But immediately after this sentence came the old claim: "For men who believe in Christ and have been properly baptized are brought into a certain, though imperfect, communion with the Catholic Church." In essence, this concession is a repetition of the Catholic thesis that Protestants are Christians to the extent that they are conscious or unconscious Catholics.

Most Protestants welcomed the new warmth and graciousness in Catholic terminology, even when they had some doubts about the ultimate meaning of the new courtesy. But they did not fail to note that at no point in the decree on ecumenism was there any specific repudiation of the doctrine that Christian unity means return to the Catholic Church. The decree still put Protestants in their place by saying:

> Nevertheless, our separated brethren, whether considered as individuals or as Communities and Churches, are not blessed with that unity which Jesus Christ wished to bestow on all those whom He regenerated and vivified into one body and newness of life—that unity which the holy Scriptures and the revered tradition of the Church proclaim. For it is through Christ's Catholic Church alone, which is the all-embracing means of salvation, that the fullness of the means of salvation can be obtained.

The leader of the World Council of Churches at that time, Dr. W. A. Visser't Hooft, expressed the truth quite frankly when he said: "Catholic Ecumenism is tied up with the Catholic concept of the papacy in Rome . . . despite its broadness and despite all its readiness to take the other Churches seriously, nevertheless it ultimately implies an invitation to join the unity which already exists under the pope."[3]

How much did the final decree on ecumenism mean in practice? Its significance depends largely on the future activities of leading Catholics and non-Catholics in their local communities. In the United States it led immediately to many "little Vatican Councils," exchanges of speakers between Catholic and Protestant assemblies, ecumenical interfaith forums, and very cordial joint public utterances by Protestant and Catholic leaders concerning the things they held in common. The Catholic-Protestant atmosphere in many parts of the world became more irenic than it had ever been before.

In England, however, there was more caustic criticism than in the United States. The late Evelyn Waugh, the novelist who had become a Catholic convert, sounded a sour note in a letter to the London *Tablet* in reply to one of England's most distinguished Catholics, Abbot Christopher Butler of Downside:

> The early Christians sought no accommodation with their enemies. They offered something new and quite unreconcilable with contemporary tastes and superstitions. They died to preserve their unique position in opposition to what was the spirit of their age.
>
> Instead of "dialogue with separated brethren" why do we not revert to the old-fashioned effort to convert the Protestants, the Jews and the Heathen, to show them their errors and present disagreeable truths in full and sharp detail? . . .
>
> I write this because I am told on what seems good authority that in this country and the USA conversions to the Church have much declined since the assembly of the Council.[4]

Although such sentiments seemed petty when published at a high moment in ecumenical developments, Waugh's attitude was typical of many opinions expressed in the American Catholic press, even during the Council. There was some apprehension among Catholic prelates because conversions from Protestantism to Catholicism had fallen off in many parts of the world. This was natural enough since such conversions had often been based upon the conviction that Protestants were not Christians at all but heretics.

In the whole discussion both Protestants and Catholics were somewhat embarrassed by the official character of anti-Protestant statements by the Church in the past. Although the irenic title "separated brethren" was adopted at the Council with papal sanction, all Protestants are still rated as heretics in official teaching. Wilful heretics are bound to go to hell unless their heresy is based on invincible ignorance or unless God in his infinite mercy grants them a last-minute reprieve. Since most Protestants would rather be consigned to hell by the Catholic Church than be classified as guilty of invincible ignorance, the conditional salvation offered by the Church was not welcome.

The official teaching of the Catholic Church concerning Protestants is still quite appalling. Every convert from Protestantism to Catholicism is supposed, under the rule of Canon 752 and various instructions from the Holy Office, to abjure Protestant errors in very specific terms. The wording is quite recent and was transmitted to the American faithful in March 1942 by Archbishop Cicognani, then Apostolic Delegate in Washington and later Vatican Secretary of State. Here are some of the statements that every Protestant convert to Catholicism is supposed to profess:

> I ——— years of age, born outside the Catholic Church, have held and believed errors contrary to her teaching. Now, enlightened by divine grace, I kneel before you, Reverend Father ———.
>
> I admit and embrace most firmly the apostolic and ecclesiastical traditions and all the other constitutions and prescriptions of the Church.
>
> I admit the Sacred Scriptures according to the sense which has been held and which is still held by Holy Mother Church,

whose duty it is to judge the true sense and interpretation of the Sacred Scriptures, and I shall never accept or interpret them except according to unanimous consent of the Fathers ———.

I recognize the holy Roman, Catholic, and Apostolic Church as the mother and teacher of all the Churches and I promise and swear true obedience to the Roman Pontiff, successor of St. Peter, Prince of the Apostles, and Vicar of Jesus Christ.

Besides I accept, without hesitation, and profess all that has been handed down, defined and declared by the Sacred Canons and by the General Council, and in a special manner concerning the primacy and infallibility of the Roman Pontiff. At the same time I condemn and reprove all that the Church has condemned and reproved. This same Catholic faith, outside of which nobody can be saved, which I now freely profess and to which I truly adhere, the same I promise and swear to maintain and profess, with the help of God, entire, inviolate, and with firm constancy until the last breath of life; and I shall strive, as far as possible, that this same faith shall be held, taught, and publicly professed by all those who depend on me and by those of whom I shall have charge.[5]

Nominally this profession of faith commits a Protestant convert to all the condemnations and anathemas of the Church in the past, including the package of anathemas in the *Syllabus of Errors* of Pius IX. It commits him to believe that the state may, with perfect propriety, exclude all other forms of religion except Catholicism.

The leaders of the Church at Vatican II made no attempt to conceal or retract these ancient anti-Protestant teachings. Even Cardinal Bea, when he came to Harvard to deliver a series of three lectures before huge audiences in 1963, did not attempt to dilute the Catholic gospel lying behind its separatism. He declared that John XXIII had no intention of using the word "ecumenical" to designate that which is common to all Christians, hence to discuss unity. John, he said, gave the word "the meaning which it had for many hundreds of years in the terminology of Catholic canon law, namely: a council to which all the bishops of the *oikoumene* (the whole world) who were in communion with the See of Peter were invited."

Bea, after he had delivered two lectures to an enthralled audience, calmly announced: "First and foremost the fundamental teaching of the Catholic Church will not be changed. Compromise on points of faith which have already been defined is impossible. It would be quite unfair to our non-Catholic brethren to stir up false hopes of this nature. Nor is there a possibility that the Church —even in its zeal for eventual union—will ever be content with a recognition only of 'essential dogmas,' or that she will reverse or withdraw the dogmatic decrees drawn up at the Council of Trent. Again it would be simply dishonest to suggest that there is any likelihood that the dogmas of the primacy or the Infallibility of the Pope will be revised."[6]

Long before Vatican II, Protestant leaders and some Orthodox leaders had attempted to talk unity and cooperation with the Roman Catholic Church and had been brusquely repulsed. The leaders of the World Council of Churches, organized in 1948, had tried desperately to persuade the Catholic Church to participate. In the beginning they were thoroughly snubbed, and the Vatican forbade any Catholic to attend the organizing section of the World Council at Amsterdam in 1948.

Catholic exclusiveness had begun long before 1948. In 1857, when a Society for the Union of Christendom was formed in London, it was promptly boycotted by Rome. Catholics were forbidden by the Holy Office in 1864 to participate in meetings of such organizations. In 1919 the prohibition was repeated and applied to "meetings or conferences of whatever kind, public or private, called by non-Christians for the purpose of promoting the union of all churches claiming to be Christian." The inference that non-Catholic Churches only "claimed" to be Christian has always been considered a supreme act of unfriendliness by Protestantism.

For a large part of the twentieth century it continued to be the official attitude of the Church toward "separated brethren." When the Canon Law was promulgated in 1918, Canon 1325 forbade all

Catholics to discuss "matters of faith" with non-Catholics. Pius XI in his 1928 encyclical *Mortalium Animos* put the Catholic position bluntly when he said: "The Unity of Christians cannot be otherwise obtained than by securing the return of the separated to the one true Church of Christ from which they once unhappily withdrew." He reminded the faithful of Leo XIII's rebuke to Catholics for participating in promiscuous religious meetings after Cardinal Gibbons had been so rash as to recite the Lord's Prayer before a mixed religious group in 1893.[7]

The Catholic policy of aloofness had persisted down to the 1950's, when the World Council of Churches met for its Second Assembly in Evanston, Illinois, in 1954, largely to discuss greater unity among Christians. The Catholic Church not only refused to accept an invitation to send observers but it also issued through Cardinal Stritch of Chicago a special warning to its people not to attend any of the sessions. (This World Council is now a consultative body for 214 Protestant and Orthodox churches of the world that have a total membership of more than 35,000,000.)

A new *rapprochement* between the World Council and Rome began before Vatican II. Rome sent five observers to the World Council's Assembly in Delhi in 1961, and the World Council reciprocated by sending observers to Vatican II. But it was apparent that many leaders of the Church were apprehensive about any overcharitable interpretation of cooperative hospitality.

In spite of his eloquent words of remorse concerning past Catholic offenses against Protestants, it became quite evident during the Council years that Pope Paul still regarded Protestantism as something akin to modernism, that most obnoxious of latter-day heresies. In one of his great general audiences, the one on November 4, 1964, Paul coupled Protestantism and modernism in a most revealing paragraph. He classed them both as champions of the religion of the spirit in a narrow sense, as contrasted with the Catholic religion of authority, and he championed the religion of authority. "All can perceive," he said, "that there is spread a little everywhere the mentality of Protestantism and Modernism, denying the need and the legitimate existence of an intermediate authority in the relationship of the soul with God. 'How many men between God and me!' exclaimed the well-known voice of a child of this mentality [Rousseau]."

Although Pope Paul went on to disown purely temporal authority, his meaning was made clear enough when he underscored his own supreme authority "over the entire community united in the name of Christ; a power that is not only purely external but is capable of creating or annulling internal obligations for consciences; and not indeed something left to the optional choice of the faithful but necessary to the structure of the Church; and not derived from the latter but from Christ and God."[8] It would be difficult to find words more clearly in conflict with the Protestant outlook.

Pope Paul's words served to remind the Protestants at the Council that the Church still preserved and imposed upon its most important intellectual leaders the Oath Against Modernism, prepared by one of the Church's most reactionary theologians, Pius X, recently made a saint. This long and detailed oath binds Catholic leaders to reject most of those elements of liberal Protestantism that have been developed in an effort to adapt Christianity to modern science and modern biblical scholarship.[9] The oath-taker must formally renounce "the heretical misrepresentation that dogmas evolve and change from one meaning to another different from the one which the Church held previously," and he must accept fully "miracles and prophecy as the surest signs of the divine origin of the Christian religion."

During the Council the conservatives attempted to maintain the fundamentals of the old anti-Protestant position, but they were opposing a new tide of tolerance and decency. Monsignor Francis J. Connell, for many years Dean of the School of Sacred Theology of the Catholic University, had published in 1956 his famous pamphlet, "Cooperation of Catholics in Non-Catholic Religious Activities," in which he had declared, among other things, that no Catholic had a moral right to participate in the erection of a non-Catholic Church, that no Catholic should participate in the public worship of any non-Catholic Church, and that if a Protestant clergyman requested a priest to lend or give him some altar breads for his religious services he should be met with a courteous but firm refusal. Connell had laid down the rule that Catholic priests should never join ministerial associations or even participate in any campaigns that had such heretical slogans as "Worship in the Church of Your Choice."[10]

Fortunately for the future of ecumenism, many of these old pronouncements, although they came from the highest theological sources in American Catholicism, were openly scorned by the Fathers in the Council. The spirit of Pope John triumphed over the spirit of Pius X. All over America in the closing year of the Council Catholic bishops and priests participated in joint services with Protestants and were frequently admitted into predominantly Protestant ministerial associations. Protestant and Catholic congregations united in helping each other. If the old rules were still on the books, it was clear that they no longer controlled either the Protestant mind or the Catholic mind.

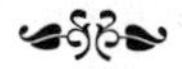

At the beginning of the first session there were 49 non-Catholic observers and guests from the Protestant and Orthodox world, 17 of whom were Americans. Many of them stayed only a short time, and very few remained for all four sessions. Altogether there were more than 100 non-Catholic observers who sat as honored guests at one time or another during the four sessions. In theological outlook they ranged all the way from Bible fundamentalists to near-humanist Unitarians, who were admitted as observers by virtue of their affiliation with the International Association for Liberal Christianity and Religious Freedom. The American Protestant observers were somewhat handicapped because they did not, in any sense, represent the largest Protestant grouping in the United States, the Southern Baptist Convention, which not only refused to accept any invitation from Vatican II but has consistently refused affiliation with the National Council of Churches of the United States and the World Council of Churches.

The Protestant observers were not only observers but guests, a somewhat embarrassing position. The Vatican had graciously offered to pay their board and lodging in Rome, and many of them had accepted. Although most of them came to Rome with the official approval of their denominations, they had been warned not to speak for those denominations. They were under great pressure at various times during the Council to speak as a group for the Protestant outlook, but they refrained. Consequently there was never any official statement issued at the Council expressing the opinion of Protestant observers as a group.

This attitude of reserve was probably necessary, but in many ways its results were unfortunate. In spite of strictures, many individual Protestant observers issued complimentary statements about events at Vatican II, omitting critical remarks, and thus creating an impression of starry-eyed naïveté. In fact, most of the Protestant observers could be described as "concessionists." They had been chosen for their friendliness to Catholicism in the first place, and the warm hospitality at the Vatican tended to accentuate that friendliness to a point at which their own Protestantism was expressed in almost apologetic terms.

Among the Americans, the most effusive of the Protestant apologists was the highest ranking Methodist, Bishop Fred Pierce Corson of Philadelphia, a leader who had frequently attacked the Supreme Court's policies on the separation of church and state and warmly praised Catholic policy. Although he was present at the Council for a very short time, he was given the exceptional distinction of several private papal audiences, and in the United States he received many honorary degrees from Catholic colleges.

More critical and intelligent in his approach was the second-ranking American Methodist among the observers, Dr. Albert C. Outler of Southern Methodist University, but he too gave an appearance to the world of bland acceptance of Catholic policies. When he was chosen in the last session to give the final public address for Protestant observers in the presence of many high-ranking Catholic prelates and the press, he spoke with captivating eloquence of "your budget of unfinished business" but he failed to speak specifically of the great barriers of Catholic policy that lie between American Protestantism and Catholicism.

Dr. Outler's silences were, unfortunately, characteristic of the attitudes of many of the guest observers. No guest observer cared to stand up and say, even in Bar Jonah and Bar Abbas, the two coffee bars in St. Peter's, that Western Protestantism had moved steadily toward complete internal democracy since the days of Luther while Catholicism had remained as essentially imperialistic in its government as it had been in the sixteenth century. Thus the gap between the two great branches of Christianity had been increased. How impolite it would have been to say: Your Church is an obsolete monarchy and mine is not!

Nevertheless the private remarks of some Protestant observers undoubtedly had some effect in shaping Council policy. Many an episcopal orator turned to the Protestant observers in the aula as if to say, See! I think you will like this. We are moving in your direction even if we have to move slowly. And some of the Protestant observers wrote publicly with considerable effect, expressing mild but useful skepticism concerning the nearly frozen archaisms of the Church.

Perhaps the most useful of these mild Protestant critics was Dr. Robert McAfee Brown of Stanford University, a Presbyterian who had formerly served as a professor at Union Theological Seminary in New York. In some senses he could be described as a concessionist since he had not publicly opposed Catholic demands on the public treasury for the parochial school system and he had steadily advocated more friendly relations with Catholics. But, in *Look* magazine and in his book, *Observer in Rome,* he put many key questions that needed to be asked.[11] To paraphrase them roughly, Dr. Brown asked (1) How about religious liberty? (2) How about a good, clear declaration concerning the Jews? (3) How about giving laymen more voice in your Church, especially since a more adequate theology of marriage may come from laymen than from celibate priests? (4) How about a genuinely biblical doctrine concerning Mary, without the polemics of the past? (5) How about birth control? (6) How about mixed marriage and the rule that requires a non-Catholic to sign away his spiritual birthright? (7) How about genuine ecumenism, not designed as a soft-sell technique to get non-Catholics back into the Roman Catholic Church? (8) How about forbidden books and intellectual freedom for your own flock?

These were enormously important questions, the best published by any Protestant observer at the Council, but they illustrate the weakness as well as the strength of liberal Protestantism vis-à-vis Catholic policy. Papal infallibility* and primacy, the key to the whole power structure of Catholic autocracy, was not mentioned, nor was the separation of church and state, American style. The money question—the billions of tax dollars demanded from American taxpayers for Catholic schools—seemed to be outside the range of Dr. Brown's otherwise effective probing. Oddly enough, these basic questions were being asked during the Council sessions in the United States more by the conservative wing of American Protestantism than by the liberal wing. But in England the liberal skeptics spoke up quite frankly. Few liberal Protestant journals in the United States would have ventured to express non-ecumenical sentiments so bluntly as the *Manchester Guardian Weekly*'s John Grigg did in January 1966: "For those of us who feel that the Protestantism relevant to our time—though not, in many respects, identical with the Protestantism of our ancestors—is still quite distinct from Roman Catholicism, the rather naive eagerness with which Anglican divines are proclaiming the birth of a new ecumenical age arouses suspicion and pity. They are traveling on a road where the traffic moves only in one direction. The Second Vatican Council has left unchanged that aspect of the Roman Church to which Protestants can most legitimately object—the spiritual autocracy of the Bishop of Rome."[12]

This caustic comment is probably symptomatic of majority sentiment in Great Britain. Because of their history the British people are deeply aware of the gulf between their outlook and that of Rome. Great Britain still has a great residue of specific

* But Dr. Brown later criticized papal infallibility before a Catholic group.

anti-Catholic feeling, probably much more specific than the vague and evaporating anti-Catholicism of the United States. Although Catholicism is increasing a little in Britain at the expense of Protestantism, the Catholic proportion in the population is still under 10 per cent, and Church leaders betray great anxiety over the drift of their people away from manifestations of their faith.

The thought that the Anglican Church constitutes a natural bridge between Protestantism and the Roman Catholic Church will not bear analysis. The fact that they are both state churches and that they both secure public money for their schools does not soften their natural rivalry. It is partly a political and national rivalry. There could never be a union of the Church of England and the Church of Rome without the approval of a political parliament. The Anglo-Catholic movement within the Church of England is by no means representative. It is only in ceremonialism and pageantry that Anglicanism and Romanism seem so much alike. In breadth of intellectual outlook they are worlds apart.

This was not apparent in March 1966 when the Archbishop of Canterbury, Arthur Michael Ramsey, made the first formal visit to a reigning pope by an Anglican bishop since the sixteenth century. The reaction in Britain, however, was mixed, particularly when aides of the Archbishop knelt and kissed the Pope's ring before television cameras while Rome's cardinals merely shook hands with the Archbishop. The British public will not tolerate anything that looks like a surrender to imperial Rome. In any case, no leader of the Church of England could carry much of England along with him in anything approaching surrender, since approximately nine-tenths of the English people never go near an Anglican church more than once a year.[13]

At an international level world Protestantism and world Catholicism are steadily moving toward more friendly relations, but it is much too soon to talk in terms of any kind of reunion. The World Council of Churches and the Vatican have appointed committees for consultations, and there is no doubt that they will lead to various types of cooperative effort. But leaders of the 214-church combination of Protestant, Orthodox and Anglican organizations are wary of any reunion efforts by Rome that might imply subordination to a pope, and thus far Rome has not abandoned this notion of subordination. Valiant efforts are being made within American Protestantism by the Consultation on Church Union to work out a major combination of eight Protestant denominations embracing 24,000,000 members and including Methodists, Presbyterians, Episcopalians, and several smaller denominations, but it is not at all certain that such a combination, if effected in the distant future, would bring Protestantism any nearer to unity with Rome. The unity movement has been strengthened by the election of the American Presbyterian leader, Dr. Eugene Carson Blake, to the chief executive post in the World Council of Churches, but his position carries with it little ecclesiastical authority.

It is difficult to avoid the conclusion that, on the whole, the events of the Council constituted a major defeat for Protestantism. The Protestant image was subordinated and blurred in a great wave of favorable Catholic publicity in which Protestant objections to Catholic policy were virtually ignored. When all the ecumenical manifestations of the Council were added up, they did not amount to much in Protestant terms. A new geniality of manners had emerged. The Protestant churches had been recognized as churches, and this was an important verbal victory. The Bible had been given a slightly higher place alongside of tradition in Catholic thinking, and this would make theological cooperation less difficult. Genuine regret had been expressed for the most cruel and unusual features of past Catholic abuses of Protestants. A limited amount of common worship had been endorsed. A great deal of splendid and free discussion had taken place between Protestant and Catholic leaders.

But, balancing these ecumenically favorable phenomena, there had been many reaffirmations of old, narrow dogmas and many flat refusals to change discriminatory practices. On the debit side of the Protestant ledger there were at least nine items, most of which will be discussed in detail in later chapters:

1. Papal infallibility was reaffirmed without serious discussion.
2. Papal primacy was modified slightly by the doctrine of collegiality, but the central power structure remained authoritarian.
3. The prohibition against birth control was continued.
4. The prohibition of divorce was continued.
5. Changes in mixed marriage discrimination were very slight.
6. Mariology, although denied a separate chapter, was still reaffirmed with many flourishes.
7. The partial union of Church and state with tax payments to Catholic schools was, in effect, confirmed.
8. The medieval pomp of the Vatican was only slightly reduced.
9. No substantial changes were made in the vast underworld of Catholic superstition represented by such phenomena as relics, saints, indulgences, and purgatory.

At first glance the problem of reunion between Rome and Greek Orthodoxy may seem more simple than the problem of reunion between Rome and Protestantism. The religious ceremonies of the Greek Orthodox and the Roman Catholic Church have much in common. Their creeds are similar, though not identical, and the Orthodox church employs the same liturgy as the Roman Catholic churches of the Eastern rites. Both institutions emphasize hierarchical control. Rome and the Orthodox East, as Father Clement Englert has put it, have a "huge body of Christian faith and practice, which both East and West have inherited from the early undivided Church. . . . What still divides them is now an immense accumulation of mutual distrust, real and imagined grievances, and the remembrance of personal and diplomatic mistakes made in the past."[14]

Vatican II began amiably in dealing with the Orthodox because Pope John had made many Orthodox friends when he had served as apostolic delegate in Bulgaria, Rumania, Greece, and

Turkey. Pope Paul followed Pope John's lead by making effective gestures of amity toward the Orthodox. His most striking gesture came in January 1964 when, in the course of a visit to Jordan and Israel, he met and embraced Orthodox Patriarch Athenagoras of Istanbul, and prayed with him before the Holy Sepulcher. Since Athenagoras is technically the spiritual leader of the Orthodox world, his meeting with a Pope on neutral territory was rightly accepted as significant. The ecumenical significance was increased when, in December 1965, during the last week of the Council, Pope Paul and Athenagoras issued mutual declarations canceling the old anathemas and excommunications Rome and Constantinople had exchanged during the bitter quarrel leading to the Great Schism of 1054, when Orthodoxy and Roman Catholicism finally parted company.[15]

Pope Paul was as deeply interested as John had been in persuading Orthodox observers to attend Vatican II. Two months after his election as pope, Paul delivered a passionate speech addressed indirectly to the Orthodox at an Eastern-rite monastery near Frascati: "Let fall the barriers that separate us! . . . Let us seek to make our creed common and firm. Let us seek to articulate and compose our hierarchical union. We want neither to absorb nor to kill this great flourishing of the Eastern Church, but we wish to re-graft it to the single tree of the unity of Christ!"[16]

That last sentence clearly illustrates the insensitivity of so many Roman leaders to the feeling of leaders in the Orthodox Church who have long held that the Western or Latin branch of the Church should be regrafted to the single tree to which *they* had belonged, the tree originating in the East and not in Rome. In 1963 ten of the autonomous Orthodox churches meeting at the Pan-Orthodox conference in Rhodes announced that they would open a dialogue with Rome only on condition that the Pope would speak to them "on equal terms." At the 1964 Rhodes conference ecumenism did not make any advance beyond that point.

Athenagoras, who received Paul so warmly in Jerusalem, is only the honorary leader of the Orthodox world, not a pope or the counterpart of a pope, since Orthodoxy will not permit any single leader to rule its ecclesiastical organization. "First among equals," his actual power is much less than some of the other Orthodox patriarchs. Today his flock is relatively insignificant and he is virtually a prisoner of the Turks in his home city.

In terms of organization the Orthodox Church is really fifteen autonomous and semiautonomous churches, very much divided along national and political lines and badly split between Communist and capitalist inclinations. The world of Orthodoxy is almost as badly fragmented as the world of Protestantism, and there is a strong underlying hostility to Rome because of the long and bitter history of conflict between Rome and Constantinople.

At the beginning of the Council the Roman leaders, even Pope John, seemed blissfully unaware of the deep hatred for the doctrine of papal infallibility among the Orthodox. Cardinal Cicognani, acting as Pope John's Secretary of State, made a speech in Naples in November 1961 in which he not only reemphasized papal infallibility but attacked the historical claims of Constantinople as "pure legend." Then, in January 1962, three years after he had decided to create a Council, Pope John issued a special encyclical, *Aeterna Dei Sapientia*, glorifying St. Leo the Great, a fourth-century pope who had rejected the primacy of Constantinople and exalted the primacy of Rome.[17] John rubbed salt into the wound by stressing that the indispensable thing in Christian reunion must be "the harmony of bishops among themselves in communion and submission to the Roman Pontiff."

Although the Vatican made strenuous efforts to see that all the main branches of Orthodoxy sent observers to Vatican II, it was only partially successful. Oddly enough, Rome was more successful in wooing Orthodox observers from Communist countries than from capitalist countries. The Russians were the first among the major Orthodox groups to send observers, and Bulgaria, Rumania, and Czechoslovakia followed suit. Nominally this meant that the majority of the Orthodox people of the world were represented by observers, since the Russians, if old statistics can be accepted as reliable, have much more than half of the world's alleged Orthodox membership of 142,000,000.

But the solid core of Orthodoxy in Greece, suspicious of both Rome and Moscow, refused to send observers to Vatican II. Many Greek leaders denounced those prelates of other Orthodox nations who had succumbed to Roman blandishments. Archbishop Chrysostomos, Primate of Greece, declared that Russia's decision to send observers to Vatican II was "a great blow to Orthodox unity," a relatively mild comment compared with his later denunciations of those who were being beguiled by Rome. At one time he told the Greek Synod: "As long as I live there shall be no *rapprochement* with the Roman Catholic Church, and to this end I am prepared to sacrifice my life."[18] Such words, coming from the head of the Orthodox Church in Greece, were embarrassing to both Rome and to Western Protestantism, since this Orthodox Church of Greece is affiliated with the predominantly Protestant World Council of Churches.

At the present time the attitude of most Orthodox leaders toward Rome is one of wait-and-see. The Russian Orthodox are evaluating the new expressions of personal kindness toward atheism. They do not want to move toward Rome at a moment when Rome is launching a new crusade against an atheist and Communist regime that has control over them. Although they deplore atheistic Communism, they are compelled to live with it. The Vatican on its side is equally cool in adjusting its relationships to the Soviet regime with a view to its own institutional advantage. When Pope Paul received Andrei Gromyko in April 1966, the exchange did not indicate any yielding of principles on either side but only a realization by two great authoritarian powers that somehow they must live in the same world with a minimum of wasteful conflict. Although the Orthodox Patriarchate of Moscow sent observers to Vatican II, the primary motive was probably political. The Kremlin probably hoped for immediate political advantage in dealing with the people of Italy, where Communism is blandly wooing Italian Catholics. It would be quite inconceivable that the Soviet government should ever permit any Russian Orthodox Church to come under control of Rome while Communism remained dominant in the home country. It was primarily

Communist pressure that kept more than half of the Catholic bishops in Communist-ruled countries from attending the fourth session of Vatican II.

Meanwhile, there is much more animosity between Orthodoxy and Roman Catholicism in Europe than appears on the surface in the relations between Orthodoxy and Roman Catholicism in the United States. For most Americans the 3,000,000 Orthodox members in the United States, divided among some 20 national and language groups, remain almost invisible except at presidential inaugurals, when bearded priests demonstrate that their prayers can be as intolerably long as Catholic and Protestant prayers. In the American atmosphere the full European animosity between Slav-Orthodox groups and Polish, Czech, and Serbian Catholic groups rarely breaks out in public view. There is even an ecumenical movement on foot to produce closer cooperation in the United States between the Orthodox and Catholics. In many parts of Europe, however, the memory of bloody struggles between Catholics and Orthodox is still too vivid to permit such mutual charity. The Orthodox remember the cruel persecutions to which their Church was subjected even in times of peace in Catholic Poland, Catholic Czechoslovakia, and especially in the Catholic regions of Yugoslavia. One Orthodox Archbishop has declared that in the general massacre in Yugoslavia more Orthodox were killed in four years than were killed by the Inquisition in three hundred years of persecutions in Eastern Europe.[19]

Vatican II went out of its way to erase this old hostility by gentle words. In the Decree on Ecumenism the Orthodox were assured that because "they possess true sacraments, above all—by apostolic succession—the priesthood and the Eucharist, whereby they are still joined to us in a very close relationship," some common worship is recommended. In order to reduce the antagonism to papal primacy the Council solemnly declared that "the Churches of the East, while keeping in mind the necessary unity of the whole Church, have the power to govern themselves according to their own disciplines." But the concession was useless since the phrase buried in the heart of it, "keeping in mind the necessary unity of the whole Church," was regarded by the Orthodox as a verbal trap.

❧

Nominally the Roman Catholic Church has a natural bridge between itself and the world of Orthodoxy in the approximately 11,000,000 Catholics of the Eastern rites who are still loyal to Rome and who still consider themselves Roman Catholics in spite of variations in liturgy. In the Council's Decree on Eastern Catholic Churches, the Fathers declared that: "The Eastern Churches in communion with the Apostolic See have a special role to play in promoting the unity of all Christians, particularly Easterners"—meaning the Orthodox. To which one Orthodox leader replied brusquely that even after the Council's "positive, irenic and constructive intentions," the whole policy still seemed to be clouded in a "deep ambiguity," reeking with a Latin point of view.

The truth is that the Orthodox regard the Eastern-rite Catholics as Vatican decoys, not as an acceptable bridge between Rome and the East. They are suspicious of them as the "Uncle Toms" of Byzantine Christianity who have become traitors to their original faith. Maximos IV Saigh, the Melchite Patriarch of Antioch, tried vainly to woo the Orthodox, declaring that "By our example we must enable the Orthodox Church to recognize that a union with a great Church of the West, with the See of Peter, can be achieved without their being compelled to give up Orthodoxy." His appeal was scorned by almost all of the Orthodox world.

For their part, the Eastern-rite Catholics at the Council had their own problems of competitive prestige with the leaders of Rome. Ruled by patriarchs whose titles go back long before the Great Schism, they claimed that since their patriarchs had come before cardinals, they should be given at least as much status as the cardinals. Their resentment boiled up during the second session because the patriarchs had been given green upholstered seats of slightly lower status than the red upholstered seats of the cardinals. In November 1963 their injured pride was somewhat appeased when six of their leading patriarchs who had been sitting with mere archbishops were moved across the aisle in St. Peter's and given special red upholstered seats opposite the cardinals. Later, in 1965, when Pope Paul, somewhat to the surprise of the Council, persuaded some of these patriarchs to become cardinals, including the effervescent Maximos Saigh, the Eastern-rite leaders who had accepted the honor were immediately denounced by Greek Orthodox leaders for accepting the rank of cardinal when they should have remembered that patriarchs had acquired a higher status than cardinals many centuries before.

Vatican II not only failed to bridge the gap with Orthodoxy in any substantial way; it also failed to unsnarl the competing jurisdictions, national and ethnic, that still exist among Eastern-rite Catholics. There is still within the Roman fold a confusing multiplicity of Eastern-rite survivals: Maronites, Melchites, Chaldeans, Syrians, Coptics, etc. Rome, while criticizing Protestantism for fragmentation, continues to retain this Eastern fragmentary world of its own.

CHAPTER NINE ❧ MARY, SCRIPTURE, AND TRADITION

Most nontheologians are bored with disputes in the field of theology because the whole field is so speculative and because many of the conclusions reached are so ambiguous. This was not the case at Vatican II. Theology came alive because it was a tool in a power struggle within the Church and because it assumed critical importance in the attempt to work out an adjustment between the Church and non-Catholic Christians.

The first theological battle at Vatican II, the struggle over the use of Latin or the vernacular languages in Catholic liturgy, was not considered a problem in the external relationships of the Church. Nominally at least, it belonged exclusively to internal affairs. But Protestants noted joyfully that, after a long and heated debate, the right to introduce the vernacular into archaic Latin ceremonies was established—a move away from magic toward intelligibility. The reform helped to prove that Catholicism was no longer as glacially monolithic as it had been in the past.

The two most substantial theological barriers to Catholic-Protestant cooperation mentioned in the debates at the Council were the differing emphases on scripture and tradition, and the Catholic phenomenon called Mariology. The scripture-and-tradition debate consumed much of the first session; the Mariology debate came to a climax in the second session. Often the issues involved appeared to the secular world quite unreal, but in the world of Catholic and Protestant theology they presented very substantial barriers to unity. The first of these issues, that of scripture and tradition, was neatly compromised for the time being.

The second, Mariology, was not compromised. It still remains a serious obstacle to future Catholic-Protestant cooperation.

⁂

In October 1963, the fifth week of the second session, there were some surprising headlines in the European and American press. The Virgin Mary made the first page of the *New York Times!* "Schema On Mary Barred in Rome," read the slightly inaccurate headline. "Council Votes De-Emphasis of Mary," was the headline in the Rome *American*. The story in the *New York Herald Tribune* summarized the news most correctly by saying:

> After days of intense lobbying, which went as far as distributing pamphlets on the steps of St. Peter's Basilica, the Vatican Council moved today to de-emphasize the place of the Virgin Mary in the Church.
>
> On its face, the vote was procedural. The fathers agreed by a slim majority of 40 that a chapter on the Virgin Mary should be included in the Schema on the Church.
>
> Behind the vote is the Council's deep division on the issue, with two different conceptions of Mary's role in the Church.
>
> One, called the maximalist, insists on giving the utmost possible devotion to Mary and associating her in the Mystery of Redemption. The minimalists stick to Scripture and view Mary as the most perfect member of the Church, but insist that she should not be venerated separately.
>
> Today's vote was felt by experts and Council fathers to be a narrow victory for the minimalists and for the Christian-unity movement. Stressing devotion to Mary is criticized by Protestant and Orthodox Churches alike.[1]

Among the correspondents as well as among the fathers on the day of the vote on the Virgin Mary, it was a day of considerable excitement. The atmosphere outside the basilica reminded one of a political convention or a racial demonstration, and the conduct of some of the bishops and theologians approached that level. Ukrainian bishops of the Eastern rite of the Church, ardent devotees of the Virgin Mary, distributed on the steps of St. Peter's a propaganda leaflet signed by both Ukrainian and Indian functionaries opposing the placement of the chapter on Mary in the schema on the Church, a blow, they argued, to her prestige as the Mother of God. They were accused of deceptive collaboration with Cardinal Ottaviani and the Holy Office because one of their pamphlets, written by a Yugoslav Mariologist named Balic, urging a pro-Mary vote, bore not only the imprint of the Vatican Press Office but also had the exact form of official literature! It was said that in the excitement over the handbills one bishop hit another bishop, but this was never verified. The arguments split the bishops in an unusual way. Regional loyalties were overcome by Marian loyalties. Bishops from Chile and Uruguay distributed literature favoring the incorporation of the Mary chapter into the schema on the Church, while most Latin American bishops took the other side.

The Fathers had recognized the critical nature of the discussion by calling on two cardinals to speak for and against the proposal to include the Blessed Virgin Mary in the Church schema —Cardinal Koenig of Vienna for and Cardinal Santos of Manila against.[2] Although their speeches were dull and cautious, relying much on authority and tradition, there was no doubt about the genuineness of the clash of opinion. Each professed undying loyalty to the Virgin and the Church, and then proceeded to argue for different locations for the B.V.M. (Blessed Virgin Mary) declaration. Cardinal Santos had his eye primarily on the millions of faithful Catholics in Latin countries who have treated Mary as a virtual goddess for centuries. He implied that the best way to honor her was to give her a whole chapter by herself. Cardinal Koenig, probably no less loyal to the Virgin, was anxious not to erect new Mariology barriers against the Protestants. Koenig won 1,114 to 1,074, and the section on Mary was relegated to the chapter on the Church.

When the close vote was announced, there was an audible sigh, but otherwise dead silence. The progressives in the Council had won, but they were somewhat aghast at the narrow margin of their victory. Cardinal Agagianian, moderator for that day, had smoothly explained to the Fathers before the vote that they were not voting for or against the Virgin Mary. They were voting simply for or against the *location* of a chapter on the Virgin Mary. "No vote on either side," he protested, "can be construed as constituting any lessening of the dignity of the Blessed Virgin or any downgrading of Her preeminent role in the Church." But everybody knew that this was not the whole truth.

The question of the location of the chapter on the Virgin Mary may not have been designed deliberately to raise matters of doctrine or fundamental policy, but it became an important test question in one of the most sensitive controversial areas now dividing Protestantism and Catholicism. To devote a whole independent chapter in the agenda to Mary meant at least an implied endorsement of the present very exaggerated Catholic emphasis on the Virgin and her role in Christian development. To relegate Mary to a subchapter in the chapter on the Church was, in fact, a slight downgrading of her place in theology, indicating some willingness on the part of the Church to discuss Mariology with Protestantism in a mood of give-and-take.

The large opposition vote served notice on the progressives that nearly half of the Council Fathers wanted to stand pat in emphasizing the significance of Mary in Catholic theology. The Protestant observers were depressed. They had long realized that Catholic Mariology is, next to papal infallibility, the greatest purely theological stumbling block to Christian cooperation and Christian reunion. Many Catholic progressives had become keenly aware of the critical nature of Mariology as an obstacle. Father Hans Kung had described Marian devotion as the chief difficulty in the sharing of the common life of prayer, and had viewed with apprehension the "flood of Marian books, Marian sermons, Marian sodalities, Marian congresses, Marian apparitions, Marian pilgrimages."

The closeness of the vote on Mary at the Council could not be explained in terms of haste or temporary emotionalism. A carefully prepared document on the subject had been before the Council Fathers for at least twelve months. The original list of sixty-nine subjects for Council consideration had conspicuously included the B.V.M. (These initials are respectfully used throughout the Catholic world for the Virgin Mary.) A 12-page summary called "Some Ideas on the Mariology of Today" had been distributed to the Fathers, describing her as "The first to believe in Jesus Christ," "the first among the Elect," and "the first to intercede." Somewhat more cautiously, the document had declared that "one can also affirm the possibility of speaking of Mary as 'Co-Mediatrix.' "

All of this tremendous adulation of Mary had become virtually routine in the Catholic Church, especially during the last century. Catholic leaders take it for granted, and wonder why Protestants question it. Pope John, probably without any conscious intention of stressing a controversial point, declared Vatican II open in his inauguration address "under the auspices of the Virgin Mother of God, whose maternal dignity is commemorated in this feast." Earlier, in 1959, he had declared in praising the Mary cult: "It is through Mary that one goes to Jesus"; and throughout the Council sessions John prayed publicly to the Virgin as a possible major force in making the Council an ecumenical success. Quite naturally, Pope Paul followed the same Marian line in his opening speech at the second session, although he announced that the session was "under the aegis of St. Michael the Archangel." "Certainly," he said, "the Virgin Mother of Christ is helping us from Heaven."

Under the circumstances, the debate over the Virgin Mary at the Council seemed to many non-Catholics a debate over nonessentials. No speaker touched on the basic reasons for Protestant discontent. Cardinal Santos and Cardinal Koenig were near to agreement in principle in exalting the Virgin. One called her "the author of all sanctification," and "in some way above the Church." The other described her as "a most Exalted Co-operatrix with Christ"—whatever that means.

The real objection of the Protestant world to Catholic exaltation of the Virgin Mary never reached the basilica floor, partly because no Protestant observers were permitted to speak and partly because there was no Catholic bishop or theologian who dared to challenge any of the basic *additions* to Mariology adopted by the Church since the Protestant Reformation. It is these *additions*, not the New Testament passages about Mary or the original doctrine of the Virgin Birth, that disturb Protestants most. Most Protestant leaders stress the non-biblical character of Mariology and the audacity of the Church in manufacturing its own supplementary Mariological faith without support in scripture or ancient tradition. Sometimes Mariology is called Mariolatry to emphasize the Protestant criticism that it approaches idolatry. As Reinhold Niebuhr put it in the *Atlantic Monthly*, in an article published just two months before the Council began:

> Another basic cause of tension [between Protestants and Catholics] is the increased Mariolatry of modern Catholicism. By dwelling on Catholic piety with roots preceding even the medieval period, the Church, for some mysterious reason, has chosen to widen the breach between it and modern culture. In a series of dogmas promulgated in the late 19th century and extending into this very century, it has virtually lifted the Virgin Mary into the Godhead (some say into the Trinity), replacing the less historical Holy Spirit. To Protestants this is offensive because it has no scriptural warrant.[3]

Many scholars, both Catholic and non-Catholic, have acknowledged that the scriptural part of Niebuhr's criticism is sound. There is absolutely nothing in the Bible to justify the extra dignity and status of the Mary of Catholic Mariology.[4] Mary is mentioned explicitly in the New Testament in only a few passages and not one of the passages indicates that she was particularly important in the early Church or that she took any leading part in promoting it. As to the three great miracle stories involving Mary, the Virgin Birth, the Immaculate Conception, and the Assumption, the New Testament does not indicate that either Jesus or Paul ever heard of them.

Catholic theologians in press conferences at the Council admitted quite frankly that Catholic Mariology cannot be based primarily on scripture. There are, of course, several respectful or noncommittal references to Mary in the New Testament, but there are also several references that clearly imply that Mary was not on the best of terms with her son and that she may not have been a believer throughout his ministry. Mark, the attributed author of the earliest Gospel, does not mention her; nor does Paul, whose Epistles come first chronologically. Nowhere in scripture is she described as having any particular authority in the early Church or as sharing with her son and the apostles any theological or ecclesiastical distinction. She is mentioned casually in Acts I as part of a faithful congregation, but she does not even appear after the launching of Christian enterprise in the first Pentecost. At the marriage in Cana, Jesus said of his mother rather brusquely: "Woman, what have I to do with thee?" In Matthew 13:57, when Jesus was being criticized by the people of his own town, he remarked somewhat acidly: "A prophet is not without honor save in his own country, and in his own house." When an enthusiastic woman cried out (Luke 11:27), "Blessed is the womb that bare thee and the paps which thou hast sucked," Jesus did not say a single complimentary word about his mother, but replied: "Yea rather, blessed are they that hear the word, and keep it."

Both Protestants and Catholics, of course, honor Mary as the mother of Jesus. Beyond that simple expression of reverence and respect lie five doctrines about Mary which may be accepted as progressive steps beyond the original New Testament attitude: (1) The Virgin Birth of Christ; (2) the perpetual virginity of Mary; (3) the Immaculate Conception of Mary, the dogma that she was free from original sin at her own conception; (4) the Assumption of Mary, the dogma that at the time of her death her soul was received directly into heaven, and (5) direct revelations by Mary in apparitions at Lourdes in France, Fatima in Portugal, Guadalupe in Mexico, etc.

Most Protestant bodies throughout the world reject all of these five steps in Mariology except the first, and even the Virgin Birth is doubted by many American Protestant leaders. They have noted that many religions have legends concerning the virgin birth of gods or goddesses, and that the genealogies of Jesus in the first chapter of Matthew and the third chapter of Luke, while contradicting each other, trace the ancestry of Jesus down through Joseph, and only skip over to Mary as if by an afterthought. Concerning the perpetual virginity of Mary, there are nine passages in the New Testament referring to the brothers of Jesus, and they see no reason to believe that these brothers were not born in a normal manner.[5] In any case, they are not anxious to glorify as perfect marriage a union between Joseph and Mary that was never blessed by sexual fulfillment. In addition several of the passages mentioning the brothers of Jesus name them in a family grouping so unmistakable that it seems to nullify the Catholic claim that the word "brothers" is intended to apply to cousins or friends.

The sharpest differences between Protestants and Catholics in this whole area have developed concerning the two final dogmas: the Immaculate Conception, promulgated by Pius IX in 1854, and the Assumption, promulgated by Pius XII in the Holy Year of 1950. The Immaculate Conception seems to them an unnecessary clerical invention without any scriptural basis whatever, a nonlogical exception to the Catholic doctrine of original sin.

The most severe Protestant criticism, however, is reserved for the dogma of the Assumption, a doctrine with no biblical authority whatever. At the time of its promulgation it was widely reported in Rome that careful priestly research had revealed the complete absence of any scriptural authority for it. Despite this finding, Pius XII proclaimed it, and it is apparently the first infallible utterance since the adoption of the doctrine of infallibility —with the exception of papal saint-making declarations.[6]

Catholic leaders strenuously deny that they worship Mary. They adore, venerate, glorify, and petition her, but they do not worship her. For Protestants the distinction seems to be a quibble. The innumerable altars, chapels, statues, and special prayers of Mariology have virtually exalted Mary to the level of a goddess in the eyes of common people. Beyond this there is the elaborate system of shrines based upon the sixteen most notable apparitions of the Virgin in various parts of the world. It is impossible to convince non-Catholics that the worshipful processes in vogue at these shrines do not constitute the worship of Mary as part of the Godhead.

Many Catholics have recognized and deplored the factors in Mariology to which Protestants object. François Mauriac in *The Stumbling Block* has declared that people are shocked by "the inventions on the margin of dogma, the ratiocinations, the alterations," and he says of his own experience: "We have many times heard priests proclaim from the pulpit that it was impossible to attain to Jesus Christ without Mary's intervention, and I confess that the reasons given for this statement have always seemed to me to be pure verbalisms."[7] During the second session, *Commonweal*, edited by American Catholic laymen, announced in an editorial: "Though usually denied prior to the Council, the Fathers now appear ready to recognize that devotion to Mary has, in some places, usurped the primacy of devotion to Christ . . . there have been excesses in the kind of homage many Catholics offer to Mary. Part of the renewal of the Church ought to encompass their removal."[8] The Jesuits' *America* did not go quite this far, but in an editorial the magazine pointed out that when you "mention Mariology . . . you conjure up in the Protestant mind visions of banners swaying and throngs marching at shrines, of volumes on the glories of Mary, and myriad flickering vigil lights in Latin churches. For the Protestant, what could be more calculated to obscure the Unique Mediator and the Trinity?"[9]

The Council's final, long statement on the Virgin Mary, Chapter 8 of the Constitution on the Church, stopped just short of the so-called maximalist position in its Mariology. It was flamboyantly eulogistic, inflating scriptural "sources" about Mary beyond recognition, but it did not in so many words call Mary Co-Redemptrix on a plane of equality with Jesus. The minimalists could find little comfort in it. It was a panegyric to virginity as well as to Mary herself, the "ever virgin," emphasizing the glories of her sexless marriage. In deference to Protestant apprehensions, the text warned against "the falsity of exaggeration," but then it proceeded to describe Mary as engaged in "constant intercession" and declared that "this Holy Synod" would teach and promote "the cult" of Mary.

Pope Paul gladdened the hearts of all the conservative Mariologists at the end of the third session when, in his closing address, he proclaimed Mary the Mother of the Church, apparently acting wholly on his own authority. And he added: "We wish that the Mother of God should be still more honored and invoked by the entire Christian people by this most sweet title." He closed his appeal with a special prayer addressed directly to the Virgin and an announcement that he was sending a Golden Rose to the sanctuary at Fatima, Portugal, where the Virgin is said to have appeared in 1917 to three illiterate peasant children, transmitting to the world through them a special warning against Communism.

These two gestures, toward Mary as Mother of the Church and toward Fatima as gospel truth, could scarcely have been excelled in tactlessness. The assertion that Mary is the Mother of the Church seemed to many Protestants another way of saying that there is only one Church and that it is the Holy Roman Catholic Church, since no other church grants Mary such a unique status. And the reverent nod in the direction of Fatima, the site of one of the most questionable "miracles" in the underworld of Mariological apparitions, served to remind the Protestants that Catholic Mariology is not only a theology but a practical and lucrative device for holding the loyalty of the poor and the ignorant.

❧

The struggle over scripture and tradition was the most bitter and time-consuming of the Council's purely theological disputes. It began in the first session when Cardinal Ottaviani introduced an unpopular and nonecumenical schema, which was then called "The Sources of Revelation," and it continued through 105 speeches in that session until it was rejected by the Fathers by a vote of 1,368 to 822. Sent for revision to a Mixed Commission, coming back after many alterations to the third session in the form of majority and minority reports that were discussed for 5 days in 69 more speeches, it was finally adopted under the title "The Constitution on Divine Revelation" in the fourth session with so many compromise phrases in it that the public wondered which side had really won the long battle.

Nevertheless, in spite of many ambiguities and much theological double-talk in the text, the very fact that a compromise was reached on so controversial an issue was a substantial victory for those who wanted increased friendship between the Church and other Christian bodies. The debates revealed that the ancient quarrel over the relative value of the Bible and tradition as sources of Christian knowledge had been inflated beyond reason by partisans on both sides. In effect, both sides in the argument came closer together during the Council because it was revealed that neither side possessed all the truth.

At the same time, however, the final pronouncement on divine revelation reaffirmed the essentially conservative Catholic position on the authority of revelation. Modernists and liberal Protestants could not get much encouragement from it. Certainly the honest-to-God Anglicans in Great Britain and the God-is-dead theologians in the United States must have looked on the final text with horror. The biblical scholars of liberal Protestantism could not find in its phrases any clear sanction for complete intellectual freedom. While the bishops tipped their miters in the direction of modern scholarship, their orthodox findings justified the conclusion that the Church is still a fundamentalist church, not in the style of the Bible belt but in the traditional Roman style. Oddly enough, their conservative theological conclusions brought them nearer to the very Protestants who rejected their ecclesiastical claims most vigorously. Their liberal Protestant critics could say with some justification that these Catholic bishops appeared to be trapped, along with their conservative Protestant counterparts, in the web of their own over-beliefs. They had gone so far in proclaiming old "certainties" that they could not face up to the devastating conclusions of modern biblical scholarship.

The scripture-tradition dispute at Vatican II went back to

the "two-sources" doctrine of conservative Catholic theology, favored by the Council of Trent, that all legitimate revelations about God and Christ come from two distinct sources, the Bible and tradition. Protestants have emphasized the Bible as the chief—some say the *only*—source of such truth, while Catholics have tended to emphasize tradition partly because this emphasis strengthens their claim to unique ecclesiastical authority. By "tradition" they have usually meant the whole complex of oral information, Church teaching, and patristic writings in early Christian history outside the Bible. They have argued that during the first two centuries Christian faith was dependent wholly on this tradition. It was obvious at the Council, though it was rarely expressed in words, that any new emphasis upon tradition rather than scripture would imply a drift away from ecumenical relationships with Protestants.

At the beginning of the argument in the first session, Cardinal Ottaviani tried to railroad through the Council a "two-sources" statement which, in the words of one of his critics, Cardinal Frings, was "offensive to our separated brothers in Christ and harmful to the proper liberty required in any scientific procedure." Ottaviani was met by spirited opposition, particularly from German and French prelates who wanted to open the Church's doors to modern biblical research. Behind the clash was the fundamental question whether the Pontifical Commission of Biblical Studies in Rome—founded in 1902 by Leo XIII—and the great theological seminaries of the Church in Rome would be free to explore and publicize new facts about Christian sources even if those facts proved to be contrary to past Church teachings.

The champions of tradition were fearful of too much exposure to new discoveries, holding that the Church already possesses enough "amplitude of tradition" without any more additions or interpretations. The liberals took the line that scripture and tradition should be considered as one open-end and interconnecting source of knowledge. To most of these liberals the long quarrel between scripture and tradition seemed sterile and meaningless, since they wanted their Church to be openminded in receiving truth from any source.

While Cardinal Ottaviani and the Holy Office lost the first round of the struggle in the first session, the final outcome could be called a draw. In the Constitution on Divine Revelation, the "two-source" doctrine was virtually abandoned in favor of a one-source doctrine combining both scripture and tradition in one fused "sacred deposit," but in the same document the Church asserted its most arrogant claims to pre-eminence in interpreting all scripture and tradition, regardless of what other churches might say about their validity.

In one irenic paragraph the final statement declared that "both sacred tradition and sacred scripture are to be accepted and venerated with the same sense of loyalty and reverence"; and a few sentences later the text asserted that "the task of authentically interpreting the word of God, whether written or handed on, has been entrusted exclusively to the living teaching office of the Church. . . . It is clear, therefore, that sacred tradition, sacred Scripture and the teaching authority of the Church, in accord with God's most wise design, are so linked and joined together that one cannot stand without the others." In respect to Protestantism, the Church gave with one hand and took back with the other. It lifted the Bible to equality with tradition, and then proceeded to declare that both Bible and tradition come under the teaching authority of the one true Church.

The same kind of adroit ambivalence was demonstrated in handling the rights of modern scholars in interpreting scripture. For many years restless biblical scholars connected with the Pontifical Biblical Institute in Rome had been chafing under the repressive rules of the Holy Office. They had been hoping that a kind of Magna Charta for free biblical criticism might come out of the Council. Their hope was based partly on some slightly progressive phrases used by Pius XII in his 1943 encyclical, *Divino Afflante Spiritu*, in which he praised the explorations of Catholic biblical exegetes and released them from their hitherto exclusive allegiance to the Latin Vulgate text of the Bible. Pius' encyclical was only half a Magna Charta, since he insisted on repeating the old claim concerning the New Testament that the Church "received it intact from the hands of the Apostles."

When the section on the interpretation of scripture was finally adopted by Vatican II, it acknowledged the right of scholars to "investigate what meaning the sacred writer intended to express and actually expressed in particular circumstances as he used contemporary literary forms in accordance with the situation of his own time and culture," a distinct concession to the modernist advocates of form criticism of the Bible. But in the same section the final text proclaimed that all books of the Old Testament and the New Testament were written under the inspiration of the Holy Spirit and that they "must be acknowledged as teaching firmly, faithfully and without error that truth which God wanted put into the sacred writings for the sake of our salvation."

This kind of double-talk is not new, but it is fundamentally dishonest, since it excuses from all error those biblical writers who wrote bad history because they had not been trained to distinguish between fact and myth. The final Constitution on Divine Revelation perpetuated the dishonesty by pretending that "the four gospels are of apostolic origin" as "the Church has always and everywhere held," setting forth without error the actual facts of Jesus' life. This standard conservative line had been reiterated in May 1964 in a long Instruction on the Historical Truth of the Gospels by the Pontifical Biblical Commission, contending that "the Gospels were written under the inspiration of the Holy Spirit, and that it was He Who had preserved their authors immune from all error." The Instruction had warned all Catholic priests and scholars against those innovations that might undermine the faith of believers.

Biblical scholarship has long ago dismissed as unproved the contention that "the four gospels are of apostolic origin."[10] They were written long after Jesus' death in a language (Greek) he did not speak by men who had not even been eyewitnesses to those events they recorded. No one knows who wrote them. Their narratives contain many contradictions which make it mathematically impossible to argue that they are errorless.

The biblical scholars at Vatican II knew these things, since the writings of Protestant theologians such as Rudolf Bultmann had quite clearly established the concept that myth and fact have been inextricably mixed in New Testament accounts of the historical Jesus. But, in the face of unpleasant threats to established Catholic doctrine, Vatican II chose to stick its head in the sand and to pretend that modern scholarship and an "errorless" New Testament could exist in harmony in the same fuzzily worded pronouncement.

Although the Fathers at the Council failed to reconcile integrity with orthodoxy in their conclusions about revelation, they made a great advance toward cooperation with Protestants in the use of the Bible. For several centuries the emphasis of the Church —a kind of reflex against Protestantism—had been opposed to the use of the Bible by the common people. The Bible was God's word, entitled to great reverence, but primarily designed for the use of priestly experts. There had been many instances of outright prohibition of Bible-reading for the untutored Catholic masses.

At Vatican II all that was changed. An illuminated copy of the scriptures, a kind of Holy Golden Book, was enthroned every morning by a bishop at the beginning of each session in St. Peter's. Almost every declaration about divine authority appealed to the Bible; almost every speech, if there was any excuse for it, brought in biblical sources. From the Protestant point of view the greatest single theological advance of the Council was this new and reverent emphasis on the Bible. If the Church still claimed exclusive right to interpret the Bible correctly, it also demonstrated that it regarded biblical treasures with the same worshipful esteem that had characterized Protestantism for so many centuries. Thus, while the scripture-tradition conflict ended in a draw, ecumenism triumphed in a new and common veneration for the Bible. The Church demonstrated a new loyalty to the scriptures and a new willingness to cooperate with Protestants in biblical promotion.

Vatican II also produced a new and powerful movement toward a Common Bible, a modern translation of the whole Bible that would be acceptable to both Catholics and Protestants. Indeed, the accomplishment of this purpose may be one of the few quick and specific achievements of the Council. Already—published in June 1965 in London—there has been a Catholic edition of the Protestant Revised Standard Version of the New Testament, which was derived from the Protestant King James Version. Ancient theological disagreements will remain for a long time, perhaps forever. They need not include the fruitless and often petty disputes about textual details that have characterized Christian history since the sixteenth century.

How much does the joint acceptance by Catholics and Protestants of both scripture and tradition as sources of knowledge mean in actual practice? Apparently not much when any basic dogma of Catholicism is involved, particularly when Paul VI is pope.

The new irenic theological atmosphere produced by Catholic-Protestant biblical cooperation suffered a rather rude jolt just before the beginning of the last session when, on September 3, 1965, Pope Paul issued an encyclical critical of theologians in his own Church who had seemed to question the "real presence" of the body and blood of Christ in the eucharist. Strongly worded, the encyclical, *Mysterium Fide*, was appropriately issued on the feast day of Pope Pius X, the Church's most reactionary pope of this century.[11] Although it did not mention Protestants, it seemed to be directed against one of the most typical items of Protestant teaching. It represented a backward step away from ecumenical dialogue not only because of its content but also because of its sharp, belligerent tone. Upon reading it, some Protestants must have recalled the polemical style of sixteenth-century Catholic-Protestant debates when Luther, Calvin, and Zwingli assailed the Catholic doctrine of transubstantiation.

In the Netherlands during the course of the Council two

Catholic theologians had advanced interpretations of the real events of the eucharist—called by most Protestants Holy Communion or the Last Supper—which seemed to suggest modification of the Catholic doctrine of transubstantiation in the direction of Protestant thought. They had interpreted the central event of this sacrament not as an actual transformation of bread into flesh and wine into blood but as a "transignification," a symbolic event that nevertheless contained what Catholics describe as the Real Presence.

The alleged heresy of these Dutch theologians seemed very mild to most Protestants, since the great majority of the world's Protestants have long treated the Last Supper as largely symbolic, commemorating Christ's life and death but not actually involving an instant physical miracle. They do not accept the full antinaturalistic magic of the Catholic interpretation.

Cardinal Alfrink of Utrecht, much disturbed by the charge of potential heresy against some of his prelates, held an emergency press conference at the last session of the Council, claiming that the pope's rebuke did not apply to his theologians. Actually it did, and there was no escaping the harshness of the pope's impeachment. Paul, at the mere suggestion that a realistic and scientific interpretation should be given to an alleged miracle for which there is no chemical evidence, not only rebuked the theologians who were trying to adapt theology to modern knowledge but also reiterated the old dogmas of magic in a very heavyhanded manner.

Striking at those who "spread abroad opinions which disturb the faithful," Pope Paul reprimanded theologians who challenge the findings of the anti-Protestant Council of Trent in this area, declaring that "it cannot be tolerated that any individual should on his own authority modify the formulas which were used by the Council of Trent to express belief in the Eucharistic Mystery." He declared that it was not allowable to treat the eucharist as if its symbolism expressed the full reality, although many Catholic theologians had accepted this interpretation in the past. Then he reaffirmed the ancient Catholic teaching that there is in the eucharist "the change in the whole substance of the bread into his Body, and of the whole substance of the wine into his Blood, and that this unique and truly wonderful change the Catholic Church rightly calls transubstantiation."

Paul had rushed into a theological controversy involving Protestant sensitivity apparently without any thought about the ecumenical effect. He had strengthened the image of the Catholic Church as a church of rigid dogma and primitive magic, relying more on ecclesiastical mechanics than moral suasion.

CHAPTER TEN ❧ SEX, CELIBACY, AND WOMEN

THE first formal mention of sex at Vatican II occurred at the second session when the revival of the once-important order of deacons was discussed. In early Christianity deacons constituted a significant order in the Church, separate from the priesthood and just below it. More recently the rank of deacon had become in most parts of the world simply a steppingstone for seminarians on their way to the priesthood, subject to the same rules of celibacy that applied to the priests.

There is a desperate need for deacons, particularly in South America, where it has been impossible for many years to recruit a sufficient number of priests. Many bishops at Vatican II believed that deacons could be trained to perform almost all of the pastoral functions of the priesthood except the administration of the sacraments, an obvious labor-saving solution in countries with too few priests.

Sex entered the picture when the question arose whether deacons today should be allowed to marry. For a long time in the early days of the Church they had been permitted to do so. Why not now, when the need was so desperate?

Most of the Latin American bishops heartily approved of the idea. Cardinal Spellman took the lead in saying "No." Cardinal Ottaviani and the Holy Office—now the Congregation for the Doctrine of the Faith—and most of the other conservatives of the Curia went along with the concept of prohibition. Reasons galore were given, theological, financial, and practical, but the underlying reason was quite apparent—a fear of sex and what sex might do to institutional holiness. Could the Church put young priests without wives side-by-side with married deacons and expect the priests to be happy in their chastity? Would not the card-house of celibacy come tumbling down?

Many bishops believed that any relaxation of celibate standards would lead to all-out disaster for celibacy. Perhaps they were right in their apprehensions. It is hard enough at the present time to recruit young priests into a life of sexual abstinence. Some of the seminarians, it was averred, might actually accept demotion and become deacons rather than priests in order to marry. Probably many more would forsake the priesthood altogether for the world and the flesh. Were not thousands of seminarians throughout the world deserting their classrooms for this very reason? Cardinal Cushing said facetiously that under the proposed plan: "The bishops will govern the Church, the priests will do all the work, and the deacons will have all the fun."

Desperately the South American bishops and some missionary bishops from other regions argued for facing the issue, perhaps with married deacons who could work part-time. Bishop Jorge Kemerer, speaking in the name of twenty bishops from Argentina, Uruguay and Paraguay, declared that, "The restoration of the diaconate is our great hope." Then he argued: "Something serious must be done in order that the great and urgent problem of shortage of priests around the world may be solved . . . nearly every diocese [in Latin America] has many parishes with a single priest caring for 10,000 and 20,000 and even 30,000 souls! What we need is the restoration of the order of diaconate without the obligation of celibacy. . . . We graciously beg you not to close the door on us."[1] The Fathers gave Bishop Kemerer a good round of applause, but the conservatives finally defeated him. In the third session Cardinal Spellman and his allies scored a partial victory on the issue by a vote of almost 3 to 1.

The Constitution on the Church, promulgated during this session, provides that "the diaconate can in the future be restored as a proper and permanent rank of the hierarchy," by national conferences of bishops with the approval of the pope, but, presumably, no young deacons may be used unless they are celibate.

Men "of more mature age," already married, may be allowed to continue in the married state under certain circumstances. For young men "the law of celibacy must remain intact." The proposal to open the door to marriage for young deacons was finally defeated by a vote of 1,364 to 839. So the concession concerning married deacons amounted to very little, although it was welcome because it was the first official crack in the bastion of obligatory celibacy since the eleventh century.

Cautious conservatism characterized Council proceedings whenever the awesome subject of sex was approached. One could almost feel the currents of apprehension in the air when any proposal skirted the edge of sexual reform. These Fathers, all male, all celibate, and most of them quite old, were the men who had worn the hair shirt of sexual denial more or less successfully all their lives. They did not want their life agonies to go unappreciated. Following St. Paul, they had come to regard sexual starvation as a high virtue and they could not face the suggestion that the long, weary years of self-denial had been a foolish blunder imposed upon them by celibate superiors who were no wiser than they were. Pope Paul himself seemed quite typical of the Church's celibate clergy in his attitude toward sex and women. In addressing the Thirteenth Congress of the Italian Women's Center in 1966 he said: "Conjugal chastity . . . throughout the centuries has redeemed woman from the slavery of a duty submitted to through force and humiliation."

This reluctance to face sexual issues squarely was apparent whenever anyone tried to discuss the real merits of a celibate clergy. Never once in all the four sessions was there a direct debate on the policy as applied to ordinary priests. There were only tangential references to the problem. Although these unmarried gentlemen were quite willing to talk at length about the problems of marriage, they avoided any head-on discussion of their own unmarried state.

When, in the third session, the issues of marriage and birth control threatened to bring the whole dark territory of sex into open debate, Pope Paul took the questions of birth control and celibacy out of the hands of the Fathers and reserved decision for himself and his private advisors. There was no substantial opposition to this intervention; in fact, the general attitude of the Council Fathers seemed to be overwhelmingly in favor of the status quo in most sexual matters except birth control. In the fourth session the Fathers voted almost unanimously to continue training seminarians for celibacy and to maintain celibacy in the priesthood. In that same session they applauded warmly when Pope Paul took the discussion of celibacy away from them as "too delicate," and pronounced unwavering support for the present prohibitions.

Earlier in the third session, the Mexican bishop from Cuernavaca and the German bishop from Mainz had talked about the glories of celibacy for seminarians. "Virginity must be regarded as a gift of God," said the Mexican bishop, although he admitted that celibacy was in considerable danger because of "the solitude in which so many priests must live." He suggested that priests who slipped and fell into the morass of infidelity might be reduced to the lay state without excommunication. That was the nearest approach in the whole Council to a facing up to the agonies and frustrations of celibate rule.

At an English press conference in the second session, three of England's top clerics, Archbishop (now Cardinal) John Heenan, Abbot Butler of Downside, and Bishop Holland of Salford, were asked directly about the wisdom and the necessity of celibacy. Bishop Holland replied that the question of altering the fundamental Church rule on the subject would most certainly not even be discussed at the Council. Cardinal Heenan was asked—by this writer—why a poll of all the priests in the world could not be taken to see whether they actually favored celibacy. He replied that such a poll would take too long in operation. An air-mail poll covering more than 90 per cent of the world's priests could have been taken in a month.

Of course, the men who should really be polled on celibacy

are the hundreds of thousands of seminarians, ex-priests, and young priests throughout the world, many of whom have left their seminaries or the priesthood itself for marriage. According to one estimate there are fifteen thousand ex-priests in Italy alone, most of whom have left their vocations to choose marriage. Probably half of all the young seminarians in the world finally drop out of seminary and reject their priestly vocation for this same reason, although there is no way to prove this fact statistically.

During the discussion on the Church in the Modern World, Cardinal Suenens of Belgium was credited with breaking the subject of sex and marriage wide open in an historic speech in October 1964. He demanded "an objective study of the theology of marriage." Although his speech was not revolutionary by non-Catholic standards, it was so unusual for a cardinal to question the ancient sexual standards of the Church that his address gained world-wide publicity. "We have learned much since the time of Aristotle and even since the time of St. Augustine," he said. "It is true that the Church cannot abandon a doctrine which has been accepted and which clearly comes from revelation. But there is nothing to prevent the Church from making a thorough inquiry to see if all facets of a problem have been sufficiently explored. . . . The Council should take care to avoid a new Galileo case."[2]

This relatively cautious speech by Cardinal Suenens was followed by a much bolder and more specific speech in favor of birth control by the aged Melchite Patriarch of Antioch (later a Cardinal), Maximos IV Saigh. "Frankly," said His Beatitude, "the official position of the Church on this matter [birth control] should be revised on the basis of modern theological, medical, psychological, and sociological science. . . . We are entitled to ask for some new thinking on certain official positions which may derive from out-moded ideas and perhaps also from a 'bachelor psychosis' on the part of individuals unacquainted with this sector of life." A celibate priest had dared to twit his celibate associates on their celibacy. Cardinals Ottaviani and Browne struck back sharply, insisting that the teaching on family morality of Pius X and Pius XII was good enough for them and for the Catholic people.

Ottaviani and Browne, of course, had the balance of precedent on their side. Over the centuries the teachings of the popes on sex and marriage have been doctrinaire and monastic. In 1930 Pius XI tried to sanctify the most conservative traditions on sex by listing them in his famous encyclical *Casti Connubii*, still considered the Bible of Catholic marriage doctrine.[3] It prohibits divorce and contraception, lays down very strict and narrow rules for mixed marriage, and condemns sterilization. It holds up as "a striking example to all" the marriage provisions of the 1929 Mussolini-Vatican pact under which the Italian government recognizes Catholic canon law as the supreme law for the marriage of Catholics.

Cardinal Suenens in his 1964 speech was questioning primarily the Church's position on birth control, but his demand for "an objective study of the theology of marriage" went far beyond birth control and reached the heart of the whole problem of sexual standards in the Church. Those standards are antiquated because they were developed in an age of general ignorance about sex by men who were themselves extraordinarily ignorant of the subject because of their celibate condition. They described their philosophy as "Christian," but there is no proof for this claim.

Celibacy was not specifically prescribed by Jesus for either priests or laymen. It is and was a strictly clerical invention of the later centuries. The two greatest villains of what Cardinal Suenens called "the theology of marriage"–the word "theology" is often used to cover the whole field of moral teaching–are St. Paul and St. Augustine. (St. Thomas Aquinas was almost as bad.) Suenens ventured to attack St. Augustine but not St. Paul. St. Paul was deeply prejudiced against women, and if he was ever married, it must have been unhappily. During his ministry he seems to have been a celibate, and he looked on marriage as a way of handling lust, not to be resorted to if men could maintain higher spiritual values. A woman, he argued, must "learn in silence with all subjection." "I suffer not a woman to teach," he added, "nor to usurp authority over the man." "Wives, submit yourselves unto your own husbands as unto the Lord. For the husband is the head of the wife even as Christ is the head of the Church." "He that is unmarried careth for the things that belong to the Lord, how he may please the Lord; but he that is married careth for the things that are of the world, how he may please his wife." Both Leo XIII and Pius XI supported St. Paul's antifeminism by declaring: "The man is the ruler of the family, and the head of the woman."

St. Augustine was so extreme on the subject of sex that even a cardinal could disagree with him openly without losing face.[4] Laden with sexual guilt because of an unsatisfactory experience of concubinage, Augustine taught that all sexual intercourse was irrational and nonspiritual and that Adam and Eve in resorting to intercourse had indulged in "a shameless novelty which made nakedness indecent." He regarded his own early life as thoroughly indecent since he had lived from the age of eighteen to the age of twenty-nine with a girl he refused to marry; then, under the influence of a dominating mother, he had contracted a legal marriage which lasted 11 years.

It was Augustine who evolved the novel theory that in marriage sexual intercourse only for the sake of procreating children is wholly moral. Somewhat inconsistently, he evolved the accompanying doctrine that when one spouse seeks intercourse the other must ordinarily acquiesce. In combination, his two theories, if consistently carried out, might soon people the world with billions of unwanted Catholics.

The moral rules now governing sex in Catholic teaching are much less permanent than most people suppose. For many centuries priests in all divisions of the Church were allowed to marry, and even divorce was permissible. Today Roman Catholic priests of the Eastern rites are permitted to marry before ordination, and most of them rush to the altar for marriage at the opportune moment. They suffer some discrimination because they may not become bishops while married, but this does not deter many of them in their choice of normal family life.

Celibacy, which was imposed on all priests and deacons of the Latin Church in the fourth century and confirmed by the Second Lateran Council in 1129, has always been a subject of bitter controversy within the Church. There is not much doubt that if it were submitted to a secret vote of all seminarians as well as priests it would be voted down. It has actually been voted down in some informal referenda on the subject–by the priests of Czechoslovakia, for example, after World War I. In 1963 the French Public Opinion Institute reported that almost half of the practising Catholics of France said that they would not object to married priests.

Perhaps it is the awareness by the popes of a potential rebellion against celibacy that has led them to be overly vehement in their insistence upon it. When Benedict XV in 1920 saw that the priests of Czechoslovakia were apparently winning the majority of their fellows and of Catholic laymen to the concept of abolishing celibacy, he issued a blistering Allocution against them, and sent an indignant letter to the Archbishop of Prague: "It can hardly be necessary to insist once again that the Apostolic See will never consent to the introduction of 'democratic' innovations in the Church, or to the mitigation or abolition of the obligation of celibacy."[5] Thirty-four years later Pius XII in his encyclical on virginity deplored the fact that some persons "so extol matrimony that in practice they put it above virginity."

Pope Paul revealed no inclination to relax the celibacy rule of the Church, and even Pope John, while confessing that he sympathized with the agony of young priests, still adhered to the Church's traditions on this subject. The general rule, now embodied in Canons 132 and 1072, imposes celibacy on all priests, brothers, and nuns except the priests of the Eastern rites before ordination. In one respect it discriminates against widowers and second marriages in an archaic manner that has no affirmative relationship to morals. A priest of any Eastern rite who marries just before ordination may not remarry after ordination even if his wife dies and he has several young children.

On one point all the theological experts at Vatican II agreed; in spite of St. Augustine, St. Paul, and Pius XI, there is nothing in divine law to bind the clergy to celibacy. The rule is a Church regulation that may be relaxed or abolished by ecclesiastical authority at any time. No one could deny that most of the apostles, including St. Peter himself, had been married and that for many centuries the priests of the Church were not compelled to be celibate.

Although very little discontent with celibacy was evident on the floor of the aula at Vatican II, the silence and evasion were not maintained in the liberal Catholic journals in the United States. Several of them spoke up against celibacy with courage and frankness. *Commonweal*, in a lead editorial published between the second and third sessions of the Council, came out flatly for "a certain portion of married priests," claiming that "there are many married laymen who would make excellent priests, but who do not feel called to celibacy. Since Christ did not demand celibacy of His Apostles, it ought to be possible for the Church to accept among its clergy married men." The editors, acknowledging that no one had intervened at the Council to modify the Church's general rule, still contended that "history has a way of putting questions to the Church which individual men may not dare to raise or may not even see. Clerical celibacy is one of them." The editors were careful to praise the "total dedication" of celibate priests but they pointed out that the connection between suitability for the clerical state and celibacy was an "essentially accidental link."[6]

Other lay voices in America were even more challenging. The *National Catholic Reporter* of Kansas City decided to open its columns to frank discussion of a subject that had long been considered taboo in nearly all diocesan journals. The result was astonishing. For issue after issue long letters written by celibate priests attacked celibacy. They appeared under such headings as "Celibacy: Legacy from Another World"; "Should the Council Look at Celibacy"; "Priest Questions Law on Celibacy." Most of the priests wrote under pseudonyms because they feared reprisal, and what they said shook the American Catholic world. *Sacerdos Midwesternensis* wrote:

> I am not saying celibacy is not a good and holy state (for those who can take it), but I am saying that because of its difficulty it should be a free act at every moment of a priest's life—not one forced on him by reason of his state of life. When will the Church realize how burdensome this is to many priests—to be what they are many times out of fear of hell? If this freedom were suddenly restored I wonder how many priests would remain celibate? . . .
>
> Perhaps we should take a closer, less hypercritical look at our Protestant brothers who were 400 years wiser than we in adopting the vernacular to make worship more meaningful. Likewise their views on married clergy and the success of these clergymen certainly should raise some doubts in our minds as to the total effectiveness of our celibate clergy.[7]

Sacerdos Occidentalis went a little further. "The seminary," he said, "introduces an element of unreality into the life of the priest to be. From the time he enters the seminary, at the end of grade school or following high school, he is cut off from all female relationships. Even during vacation, the directives of the seminary, his family and the attitude of the Catholic community see to it that he avoids the companionship of the opposite sex. In this atmosphere of unreality he makes his choice." And *Sacerdos Occidentalis* added: "Another problem is the problem of defections. It is reported that there are 15,000 priests in Italy who have left the ministry, 5,000 in France, 4,000 in the United States, and many thousand more in Latin America and the rest of the world. The great majority of these men, so the reports assert, are married. . . . With the present shortage of priests, what would be wrong with accepting these men back into the ministry as a married clergy?"

Another pseudonymous priest, writing as Father Stephen

Nash in the *Saturday Evening Post*, expressed his agony even more eloquently. Describing himself as wholly committed to the priesthood and the faith, he charged that: "The Church has never come to grips with this problem, never really been honest about it . . . the Council Fathers merely re-echoed the mossy accents of the past." Although he declared that he would lead no crusades, he said: "I am tired of examining my motives, increasing my penances, in order that I might live in a way that I do not believe Christ intended." And he added: "I want to be a man, not an ideal; a lover and not a preacher; a father, not a father image."[8]

Those American Catholic liberals who asked for a modification in the celibacy rule were given short shrift in the standard diocesan papers in the United States. For the most part, these journals evaded discussion of the merits of the question and fell back on authority and tradition. The *Register* said: "No one could deny the abstract possibility [of a change in the celibacy rule] inasmuch as clerical celibacy is not of divine law. But we can say that probably no great inroads into clerical celibacy will ever be made in the Western Church. . . . Clerical celibacy, though not a divinely imposed law, is so entrenched in tradition, so well supported in scripture, so obviously favored by Christ's teaching of the superiority of virginity to marriage, so suited to the service of souls, that it appears improbable that it should ever cease to be the rule."[9]

The *Register* did not raise those delicate questions of economics which underlie the Church's policy on the subject. It would be extremely expensive for the Roman Catholic Church to discontinue celibacy and support all priests and other religious workers as normal human beings entitled to a family wage.

The debate on the merits of celibacy had created such a stir in various parts of the world during the Council that at the final session a number of bishops sent in their speeches on the subject to the Council moderators. It was reported that Cardinal Alfrink of Utrecht and several African bishops were ready to bring the whole subject to the aula floor. Cardinal Alfrink had said previously that "it must not be thought that the problem is nonexistent simply because no one has the courage . . . to express himself publicly on this point."

❧

What the liberal bishops intended to say about celibacy will never be known. It was at that moment, on October 11, 1965, just a week after his triumphant plea for peace and freedom at the United Nations, that Pope Paul stepped in and stopped all public discussion of the question. In a letter addressed to Cardinal Tisserant, ranking member of the Council's Presidency, Paul declared: "It does not seem expedient that there should be a public discussion of a topic which calls for such delicacy of treatment and which is of such far-reaching importance for the Church . . . the existing discipline must be retained and strengthened, especially today . . . through it priests are able to consecrate all their love completely to Christ and to dedicate themselves exclusively and generously to service of the Church and to souls."[10] Then the pope added that if any of the Council Fathers wished to make any observations on the topic they might do so in writing. Paul seemed to rub salt in the wound by declaring blandly that his action was taken "without limiting the liberty of the Fathers in the least." Actually, the Fathers had already committed themselves to celibacy in several schema.

The Fathers, with the honorable exception of one Dutch bishop, took the papal order without protest. In St. Peter's the pope's decision was greeted with a sigh of relief, then with two waves of applause. Cardinal Tisserant assured the pope in a letter: "For our part, Holy Father, we are always ready to accept your will and to obey your commandments." The subject was closed.

Or was it? Across the world in many places and among many types of Catholics, liberal laymen and many young priests and seminarians have begun to think the unthinkable, that the real trouble with the sexual policy of their Church is the sexual ignorance of the rulers of their Church. Is repression a good thing in itself? Is a hair shirt the holiest kind of shirt after all? Have not the Eastern-rite Catholics, the Orthodox, and the Protestants demonstrated that a clergyman can be a servant of the Lord without suppressing sex?

A few days after Pope Paul had taken the whole question of celibacy away from the bishops of the Council, 81 Catholic laymen from 12 countries sent a petition to the Fathers asking for a reconsideration of the celibacy question. "Faithful priests," the laymen said, "are finding it increasingly difficult to radiate the new glory of the Church in a state of celibacy, which to many true followers of Christ appears to be imposed by law rather than embraced by one's own free will."[11]

The shock of the arbitrary suppression of the debate by the pope brought into the open many estimates about the great number of priests and seminarians who have been dropping out of clerical careers because of the will to marry. One priest "with good Curial connections" told a United Press reporter on the day of the pope's suppression that "the Holy Office presently has on file more than 10,000 requests from priests for a dispensation of vows. Many of these are from priests who want to marry." Further unofficial reports in Rome–impossible to confirm with documentation–indicated that an estimated 15,000 Italian and French priests had already filed requests with the Holy Office for permission to demit from the priesthood, chiefly on account of marriage already accomplished or marriage intended. The statistics are probably worthless. Such facts are never made public by the Church.

When the Council finally passed and the Pope finally promulgated the Decree on Priestly Formation, the philosophy of celibacy for the priesthood was continued as before. Said the Decree: "Students who, according to the holy and fixed laws of their own rite, follow the revered tradition of priestly celibacy should be very carefully trained for this state. By it they renounce the companionship of marriage for the sake of the kingdom of heaven; they devote themselves to the Lord with an undivided love. . . . May they deeply sense how gratefully this state deserves to be undertaken."

As they were about to indulge in a hunger strike, Emmeline Pankhurst is reported to have said to her English suffragettes: "Now, put your trust in God and She will protect you." Apparently Miss Pankhurst's female deity was not present at the first session of Vatican II. Women were almost entirely overlooked in preparations for the Council and finally squeezed in only as auditors in later sessions. In this sense the Council was a Pauline Council, demonstrating bland condescension to all females, even to those hundreds of thousands of religious women throughout the world who perform the basic work in the Church's vast system of schools, hospitals, and charitable institutions. Some of these nuns appeared in the balconies of the aula during the open meetings of the first session in their quaint black, white and gray costumes, and a few nuns appeared as journalists at press conferences. Usually they were silent, at least until the fourth session when Mother Mary Luke, Chairman of the Conference of Major Superiors of Women's Institutions in the United States, the only American religious woman to be appointed an auditor at the Council, made an excellent speech. After that, press conferences heard short talks by other women.

But the general rule for women at the Council was silence and subservience. They served in an advisory capacity on several commissions in the later stages of the Council but they were not given any power. They still have no place even on the staff of the Sacred Congregation of Religious which supervises the Church's female orders throughout the world. Even when females are canonized in Rome, the males walk in elegant isolation up to the altar of God where a woman is being elevated almost to the divine level.

Of course, one reason why there were no women with power to vote in the Council is that there are no women bishops or archbishops or priests in the Catholic system. American Protestantism, in 63 denominations, can boast of nearly 7,000 women preachers. Catholicism has not yet crossed that bridge, although agitation for female Catholic rights is growing. In the first session, as one Catholic woman critic put it, aside from a few silent women journalists there was "not even a cleaning woman." At the beginning of the third session 17 women, including 9 sisters, were admitted as auditors. Three of them were Americans, none currently married. For these American Catholic women, subservience was an old story. Although nuns in the United States outnumber priests more than three to one, they do not participate in the Church's machinery of power.

When Cardinal Suenens complained that "in our age when woman almost travels to the moon," the Church should give her greater recognition, almost all the bishops agreed in part. By the middle of the last session 16 Fathers had made speeches asking for a more important role for women in the church, but their suggestions for reform were minor and vague. Archbishop Paul Hallinan of Atlanta wanted new rules permitting women to serve as acolytes and deaconesses, as teachers in theology and, above all, as consultants both for the Commission on the Revision of Canon Law and for the Congregation for the Religious. He did not ask that women should have the right to be ordained but he did say: "The Church has been slow to offer to women, in the selection of their vocation, any choice but that of mother or nun. In fact, among the Saints, there are only three groups: martyrs, virgins, and the vague negative category called 'neither virgins nor martyrs.' "

Although the Council began to correct some of these deficiencies by minor concessions as early as the second session, the Church was almost as much a male power-monopoly at the end of the Council as it had been at the beginning. The concessions did not satisfy a small but militant group of Catholic feminists who belong to an international organization called St. Joan's International Alliance. In Rome during the fourth session they held a public meeting and presented a petition to the Commission on the Revision of Canon Law, asking that women should be allowed ordination as priests and that the canon law should be thoroughly revised to treat women as adults rather than minors. Their request for the right of ordination was received with mild amusement, but their demands for advisory roles in many Church departments in the future are quite sure to be granted.

It is the subjection of religious women to petty and childish restrictions in convent life that is now causing real turmoil in religious orders, particularly in the United States. To a certain extent the new turmoil is a product of that *aggiornamento* which began with Pope John.

Convent life had begun to lose its lure in the United States even before the Council was called and the recruitment of nuns had suffered a relative decline in many countries. After some medieval and repressive features of the life of modern nuns had been exposed to critical comment at the Council, the reverberations spread rapidly. In Kansas City the *National Catholic Reporter* opened a special department for letters from nuns, calling the department a "Sister's Forum." The letters of protest which poured in from the submerged convent world created a sensation. For the first time Catholic liberals like Michael Novak, a correspondent at the Council, questioned the whole tradition of silence about the suppressions and repressions of convent life, charging that there had been "a breakdown in candor in American Catholic life." "There is a conspiracy of gentility, politeness and adulation, which inhibits honest sentiment and direct speech," he charged. Then he added:

> The layman can't help feeling that the sister, once formed by novitiate and juniorate into the convent code, and then kept isolated by her rule from mingling with the men and women of our society, slowly adopts as the normal way of viewing the world the imperatives and the delicatenesses she has been taught to observe. Her mentors may think of these as particularly civilizing, as leaven in a harsher and more vulgar world, as a genteel tradition worth preserving. But if this is the choice that nuns in America make, they should realize that it deprives them of the chance for leadership; it robs them of positive spiritual force, with its multiplier-effect among their students; it makes them, not apostles, but guardians; it takes them out of the mainstream and the center of the fray and–to use the harsh, honest word–it makes their work defensive and ephemeral.[12]

Novak even ventured to suggest that "the fears and uncertainties concerning sex felt by many of the girls who graduate from Catholic schools are scarcely due to Christian modesty alone, which need have no fear; they seem due to the sexual uncertainties of their teachers (and parents)."

James O'Gara, associate editor of *Commonweal*, describing "an internal crisis of considerable proportions" in American convents, said bluntly: "By Canon Law and long-standing traditions, nuns are treated like the children most of them spend their lives with."[13] It is well known that in many American convents nuns are forbidden to return home for visits with their families even in case of serious illness. Having taken their vows, they are frequently cut off from home environments for life.

In the United States, public criticism of convent life centered at first on such details as cumbersome and unsuitable dress, often so clumsy as to handicap sisters in their daily work as nurses, teachers, and social workers. Under pressure some of the most unusual headdresses of religious orders—especially the "flapping wings of white geese"—were eliminated during the Council years. In this movement the chief opposition to change seemed to come not from male overlords but from older sisters who had become accustomed to ruling convent life as autocrats. A few American religious orders transferred their sisters into new habits more consonant with modern industrial life. One new costume was described as "a navy blue dress with a belted waist and skirt extending to mid-calf," with a loose-fitting white collar replacing the old white, starched coif.

Several exposures of the convent system in book form appeared during the Council, revealing quite astonishing abuses. In one book, *Convent Life,* published under official imprimatur in the United States in 1964, the "Balkanized" condition of American female religious orders was exposed. The United States has 480 religious orders for nuns with competing and overlapping jurisdictions and varying rules of conduct. They are often presided over by very jealous superiors who fight for tradition and their own supremacy. Sister Mary Gilbert, describing the embarrassing predicaments involved when several nuns from various houses decide to go together in an automobile for an afternoon outing, said:

> Sister A may go for the ride, but she can't get out of the car or eat an ice-cream cone on the way. Sister B may go for the ride and get out of the car, but refreshments are taboo. Sister C may go for the ride and have her ice-cream, but all within the sanctuary of the car. Sister D may go for the ride, get out of the car, and eat the ice-cream cone. She may even name her flavor if Mrs. X isn't a dictator. Sister E? She may come out to the car and wave good-bye to the others.[14]

In 1965 two faculty members from Fordham University, one of them a priest, published in *Harper's Magazine* an article on "The American Nun, Poor, Chaste and Restive" that raised some of the fundamental questions about the imposed chastity of the convent system and its sad effect on both nuns and pupils. The authors pointed out that in the recruitment of young girls for a convent life in Catholic high-schools: "The decision to become a sister is usually made during the teen years, commonly under the influence and inspiration of teaching sisters. This magnifies the danger of unrealistic and immature decisions."[15] The authors might have added that the primary danger lies in the recruitment for a single occupation by ardent devotees of that occupation, without due consideration of other occupations, at a time when adolescent sexual guilt and the adolescent tendency toward "crushes" are most likely to produce unbalanced judgment. The Fordham authors also quoted studies showing that nuns have a higher incidence of schizophrenia and psychoneurotic disorders than American women in general.

The new realism in regard to convent life is having a profound effect on the position of religious orders in Catholicism. Cloistered nuns are declining in numbers and importance, and service orders are becoming more militant. Rebellion against petty tyrannies in convent life has revealed itself in many parts of the United States. Nuns, with the sanction of progressive superiors and bishops, have occasionally taken an active place on picket lines and in racial demonstrations from Selma to California. A Sister Formation Movement is attempting to raise convent standards of training to the level of the best public schools and public hospitals. The American nun can never again be quite so submerged in an antisexual and antisocial ghetto as she was before the Council began.

But apparently the highest authorities in the Church have not learned the lesson that there is a female *aggiornamento* in Catholic life. In March 1966, a nun specializing in the study of drama at the University of Detroit (a Catholic university), Sister Marie Bernadette of the Glenmary Sisters, had worked for weeks to prepare herself for the stellar role in a perfectly decent play to be put on by Catholic students for the public. She was to be disguised as a man for a farcical portion of the play and she was to embrace a would-be lover briefly and in a chaste manner. From 4,000 miles away, as the *National Catholic Reporter* tells the story, came the order from Cardinal Ildebrando Antoniutti, prefect of the Congregation of the Religious, transmitted through the Apostolic Delegate in Washington, then through the office of Archbishop John F. Dearden of Detroit, and finally to Sister Marie Bernadette, prohibiting her from appearing in this role. Sister Bernadette had not taken her final vows, was in fact only a senior at the university itself who had won the lead role in the play in open competition. The *National Catholic Reporter* could think of only one adequate analogy, a "cable from Secretary of Defense McNamara administering a personal reproof to an army corporal for appearing out of uniform in a tea shop in Johannesburg, South Africa. But you'd have to stipulate that the corporal had permission from his unit and post commanders, his parents, his wife and the owner of the tea shop."[16]

In all the agitation for improvement, no one at the Council suggested abandonment of celibacy for nuns. It was admitted that such a reform would be unthinkable. Priests might marry and continue to function as both pastors and heads of families—they already act in these dual roles in the churches of the Eastern rites. But it is universally admitted that this type of liberty would never be feasible for women. If they married, they would become mothers and housekeepers, and the convent system would collapse.

Meanwhile, no one can deny the truth in a petition demanding women's rights that was filed with the Council in 1961 by a leading Catholic of Zurich, Dr. Gertrud Heinzelmann. It expressed "the complaint and accusation of half of humanity . . . in whose oppression the Church, through its theory on women, did and still does play a part, in a way that gravely violates the Christian conscience." That was an improvement over St. John Chrysostom, who had described woman in the fourth century as "a necessary evil, a natural temptation, a desirable calamity, a domestic peril, a deadly fascination, a painted ill."

CHAPTER ELEVEN ❧ MARRIAGE AND DIVORCE

PROBABLY the two most controversial subjects of the entire Council were mixed marriage and contraception. The Church's willingness to modify the discriminatory laws against Protestants and Jews in mixed marriage was considered by most Protestants to be the touchstone of Catholic sincerity in proclaiming brotherhood. The Church's opposition to contraception was considered by almost all Protestants and Jews, and by millions of Catholics also, to be the worst survival of ignorance and superstition in the Church. It was hoped that the Catholic policies on these two subjects could be thoroughly ventilated on the aula floor and that the resultant reforms would come quickly.

These hopes, alas, were soon dashed. In the second session Cardinal Frings of Cologne, during the discussion on ecumenism, made headlines by suggesting a slight change in the mixed marriage laws that would make the marriage of a Catholic by a non-Catholic minister "valid" under Catholic law. He was joined by a Melchite superior general. But simultaneously Cardinal Frings suggested that any non-Catholic contemplating a mixed marriage who felt that it was against his conscience to sign away the religion of his children should give up any idea of marriage. It was evident that even reasonably liberal prelates did not appreciate the strength of non-Catholic criticism of Catholic marriage discipline throughout the world.

A brief and spirited debate on marriage and birth control broke out in the third session, and a short discussion of some of the marriage issues continued in the fourth session, but the debate in both sessions was superficial and theoretical. When the wide differences of opinion among many prominent Church leaders caused sensational headlines in journals throughout the world, both the pope and the bishops acted to suppress public discussion. The pope took over the birth control question for himself by a direct intervention. The bishops themselves voted in the third session to turn the subject of marriage laws over to the pope and his advisors for final decision. The abrupt manner in which the marriage debate was terminated in this session seemed to indicate that the order for termination came from the "Higher Authority," meaning the Pope. Many bishops were waiting to be heard on the subject when suddenly, on October 29, 1964, the presiding officer of the day, Cardinal Agagianian, acting without warning at a time when many bishops were absent, called for a standing vote on the question whether to end the debate. No count was taken. The debate was ended.[1]

In spite of this abrupt termination of what might have been the most important debate of the entire Council, enough opposition to the Church's archaic marriage rules had already reached the public to make Catholics throughout the world aware that the traditional philosophy of their Church was under fire. Several cardinals came as close to challenging the Church rule on contraception as they dared, and in the whole field of sexual philosophy the conservatives were placed on the defensive. Among the liberals, the lead was taken by Cardinal Leger of Quebec, Cardinal Suenens of Belgium, and Patriarch (now Cardinal) Maximos IV Saigh. Predictably, Cardinals Ottaviani and Browne of the Holy Office took the lead in proclaiming that the Church's present philosophy of marriage was eternally right.

In introducing the *relatio* on marriage, Archbishop John F. Dearden of Detroit had stacked the cards slightly in favor of the conservatives by declaring that: "Nothing can be permitted which is opposed to the natural orientation of the marital act or which destroys the conjugal act's expressiveness of personal and marital love." But he did not mention the birth control pills specifically.

In retrospect the stand of the liberals does not seem as original or as daring as it seemed at the time. This, at least, can be said for the position of the European liberals. Maximos IV Saigh of Antioch showed greater courage; he actually advocated the junking of many of the Church's archaic marriage rules. Cardinal Suenens spoke of those Catholic couples who try "with anguish to live in double fidelity to the doctrine of the Church and to the demands of conjugal and parental love," but he hedged his liberalism with many safe reaffirmations of Church doctrine. He declared that "it is not a question of modifying or of casting doubt on the truly traditional teaching of the Church. That would be folly! . . . the Church has never to repudiate a truth that it once taught, but . . . she must integrate this truth in a richer synthesis." This last phrase is a standard verbal artifice for dismissing an outworn doctrine without officially denying its truth. Maximos IV Saigh was more forthright, as usual. "The Council must find a practical solution [to the impasse on birth control]," he said. "Frankly, can the official positions of the Church in this matter not be reviewed in the light of modern theological, medical, psychological and sociological science?"

Cardinal Browne, Irish Dominican from the Holy Office, assumed the main burden of defending the Church's present scholastic philosophy on marriage. "The primary end of marriage," he proclaimed, "is procreation and the education of the children. The secondary end is, on the one hand, the mutual aid of the spouses, and on the other a remedy for concupiscence. . . . Love forms part of marriage, but we must distinguish between the love of friendship which desires the welfare of another and the love of concupiscence which seeks what is good for oneself. The kind of love required for the stability of marriage is the conjugal love of friendship." Apparently Cardinal Browne, born in 1887, could not visualize a marriage in which the love of concupiscence was entirely mutual and equally satisfactory to both man and wife. His philosophy seemed to come straight from the writings of St. Augustine.

When the section on Fostering the Nobility of Marriage and the Family (Part II, Chapter I of the schema on The Church in the Modern World) was finally promulgated at the end of the last session, it adhered, for the most part, to the basic philosophy and theology of the conservatives. Marriage was proclaimed a sacrament since "God Himself is the author of matrimony." The procreation and education of children were proclaimed as primary aims. There were a few warm words of approval for mutual love but they seemed to be thrown into the clerical stew as a kind of afterthought. Graciously the Fathers, in discussing the merits of marriage, conceded that "the excellence of this institution is not everywhere reflected with equal brilliance."

There seemed to be no necessary connection between the various theological ingredients in the marital stew and the modern reality of marriage. The stew was not well integrated. Official Catholic thinking about marriage had been for centuries a purely clerical concoction. The farther the priests were removed from the realities of marriage and sequestered in their institutional celibacy, the more unrealistic their book formulas seemed to become.

Over the centuries, an interconnected network of formulas had been worked out in Catholic teaching covering marriage, divorce, annulment, and birth control.[2] Gradually, in formal teaching, the realities of love, hate, mercy, and cruelty had been subordinated to verbal conformity. A whole system of marital jurisprudence had been developed outside the laws of the state, operating under exclusive Church control. The system included marriage courts operating at the local diocesan level and, after appeal, progressing upward to the Roman Rota, the highest Catholic Court.

The complicated clerical rules in this network of marital jurisprudence had often become more binding than the demands of human happiness. The parties to a marriage had little to say about it since the formulas were all made and interpreted by the priests in the light of ecclesiastical tradition. Even when they wanted to, the priests were not permitted to approach a marriage problem with a simple direct question: What is the best thing for the welfare of the persons involved?

Often the answers of ecclesiastical courts about sexual problems seemed to be buried in unreal verbiage. Here, for example, is a key part of the decision of the Roman Rota in a 1958 case in which a Catholic wife asked nullification of her marriage because her husband insisted that she wear a pessary during sexual intercourse.

> By the contract of marriage there is not conferred a *ius in re* or right in the body, that is ownership of the body simply as such; but what is conferred is the right to the use of the body, and to a very determinate use, i.e., for truly conjugal acts. Therefore, just as you cannot have a right to the use of a thing without the right to use that thing, so the right to the use of the body for conjugal acts cannot be transferred without the right to use the body for these same acts; and a condition which excludes those acts, or the use of the right to those acts, excludes consent and consequently the right to those acts. So one who contracts marriage with a condition excluding the use of the right to conjugal acts, transfers a right to the use, without the right to use; that is, he transfers the right and excludes the right to one and the same thing, which is a contradiction. Since the right which is given and accepted in marriage is the right to use, and to a very determinate use, and consequently cannot be conceived without the right to use, the distinction between the *ius radicale* and the *ius utile sen expeditum* in regard to marriage, involves a contradiction.[3]

The lady got her annulment.

Priests were not so unrealistic in the early centuries of Christianity. In fact, the present clerical monopoly of Catholic marriage with its antisexual implications is of relatively recent origin. The Church's position on marriage, divorce, and many of the kindred problems of family life has become steadily more reactionary and more priest-centered in the last two centuries. The Council of Trent in the sixteenth century made the celebration of marriage by a priest essential to its validity but for many years that Council's very strict clerical rules about marriage were applied unevenly to various countries. There were plenty of special dispensations to ease what Cardinal Suenens might have called "the anguish" of living in double fidelity to Church law and conjugal happiness at the same time.

The strict rule of the *Ne Temere* decree, which required the presence of a Catholic priest to make every marriage of a Catholic valid, was not imposd upon Catholics in the United States until 1908.[4] As W. E. H. Lecky pointed out in his *Democracy and Liberty*, the Church in its early days acquired control of the marriage field very gradually. There was nothing in the earliest Christian teachings to require such control.

> The civil law of the early Christian emperors and of the early period of the Middle Ages diverges widely from the ecclesiastical conception of marriage, and for a long period of Christian history no religious ceremony of any kind was deemed by the Church necessary for its validity. . . . In the Middle Ages a religious ceremony appears to have been made obligatory by law, and marriages without the intervention of a priest were considered clandestine and irregular; but they frequently occurred, and their validity was perfectly undisputed.[5]

It was during the nineteenth and twentieth centuries that the Papacy finally made its present extreme claims in regard to the invalidity of civil marriage for Catholics. Pius IX in 1852, twelve years before his *Syllabus of Errors*, issued an allocution, *Acerbissimum*, in which he outlined what his followers called "the ideal harmony of Church and state," which, in the marriage field, required an outright condemnation of civil marriage for all Catholics as "abominable concubinage." Twenty-six years later Leo XIII virtually repeated the condemnation of Pius IX in an encyclical of his own, and added some strong words about the sacredness of marriage and the Church's desire to "maintain intact the holy modesty of the marriage bed."

In the decade before that, by a decree of the Third Council of Baltimore, Catholics in the United States who attempted to marry before a non-Catholic clergyman had been ordered excommunicated. Thus the Church established the principle in America that Protestant marriage for Catholics was even worse than the "abominable concubinage" of civil marriage, at least in its ecclesiastical consequences.

All of these relatively new dogmas about marriage were made official by Benedict XV when he promulgated the new Code of Canon Law in 1918. A whole chapter of canons was adopted going into the most excruciating details about the regulation of family life and ending with the arrogant claim of Canon 1038: "The supreme authority of the Church alone has the right to authentically declare in what cases the Divine Law forbids or annuls a marriage." After that, in 1930, Pius XI added in his famous encyclical *Casti Connubii* a few final doctrinal touches, including the prohibition against birth control. Pius XI's encyclical was considered, on the whole, just as binding as canon law itself, since it was promulgated with great solemnity.

So the Church came to Vatican II with a marriage code which, in a sense, was worse than medieval. It represented the growing clerical arrogance in marital matters that had progressed steadily to new heights of self-assertion. The Code declared that (1) all valid marriage for a Catholic must be performed by a priest under priestly rules; (2) no Catholic could marry a non-Catholic without express permission from his bishop and the written pledge by the non-Catholic party to raise all children of the marriage as Catholics; (3) no consummated marriage under full Catholic auspices could ever be dissolved by divorce with the right of remarriage; (4) no direct resort could be made to contraception; and (5) direct therapeutic abortion even to save the life of a mother was absolutely forbidden.

It should not be supposed, of course, that such a narrow code ever met with approval by all Catholics. It is a code of the priests imposed on the people without recourse. The Fathers at the Council were aware that the narrowness of the code had been considered by many laymen to be the most common cause of anticlerical sentiment throughout the world. Frequently Catholic majorities in Catholic countries had rebelled against it and enacted marriage laws quite contrary to Church concepts. Almost every Catholic country in the world had passed laws allowing civil marriage for Catholics in spite of the fact that the hierarchy would like to preserve its monopoly control over such marriages, as it did in the Middle Ages.

Occasionally in a Catholic country a Catholic who has been married in a civil ceremony has rebelled openly against the teaching of his priests that he was living in "abominable concubinage." Such, for example, was the famous Italian incident at Prato that began under Pius XII and was not settled until the reign of John XXIII.[6] It all started in 1956 when an Italian grocer named Mauro Bellandi, a resident of the little Tuscan town of Prato and a baptized Catholic turned atheist, persuaded his fiancée, Loriana Nunziati, a practising Catholic, to forgo a Church wedding and be married by Prato's Communist mayor. Immediately the bishop of Prato, Pietro Fiordelli, ordered a local priest to read to his parishioners at a public gathering a denunciation of the Bellandis as "public sinners" engaged in something "absolutely not matrimony but only the beginning of scandalous concubinage." The Bellandis brought charges against their bishop of "criminal defamation of character," and a three-judge Italian court found the bishop guilty.

The decision rocked the nation and the church. It was the first time in recent years that a Catholic bishop had been tried in an Italian court on criminal charges. Some bishops ordered their churches to toll their bells in protest and drape their buildings in mourning. *Osservatore Romano*, in recording the awful verdict, pointed out that all the Catholics involved, including the three judges, must be considered excommunicated, since no Catholic is permitted to cooperate in bringing a Church official into a civil court on charges involving his clerical duties. The Church finally won the Prato case on appeal to a Florence court on the ground that Bishop Fiordelli's sanctions against the Bellandis "were not temporal ones but exclusively spiritual," authorized under Canon Law. The free expression of such doctrines, it was held, are guaranteed by the Italian Constitution as part of the Church's liberty.

Americans had an opportunity in 1962 to see how this Prato rule concerning "public sinners" could operate even in the United States during the period of the Council. In March of that year two students at America's largest Catholic university, St. John's University of New York, were married in a civil ceremony in the Municipal Building in Brooklyn with the assistance of two other students as witnesses. All four were dismissed by the Catholic authorities of the university on the ground that their action was "gravely sinful," was in violation of ecclesiastical law, and in contravention of a university ruling to the effect that the institution must operate "in conformity with the ideals of Christian education." Although the young couple had been remarried by a priest about one month after the civil ceremony, university authorities still held that the original "sin" had not been expunged. When the New York Civil Liberties Union helped three of the ousted students to appeal to the courts on the ground that their civil rights had been impaired, Justice George Eilperin ordered them reinstated, but a month later St. John's University won on appeal.[7]

It is fair to ask: Where did all this extreme narrowmindedness about marriage and sex come from? Catholic textbooks teach that it came from Jesus, but there is no evidence whatever for this claim. So far as we know, Jesus never performed a marriage ceremony for anybody or prescribed any clerical monopoly of marriage or gave any lectures in favor of celibacy or against sex. He once was present at a marriage feast in Cana and is said to have blessed the wine used at the wedding, but this is a far cry from the rigors of present-day Catholic marriage dogma. Marriage is alleged in Catholic textbooks to have been "elevated by the Divine Founder of Christianity to the dignity of a sacrament." "Therefore," says Canon 1012, "it is impossible for a valid contract of marriage between baptized persons to exist without being by that very fact a sacrament." This is the basic theological and scriptural premise on which the whole set of priestly marriage claims is based. It was the assumption on which the entire discussion of marriage took place at Vatican II. It remains a premise without any real historical or scriptural foundation, a thesis manufactured by priests several centuries after the death of Jesus.

Until the very last days of the last session there was some hope that the present rules of the church on mixed marriage would be substantially changed by the Council itself before adjournment. Long before the Council began, various Protestant leaders had declared that the Church's willingness to change these discriminatory rules would be the acid test of its good faith in favoring ecumenism. Dr. W. A. Visser't Hooft of the World Council of Churches put it very mildly when he said in 1963: "It would greatly help if the [Vatican] Council taught that the Catholic [in mixed marriage] should take seriously the faith of the non-Catholic partner who is a convinced Christian. For what is shocking to the Protestant and to the Orthodox, too, is that the non-Catholic party is treated as though he or she had no Christian faith to be taken seriously."[8]

The mixed marriage problem had received plenty of advance consideration at the Council, since there had been some discussion of the problem in three preparatory drafts of schemata put out by three different preparatory bodies. Although the suggestions made in the original drafts were not discussed in the aula at the first session, there was a great deal of unofficial discussion elsewhere, and it was finally agreed that the three differing preparatory treatments of the subject should be resubmitted to a joint mixed commission for consolidation or revision before the second session. A revised statement on mixed marriage finally reached the aula in the closing hours of the third session.

Protestant observers, who were deeply concerned about a change in the mixed marriage rules, did not give up all hope of a change even in the final hours of the third session when the whole problem of mixed marriage was transferred to the pope and the Commission on Canon Law. Paul, they felt, might be amenable to public and Protestant pressure. Apparently Paul was wholly unmoved by Protestant pressure. He had lived all his life in a nation with a very small Protestant minority and he apparently took for granted the Catholic right to control all marriages of Catholics. Was that right not written into the Church's concordats with Mussolini as well as with Franco?

In the fourth session Pope Paul was about to make public a *Motu Proprio* on mixed marriage that crystallized and confirmed present Church policy. The proposed contents of the document had become so nearly public that it was widely discussed at the coffee bars. The papal pronouncement, it was said (1) had already been signed; (2) was about to be signed; (3) would be signed and released in such a way that the world-wide publicity coming from Paul's visit to the United Nations would help to drown out its very sour implications.

It was generally agreed among all the journalistic detectives at the Council that the document made such a small concession to Protestant sensitivity that it was almost an insult. The only change it made in the present rule, it was said, concerned the form of expression of the pledge of the non-Catholic party in a mixed marriage obliging him to raise all his children as Catholics. This non-Catholic party, it was said, would be "trusted" in the future to make his pledge verbally instead of being subjected to the more humiliating requirement that he sign a paper on the dotted line. It was also rumored that the Church might alter its official policy of excommunicating a Catholic for marriage by a Protestant minister.

It was at this period, in September and October of the final session, that the Protestant observers at the Council came nearest to a useful collective rebellion. They met and discussed the coming *Motu Proprio* with much apprehension, realizing that if it were issued without alterations much of the good will between Catholics and Protestants throughout the world would be dissipated. Some of them wanted to speak out collectively in public but the majority prevented this because of the agreed policy that no public statement should be made by the observers as a group.

Having lived with the Council for three years, the Protestant observers did not see any great hope of persuading Catholic leaders to grant absolute equality in mixed marriage. All they hoped for was a somewhat greater concession than the almost meaningless modification in the form of the pledges. A number of Protestant observers sent written memoranda to the appropriate

Catholic leaders asking for delay and further consideration of a more substantial concession. In the end the Council had to adjourn while the matter was still hanging in the air.

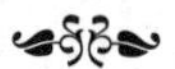

Much Catholic as well as Protestant agitation against the hardships of the mixed marriage rule had broken out in Europe during the Council, particularly in Germany, where there had been a great intermingling of Protestants and Catholics after World War II. The agitation was less vehement in the United States although, even here, the problem had become acute. Probably no single policy except that of opposition to birth control has troubled American priests and laymen more deeply. American mixed marriages have been increasing steadily even while local priests have continued to inveigh against them. And, in spite of the attempt to keep all children of such marriages in the Church, it is now generally admitted that the great majority of such children are permanently lost to Catholicism.[9]

The unfairness involved in the pledge to raise all children of such marriages as Catholics has angered Protestants without proportionately increasing the Catholic population. Millions of American Catholics have admitted the unreasonableness of the present rules, and so many Catholics have been "married" to non-Catholics by Protestant ministers and public officials without benefit of the Catholic clergy that, if all these so-called "invalid" marriages were added to the "valid" mixed marriages performed by priests, it is possible that half of all of the marriages of Catholics in the United States could be described as mixed marriages. (When a Catholic is married by a public official it is almost always to a non-Catholic; otherwise a priest is chosen.)

Strictly speaking, the issue of mixed marriage is not primarily a sexual issue, although it may involve for the non-Catholic party some incidental surrenders to Catholic sexual policy. It is an issue of the exercise of unilateral Catholic clerical power against non-Catholics and against the state. In Catholic teaching the state is denied the right to marry any Catholic validly or to grant a divorce to any Catholic validly. The state's action in marriage covers only the "civil effects," not its essence. Similarly, every non-Catholic religious body is denied the right to equality of treatment with the Catholic Church in a mixed marriage. The non-Catholic is made into a second-class citizen because the marriage is made into an instrument of proselytism.

Some American Catholic leaders came out quite boldly during the Council in denunciation of the unfairness and deceit involved in the present mixed marriage rules. Bishop John K. Mussio of Steubenville, Ohio, writing in the Catholic monthly *Marriage* said: "To many sincere non-Catholics, the promises are nothing more than an attempt to force them to violate their consciences. No good can come of a method that is forced upon a non-Catholic as the only means of marrying the person of his choice. This type of forced conformity is oftimes the source of a resentment and indignity that is far more harmful to marriage than can be imagined."[10]

Commonweal went even farther in an editorial in its issue of March 5, 1965. It said:

> The mildest thing which can be said about the Church's laws on mixed marriages is that they are merely troublesome and awkward. But mild things have rarely been said. Catholics have never found it easy to defend these laws; or at least have rarely been able to make their purported reasonableness plausible to the non-Catholic. For their part, non-Catholics have felt that the Church's demands are both unreasonable and unjust, little more than another cog in the vast machinery of Catholic imperialism, but all the more odious since they impinge intimately on their consciences and their rights. . . .
>
> But the price of this policy has been high. It all but totally ignored the conscience of the non-Catholic marriage partner. It practically forced many Catholics to marry outside the Church—by telling them that they had no choice, should the non-Catholic assert his or her rights, but to give up their prospective husband or wife. It opened the way for hypocrisy since, as it often turned out, promises were made for the sake

of a respectable "church wedding" and family blessings which were never intended to be kept.

This was strong medicine for the Catholic hierarchy, and *Commonweal* cannot be praised too highly for speaking out so frankly. But, at the Council itself, it soon became apparent that the conservative pressure for preserving the mixed marriage rules was quite overwhelming. Several cardinals and many bishops spoke optimistic words about minor changes in the rules, and these optimistic words became overoptimistic headlines in the American press. But even Cardinal Cushing, who had been one of the first to suggest possible changes in the present rules, soon admitted that he expected little reform.

The Boston cardinal, who has nearly 1,700,000 Catholics in his archdiocese, said in 1963: "As it is now, the requirement that a non-Catholic partner make the famous promises before marriage is an irritant to many, and some, it is clear from what happens subsequently, make the promises in bad faith. If we no longer required the promises, we would not be revoking any divine law; we would not be changing any dogma of the Church. . . . Many people forget that it was only half a century ago that we had changes in the Church's marriage legislation."[11] Cardinal Cushing's appeal was not accepted.

While Protestants throughout the world appreciated the attitude of Cardinal Cushing and other liberal leaders, they were not disposed to forgive or forget the failure of the Council to effect a reform in this elementary matter of interdenominational fair play. A leading Lutheran pastor in Germany declared that improvement in Protestant-Catholic relations is "inconceivable" unless the Catholic Church changes its rules on mixed marriage. He declared that a "guerilla war" is in progress over mixed marriage in almost every community in West Germany and that the Catholic Church has aggravated the situation by regarding a million valid marriages as "non-existent." The Church of Scotland was equally forthright. In a report issued between the first and second sessions of the Council the General Assembly of the Kirk declared that the

Catholic policy on mixed marriage "cannot escape unqualified moral condemnation."

But even the American bishops at the Council, liberal in so many other matters, were not united in asking liberalization of Catholic mixed marriage rules. When a draft statement called "Suggestions on the Sacrament of Marriage" finally reached the aula floor on the next to the last day of the third session, its mild suggestions for reform in mixed marriage rules met with considerable opposition. Cardinal Ritter of St. Louis favored liberalization, but Bishop John Fearns of New York, speaking for Cardinal Spellman, opposed "dangerous changes which might do serious spiritual harm in our country."[12] Archbishop John Krol of Philadelphia joined Spellman in the attack, suggesting that any relaxation of the present severe rules might promote secularism and indifferentism.

The Spellman-Krol criticism was directed at a mild provision in the proposed drafts which would have allowed local bishops to determine for themselves when it was advisable to enforce all the present requirements in the mixed marriage form. The drafts also called for the abrogation of the present rule excommunicating any Catholic who is married before a non-Catholic minister. The draft suggested that the responsibility for pledging a Catholic education for all offspring in mixed marriage should be shouldered by the Catholic party and not by the non-Catholic party, leaving it to the Catholic party to make known these pledges to his non-Catholic spouse "when the occasion presents itself." In vain Cardinal Ritter argued that the suggested reform proceeds "wisely and prudently and offers a middle course between the extremes of inflexible retention and complete relaxation of the form." He especially emphasized the ecumenical necessity of reform. The bishops on that day voted to send the whole question to the pope and a commission.

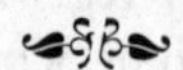

In the heated discussion about the injustices meted out to non-Catholic Christians in mixed marriage, the injustices meted out to Jews in Catholic-Jewish mixed marriage were virtually ignored. Even in the coffee bars there was no suggestion that any effort be made to eliminate the anti-Semitism of present rules. Perhaps the Fathers reasoned that they had had enough Jewish headaches in the discussion of the declaration on the Jews. In any case, they had more to be ashamed of in Church rules about Jewish-Catholic marriages than in the rules about mixed marriages with baptized Christians. For every archaic and discriminatory feature in marriages with non-Catholic Christians there is an extra discriminatory feature prescribed by canon law for mixed marriages with Jews.

Marriage with a non-Catholic Christian is rated by canon law as bad; with a Jew worse.[13] The caste line is clearly drawn by describing mixed marriages with Christians as acts forbidden by the impediment of mixed religion, while the same kind of marriages with Jews are forbidden by the impediment of the disparity of cult. This latter impediment is so serious that it involves two extra disabilities; a marriage to a Jew without special dispensation is not only forbidden but it is also absolutely invalid; and any dispensation by a bishop for a Catholic-Jewish marriage must be sanctioned by Rome, either directly by the Vatican or by a representative of the pope. Marriage by a rabbi which involves a Catholic is, of course, no marriage. There is even less reciprocity here than there is in Catholic-Protestant marriage relations. The extra narrowmindedness, however, flows naturally from the basic bigotry of the general rule. All mixed marriages to any non-Catholics are absolutely forbidden under Canon 1060 unless the appropriate bishop grants an exception to the prohibitory rule after he is satisfied that there is no "danger of perversion for the Catholic party." If there is such danger, "the marriage is forbidden also by the divine law itself." The "danger" to the faith of the non-Catholic party is disposed of by a requirement that the Catholic bride or groom in a mixed marriage must do everything possible to bring salvation to that party through conversion to the Catholic faith.

A special flank attack on the narrow mixed marriage rules of the Church came with considerable force from Eastern-rite sources during the Council. A Coptic bishop from Egypt, speaking in the aula, made a deep impression when he pointed out the fearful nonecumenical effect of these rules in his own territory and throughout the Middle East, where Greek Orthodox and Eastern-rite Catholics live side by side and are intermarried.

Until 1949 the Roman Catholic Church had recognized the validity of mixed marriages involving Orthodox and Catholic parties when the marriages were performed by Orthodox priests. Then, in direct opposition to ecumenical tendencies, the Church issued a decree, promulgated in 1949, which provides that in the future all marriages of Catholics, even Eastern-rite Catholics, by Orthodox priests should be considered as no-marriages. Grotesque tales circulated in the Council's coffee bars about mixed marriages in which bewildered couples were married twice in one room by two priests of Catholic and Orthodox persuasion. The Coptic Egyptian Bishop who protested against the new and more narrow rules regarding such mixed marriages, Isaac Ghattas, pointed out that: "This new legislation has, in fact, not only increased the obstacles to union and enlarged the gap of separation [between Orthodox and Eastern-rite Catholics] but has also turned quite a few Catholics away from the Church and led some to apostasy."[14] Bishop Jean Nuer of Egypt declared: "It hardly makes sense, for instance, when two brothers of the same family, one a Catholic and one an Orthodox, are being married on the same day, to have the Orthodox priest performing one ceremony with his back turned to the Catholic priest, or to have the Catholic priest do the same with his back turned to the Orthodox."[15]

When the decree on Eastern-rite Churches was drawn up and promulgated in the third session, it recognized the necessity for changing the narrow and restrictive 1949 rules on mixed marriages with the Orthodox. The decree provided that a marriage of an Eastern-rite Catholic by an Orthodox Christian could be considered "valid," though not "licit," when performed in the presence of "a sacred minister." This confusing verbiage was tantamount to saying: Don't be married by an Orthodox priest because it is morally wrong, but if you insist you will still be legally married.

Pope Paul, weaving back and forth like an ecclesiastical shuttle train, finally came forth in March 1966, three months after the end of the Council, with his special document on mixed marriage, *Matrimonii Sacramentum*, in which he embodied many of the worst features of the rumored documents on the subject that had been discussed in the coffee bars at the Council.[16] The one concession having substantial meaning in the document was that: "The excommunication provided by canon law for those who celebrate marriage before a non-Catholic minister is abrogated. The effects of this abrogation are retroactive." But marriage by a Protestant minister was still branded as a dreadful sin, and the document declared that "There must be avoided absolutely any kind of celebration in the presence of a Catholic priest and a non-Catholic minister, performing simultaneously their respective rites." A non-Catholic minister at most is permitted to stand around during a mixed marriage ceremony, and address some words of "congratulation and exhortation, and prayers" to the assembled guests at a wedding, "with the approval of the [Catholic] bishop."

The text of the new mixed marriage pronouncement was so confusing that some priests publicly protested against its ambiguities. In general it condemned all mixed marriages and said that the Church "strives with the greatest concern and vigilance to ensure that Catholics marry Catholics." It preserved intact the insulting discrimination in mixed marriage against all Jews, saying that pastors should warn their young people "solemnly about the difficulties and dangers inherent in contracting marriage with a non-Catholic Christian and even more with a non-Christian." It reiterated the rules of Canons 1060–1064 forbidding mixed marriage with other Christians but allowing such marriages to be considered valid when consummated, whereas marriage contracted with a Jew without all the special dispensations was still branded absolutely invalid under Canons 1070–1071.

On the all-important question of the pledges now extracted by priests from mixed marriage partners to raise all their children as Catholics, the new rule is confusing in its phraseology but substantially as severe as it was before the Council began. The promise of the Catholic party to raise the children as Catholics must be explicit, since such Catholic upbringing is a "necessity." The non-Catholic party must also make a promise, but it is not quite so formal and it need not be in writing. This non-Catholic party, after being informed of the Catholic party's obligation, "should be asked to promise sincerely and openly not to place any obstacles in its way." The present promises by the non-Catholic party are usually required in writing after a period of compulsory indoctrination in Catholicism; both of these requirements are now made optional. The Catholic bishop is permitted to decide how the commitment to Catholic education for the children "is to be included in the documents of the marriage."

Although Catholics married by Protestant ministers will not be automatically excommunicated in the future, as they were formerly under Canon 2319, "as such marriages are still regarded as invalid, the couples concerned would be regarded as living in sin and Catholics involved would still be barred from the sacraments." The document seemed to reach a climax in hypocrisy when it declared that one of the reasons for the new regulations was to ensure that "mutual relations between Catholics and non-Catholics may be marked by a greater sense of charity." In actual practice it is probable that the only visible variation in mixed marriage procedure in the future will be the celebration of some mixed marriages "with sacred rites and with the usual blessings and a sermon."

From the Protestant point of view, the new reformed practices seem almost as objectionable as the old—although, when the pope's new statement was made in March 1966, a few American Protestants rushed into print with milquetoast hosannas over the "welcome development." For most Protestants the changes in mixed marriage rules seem merely nominal so long as the one-sided pledges to raise all children as Catholics are preserved. The shifting of the style of the pledge for the non-Catholic party from a written to an oral promise will reduce the humiliation but it will not eliminate it. In fact, the very indefinite character of a pledge taken in writing by the Catholic party, and then supposedly imposed in oral form by persuasion on the non-Catholic party, may only increase the likelihood of tension in a mixed-marriage family. Most Protestants consider that there is a triple indignity in these pledges because (1) they are imposed at a moment of high emotion when a non-Catholic bride or groom is rendered somewhat defenseless by young love; (2) if strictly interpreted they commit all future children not only to Catholic religious training at home but also to education in parochial schools; and (3) any challenge to the doctrinal correctness or validity of the arrangement must go on appeal to the most bigoted of all the Church's agencies, the Congregation of the Doctrine of the Faith.

It should be remembered that Protestant churches have recognized the validity of the marriage of their people by Catholic priests for centuries. A slight and long-delayed move toward reciprocity in this area is welcome to Protestants but relatively meaningless unless the Catholic Church is prepared to accord complete and genuine reciprocity.

After Pope Paul's minor modifications in the existing rules, *The Christian Century* reflected American Protestant sentiment by saying that "these laws deal unjustly with the sacred rights of men and women by playing against each other two of the most elementary and powerful human drives: romantic sexual love and religious devotion. For the non-Catholic contemplating marriage to a Catholic the church's laws compel the betraying of one or the other of these drives—his love or his religion. . . . To us it does not appear possible for the Declaration on Religious Liberty and the mixed marriage laws to exist in the same church without colliding."[17]

The strength of the Protestant feeling on this subject was manifested in March 1966 when the Archbishop of Canterbury,

Arthur Michael Ramsey, was making his formal visit to Pope Paul in Rome as a representative of the Anglican Church. Although Dr. Ramsey is a genial concessionist in most matters relating to Roman Catholic policy, he decided to speak out on the unsatisfactory character of the mixed marriage ruling by Pope Paul, which had just been made public. In making this public protest he represented unofficially the whole Protestant, Orthodox and Jewish world, which had for too long endured with too much patience a system of denominational discrimination quite contrary to the principles of brotherly love espoused by Pope John. He had a particular interest in Catholic policy on this subject because in Britain one in three Catholics marries a non-Catholic. (In the United States the proportion is probably higher still.)[18]

"What God hath joined together, let no man put asunder," quoted Cardinal Journet of Switzerland in an eloquent Council speech against divorce on September 30, 1965. "The teaching of the Church on the indissolubility of marriage," he said, "is the doctrine of Christ himself as revealed to us in the gospel. . . . The Church has no right to change what is of divine law."

Most of the bishops in their long green rows probably nodded assent because they had been taught this thesis all their lives. Perhaps some of them did not even know that (1) there is good authority for the claim that Jesus did *not* teach the indissolubility of all marriages, and (2) the Church itself permitted divorce for many centuries. Moreover, the Church, while officially denying the right of divorce, permits a system of annulments for causes that would be considered much too flimsy for serious consideration by any civil divorce court in the world.

The occasion of Cardinal Journet's passionate defense of Orthodox teaching was an unusual speech in the Council the day before in favor of the right of remarriage after a marriage failure by an Eastern-rite archbishop from Egypt, Elie Zoghbi, a Patriarchal Vicar of the Melchites.[19] Journet's speech was essentially a reply to Archbishop Zoghbi and also a rebuke. Zoghbi's speech was the only one in the entire four sessions which could be construed as an appeal in favor of the right of remarriage after divorce. His speech came with special force because it dramatized the long conflict over sex and marriage between the Latin Church and the Catholic Churches of the Eastern rite. The Eastern-rite Churches believe in women and their priests marry them. Also many of the Eastern-rite Roman Catholics live surrounded by Greek Orthodox Christians who employ married priests and permit divorce under certain circumstances. Hence, when Zoghbi talked about divorce, annulment, and remarriage, and the unrealistic rules governing them in the Western Church, he was opening an old wound.

However, he did not dare to use the word "divorce." He asked for some kind of relief for certain Christians in distress. He dramatized their distress very effectively, calling it a problem "more agonizing than that of birth control."

> It is the problem of the innocent spouse who at the height of his powers and without any fault on his part, finds himself definitely alone through the fault of the other. The innocent party when he goes to his priest receives only one dogmatic answer: "I can do nothing for you." He is directed to keep continent for the rest of his life. This rule presupposes a heroic virtue, a rare faith and an uncommon temperament. This is an impossible solution for most men. . . . It does not seem normal that perpetual continence which calls for a state of perfection can be imposed forcefully like a punishment on an innocent spouse because his own spouse has deceived him.

"Does the Church have a right," asked Archbishop Zoghbi, "no matter what the nature of the problem, to speak in this way to a tormented innocent member of the faithful?" He pointed out that young people who are denied the right of divorce and remarriage often end by contracting an illegitimate union outside the Church.

Zoghbi's speech made such a sensation that he almost apologized for it in a later appearance, obviously acting under pressure.

He explained that he had never actually used the word "divorce," nor attacked the indissolubility of marriage as such. But he stood by his major suggestion for some easing of strict rules.

The two-speech debate between Archbishop Zoghbi and Cardinal Journet opened up briefly the whole troubled question of the Church's ancient prescriptions for marriages that fail. Probably no part of the Church's marital code is more deeply encrusted with hypocrisy. In general, the Church's only "remedy" for a marriage that has failed is separation without divorce, preventing both parties from finding a renewal and happiness in a new marriage—unless some ecclesiastical technicality can be discovered which "annuls" the existing marriage.

At present the Church is very active in maintaining this policy throughout the world and in attempting to block all legislation which liberalizes divorce. In those nations where it has the power to do so it prohibits divorce through concordats with civil powers. During the fourth session of the Council Luis Cardinal Concha of Colombia led the fight in his country against a new divorce law by making a public pronouncement that divorce was forbidden by the Vatican-Colombia Concordat and that: "The state cannot establish divorce without transgressing the natural law."[20] In Italy at the moment when the Zoghbi-Journet discussion took place the no-divorce situation had become a national scandal. At present only a few rich and fortunate Italians can ever secure release from holy deadlock. A strong new movement had begun in Italy during the Council years to legalize a system of "little divorce," that is, divorce on a few highly restricted grounds.

Italy has millions of extra-legal unions plus a prodigious amount of prostitution. It is estimated that the nation, with 100,000 to 200,000 prostitutes, now has the second highest venereal disease rate in the world.[21] During the fourth session of the Council, in September 1965, the Christian Democrats and the Italian government were embarrassed when a woman Socialist Deputy, Loris Fortuna, introduced a bill to allow limited divorce. It was the tenth bill aiming to permit divorce submitted to the deputies since 1878. Since Signora Fortuna belonged to a party in the government coalition, there was much speculation whether the Christian Democrats, who owe their very existence to Church support, would dare to go along with her suggestion for divorce reform. Probably the majority of the Italian people want reform, but the Church blocks it. Whatever the immediate legislative outcome, there is little chance of an effective divorce law in Italy because the 1929 concordat between the Vatican and Mussolini prevents it.

By a strange coincidence, during that same month of September 1965, the second most scandalous divorce situation in the modern world was also being revealed, this time in a public hearing in Albany, New York. In both cases the primary responsibility for delay in the passage of intelligent laws has been that of the Catholic Church. New York State, laboring under the anomaly of a divorce statute passed 179 years ago, which permits divorce for adultery only, has been fighting for at least 30 years to liberalize its divorce regulations. As *The New York Times* said only a week after the Zoghbi speech in Rome: "Evidence of adultery is flagrantly fabricated, making bar and bench the knowing partners in shameful collusion. Justice becomes a mockery. Those who can flee the jurisdiction migrate briefly to Mexico or Nevada for a quickie divorce. So a double standard of law is established; the well-to-do can afford to evade New York's bad law, while the less affluent cannot."[22]

Fortunately, virtually every important religious, charitable, and civil liberties group in New York State, with the exception of the Catholic Church, committed itself to divorce reform. When, in February 1966, after the New York legislature had taken 1,700 pages of testimony on the divorce racket, the Church asked legislative leaders in Albany to postpone further action, the Church met determined opposition from many of its own people. A new group was formed calling itself the Committee of Catholic Citizens to Support Divorce Reform, including some of the most famous political and legal figures in the state. It declared that the "social consequences of our narrowly restrictive divorce statutes are far more damaging to the common good than any possible benefits that may result from it."[23] Senator Robert Kennedy joined the chorus against "archaic" divorce laws which "undermine the administration of justice."

Even when it became apparent that some divorce reform was inevitable, the forces under Cardinal Spellman attempted to persuade the New York legislature to adopt an inadequate and cumbersome bill that would have made divorce and remarriage almost as difficult as before. They failed in this attempt but persisted in their efforts.

In April 1966, the Catholic bishops of New York State, headed by Cardinal Spellman, issued a public denunciation of divorce reform on the day before a mild reform bill was scheduled for a vote in Albany, misrepresenting a provision in the proposed bill as "divorce by mutual consent" when the provision actually permitted divorce only after a couple had entered into a separation agreement and then lived apart for two years.

In spite of this last-minute drive against reform, a bill was finally adopted almost unanimously which makes it possible to secure divorce in New York for cruel and inhuman treatment, abandonment for two years, imprisonment for three consecutive years, sodomy, and homosexuality, as well as adultery. Although the new law is a great improvement over the adultery-only statute that had created New York's divorce racket, it still contains so many requirements for unnecessary delay that it can be considered a partial victory for celibate Catholic power.

At the Council, Archbishop Zoghbi managed to bring in several important biblical and historical points in defense of his demand for a more liberal attitude toward separation and remarriage. He cited Matthew 5:32 and 19:9 to show that Jesus in at least two Bible passages sanctioned "putting away" one's spouse for adultery. He reminded his hearers that the Eastern Church during ten centuries of union with the West had permitted divorce for adultery, and he remarked modestly: "The Eastern Church has not been any less moral than the Western Church." But Zoghbi's valiant effort to nibble away at the edges of the Church's arbitrary no-divorce rule produced no appreciable results. The final section on marriage in The Church in the Modern World denounced "the plague of divorce," and described the covenant of marriage as rooted in "irrevocable consent" without any attempt to face the realities of ill-adjusted marriage.

Archbishop Zoghbi's most telling point was his brief attack on another phase of Catholic policy, the Church's annulment racket, often resorted to by wealthy Catholics as a substitute for divorce. Under the annulment system a marriage may continue in ostensible existence for many years, with children and outward acceptance of the family by the community, when suddenly the marriage is declared by the priests never to have existed at all because of the discovery of some purely technical "defect of form." The Western priests, according to Archbishop Zoghbi, try "through subtle casuistry, which occasionally performs acrobatics, to find all obstacles possible that can vitiate a marriage contract. After ten or twenty years, an impediment is discovered in the marriage hitherto unsuspected, which permits all to be dissolved as if by magic. The jurists find this natural and normal. We must realize, we pastors, that our faithful are occasionally stupified and scandalized."

The leaders of the Church are not proud of what Archbishop Zoghbi described as the "acrobatics" of the annulment system. They are aware that there is widespread belief even among the Catholic faithful that annulments can be bought for cash. Strictly speaking, this is not true, although in some cases money may be a factor in covering the very high cost of taking an annulment appeal to the Rota in Rome. When Princess Lee Radziwill, sister of Jacqueline Kennedy, received two judgments of nullity during the first session of the Council in 1962 in Rome, her lawyer, Fernando Della Rocca said: "It took four years, several hundred pages written in Latin and many witnesses before the matter was concluded . . . canonical legislation regarding matrimonial cases was applied with unimpeachable justice after an inquiry so strict that it made one think of a mathematical table."

In this case it was necessary for Princess Radziwill to receive two judgments of nullity allowing her to consider herself safely married to her present husband, Prince Stanislaus Radziwill, a member of the minor Polish nobility who had been twice previously married and once previously divorced.[24] The Prince's second marriage did not count as marriage since it was a civil one. Princess Radziwill herself had been previously married to a non-Catholic in a Catholic ceremony in Washington, D.C. The feat to be accomplished in this case was to wipe out three past marriages, two of Prince Radziwill's and one of Princess Radziwill's, without admitting that the Church ever departs from the doctrine of the indissolubility of marriage. The Prince's marriages were relatively easy to erase; the problem of the Princess' raised more difficulties. In this case the key fact was that Michael Canfield, a non-Catholic, had married the former Caroline Lee Bouvier without any intention of having children. But he had one child by her! According to a learned priest who writes the question and answer column for *The Register* on such matters, this made no difference at all. "Consent," he said, "is necessary for the validity of the marriage contract, as of any contract, and the consent must touch its essence, which is primarily the procreation of children. If the right to procreate children is excluded, there is no consent, hence no marriage."[25]

When the Church's whole pattern of no-divorce plus contrived annulments is considered in perspective, it is not surprising that the bishops at the Council did not wish to debate it in the aula. Only two speeches on the subject by Archbishop Zoghbi and Cardinal Journet took place during all four sessions. Then the situation returned to the status quo. It was Montaigne who said once: "Laws remain in credit not because they are just but because they are laws."

CHAPTER TWELVE ❧ BIRTH CONTROL AND SO FORTH

THE anticlimax of Vatican II came not in the basilica of St. Peter's but in the great hall of the United Nations on October 4, 1965, when Pope Paul was addressing the delegates. Millions throughout the world were watching and listening as national television and Early Bird, 22,500 miles above the earth, carried the image of the Roman Pontiff to both hemispheres.

The Pope spoke eloquently and effectively of the necessity of peace through world organization "convinced as We are that this Organization represents the obligatory path of modern civilization and world peace." Then, when he was talking about the "sacred character" of life he added: "Respect for life, even with regard to the great problem of birth, must find here in your Assembly its highest affirmation and its most reasoned defense. You must strive to multiply bread so that it suffices for the tables of mankind, and not rather favor an artificial control of birth, which would be irrational, in order to diminish the number of guests at the banquet of life."[1]

Millions of his listeners had been told that the problem of birth control had been sent by the Pope at the Council to a special commission of experts for recommendations. Catholics had been warned not to express opposition to standard Catholic doctrine until the commission and the Pope had spoken, yet here was the Pope refusing to wait for the report of his own commission, prejudging the results with a flat rejection of contraception as "irrational." *The New York Times,* which had been very gracious to the Council and the Pope, announced: "In only one important particular do we dissent from the Pope's remarks. His allusion to birth control as 'irrational' seems to us an unnecessarily narrow, old-fashioned interpretation of natural law doctrine on this issue at a time when the world's people, including many of his fellow Catholics, had been looking to him to provide a new, more constructive lead on the population question."[2]

There was wide speculation in Rome concerning the motive behind the Pope's birth control paragraph. Apparently inserted at the last minute, even high insiders were caught by surprise. During the period just before his trip to New York the Pope had violated all papal traditions by giving a personal interview to a journalist of Milan's *Corriere della Sera*, Alberto Cavallari, in which he had said, with characteristic indecision, of birth control: "The world asks what do we think of it and we find ourselves having to answer. But answer what?" However, this indecision was soon overcome and he committed himself to a negative and traditional view in a way that most observers considered irreversible.

On the day when he returned to St. Peter's, walking up the center aisle at noon with a still-spry step after his 30-hour trip to New York and back, Pope Paul was received with a kind of embarrassed adulation. His personal triumph as agent of the Church was immensely impressive. Since he was the Pope, no one at the Council in that moment of triumph ventured to question publicly his astonishing judgment on birth control, made before an assembly that was largely hostile to the Catholic concept on the subject. If the bishops questioned his good faith in going over their heads on an issue which he had withdrawn from Council discussion, they did not say so. He had exercised his divine primacy once again and they submitted.

Was Pope Paul operating on the principle of diversionary noise, hoping that his reactionary statement on birth control would be buried in such a mass of favorable publicity about his peace concepts that it would be virtually ignored? Some commentators reasoned that he was practising shrewd political balance by putting in one speech a traditional denunciation of birth control to offset his rather surprising advocacy of an open United Nations that might include Red China.

It would be difficult to imagine a worse faux pas than the Pope's figure of speech about "the banquet of life." One could almost hear the hungry millions of the world jeering in derision: Whose banquet? At the moment when the Pope used that phrase, the United Nations was telling the public that over half of the earth's population was suffering from malnutrition, and that hungry mouths were multiplying so rapidly—an increase of 50 to 60 million people per year—that there would be six to seven billion people on the globe by the end of the century, about twice the world's present population.

In fact, just four days before the Pope's New York speech the United Nation's special agency, the Food and Agriculture Organization (F.A.O.), with headquarters in Rome, had made public a report on food and the world's hunger that completely undermined the Pope's optimism. In Asia and the Far East, where the population explosion is most ominous, the per capita food production is about 8 per cent lower than it was twenty years ago.[3] With the present lag in food production in undeveloped countries, it is only a matter of time until the increase of population, caused primarily by death control, condemns to starvation the surplus millions still to be born. The death-squeeze between rising population and the relatively declining food supply is bound to come some time. Experts differ only on the timing. It took man 100,000 years to reach the level of a world population of one billion in the nineteenth century. It will take him far less time to reach a level of world starvation unless, as Sir Julian Huxley has put it, he develops "either birth control or death de-control." As General William Draper said in a 1966 analysis:

> I would sum up the world problem as follows: Every year the 1 billion in the industrialized countries are increasing their population 1 per cent and their food 2 per cent. Every year the 2 billion people in the developing countries are increasing

their population 2½ per cent and their food less than 1 per cent. As a whole, the world is increasing its population 2 per cent and its food 1 per cent. This means that the world is falling behind 1 per cent a year—or, to put it another way, food production is falling behind minimum needs by 30 million people more each year. This is why disaster for the human race lies just ahead.[4]

One very valuable conclusion about birth control doctrine came from the press conferences at the fourth session following Pope Paul's speech at the United Nations. It was admitted by many *periti*, both conservative and progressive, that there is no clear biblical authority for the Catholic doctrine against birth control. The doctrine may come from natural law; it may come by inference from various patristic and medieval writings; but it cannot any longer claim direct support in the Bible.

This in itself was a substantial triumph for modern scholarship. Standard Catholic works of instruction and standard Catholic journals have long been contending that "the Bible condemns birth control." One American Catholic journal, the right-wing Brooklyn *Tablet*, claimed for a time that birth control was "forbidden" by the sixth commandment, "Thou shalt not commit adultery."

Pope Pius XI in his 1930 encyclical on *Casti Connubii*, had cited the story of Onan spilling his seed on the ground, from the 38th chapter of Genesis, as biblical authority for the conclusion that "any use whatsoever of matrimony exercised in such a way that the [sexual] act is deliberately frustrated in its natural power to generate life is an offense against the law of God and Nature, and those who indulge in such are branded with the guilt of grave sin." Pius XII had followed up this prohibition with an Allocution to Obstetrical Nurses in October 1951, quoting his predecessor with approval and declaring: "This precept is valid today as it was yesterday; and it will be the same tomorrow and always, because it does not imply a precept of human law, but it is an expression of a law that is natural and divine." One month before his death in

1958 Pius XII included the new birth control pill in his broad condemnation in an address to the Seventh International Congress of Hematology. The use of drugs to prevent ovulation, he declared, is "a matter of direct sterilization" and therefore unlawful.

The one loophole in Catholic policy both Piuses left open was the somewhat ambiguous permission to abstain from sexual intercourse during the time of ovulation, according to a specific plan. Out of this vague and permissive teaching there has been developed the inefficient and now generally discredited method of birth control known as the rhythm method under which abstinence must prevail during the fertile period of each menstrual cycle. Pius XI condemned even this method if used systematically, and Pius XII limited its use to those having "serious economic, medical or eugenic motives."

Pius XI, speaking from the safe harbor of bachelorhood, declared: "There is no possible circumstance in which husband and wife cannot, strengthened by the grace of God, fulfill faithfully their duties and preserve in wedlock their chastity unspotted." Although the rhythm method has been a miserable failure in the United States and abroad, particularly in India, Catholic family organizations still solemnly promote it. A Natural Family Planning Association was formed in Connecticut in 1965 "to promote family planning through periodic continence."

The famous story of Onan in Genesis is not primarily a story about contraception. The birth control incident involved carries no hygienic moral. In the classic words of the King James version:

> And Judah took a wife for his firstborn, whose name was Tamar.
>
> And Judah's firstborn, was wicked in the sight of the Lord; and the Lord slew him.
>
> And Judah said unto Onan, Go in unto thy brother's wife, and marry her, and raise up seed to thy brother.
>
> And Onan knew that the seed should not be his; and it came to pass, when he went in unto his brother's wife, that he spilled it on the ground, lest that he should give seed to his brother.

And the thing which he did displeased the Lord: wherefore he slew him also.[5]

Probably Onan was not killed for *coitus interruptus* per se but for defying his father and for violating the spirit of an old Levirate law of inheritance which, in order to keep land in a Jewish family, directed a man to take unto himself his brother's widow, not for pleasure but for the purpose of ensuring an heir of the deceased. Such an interpretation is now generally accepted by Jewish authorities. Dr. John B. Noonan, a Catholic scholar, in his recent exhaustive study, *Contraception*, concludes that the facts "support the view that contraception is not the act for which Onan was killed."

The misinterpretation of the story of Onan has been only one item in an unrealistic policy of family limitation promoted by the more conservative elements of the Catholic clergy. *Coitus interruptus* has been officially condemned in various documents since 1822, and the use of condoms, even the permissive acceptance of such devices by women, has been condemned since 1953. In standard Catholic sociology works today the ideal family is still, under most circumstances, considered to be the large family. The planned family is morally more questionable. During the first session of the Council the conservatives who publish the *American Ecclesiastical Review* at the Catholic University in Washington produced a series of articles on "The Regulation of Offspring" that even opposed any campaign for the adoption of the rhythm method. "Ideal family life," said the author, "must be that form which is the most perfect for parents and children, when all factors are considered. Undoubtedly this is the large family."[6]

This type of advocacy of large families was resorted to by Cardinal Ottaviani when the question of family limitation came to the floor in the third session. The bishops had begun a brief discussion of the section on family life in the schema on The Church in the Modern World. Cardinal Alfrink of Utrecht had pleaded for a broader view of marital relations, suggesting that there might be a more sensible rule than the old rule under which "complete or periodic abstinence is the only efficacious, moral and Christian solution possible." Ottaviani, wholly unconvinced, reminded the bishops that the Lord had said "increase and multiply," and he added that he was himself the tenth of twelve children in a family of humble birth. "My parents never doubted Divine Providence," he said, and he quoted Matthew 6:28 to the effect that the lilies of the field they toil not neither do they spin but the Lord takes care of them. That afternoon an expert at the American bishops' press panel pointed out that when God said increase and multiply it was in the Garden of Eden, where the population was two people to the square world.

It was on this day that the bishops voted to cut off further discussion on the floor concerning the marriage sections. But before they cut off discussion it was revealed that a considerable number of the leaders wanted to move in the direction of personal rather than priestly responsibility for decisions on family size. The draft section on family life in the form announced during the fourth session, declared: "It pertains to the individual couples, according to their conscience formed in keeping with the law of God to determine the number of their children." This statement did not approve contraception but it certainly opened the door in that direction.

Long before Pope Paul's address at the United Nations it had become apparent that he was an arch-conservative on the issue of birth control. His New York speech was only the climax of a long series of warnings against "illicit" ideas that might disturb the Church's teaching on family life. In his first Christmas broadcast to the world as Pope, in December 1963, he sounded a warning in words quite similar to the words he chose at the United Nations in 1965. Acknowledging that "Hunger can become a subversive force with incalculable results," he still warned against "recourse to remedies that must be regarded as worse than the problem itself, if they consist in attacking the very fecundity of life by means that human and Christian ethics must condemn as illicit."

It was, therefore, very bad news for Catholic progressives when, in the third session, Pope Paul calmly took the problem of birth control, along with some other marriage problems, out of the hands of the Council and put it into the hands of a Commission appointed by himself. In announcing in June 1964 the proposed study of the birth control problem, Paul sounded a special warning against those Catholics in all parts of the world who were pressing for immediate reform of the Church's present policy. "We say frankly," he concluded, "that up to now we do not have sufficient motive to consider out of date, and therefore not binding, the norms given by Pope Pius XII in this regard. Therefore they must be considered valid, at least until we feel obliged in conscience to change them."

The unhappiness of the progressives was increased by the secrecy surrounding the personnel and the operations of the new commission. No one knew precisely who belonged to the group, although speculative lists appeared in Catholic papers in Europe and the United States. The first meeting of the commission was held at the Vatican in July 1964 in such complete secrecy that the very fact of the meeting was unknown for several months. The best information, leaked tangentially to the public through various sources, seemed to be that the commission started out with approximately 20 members and was finally increased to 57 or 60 members, including 8 Americans and a few married women in addition to bishops, priests, and other lay individuals. It was reported that the commission was about evenly divided between those who wanted to recognize some moral validity in the new birth control pill and those who wanted to adhere more or less strictly to the old law.

Real doubts arose in many quarters as to whether the commission was actually making a study of birth control or merely engaging in a doctrinal tussle. The composition of the commission, as unofficially given out, did not inspire confidence among the liberals. While there were a few advanced thinkers on the panel, such as Canon Louis Janssens of the Catholic University of Louvain, an advocate of the pill, there were also several theologians who were publicly committed to the most strict interpretation of traditional birth control rules. Absent from the lists was the name of the Catholic scientist who had made the most extensive studies in this field, Dr. John Rock of Harvard, author of *The Time Has Come.*

Liberals in the United States attempted with little success to influence the papal commission on birth control. A group of 37 American Catholic scholars, financed by the Ford Foundation, made at Notre Dame an extensive study of some aspects of the issue and sent the results of their study to the Vatican through two intermediaries. The American study gave cautious and qualified endorsement to contraception. Six months after the study had been sent in, John Cogley reported in *The New York Times* that it had never reached the papal commission.[7] Even after this exposure it was some time before a commission official finally deigned to admit that it had been received.

One reason why Curial officials wish to continue an ostrich policy on birth control is that the situation vis-à-vis birth control in Italy is as overburdened with hypocrisy as the situation vis-à-vis divorce. Anyone with money and a doctor's prescription can buy contraceptive supplies at any drug store within the shadow of the Vatican. The old fascist law on the subject simply forbids instruction in birth control. Early in 1966 seven members of the Italian parliament from four political parties tried to break the unholy deadlock on information by introducing a bill to legalize the dissemination of such information. Vatican forces immediately rallied against the bill.

While reform on birth control was moving very slowly in Rome, it was not moving slowly in the Netherlands, France, and the United States. The Netherlands' concern with the birth control issue is understandable because the nation has a higher population density than Japan or India, and opinion in favor of contraception has been growing rapidly among Dutch Catholics, who now constitute about 40 per cent of the national population. A

Dutch bishop, William Bekkers, described birth regulation as permissible in a radio broadcast in 1963, and in that same year a leading Dutch theologian, Louis Janssens, had defended the use of anovulants, seemingly with the support of most of the Dutch bishops.

In the United States the movement toward reform during the Council was particularly swift, partly because millions of American Catholics had begun to defy their priests on the subject. Politicians in Washington until the advent of Lyndon Johnson had been so fearful of Catholic reprisals at the polls that they had shied away from definitive support for birth control expenditures. Eisenhower in 1959 had said that, "as long as I am here," in the White House, the government will not use foreign-aid funds for birth control. His timidity on the subject seemed to be a direct result of a 1959 statement of the Catholic bishops that "United States Catholics will . . . not support any public assistance, either at home or abroad, to promote artificial birth prevention."

President Kennedy was more openminded on the subject. In an interview with me before he won the Democratic nomination for President in 1960, he declared that he, as a Catholic, respected the moral doctrine of his Church, but that as President of the United States he would do what seemed best for the American people in accordance with his oath of office, if a recommendation for government aid should come to his desk. True to his word, in December 1962 he authorized United States support for a United Nations proposal to provide birth control assistance to any needy country that requested it.

By 1964, American public opinion on birth control had changed so fundamentally that both President Johnson and former President Eisenhower publicly favored programs of tax support. Eisenhower and former President Truman agreed in 1964 to serve as co-chairmen of the honorary sponsors' council of the World Planned Parenthood movement. President Johnson included government aid for birth control in several of his federal aid programs. He publicly championed such aid no less than nine times in his first two years as President. Many Catholic journalists admitted mournfully that Catholic opinion on the whole subject had changed vitally. Columnist Paul Hallett said in the *Register:* "He [Johnson] would not have spoken so clearly if his advisors had not thought that Catholic dissension on this point presaged a change in Catholic teaching and therefore the collapse of Catholic opposition."[8]

In New York State, Governor Rockefeller, after long hesitation, finally signed in June 1965 a bill repealing his state's 84-year-old statute against birth control. The Supreme Court in that same month capped the movement for reform with a welcome, if somewhat questionable, decision declaring Connecticut's anti-birth control statute unconstitutional on the novel ground that it invaded the right of privacy.[9] Up to that moment Connecticut and Massachusetts had been the only states in the union where the enforcement of old birth control statutes made the operation of clinics definitely illegal. Cardinal Cushing expressed the new feeling of liberal Catholics about the Massachusetts anti-birth control statute by saying that: "Catholics do not need the support of civil law to be faithful to their religious convictions, and they do not seek to impose by law their moral views on other members of society."

Throughout 1964 and 1965 the movement in the United States toward the acceptance of birth control became almost a landslide. The *Wall Street Journal* announced in February 1965 that an estimated 680 public birth control clinics were being operated in 21 states in the United States, a 23 per cent jump in one year.[10] In 1964 and 1965 13 states modified their birth control procedure in the direction of acceptance. Many federal departments began to cooperate in the new reforms.

In Washington, Senator Ernest Gruening of Alaska engineered and chaired, in 1965 and 1966, a series of congressional hearings through his Senate Subcommittee on Foreign Aid, giving to the public vital information concerning the need for birth control throughout the world. Experts at these hearings dramatized the world need, and their carefully documented facts bolstered the demand for a bill sponsored by the Senator that would make it possible for the United States to disseminate birth control information more widely. When the Gruening hearings resumed in January 1966, the Senator remarked that in the seven months since they had begun the world had increased in population by 35,000,000, an increase equivalent to the population of New York and California. Eminent witnesses appeared at the hearings who testified that in 650 years, if the present rate of population increase continued, there would be one person per square foot throughout the United States.[11]

In the new movement toward acceptance of birth control, American Protestantism and American Judaism were virtually unanimous in favoring change. Liberal Catholicism also played a very important role. Rosemary Ruether, a Catholic mother writing in the *Saturday Evening Post* in 1964 on "Why I Believe in Birth Control" said: "A woman who cannot control her own fertility, who must remain vulnerable to chance conception, is a woman who cannot hope to be much more than a baby-machine. . . . The family cannot be appraised in numbers. It is, above all, a qualitative unity."[12]

Commonweal, whose lay Catholic editors had served as pioneer champions of birth control reform for a long time, came out in 1964 with a special issue on "Responsible Parenthood," written entirely by Catholics.[13] The most moving contribution came from a Massachusetts priest, Monsignor George W. Casey of Lexington, who had been compelled to face the realities of Catholic policy among his own people. He wrote:

> In practise, if not in theory, there is often a conflict between the law and people which moves us in the pastoral ministry to pray for a way out. I will say for myself that I first began to modify my adjectives in my sermons against birth control when, without bitterness or patent self-pity, a man told me that his wife had borne him nine tiny monstrosities in a row, who lived but a few weeks each. More of the fire went out when I handled the case of a poor hapless sort of mother who bore her fifth set of twins in as many years.[14]

In spite of the mounting evidence that the American Catholic people had already changed their minds about birth control, the

American hierarchy stuck to its traditional position through the four sessions of the Council. Its leaders in Rome, with the exception of Cardinal Cushing, left to Dutch, French, and Belgian bishops the task of fighting for a change in the rules. When President Johnson in his 1965 State of the Union Message declared: "I will seek new ways to use our knowledge to help deal with the explosion in our world population and the growing scarcity in world resources," the National Catholic Welfare Conference struck back through Monsignor John C. Knott, director of its Family Life Bureau. "Despite popular opinion to the contrary," he said, "the attitude of the Catholic Church toward contraception is still one of condemnation as a moral evil. It has not changed." Later he accused the Federal Government of supporting a "contraceptive, anti-life program." In championing the rhythm method, Monsignor Knott declared that it "can be not only effective for birth regulation, but more positively it can deepen the love between husband and wife and between them and God." He argued that "Evidence from all parts of the world indicates that it [the rhythm method] is an effective system. Reports from France, England, Canada, Mauritius and Latin America, as well as the United States, show that it does work and with all classes of people."[15]

During the very month when Monsignor Knott made this fantastic claim, Senator Gruening called before his Senate subcommittee a devout Catholic college professor and his wife who described in great detail their own sad experience with the rhythm method. Married in 1949, Professor and Mrs. Andre Bethune testified that, in spite of careful attempts to follow the calendar variation and the B.B.T. (basal body temperature) techniques, they had a "population explosion at home," nine children. "It is clear from the record . . . that rhythm . . . is completely impracticable for my wife and for me," said Professor Bethune. "The advice that we use the rhythm method to regulate the further growth of our family must be considered either a bad joke or a display of invincible ignorance."[16]

Apparently the American hierarchy, at least until the pope

has changed signals, is completely committed to the continuing "display of invincible ignorance." The American bishops reiterated their standard objections to birth control in August 1965 before Senator Gruening's hearings. The Church did not even modify its policy in India where 33 million live and die on the streets. In a long interview I had in Rome in 1963 with Cardinal Gracias, India's only cardinal, he told me emphatically and proudly that he and his associates would continue to fight the Indian government's birth control program with every weapon at their command.

❧

When the final sections on marriage were promulgated in the Constitution on The Church in the Modern World, the wording used in discussing birth control and all other family problems was cautious and conservative. Graciously the bishops conceded that: "Marriage, to be sure is not instituted solely for procreation." The value of "mutual love" was recognized. Education for marriage was championed. It was acknowledged that Catholic couples "sometimes find themselves in certain circumstances where at least temporarily the size of their family should not be increased." But all Catholics were warned against "dishonorable solutions," and told that they "may not undertake methods of birth control which are found blameworthy by the teaching authority of the Church."

Although one paragraph conceded that: "The parents themselves and no one else should ultimately make this judgment [about family size] in the sight of God," the context made it clear that there was no parental freedom of choice as non-Catholics understand the concept of freedom. The very section allegedly conferring freedom of choice on parents burst out in an eloquent tribute to the large Catholic family. It said:

> Thus, trusting in divine Providence and refining the spirit of sacrifice, married Christians glorify the Creator and strive toward fulfillment in Christ when, with a generous human and Christian sense of responsibility, they acquit themselves

of the duty to procreate. Among the couples who fulfill their God-given task in this way, those merit special mention who with a gallant heart, and with wise and common deliberation, undertake to bring up suitably a relatively large family.

Apparently even this text did not quite satisfy Pope Paul. His activities during the last weeks of the Council indicated that he wanted his birth control advisors to come down heavily on the traditional side of the birth control controversy. In appointing a commission to consider the problem of birth control he had conveyed the impression to the world that he was giving the members freedom to make recommendations they thought right. When rumors reached the press that a substantial number of the commission members wanted to condone the new birth control pill, Pope Paul apparently became alarmed. This was six weeks after his attack on contraception at the United Nations, and a commission report favoring contraception at that moment might have embarrassed him greatly. In November 1965, he sent his commission two letters written in the name of the Vatican Secretary of State, Cardinal Cicognani, but obviously from the Pope himself. If accepted in the spirit in which they were written, they would have foreclosed the birth control argument in favor of the traditional Church doctrine. Robert C. Doty of *The New York Times*, securing copies, gave America the story. As Mr. Doty summarized the effect of Pope Paul's action, "papal insistence on restatement of the most stern forms of the present prohibtion—a 1930 encyclical of Pius XI and a 1951 address by Pius XII—produced a chill of apprehension among progressive commission members and experts."[17]

Writing in *Commonweal* later, Father Gregory Baum, a Council expert, was very frank on the subject.[18] He pointed out that the whole question of the means of limiting families had been hushed up in the Council because of the wishes of Pope Paul—"the subject was only alluded to," then sent to a commission. The commission in November 1965 apparently wanted to leave some faint possible opening for a later change of policy. Otherwise its deliberations would have seemed a waste of time. Since Paul's interventions would have foreclosed any real reform, the members of the commission resisted his suggestions enough to leave the final conclusion still open.

There the matter rested as the Council closed. The Pope, who has the ultimate and absolute power to say what the Catholic position is, has not officially closed all avenues of reform, but his many public pronouncements against contraception seem to indicate that any change in Church policy during his reign will be insubstantial. This impression was confirmed when the section on an international community in the schema on The Church in the Modern World was made public. The section warned that any decision concerning the number of children to be born "can in no way be committed to the decision of government." The Vatican warned the United Nations to cease promoting any solution to the population problem that was "contrary to the moral law."

Meanwhile, it is quite apparent that when the theological debate on birth control doctrine is carried on among the clergy, the reasoning developed has lost all contact with reality. The logic employed is as artificial as a male falsetto voice. The struggle has become a clerical power struggle in which the celibate clerical leaders are fighting for the old rule not primarily because of their concern with human suffering but because of their desire to maintain their position and the position of the Church. They reason, and there is some justification in this reasoning, that if the Catholic people once succeed in reversing such a long-standing rule of the Church as that against birth control, their authority over their people may break down.

It was obvious at the Council that Pope Paul wanted to sidetrack all annoying revolutionary discussion and confirm the Church's standing rule against contraception. But would he dare to do this in the face of a rising tide of protest from Catholic married couples in all parts of the world? Obviously he felt impelled by the pressure of governments and his own people to make a new gesture in the direction of a solution of the troublesome issue, for, in March 1966, he announced the addition of sixteen new prelates to a reorganized form of his birth control commission. And, above all things, he appointed to head that reorganized commission the most belligerent of the "increase and multiply" orators of Vatican II, Alfredo Cardinal Ottaviani! It was like appointing Mao Tse-tung to be general secretary of the United Nations.

True, Ottaviani was not officially empowered to dominate the new commission. It included Cardinals Suenens, Gracias (see p. 250), and Shehan as well as a sprinkling of archbishops and bishops from many countries. It was evident that the outward forms of a continuing investigation were to be preserved. It is just possible that the Pope's motive in choosing Ottaviani as his top birth control aide was to neutralize Ottaviani's power as an obstructionist. If so, the motive was as objectionable as the choice. It was not a suitable moment for Machiavellian politics.

Hope for a definitive change in Church policy dwindled when, in June 1966, it was reported that the papal commission on birth control had submitted pro and con views on the subject without commitment to reform, leaving the ultimate choice to the pope. Paul VI's whole record of timid traditionalism in this area did not encourage those liberal Catholics who had been hoping for a realistic policy.

There is, however, some slight hope that the Church, under pressure, in the light of the Council pronouncement in favor of parental responsibilty in Schema 13, will decide to break away from the traditional position. Graciously the Council Fathers acknowledged in the marriage section that there is love in family life apart from the breeding of children and that it is "singularly expressed and perfected by the proper work of marriage." The Fathers' blessing of love was equivocated a little by describing, without details, how "the spouses intimately and chastely unite." This could be described as progress. When a clerical celibate congress finally admits that sex is fun and that the fun is not necessarily with benefit of clergy, the present bizarre survival of the guilt complexes of St. Augustine, known as the law of God against contraception, will go the way of all flesh. As Monsignor John C. Knott, whose views on birth control have been cited previously, said early in 1966: "Admittedly it looks as though sex is here to stay."

Sexual realism in the area of birth control arrived even in Massachusetts in May 1966 when the Massachusetts legislature passed and the governor signed a bill lifting the ancient ban on birth control for Massachusetts married couples. Officially the Church did not change a syllable of its moral teaching on the question but, led by Cardinal Cushing, it faced the fact that Catholics could no longer force such moral teaching upon their non-Catholic fellow citizens.

An outsider could read the official findings and pronouncements of Vatican II without realizing that there is a considerable area of Catholic sexual medicine lying beyond birth control in which the Church is now involved in warm controversy. The words "abortion" and "sterilization," as well as "artificial insemination," did not even appear in the final draft of the marriage section of the Constitution on The Church in the Modern World, although the word "abortion" was included elsewhere in the schema —and condemned along with murder and genocide. These subjects were discussed briefly in press conferences and behind the scenes but there was a noticeable eagerness even among the American theologians and bishops to pass on to other themes without any public discussion of the merits of the Church's position. The Council's final statement on family life said: "For God, the Lord of life, has conferred on men the surpassing ministry of safeguarding life in a manner which is worthy of man. Therefore from the moment of its conception life must be guarded with the greatest care."

The assumption behind this pronouncement was that the soul in the womb actually begins at the moment of conception, although this view has not always been held by the Church. Evidently abortion was one of those subjects that Cardinal Agagianian, acting as moderator on October 28, 1964, warned against as "too delicate" for open discussion. There were "certain points," he said, on which discussion should be avoided because it might cause possible misinterpretation and misunderstanding outside the Council. Although Agagianian could not stop the cardinals when they chose to indulge thereafter in a short, sharp debate concerning some of the theological aspects of birth control, his warning apparently prevented any full-dress discussion of a whole range of delicate points in the area of sexual medicine, including abortion and sterilization. The final draft on The Church in the Modern World lumped abortion along with suicide, genocide, and slavery as evils that "poison human society."

The present Catholic rule against abortion is one of the most rigid and sweeping in canon law. "Those who procure abortion," says Canon 2350, "not excepting the mother, incur, if the effect is produced, an excommunication *latae sententiae* reserved to the Ordinary [bishop]; and if they be clerics they are moreover to be deposed." Catholic law makes no distinction between criminal abortion and that therapeutic abortion which is deemed necessary to save the life of a mother, a type of abortion which is legal in nearly all states and nations of the world. Both types are linked together in Catholic teaching as wholly inexcusable, even if the fetus is doomed to die anyway. In general, the Church throughout the world fights any relaxation in abortion laws for any reason whatever. Catholic doctors are forbidden to make any choice between the life of a mother and the life of an unborn infant if the saving of the mother's life is to be accomplished only by a direct abortion. On this subject the Council did nothing to change the rules laid down by Pius XI and Pius XII.

Medical science and increasing Catholic sensitivity on the subject have changed the consequences of this rule quite substantially since the pronouncements of the two Piuses. Because of improvements in medical procedures, particularly the perfection of Caesarian section, genuine therapeutic abortion to save the life of a mother has declined in recent years. Lawrence Lader has supplied detailed facts about this decline.[19] One reason for the decline is that the Church has become more liberal in its interpretation of its own rule in respect to what is called the "double effect." Any diseased condition in an expectant mother that may be indirectly relieved by removal of a living fetus may justify the removal on the ground that the chief purpose is not abortion but the cure of disease. Such operations are not described as abortions.

Today the most serious problem of abortion is not therapeutic abortion in the narrow sense but abortion to save a mother's health, to avoid the birth of a monstrosity caused by such diseases as German measles, to cancel the consequences of rape or incest, or to prevent the wrecking of a home by the acquisition of a brood too large to support. The last of these factors is the most important.

Mr. Lader estimates that 1,200,000 American women, regardless of the law, resort to abortion every year. A summary by Jack Star of *Look Magazine* has put the American total at 1,000,000.[20] Mr. Lader cites three studies revealing that at least 20 per cent of all abortion patients in the United States are Catholics, close to the Catholic proportion in the American population. Contrary to popular belief, the majority of American women who resort to abortion are not single girls who have been "caught" but married women, many of whom have several children already. American law is somewhat more severe than the law on this subject in many European countries. Abortions are virtually available on request in Japan, the Scandanavian countries, Mexico, and Puerto Rico. Brazil, which allegedly has the largest Catholic population of any nation in the world, has about 2,000,000 abortions a year.

The rather startling facts about the spread of abortion throughout the world were made public in many journals during the sessions of the Council. The operation, in skilled hands, has become safer and cheaper than in earlier years. If American women act in time and have money for proper treatment—perhaps $300—the relatively simple and quick dilatation and curettage performed by a skilled physician is not more dangerous than a tonsillectomy, and the patient can usually return to work in a few days.

The Catholic Church is the main force opposing modification of present laws on the subject. The Church opposes the outstanding legal and medical organizations in the United States on this subject, not on medical but on purely theological and theoretical grounds. Its answer is bound to evoke much opposition among younger Catholic intellectuals. The Jesuit magazine *America* admitted in 1966 that there is a growing consensus in the United States in favor of permitting abortion when a mother's health is endangered. A Gallup poll recently recorded 77 per cent of persons interviewed as favoring this modification in restrictive laws.

In 1961 and 1963 in California it was the Church, through its various agencies, which defeated in the state legislature an attempt to liberalize the law in order to permit abortion in cases of rape and incest, and also in situations where "continuance of the pregnancy involves substantial risk that the mother or child will suffer grave impairment of physical or mental health." This proposal would have reformed and widened the definition of legal therapeutic abortion.[21] A similar modification had been recommended for all states by the American Law Institute and had been backed by state medical societies all the way from California to New York. The American Medical Association was about to endorse the reform in December 1965 when Catholic opposition forced delay.

The real problem here is not so much the incorrectness of the Church's rigid position on all abortion as the fact that Catholic doctors, nurses, and parents are denied freedom to analyze the moral issues involved for themselves and reach an ethical solution in the light of modern science and human necessity. They are ordered to accept a blanket and doctrinaire formula produced by celibate theologians several centuries ago. Many good men believe that the formula is correct; many equally good men believe that the formula is incorrect. The Vatican Council dodged the discussion of the problem in St. Peter's because many of its leaders realized that the opening up of the whole area of Catholic sexual medicine would reveal an underworld of outworn superstitions masquerading as morality.

The Council also chose to avoid discussion of another auxiliary but important issue on the borders of the birth control problem, voluntary sterilization.[22] Millions of individuals from India to

Latin America to Puerto Rico are resorting to the relatively mild remedy of sterilization to prevent the arrival of future unwanted children. Voluntary sterilization is now legal in all fifty American states. Of course, sterilization would be wholly unnecessary if the world had perfect birth control. In the absence of that Utopia, millions of people in the poorest sections in the world are resorting to the more desperate remedy of sterilization. The male operation for sterilization, called vasectomy, the severance or interruption of the *vas deferens*, a small tube which conducts the sperm, is relatively simple and can be performed in a doctor's office. The female operation, ligation of the Fallopian tubes, is somewhat more complicated but it is not considered a major operation when performed shortly after childbirth.

Is sterilization always a sin? Should mothers who are already living in poverty with many children be permitted to choose this remedy? (In Puerto Rico the remedy is very commonly used after the third child.)

Catholic policy may be right or it may be wrong. The objection to the Catholic answer is that it is based on preconceived theories, not on present-day knowledge of family agonies or of the latest medical developments. The rigidity of Pius XII's answer still blocks every Catholic surgeon's liberty of action. "Human beings," said Pius XI, "are not free to destroy or mutilate their members." The Pope having spoken so flatly, Vatican II did not even bring the issue to the aula floor.

CHAPTER THIRTEEN ❧ THE MIRACULOUS UNDERWORLD

ONE day during the fourth session in November 1965, the journalists at Vatican II were somewhat startled to hear that Pope Paul had turned over to the various national conferences of bishops represented at the Council a new report on indulgences with a request for the advice of these bishops' conferences on this report. Indulgences had not been noted in any Council agenda up to that moment, and no doubt the majority of the bishops did not want the subject discussed openly. Probably, if asked in advance, they would have suggested that the subject be sidetracked for private discussion and action by a committee.

Under Canon 911 an indulgence is "the remission before God of the temporal punishment due for sins whose guilt has already been forgiven, granted by ecclesiastical authority from the treasury of the Church, by way of absolution for the living and by way of suffrage for the departed." In plain English, this means that an indulgence is a device a believer can use for reducing his own stay in purgatory, as well as the stay of his dead friends, by performing certain approved acts with a contrite heart. The reduction in a purgatorial sentence cannot be transferred from one living person to another living person, but since the thirteenth century it has been transferable to the dead.[1]

The system itself, begun in the ninth century, obtained final form in the eleventh century. Pope Urban II inaugurated its most coveted reward, the plenary indulgence, in 1095 in connection with the crusades. He declared: "Whoever out of pure devotion and not for the purpose of gain, honor or money, shall go to Jerusalem to liberate the Church of God, may count that journey in lieu of all penance." The "all penance" was not supposed to include penance for future sins.

A plenary indulgence wipes out the whole temporal punishment for past sins in purgatory; a partial indulgence remits only part of this temporal punishment—usually a few days or a few months or a few years. The remission does not apply to hell or heaven but only to the rather vague intermediate state known as "the state of purification," a state that is not located geographically in this space age. Ordinarily the "state of purification" means purgatory, although many modern Catholic theologians are very reluctant to use the word "purgatory" and to define its characteristics. They refuse to give it a locus or to say what its boundaries are.

The whole world-wide machinery of indulgences is handled by a Tribunal of the Roman Curia that goes under the unfortunate name of the Sacred Apostolic Penitentiary. In this case "penitentiary" refers not to a prison but to penance. In practice the Tribunal serves as a kind of ecclesiastical parole board for prisoners in purgatory, granting them earlier release from their limited suffering in this short-term spiritual prison. It is a parole board acting under the supreme power of the pope.

The reference of this ticklish subject to the bishops' conferences was a strictly papal action, quite irregular in itself. It brought to the Council floor one of the most embarrassing and troublesome phenomena of Catholic history, a feature of Church practice most Catholic intellectuals regard with some shame.

The progressives at the Council immediately realized that the mere discussion of indulgences, unless it led to complete renunciation of the whole system, would do immense harm to the ecumenical movement by reviving the memory of old bitterness and by emphasizing the gap between Catholic and Protestant practice. The selling of indulgences for cash had once been the most unpleasant scandal of the Reformation period. Why not let the skeleton stay in the closet, for the time being, at least, particularly since it was alleged that the report on indulgences proposed only minor and inadequate reforms?

Father Thomas Stransky, young progressive of the Secretariat for Promoting Christian Unity, immediately voiced the apprehensions of his fellow liberals by publicly condemning the introduction of the twenty-page report as "a potential scandal to our Church." "I cannot conceive of any Protestant being satisfied with this document," he said. Father Gregory Baum, one of the liberal theological experts at the Council, declared that: "For Protestants the system of indulgences implies everything that is wrong with the Catholic Church."[2] Later on he attacked the report as "wholly determined by the tradition of the manuals," and as presenting "the Church's treasury of merits in almost material terms, as a kind of heavenly bank."

§

There were many puzzling things about the surprise move of Pope Paul in opening the subject of indulgences without warning to the conferences of bishops at the Council. His friends and his foes asked whether the blunder in timing was purely accidental or deliberate. Admirers of the Pope read a democratic impulse into the action and argued that it was pleasing proof that he had taken collegiality seriously, a theory somewhat weakened by the fact that, under the terms of the assignment, bishops were not empowered to discuss indulgences on their merits in the Council. They were merely asked to take a secret vote and then announce the results in public as to whether the conferences believed that the report on indulgences was acceptable.

The report had been prepared under the supervision of Fernando Cardinal Cento, the eighty-two-year-old Grand Penetentiary, and a twelve-man commission composed largely of Vatican canon lawyers. The idea of making such a report had originally been Cardinal Cento's, and probably his motive in asking the Pope's approval was sagaciously protective, the initiation of a mild reform to head off a more systematic reform. Intellectually the whole indulgence system is so burdened with inconsistencies and superstitions that an honest exposé of its features would lead to its complete elimination.

The real explanation of Pope Paul's action in opening up the subject publicly at the wrong moment was probably quite simple. At that moment in Council proceedings the Pope and the top leaders of the Council were very busy, while the bishops were not. The regular Council sessions had been suspended for many days, and many of the bishops had nothing to do. One American bishop said of the indulgences report: "It was sent to us to keep us in our seats."

The Pope's action indicated how insensitive he was to the world-wide, anti-Catholic feeling among Protestants concerning certain Church practices that seemed to them superstitious or fraudulent. Without that feeling Luther's Reformation would never have been possible and today it includes the whole range of underworld ecclesiastical phenomena such as relics, apparitions, the naming of new saints, purgatory, doubtful miracles, and, last but not least, indulgences themselves.

All things considered, it is quite remarkable that a Vatican Council pledged to *aggiornamento* could have met for more than three years without confronting some of the quite obvious abuses in this miraculous underworld of faith and superstition. There had been a few light tangential jeers at some of these abuses during the Council sessions, but there had been nothing in the way of serious confrontation. In the second session, Archabbot Benedict Reetz of a German Benedictine congregation had castigated "theological acrobatics" in his Church and had listed the system of indulgences as an "unattractive element" that is "difficult to understand for separated brethren and at times also for us."[3] But the "theological acrobatics" of the miraculous underworld of Catholicism dropped from discussion at that point. The bishops in the Council were only too glad to have the whole area left in polite silence, and the Protestant observers were too cautious to press objections to phenomena that were considered so completely a matter of internal Church policy.

The Pope's action on indulgences shattered the silence and surprised the entire Catholic world. As Abbe Laurentin remarked in *Figaro* of Paris: "For many decades one didn't dare discuss indulgences. Now public and solemn discussion at the Council brings it to the world." And he added sadly: "If the Lateran Council had taken a stand against indulgences in 1512 the face of history could have been changed."[4]

At the present time there is no *direct* financial racketeering involved in the granting of indulgences, nor is advance forgiveness for future sins obtainable under any circumstances. It was these two abuses in the indulgence system that won popular support for Martin Luther's campaign against Rome in the sixteenth century. An indulgence, Luther said, "can have no efficacy for souls in purgatory; penalties imposed by the Church can only refer to the living," and: "The Christian who has true repentance has already received pardon from God altogether apart from an indulgence, and does not need one."

Shrewdly, Luther included some keen questioning about money matters that probably had more popular appeal than his theological arguments. Why, he asked, does not the Pope empty purgatory forthwith for charity's sake, instead of cautiously for money? Why does he not, since he is rich as Croesus, build St. Peter's with his own money instead of taking that of poor believers? Luther was followed by another critic who claimed that "The Pope bids his collectors go into the whole world saying: 'He that believeth, and payeth the tenths shall be saved.' "

Luther, of course, had made indulgences the primary target of the famous 95 theses he nailed to the door of the Castle Church at Wittenberg in 1517.[5] And he had added a fierce, muckraking attack on the contemporary graft associated with indulgences, particularly a corrupt system for farming out the right to collect money for indulgences that had developed in Germany. A Dominican Monk named Johann Tetzel, nominally backed by Pope Leo X, had gone through Europe raising money for the building of St. Peter's by hawking indulgences for cash. Too often the poor peasants who contributed to his campaign thought that their purchased indulgences included permission for future sinning.

The Church repudiated many of these abuses at the Council of Trent in the sixteenth century, but it still proclaimed the practice of indulgences as "a usage most beneficial to Christians," and anathematized all "those who say that indulgences are useless." Pius V in 1567 had cleaned house to some extent by revoking all indulgences bought with money. But the memory of old scandals persisted. For a long time the Church had commissioned friars as financial and spiritual agents to raise funds by accepting gifts for repentance. The Council of Mainz in 1261 had denounced some of these clerical financial agents as—to use the colorful words of Will Durant—"wicked liars, who displayed the stray bones of men or beasts as those of saints, trained themselves to weep on order, and offered purgatorial bargains for a maximum of coin and a minimum of prayer." At Vatican II these old scandals were intensely embarrassing to the progressives, particularly to the American progressives, since indulgences have long been regarded by Catholic intellectuals in the United States as somewhat questionable survivals of medieval practice. They cannot repudiate indulgences openly without papal approval since the indulgence system is embalmed in canon law and authenticated by many papal pronouncements, but they can, and do, ignore the whole sentimental underworld as much as possible.

Apart from its naive representation of the nature of immortality, the real scandal involved in indulgences is the crazy patchwork of grants and remissions that has grown up over the centuries and continued with only minor changes down to the present day. The system is confused and irrational partly because it grew without design out of the old system of penances—a more honest and sincere system—that existed in the Church during the first one thousand years of its history. In those days the Christian sinner had to undergo a long period of penitential remorse, the punishment being graded roughly according to his offenses. Sometimes this penitential period seemed in individual cases too harsh and too long. So, beginning with the eleventh century, a gentler and easier device for punishment and forgiveness came into being. At first the indulgence system was relatively uncomplicated. Now the intricate rules have become so confused and tricky that the system has forfeited the allegiance as well as the respect of educated Catholics.

The Church has taken many precautions to see that sinners are genuinely repentant when they seek an indulgence for past sins. They must, for example, in asking for a plenary indulgence not only go to confession but also take Holy Communion and pray for "the intentions of the pope." In spite of these precautions, the whole process of gaining indulgences has become a kind of spiritual banking racket in which the sinner escapes purgatorial punishment by techniques too trivial and mechanical for acceptance by an adult mind. As the Jesuit Father Daniel O'Hanlon said in a Vatican II press conference, "among non-Catholics [the indulgence system] makes the Church seem to be an unreformed legalistic, medieval slot-machine." Cardinal Koenig of Vienna made the understatement of the fourth session when he declared in the aula: "Many things in the present practice run the risk of causing superstition among the uneducated, while at the same time, there is a further danger that indulgences will be looked down upon by the more educated." The London *Observer* expressed the characteristic attitude of intellectuals by saying bluntly: "To the uninitiated the whole idea sounds like a kind of celestial insurance policy. . . . Totting up indulgences looks rather like filling in books of green trading stamps."[6]

The spiritual green trading stamps of the indulgence system are now handed out under very specific published rules. The system attaches special rewards to certain places, certain ceremonies, and certain holy objects. The places, ceremonies, and holy objects are so plentiful in Italy, where nine centuries of grants have produced multiple layers of rewards, that no single book could possibly summarize all of them. A shrewd tourist, visiting all the holy places around Rome, could quite readily equal the record of that eleventh-century hermit who gained a thousand years remission of temporal punishment in one Lent by whipping himself in the right places at the right times—geographically and anatomically.

Such mortification is not now necessary. Even an American Catholic tourist, reading only English, could do very well by following up all the spiritual opportunities outlined in one English-language book, *The Raccolta*, edited by Father Joseph P. Christopher and published in the United States in 1952 under the Imprimatur of Cardinal Spellman. The work is a summary of available indulgences up to 1952.

Here are a few of the published rewards available in the form of reduced sentences in purgatory for the supplicant or for his deceased friends, granted always with the condition that there is true and inner repentance. The caution is added that no plenary indulgence is available without a confession, communion, and prayers for the pope.

Kissing the pope's ring—300 days.
Kissing a bishop's ring—50 days.
Kissing the foot of the bronze statue of St. Peter in St. Peter's basilica—50 days.
Climbing the Scala Santa or Holy Stairs in Rome on the knees —9 years for each step, and a plenary indulgence for the entire ascent.
Visiting the Lateran and reciting certain short prayers six times—a plenary indulgence is granted as often as this is done.
Visiting the seven altars in the Vatican Basilica—7 years for each altar if the visit is accompanied by a prayer for the appropriate saint, and a plenary indulgence if the circuit is completed in one day.
Kissing the palms of a newly ordained priest—100 days.
Helping a newly ordained priest at his first Mass, if the aid comes from kinsmen—a plenary indulgence.
Carrying and kissing a rosary and reciting the Hail Mary once a day—500 days.
Reciting a prayer: "Savior of the world, save Russia"—300 days.
Receiving the Pope's *Urbi et Orbi* blessing, even by radio—a plenary indulgence.
Ejaculating: "O God, be merciful to me the sinner"—500 days.
Wearing of the Sacred Heart of Jesus' white wool badge—500 days.[7]

Under canon law many additional indulgences, most of them plenary, are specified for very brief prayers or acts of devotion. Contrary to prevailing non-Catholic opinion, many of these indulgences have been created by twentieth-century popes. They are available for Catholics only, and their number may be increased at any time by any new pope. At times an extremely brief act of penance brings the reward of a plenary indulgence. For example, plenary indulgences are granted to any of the faithful in a state of contrition who say once a day for a month the word "Jesus" or the word "Mary" or the words "Jesus, Mary, Joseph" or the words "My Jesus, mercy."

The arithmetic of indulgences is somewhat complicated by the fact that there are sixteen approved scapulars (usually made of woolen cloth and hung around the neck), and in addition scapular medals for military personnel, all of which are more or less effective in winning surcease from a long stay in purgatory. The wearers of some of these scapulars are assured that they can gain about one hundred plenary indulgences each year by wearing them, and that the scapular assures their own liberation from purgatory on the first Saturday after death.

In recent years plenary indulgences have become so common and so easy to obtain that partial indulgences are gradually falling into disuse. Why worry about a trifling commutation of temporal punishment for sin if the whole sentence can be wiped out? Cardinal Cento, in defending his report on indulgences on the Council floor, admitted that there has been "excessive granting" of indulgences amounting to "inflation," and that the whole mathematical system has resulted in considerable confusion.

Monsignor Sesselo, Cento's assistant at the Sacred Penitentiary, presented in his *relatio* on indulgences a mild program for reform. It proposed to revise partial indulgences in order to eliminate entirely the counting of days and years, to cut down the number of plenary indulgences sharply so that no one can gain a plenary indulgence more than once a day, and to stop granting indulgences merely for wearing an object of piety. Monsignor Sesselo, however, suggested nothing to destroy the basic assumption in the indulgence system, that Catholics can secure divine commutation of their sentences in purgatory by observing certain ecclesiastical formalities. The faithful are taught that the formalities are worthless without the state of contrition and grace, but, likewise, the contrition and the state of grace are incomplete without the formalities.

This mechanization of the process of salvation cannot be called commercialism as long as no cash is passed, but it was frequently called ecclesiastical banking by its critics at the Council. Monsignor Sesselo himself compared it to a bonus system in a factory. A person enriched with an indulgence, he said, "could be compared to a worker who, besides receiving a salary for his labor, receives an additional bonus exactly equal to his salary." He defended the right of a priest at the end of a retreat or a mission to give a plenary indulgence to his entire congregation by waving a crucifix over them and making a single sign of the cross.

Many plenary indulgences are obtainable merely by passing through a particular Church door with the right intention. The most famous indulgenced door visited by thousands of pilgrims is that of the Portiuncula Indulgence in the Chapel of St. Mary of the Angels in Assisi. It is said that many faithful believers use this entrance as a kind of spiritual revolving door on the assumption that a new plenary indulgence is granted on each entrance. One of the most famous buildings in Rome, the Pantheon, bears an inscription over its main door giving a plenary indulgence daily in perpetuity for the living and the dead, extended to all those who use it.

As usual, His Beatitude Patriarch Maximos IV Saigh spoke out bluntly on this subject in his rebellious French. Nothing in the early tradition of the Eastern Church, he said, corresponded to indulgences, and nothing concrete could be found even in the history of the Western Church in the first eleven centuries. The system was a later invention. It should be reformed to eliminate the whole idea of automatic asssurances and measured days. This would be one way of forestalling Protestant objections. Cardinal Doepfner of Munich went a little further and criticized the whole spiritual banking idea that suggested a "treasury of the Church" to be drawn upon by the faithful. Speaking for the bishops of Austria and Germany, and receiving warm applause from the floor, he asked for a better study of the whole question by a more representative commission.

The bishops of the United States were caught in the middle of this controversy. Their leaders of Irish ancestry tended to be cautious about advocating the complete abolition of a system that still commanded so much devotion in Ireland. But they knew that most American Catholics pay very little attention to the whole indulgence system, and probably most of these bishops would have been relieved if the Pope had taken matters into his own hands and eliminated the whole business in easy stages. In the end, however, most of the American bishops voted for the Penitentiary report because they were confronted with no good alternative. The report proposed a number of significant reforms, and to vote against it might seem to favor the old system. So, like the majority of the Fathers in the Council, the American majority voted for the reforms with the hope that something more fundamental might come out of it. Some 28 American bishops, however, embarrassed by the Pope's tactlessness in bringing the whole question to the floor, expressed their opinion in writing that the discussion was "inopportune" and suggested that the consideration of this "intricate and delicate" subject should be postponed. Probably if they had felt entirely free to express their personal views without reprisals from Rome they would have echoed the words of one bishop who told the correspondent of *Le Monde:* "We should go much farther and bury piously all practice of indulgences, which seem entirely outdated."

In this situation Pope Paul indicated no desire to abolish the indulgence system. Indeed, he extended its operations into the post-Council program of the Church by providing that in the Jubilee Year of 1966, proclaimed in honor of the Vatican Council, Catholics who had formerly been required to visit Rome to secure the accompanying plenary indulgences could secure such indulgences in their home churches.

No one at the Council suggested going a little farther and abolishing purgatory. Purgatory is almost a Roman Catholic monopoly at the present time, although several non-Christian religions have proclaimed some form of an intermediate stage of existence beyond the grave. In spite of Dante, the prelates of the present-day Church are very reluctant to give out any specifications about purgatory. They define purgatory as "a place or state where the souls of those who have died in the state of grace suffer for a time before they are admitted into heaven, in order to be cleansed of unrepented venial sins and/or to make satisfaction for temporal punishment still due for sins." They do not try to locate purgatory in a cosmos whose outer limits are now discussed in terms of billions of light years. Presumably, in the days of a three-decker universe consisting of heaven, earth, and hell, purgatory was located somewhere below the earth and above hell.

The one thing certain about purgatory is that for many centuries it has been a kind of theological red rag for Protestant critics of Rome. Outside of a tiny minority in the Church of England, it is unanimously rejected by the Protestant world as a crude superstition, not adequately supported by scriptural texts. Accordingly, the acceptance of purgatory at Vatican II confirmed the existence of one more important road-block to Christian unity. By inference the Church stuck to the gospel of purgatory as expounded at the very anti-Protestant Council of Trent.

In the third session, the Council committed itself, in the Constitution on the Church, to the theology of purgatory, indulgences, and saints. Citing a verse in the Apocrypha to the effect that "it is a holy and wholesome thought to pray for the dead that they may be loosed from their sins," the Constitution speaks favorably of the veneration of "our brethren who are in heavenly glory or who having died are still being purified"; and it reaffirms the decrees of the Second Council of Nicea, the Council of Florence, and the Council of Trent on this subject. But the Council did have the sagacity to admit by indirection that there were many abuses in the indulgence, sainthood, and purgatorial systems, and it urged the faithful to "work hard to prevent or correct any abuses, excesses or defects which may have crept in here and there."

After indulgences had been brought up for very limited discussion for a few days in the aula in November 1965, it became apparent even to Pope Paul that calling for the public reports of the various national episcopal conferences on the subject had been a mistake. The merits and the very obvious demerits of the whole system evoked too many unhappy memories. The discussion was like the washing of unclean ecclesiastical linen in public. Abruptly, on November 13, 1965, the General Secretary of the Council, Archbishop Pericle Felici, announced that because of the time needed to read new texts and vote on them the national reports on indulgences would be suspended and all further observations would be sent in in writing. Anyway, said the Secretary, the Holy Father had never intended that the theology of indulgences should be reported on in the Council. The bishops breathed a sigh of relief and accepted cloture with enthusiasm.

It was the Council of Trent that reaffirmed and underscored another great feature of the theological underworld of Catholic practice, the naming of new saints and the veneration of their relics.[8] Trent ordained that the faithful should call upon the saints in heaven to pray for them and that "only men of irreligious mentality deny that the saints, enjoying eternal happiness in heaven are to be invoked." It proclaimed that the relics of the saints should be honored and that visits to their shrines should be promoted. Such teachings served to remind Protestants of the long history of abuses that led the leaders of the Reformation in the sixteenth century to repudiate the whole saintly system, along with the associated system of indulgences, as a survival of fetishism.

Vatican II avoided any open controversy over the whole question of saints and relics by quietly affirming the Church's present policies without any public proclamation. Pope John and Pope Paul, however, proceeded to affirm standard practices during the Council by canonizing a number of saints, although neither of them equalled the record of Pius XII in this matter. Pius had canonized 32 saints and beatified, in preparation for canonization, 164 others, which made him the largest identifier of saints since Sixtus V in 1590. John, in his short reign, canonized only 10 and beatified 5. Paul started by beatifying 4 persons in the fall of 1963, his first year, while the Council was in progress, one of them being the German-born American Bishop of Philadelphia, John N. Neumann. Neumann was the first American bishop to be beatified and the third American citizen to be so honored. The first American-born Catholic to attain sainthood will probably be Mother Elizabeth Ann Seton, a widow, Catholic convert, and mother of five children who founded the Sisters of Charity in 1809.

Paul became a major producer of saints during the third session of the Council when he canonized in one ceremony twenty-two young missionary martyrs of Uganda who had been savagely murdered there in the days when Uganda was a British protectorate. Neither John nor Paul, in spite of their many public statements of consideration and even affection for Protestants, seemed to be aware that in proceeding to name new saints and bless new relics they were widening the gap between themselves and the "separated brethren" who rejected the whole saint-making system as virtual idolatry.

Pope Paul's most dramatic gesture in the field of saint-making came in the last month of the Council when he announced to cheering bishops in an open session that he was initiating the steps to beatify both Pius XII and John XXIII. The complete process, of course, may take many years since, ordinarily, the final honor of canonization is conferred only after long inquiries. From Paul's point of view the combination of John and Pius XII as future saints was a fortunate combination, pleasing to the conservatives who honored Pius and to the liberals who honored John. It was a typical balanced ticket, as carefully arranged as that of a New York City political election. But, on the whole, the double choice was a far greater concession to the conservatives than to the liberals. The name of Pius XII was still clouded by the scandal of anti-Semitism, dramatized by *The Deputy*. Moreover, it was Pius XII who had sealed the fate of Catholic movements on behalf of birth control, and it was also this same Pius XII who had canonized Pius X, the most reactionary foe of Modernism in this century.

The beatification of John XXIII was another matter. Everybody in Italy, including the Communists, seemed to be enthusiastic about the prospect of his sainthood. A million people signed petitions for his beatification. The peasants of Bergamo, in anticipation of the proceedings for his elevation, had already produced the two "miracles" traceable to his spirit that are legally required for beatification. One of them was a four-year-old child, almost blind, who recovered his sight by touching a statue of John. At first these wonders could not be called miracles until they were solemnly investigated and approved. For the time being the peasants of Bergamo called them "special graces" and expressed supreme confidence that their beloved John would ultimately become their Holy Saint John.

The new trend toward canonizing popes was not altogether popular. It seemed to be contrary to the original practice of canonizing humble Christian martyrs. Some Catholics wondered where the new tendency would stop if popes felt an obligation to glorify their ecclesiastical predecessors. A strong movement for canonizing Pius IX had begun some years before Vatican II, but it had been held in abeyance by the Congregation of Rites during the Council, presumably for tactical reasons. Pius IX, with his *Syllabus of Errors* and his *Quanta Cura*, embodied almost everything that the modern non-Catholic world considered abhorrent. To canonize him during the Council would certainly have seemed a most nonecumenical gesture. But a movement to canonize Pius XI had started some time before the Council and had never been completed. His canonization would have been more acceptable than that of Pius IX, although it would have evoked the ghost of fascism, which he condoned, as well as the ghost of contraception, which he had not condoned.

The naming of saints and the veneration of relics is still considered in the Western world to be one of the most primitive and anti-scientific things in Catholicism. Perhaps this is the reason why American Catholicism has never exploited the system as it has been exploited in Europe. Europe is still full of competing shrines with competing, and often duplicating and spurious, relics. Millions of European Catholics still take their saints and their saints' holidays, along with relics, very seriously.

The system is also kept alive by the flat rule that no person can be canonized unless his spirit or his relics have effected four miracles after his death, two before beatification and two between beatification and final canonization. Before Bishop Neumann of Philadelphia could be beatified by Pope Paul in 1963, two miraculous cures traceable to his person had to be investigated and approved by Church authorities. One of them was the cure of Mrs. Eva Benassi Pantani, who at the age of eleven in 1922 prayed for the intercession of Bishop Neumann and was cured of peritonitis. She was present at the beatification ceremonies in St. Peter's, as were Pope Paul and this writer. The other required miracle in this case was the remarkable recovery of J. Kent Lenahan, Jr., of Ardmore, Pennsylvania, from injuries suffered in an automobile accident. In each case the theory was that the recovery was due to the intercession with God of the spirit of Bishop Neumann after the two persons in distress had asked for that intercession. As soon as Bishop Neumann had been beatified, the movement to make him a full saint began. Two new medical miracles were attributed to his spirit in the cure of two Philadelphia Catholics, Michael Flanagan, cured of lung cancer, and Alice Pittet, cured of Hodgkin's disease.

The production and veneration of the relics of saints began as early as the third century with the honoring of Christian martyrs, and ever since then the traditional practice has honored the exhumed bones of saints as sacred and miracle-producing. According to Canon 1281 and its official interpretations: "Distinguished relics of the saints or blessed are the body, the head, the arm, the forearm, the heart, the tongue, the hand, the lower part of the leg (knee to ankle), or that part of the body in which a martyr suffered, provided it be entire and not small."

The honoring of relics became an organic part of the Council proceedings through the official participation of the Fathers in many saint-making ceremonies. After a solemn ceremony in St. Peter's, attended by the Pope, Cardinal Bea interrupted his participation in the third session to carry the "skull of the Apostle St. Andrew" to the Greek Orthodox Church in Patras from where it had been taken to Rome for "safe keeping" about five centuries before. One of the interesting features of this episode was that some Greek Orthodox leaders considered the gesture of the return of the skull an ecumenical trap "prepared by the underhandedness of Catholic propaganda," and they would have nothing to do with it. Apparently they did not dissent from the underlying philosophy concerning the sacredness of the relic itself.

The system of relic veneration is kept alive partly because, since the seventh general Council in Nicea in the eighth century, every altar of a Church has been required to have some relic of a saint, usually buried beneath it. Also, saints have been honored by Church holidays for a long time, and Catholics throughout the world have learned to associate them with the relaxation and joy of vacations. The National Catholic Almanac of the United States lists 223 saints with appropriate holidays.[9] There are special saints and special days for almost every conceivable occupation and for many standard diseases including comedians, expectant mothers, funeral directors, grave-diggers, stenographers, rheumatism, poisoning, and convulsions. Prayers to the appropriate saints on the appropriate days are said to have a special efficacy. Every nation in the world has a saintly Catholic sponsor. Although most American Catholics pay little attention to saints, there are some who take the relics of such saints very seriously. A Relic of the Month Club was formed in Rome during the Holy Year of 1950 and it was said that 8,000 Americans signed up to receive their monthly fragments.

Relics of Christ and the Virgin Mary must be treated in a special category, especially "the true cross of Christ," discovered with many duplications in the fourth century; the Holy Coat in Treves, said to be existing in twenty other towns; the miraculously multiplied nails from the cross; the pillar to which Christ was bound before the Crucifixion; the spear; the sponge; and the crown of thorns. The Vatican, apparently with some reluctance, continues to exhibit about four times each year in Rome several of the most famous and most questionable relics of Christ, including the sacred sponge and Veronica's Veil–the cloth with which Veronica is alleged to have wiped the face of Christ, resulting in a perpetually preserved image of his face.

The duplication, sale, and forging of relics was one of the great themes of leaders of the Reformation, especially of John Calvin. In that period there were said to be 19,013 sacred relics of the saints in a church in Wittenberg where Martin Luther had nailed up his 95 theses. When Calvin jeered at the alleged proliferation of pieces of "the true cross" to the extent that 300 men could not carry all the wood, a Catholic polemicist "proved" that all existing pieces measured only 5,000,000 cubic millimeters, whereas the whole original cross contained perhaps 180,000,000 millimeters. Calvin's exposures seemed to have had little effect in devout Catholic circles.

Among Catholic leaders in Rome, even in the Roman Curia, there is considerable embarrassment concerning the maintenance of the relics industry and its abuses in dealing with the uneducated. In the fall of 1965 the undersecretary for beatifications and canonization in the Congregation of Rites, Monsignor Amato Frutaz, published an article in a small but official Catholic journal in Rome suggesting that if the present policy of requiring relics for altars continued, the Church would soon run out of genuine relics, and the substitution of fraudulent relics might take place.[10] He suggested abolishing altogether the whole practice of requiring saints' relics for altars, and he was quite frank in admitting the historical fact that in ancient times a "commerce in relics arose, and unscrupulous people took advantage of the good faith of the devout." Thus far, however, Pope Paul has not publicly indicated any interest in such suggestions for reform. The Council itself, in the

Constitution on the Church, urged continued veneration for "all the saints."

Catholic liberals in the United States have begun to treat the whole miraculous underworld of the Church with gentle ridicule. A news item in *Commonweal*, published during the fourth session in 1965, read:

> *Religion and Commerce:* The Bishop of Macao has loaned a major relic of St. Francis Xavier to Cardinal Spellman, who in turn "released the relic for veneration" on the fifth floor of Bamberger's Department Store, Newark, N.J. According to Bamberger's, the relic will be displayed in "a uniquely serene and reverent atmosphere." As it happens, the store is simultaneously conducting a sales promotion under the theme "Caravan Out of the East."[11]

CHAPTER FOURTEEN ❧ CHURCH, STATE, AND DIPLOMACY

FROM the point of view of American non-Catholics, the most striking omission from the proceedings of Vatican II was the absence of any solid or comprehensive treatment of the problem of church and state. There was no chapter on this subject even in the sprawling schema on The Church in the Modern World. The phrase "separation of church and state" was almost absent from Council speeches. No one, least of all the American bishops, wanted to raise the delicate subject for controversial discussion.

This reluctance to face the issue of church and state is traceable to a number of factors. The pronouncements on the subject by past popes are embarrassingly one-sided and if stated frankly could be extremely offensive to those who believe in the American expression of the principle. The Church's philosophy on the subject goes back to the days when popes crowned emperors and claimed both temporal and spiritual authority over them in the name of a God who was almost as much political as religious. This old fusion of church and state was partly a European historical tradition the Church of the present time has inherited without recourse. As George Santayana once remarked: "All ancient religions are political."

The Vatican did not abandon its papal nation in the Italian peninsula until it was forced to do so in 1870 by Italian troops, and then it never repudiated the philosophy involved in temporal power. The popes, living since then in their tiny residential territory of Vatican City State, sulked until the twentieth century when, in 1929, their restricted new 108-acre domain was made into a state by agreement with Mussolini.

From time immemorial the underlying assumption of the Papacy has been that church and state should be at least partially united, although many popes have described this partial union in confusing terms of "separation." Pius IX in his *Syllabus of Errors* had denounced as one of the principal errors of his time the thesis that "the Church ought to be separated from the State, and the State from the Church." Later popes were not quite so frank but they clung to the gospel of Pius. Leo XIII in his *Christian Constitution of States* praised Pius for speaking in his *Syllabus* in such a manner that "in this sea of errors Catholics might have a light which they might safely follow"; then he went on to say that the Church "deems it unlawful to place various forms of divine worship on the same footing as the true religion," and finally cited with approval the predecessor of Pius IX, Gregory XVI, to the effect that men could not hope for "happier results, either for religion or for the civil government" than from the Catholic method of "agreement" between the Church and state.[1]

In this century Pius X echoed the refrain in his 1906 encyclical *Vehementer*, asserting: "That the affairs of Church and state should be kept rigidly apart is certainly a false, even a dangerous, notion." Pius XII in his address to Italian jurists in December 1953, defending "the collaboration between the Church and the State" embodied in the various concordats between the Vatican and civil powers, declared: "In principle, that is in theory, she [the Church] cannot approve complete separation of the two powers."[2]

Far more important than these historic and theoretical pronouncements is the fact that everywhere in the world today where the Church has the power to effect the policy, she demands and secures partial union of Church and state as embodied either in concordats with civil governments, subsidies from the public treasury for Catholic institutions, or exclusive recognition of Catholicism as the religion taught in national schools. In some Catholic countries she secures all three of these favors while continuing to describe the resultant policy as "the separation of church and state" or "true harmony" between church and state. The Church's vocabulary in this area is full of semantic artifices.

Many countries that maintain diplomatic relations with the Vatican and favor sectarian schools with public tax grants, or give Catholicism exclusive privileges in national schools, are still called in Catholic treatises "separation countries." Even Belgium, the Netherlands, and Portugal are sometimes included in such confusing descriptions.

Exhibit A of the "true harmony" between church and state in practical operation is Italy itself, where delegates and observers at the Council could see clerical privilege at work.[3] This privilege included during the Council (1) recognition of the Pope as a foreign monarch entitled to all the honors accorded to any foreign potentate; (2) payment of public funds to the Church for the salaries of priests; (3) the recognition in a binding treaty that "the Catholic Apostolic and Roman religion is the sole religion of the state"; (4) the recognition of the Papal Nuncio to Italy as dean of the diplomatic corps; and (5) the exclusive right of the Church to teach religion in national schools with a program and teachers acceptable to the Church.

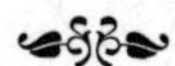

At the moment when Pope Paul opened the second session of the Council, the Vatican had full diplomatic representatives in 46 foreign capitals and religious representatives independent of the local episcopate in 15 others. (The numbers vary from month to month.) In reciprocal recognition of Catholic diplomatic machinery, 50 governments sent either full-scale ambassadors or ministers to the Holy See. They were very conspicuous in their gold braid and papal medals at all the open sessions of the Council, reminding the non-Catholic observers that the spectacle they were witnessing was a church-state demonstration deriving many of its traditions from the days when the Papacy was a considerable European nation. It was obvious that in spite of the public language of humility the Papacy intended to keep as much of its political prestige as it could defend.

The Papacy is the only religious or quasi-religious body in

the world today that still maintains direct diplomatic relations with secular powers. It still has very extensive interlocking relationships with the civil governments of Catholic countries. The heads of state in Italy, France, Portugal, and Spain still have the power to confer red birettas on the heads of new cardinals. When Pope Paul at the United Nations in 1965 referred in the third person to himself "with only a miniscule and almost symbolic temporal sovereignty, only as much as is necessary to leave him free to exercise his spiritual mission and to assure those who deal with him that he is independent of every sovereignty of this world," no realist could take his modesty seriously. His political power is not based on the 108-acre estate (with appendages) called the Vatican City State. It is based on his diplomatic-political establishments in Rome's Secretariat of State and in 46 capitals throughout the world where his papal nuncios and internuncios have full political status. These officials usually serve as the heads of the diplomatic corps in each capital where they reside, under the rules of the Vienna Conference agreement of 1815, which was renewed in 1961.

These political nuncios, who usually have the rank of archbishop, are not to be confused with the apostolic delegates, who are purely religious representatives and who serve in the United States and 14 other nonrecognition countries. The apostolic delegates exercise a great deal of surveillance over national churches but they do not have official relationships with the governments in their respective capitals.

The delegates at the United Nations who heard Pope Paul's very modest appraisal of his political state also knew that, in one sense, he possessed an advantage over all their nations. His state could share in the operation of political parties and trade unions within the territories of most of these nations while these nations could not engage in such enterprises in each other's territory without being accused of illegal or improper intervention. The Vatican's political parties and trade unions, described in affirmative terms as "Christian Democratic," function in many parts of the world as internal agents of certain Vatican policies because the fiction is kept alive that they represent a church or a holy faith rather than a political entity.

In the coronations of Pope John and Pope Paul, the Vatican did not attempt to conceal any of its claims to super-state status. Political and religious pomp were intermingled. Political claims and political personages were equally conspicuous. Heads of state mingled with princes of the Church in homage. As Cardinal Ottaviani lowered the richly jeweled, beehive crown on to the head of Pope Paul on June 30, 1963, he intoned the old challenge to the powers of the world, describing the Pope as "the Father of Princes and the Ruler of Kings." Probably no coronation of secular states anywhere in the world approaches the worldly elegance of a papal coronation. Many famous heads of state were present, and the Catholic rulers kneeled to their Pope, while the cardinal princes of the Church kneeled and kissed his hand, pledging total obedience.

Even the Jesuit magazine *America* thought that the trappings of temporal power at Paul's coronation were a little too obvious. The editors remarked that "the pageantry of flabelli and tiara are harmless reminders of a rich past. But a coronation formula which calls the Pope 'Father of Princes and Kings' and 'ruler of the world' is a different kind of anachronism."[4]

The Council made no move to terminate any of the leading political features of Catholicism except to indicate at one point that the practice of having bishops appointed by heads of state seemed outdated. We have already seen that in the Declaration on Religious Liberty a few slightly ambiguous phrases were inserted that clearly implied the right to continue the Church's privileged position in Catholic countries as long as competing sects were given some liberty. Under these circumstances it is not surprising that the American bishops and *periti* seemed especially glad to avoid any public confrontation of the facts about church and state. They had been trumpeting their acceptance of the American principle of separation very successfully, partly because few Americans were aware of the Church's policies in other countries. The American bishops were undoubtedly sincere in accepting their own interpretation of "separation" for America, although nearly all of them were squarely opposed to the interpretation handed down by the United States Supreme Court. In their seminaries they had been raised on the unreal phrases used by Leo XIII: "The Almighty . . . has appointed the charge of the human race between two powers, the ecclesiastical and the civil, the one being set over the divine, and the other over human things. Each in its kind is supreme, each has fixed limits within which it is contained." Catholic political power has not been "contained" by this formula either in Catholic countries or non-Catholic countries.

The question naturally arises: If the realms of ecclesiastical and civil power are as clearly separate as Leo XIII implied, why should the Church, a religious institution, continue to maintain both political and religious establishments? It is a good question, and it came up for some discussion both in the aula and in press conferences. The discussion in both cases was somewhat fragmentary. Naturally enough, the fact that the United States had no diplomatic relations with the Vatican entered the discussion. The late Father Gustave Weigel, S.J., the most astute and valuable of the American *periti* at the Council, had said in 1962 in discussing diplomatic relations between the United States and the Vatican: "Given the feelings of our nation as a whole, with its strong hostility against any relationship with the Vatican State, it would be an unwise ruler who would try to establish such relations. They are not necessary and the harm they would produce would be more than enough to avoid them. The diplomatic recognition of the Vatican is not a Catholic dogma, much less a Christian need."[5]

The attack on the diplomatic establishment of the Church on the Council floor took a different turn, a more superficial one. A few bishops dared to criticize the whole Church-state theory behind the establishment, but most of the critics simply sniped at the "interference" of both papal nuncios and apostolic delegates in the affairs of national churches. It was evident that there had been a great accumulation of resentment against these gentlemen as "Italian spies" who exercised altogether too much authority. These "spies," it was alleged, watched the goings on in local dioceses with a jaundiced foreign eye, not always comprehending what they saw. It was said that they sifted out the suggested names of prospective appointees as bishops and condemned to limbo the progressives who demonstrated any good, non-Roman independence. They were constantly sticking their noses into places where their noses did not belong. This, at least, was the meaning of the criticism which broke out on the Council floor and at press conferences, and it probably came as something of a shock to the august archbishops who now reside in diplomatic palaces throughout the world, living above the level of the priests and bishops who do the daily work of the Church.

Bishop Joachim Amman, a sixty-five-year-old prelate from Tanganyika, a retired German Benedictine missionary bishop, somewhat out of reach of papal reprisals, dared to raise the question in the second session whether laymen should not be substituted for archbishops as nuncios. Declaring that the whole system of apostolic delegates and nuncios "hides the true face" of the Church and "puts it into international politics" where it does not belong, he questioned the whole wisdom of the system and electrified the bishops because he said some things about papal nuncios and apostolic delegates they had longed to hear. Arguing that local bishops know their own country far better than outsiders, since they are familiar with their country's language and institutions, he suggested that the time had come to put any representation of the Holy See into the hands of leaders chosen not by the Pope or the Secretary of State in Rome but by local episcopal conferences.[6]

The notion that the entire diplomatic establishment of the Church has no place in the world of the twentieth century is not entirely new. No one at the Council claimed that Vatican diplomacy is necessarily grounded in divine law, and there is no requirement in Church doctrine or canon law for it. Pius X seriously considered abolishing his diplomatic corps after he had had some quarrels with France, Portugal, and Spain. Pope Paul could tomorrow demote all papal nuncios to the rank of apostolic delegates, thus making them purely religious representatives without political status. Many Catholics would undoubtedly welcome this kind of modernization. The pope could also decentralize the whole diplomatic apparatus without changing its political character by giving national conferences of bishops controlling power in the selection of papal representatives in their territories.

When he was Monsignor Montini, Pope Paul actually raised some of these very questions about the wisdom of a Vatican diplomatic establishment. It was in the course of a speech he made in Rome in 1951. Although his answers at that time were conservative and cautious, he indicated that he had faced some of the issues with painful reflection. In that speech, as reported by Father Robert A. Graham in his *Vatican Diplomacy*, Montini wondered: (1) whether, in view of the fact that the temporal power of the Papacy had almost ended in 1870 with the disappearance of the papal states, it would not be wise to discontinue the diplomatic system which had grown up with those states; and (2) whether diplomacy, made notorious by Machiavelli, was really suited to the Church.[7]

The bishops at Vatican II did not want to go that far in their questioning, particularly since Montini had rendered conservative answers to both of these questions and thereafter had continued to serve faithfully in the Vatican diplomatic machine. The system, the bishops realized, would continue under Pope Paul. But it needed reform.

It was obvious at the Council that in the minds of the bishops the chief immediate objection to the diplomatic system of the Vatican was not so much the mingling of church and state as the almost complete Italian monopoly of high diplomatic posts. For many centuries Vatican diplomacy had been an essentially Italian game. Although four American archbishops have held diplomatic posts at various times, carrying double passports from the United States and the Vatican, there has been very little American influence in the diplomatic work of the Church. In general, Vatican diplomacy consists of an Italian archbishop in the field reporting to another Italian archbishop in Rome, the Secretary of State, while still another Italian archbishop, the Pope himself, appoints, supervises, and controls all the diplomats.

It developed at the press conferences in the second session that there are many places in the world where the Italian representatives of the Pope are not in sympathy with the Catholic leaders of the countries to which they are assigned. The United States has a prize example in the Apostolic Delegate to Washington, already mentioned in Chapter 6, Archbishop Egidio Vagnozzi, an outstanding conservative whose sympathies with the right wing elements of the Council had been revealed in American controversies again and again. *Time* magazine quoted one United States cardinal as saying hopefully: "Maybe we can get him named Papal Nuncio to Lapland." Unsympathetic, arrogant, and uninformed papal nuncios and apostolic delegates are considered particularly obnoxious by bishops throughout the world because, ordinarily, all suggestions for the appointment of diocesan local bishops flow through their hands to the Vatican. A hostile report by a papal nuncio or apostolic delegate may ruin the future career of a bishop who is not popular with the Italian official.

The Council took a modest step in the direction of decentralizing the control of the Vatican diplomatic corps when it expressed in the decree on the Pastoral Office of Bishops, promulgated by the Pope in 1965, the desire that the office of Legate of the Pope should be more precisely determined and that such legates should "be more widely taken from various regions of the Church, insofar as it is possible." How much these words mean no one can tell until reform has actually been accomplished. The fact that Pope Paul promulgated the words is slightly encouraging, but as long as both the Pope and his Secretary of State are Italians, and all diplomatic appointments are made in Rome, the system will probably remain overwhelmingly Italian, committed to the European outlook on church and state.

The American bishops were not anxious to have any public discussion at the Council of either the separation of church and state in general or the diplomatic corps in particular. They stood to lose if such things were brought into the headlines because the news stories would inevitably reveal new evidence of the divergence between the European political policies of the Church and the American conception of church-state separation. At one moment in the second session the American bishops were quite embarrassed by the casual mention of the separation of church and state as "unfortunate" or "regrettable." The offending sentence read in part: "The faithful, mindful of the Word of the Lord, 'Give Caesar that which is Caesar's and God that which is God's,' will, on the one hand, carefully avoid the confusion and undue mixing up of religion and Church with purely civil matters, but on the other hand they will legitimately resist their unfortunate separation and the opposition of the earthly regime to God and His Church." Apparently the language was intended to indicate that it was unfortunate for certain regimes, particularly the anti-religious Communist regimes, to separate themselves from the Church's spiritual influences.

The American bishops, alarmed by the possibility of a misunderstanding, held an emergency meeting, protested against the language, and the unfortunate word "unfortunate" was dropped. At an American press panel Bishop Victor Reed of Oklahoma explained that, of course, "The American Church is in favor of the separation of church and state." But nobody in the aula wished to discuss the difference between the American conception of the separation of church and state and the Catholic conception. When the schema on The Church in the Modern World appeared, it discussed the relation between the Church and politics only in the most general terms.

This schema also omitted any discussion of the question of whether there should be a diplomatic representative of the Vatican in Washington and an American ambassador at the Vatican. Such an omission was considered natural because the issue was local and national. Nevertheless, the question was widely discussed in the coffee bars and at press conferences, and many of the arguments pro and con appeared in articles in the American press during the Council sessions. Just before President Kennedy's death, the official newspaper of the archdiocese of Baltimore had come out in favor of establishing diplomatic relations with the Vatican, partly on the ground that the lack of any great protest over Kennedy's 1963 visit to the Pope had revealed a new American spirit, and partly on the ground of "the new understanding and sympathy for the role of the modern papacy by Pope John."

The American Jesuits tried to take advantage of Pope Paul's visit to the U.N. in 1965 to argue that the time had come for the United States to break old precedents and establish official diplomatic relations with the Holy See. They had been joined in this attitude by two important American journalists, James Reston and C. L. Sulzberger of *The New York Times*. In the United States the *Register* chain of diocesan papers immediately declared: "We join with Mr. Sulzberger in saying that it is time that Washington acknowledges the need for formal contacts with the Papal government."[8]

There is no doubt that the conservative elements of American Catholicism, and the Roman Curia itself, would like to see the United States represented at Rome by a full ambassador. Pius XII practically asked for this in a letter to President Truman in 1952 after the termination of the Taylor mission to the Vatican, and Cardinal Spellman has repeatedly indicated his desire for such recognition. Probably most of the American bishops would welcome the innovation if it could be secured without a fight, but they remember too well the sad experience of 1951 when President Truman sent the appointment of General Mark Clark to the Senate for confirmation as a full ambassador, and Clark's name was withdrawn because of almost solid opposition by the national Protestant community. In fact, the 1951 battle against the appointment of an American ambassador to the Vatican may be considered the last major occasion on which American Protestantism has achieved virtual unanimity. At that time the National Council of Churches protested against the "alarming threat of basic American principles" involved in the Vatican ambassador proposals and suggested that all the desirable results involved could be achieved through an American ambassador to Italy who is "resident in Rome and readily accessible to the Vatican."[9]

The United States, of course, has never formally recognized the present three-headed amalgam of church and state formally created by the 1929 concordat with Mussolini and known in its various aspects as The Holy See, the Vatican City State, and the Roman Catholic Church. The American government did, for a few years, send officials of consular and ministerial rank to Rome when the Pope ruled the city and the hinterland as absolute monarch of the Papal States, since there was justification then for maintaining standard consular procedures. But even in those days our lesser diplomats who went to Rome were cautioned not to confuse "ecclesiastical questions" with those civil matters they were authorized to treat. The last minister-resident of the United States left the Papal States in 1868, two years before those states were conquered and secularized by the military power of the new Italy. Since then every move to establish formal diplomatic relations with the Vatican has run up against the traditional view that such a move would, directly or indirectly, demonstrate a preference for one religion over all other religions, in conflict with the spirit if not with the letter of the Constitution.

President Kennedy, as the first Catholic President, realized that he could not under any circumstances advocate Vatican-United States diplomatic relations because it would seem to be a personal reward for his own church. Moreover, he had committed himself against the idea long before election—in 1959—and he was probably entirely sincere in the feeling that the raising of the issue could have a divisive effect upon the American electorate. When, between the first and second sessions of the Council, he was asked at a Washington press conference whether it would not be fruitful to consider setting up some regular channel of communications between the United States and the Vatican, he replied: "I do not think that there is any lack of information or communication back and forth."[10]

President Kennedy's answer was very much to the point. The

embassy in Rome is now quite adequate to handle any communications with the Holy See, and there is no need of braided or plumed or salaried ambassadors specifically assigned to the Vatican, with expensive establishments and retinues. For several years the special matters of information about the Vatican arising in connection with American interests have been covered by one young man in the United States embassy in Rome, and this Vatican assignment has taken only part of his time.

Journalists of the stature of Mr. Reston and Mr. Sulzberger are very persuasive if their arguments are taken in isolation. In general, it is a good thing to establish communications with any state possessing power, and the Vatican certainly possesses great moral power. The Vatican, as Mr. Reston points out, is "a listening post of great potential." "In Catholic lands," Mr. Sulzberger says, "the Vatican has an evident influence that transcends pure theology. This can be discerned, for example, in the simple fact that Catholicism's political image, Christian Democracy, has a powerful hold in all six countries of the European Common Market. And in the Communist orbit those lands where an independent spirit is most marked are often those with large Catholic populations."[11]

Yes, but are not these facts the very facts that cause many Americans to hesitate concerning diplomatic relations with the Vatican? What lies beyond recognition? Vatican diplomacy is part of an ecclesiastical-political network that spreads across national boundaries and involves a whole chain of political parties in Europe and Latin America under Vatican influence if not under direct Vatican control. In respect to these ecclesiastical-political parties the Vatican acts as a kind of advisory super-state. Does the United States want to do anything even indirectly to promote and encourage any Church in such a political role, particularly at the very moment when liberal Catholics are doubting the wisdom of the Vatican's participation in diplomatic and political affairs?

In a sense it is unfortunate that the question of diplomatic relations should receive so much attention, because formal diplomacy is the least important part of the church-state political problem.

The diplomatic establishment is important only because it is part of a semi-political Church with its own interests to preserve. In view of those interests, it must be remembered that the Vatican is not only a diplomatic listening post but a diplomatic leakage post. Because of their special institutional interests the Vatican diplomats in all parts of the world are engaged in promoting certain political policies which they describe as "moral" but which many non-Catholics describe as anti-social—e.g., opposition to birth control and the advocacy of sectarian teaching in public schools. Such promotion goes on throughout the world quite apart from Vatican diplomacy, but it counts upon the aid of such diplomacy wherever feasible.

Recent American experience has demonstrated that American cardinals or bishops can be just as obnoxious or mistaken in matters of political policy as formally appointed Vatican diplomats. The role of Cardinal Spellman vis-à-vis Vietnam is well known: he was the chief promoter of the Catholic dictator of South Vietnam, Ngo Dinh Diem, whose elevation to the premiership by American military power proved so disastrous.[12] The American experience in 1960 in Puerto Rico was equally unpleasant, although it had its comic opera aspects.[13] On that American island the first large-scale Catholic political party on American soil was formed by the Church to defeat Governor Luis Munoz Marin and his "birth controllers and the social scientists with an itch to remake a culture." Because the "island's government promotes abortion and sterilization and puts its strength behind efforts to defeat Catholic-supported proposals for establishment of a released-time religious education program for public school pupils," three Catholic bishops on the island proclaimed in letters read in all Puerto Rican churches that a vote for Munoz' party was "sinful." They and their Christian Action Party were overwhelmingly defeated, but even Pope John did not rebuke them. During the controversy *Osservatore Romano* opined that no country provided sufficient guarantees of the rights of God and the Church if it admitted divorce.

In many countries Vatican diplomacy is inextricably entangled with two other political phenomena of Catholicism, the concordat and the Catholic political party. Although both phenomena are declining in importance, they cannot be ignored in assessing the meaning of Vatican diplomacy. In general the concordat represents the final triumph of Church diplomacy in a secular world. In spite of all the Council's professions of support for religious liberty and opposition to all kinds of discrimination, there are still many Vatican concordats in effect that give exclusive rights to Catholicism and discriminate against all other faiths.

Concordats are political treaties binding political regimes to maintain certain relations with the Vatican as a foreign state, and usually conferring upon the Church a favored position in the nation. In many cases they are deemed to be irreversible under national constitutions—the situation in Italy where, under the Vatican concordat of 1929, the Vatican claims that the Italian people have no independent constitutional right even by majority vote to change the system of Church privileges. Germany, Spain, Portugal, and Colombia also have full treaties that establish the Catholic Church as an organization with specific grants of status, or money, or both, while Belgium and France have partial concordats covering certain territories. In addition there are several nations with special favorable conventions between their governments and the Church.

Although the Vatican had no special concordat with Vietnam, the bitter memory of past political favors to the Church in that country, when it was under French colonial rule, explains a great deal of the hostility of Vietnam Buddhists to the West. The Catholic Church was the privileged Church under French rule, and government favoritism to Catholicism prevailed in the schools, the army and the public services, although Catholics never comprised more than 10 per cent of the population.

After World War II there was a temporary boom in Catholic parties in Europe. The *Register* boasted in 1957 that Catholic postwar political drives had brought into power Adenauer in Germany, De Gasperi and Scelba in Italy, Bidault and Schuman in France, van Zeeland in Belgium, Salazar in Portugal, Artajo in

Spain, Figel and Gruber in Austria, Costello and De Valera in Ireland, and Magsaysay and Ngo Dinh Diem in Asia.[14] The political parties led by these statesmen all supported existing concordats with the Vatican wherever these concordats existed and all advocated that partial union of church and state that guarantees some tax support for the Catholic faith.

This has strengthened the political and economic prospects of Catholicism, but has it helped the Church as a spiritual and religious body? Many Catholics believe that an unwelcome clericalism has been introduced into these parties and that the Church has been ultimately weakened by being represented before the public as a political organization based on self-interest. When a Catholic political party fails, it tends to drag the Church down with it. On the whole, American Catholics are not proud of the Church's political ventures in Europe and Asia since World War II. There is no disposition to form a Catholic political party in the United States, and among American liberal Catholics there is a distinct tendency to regard all Church diplomats as well as all Church political parties as of doubtful value.

In such attitudes, of course, there is no hostility to the Church's efforts on behalf of world peace, racial justice, or economic reform. No one questions the importance of the Church's role in influencing political policy by persuasion. It is part of the duty of the Church and of all churches to exercise moral influence. But should not the Church's drive for peace, plenty, and justice stand on its own legs, religious legs?

CHAPTER FIFTEEN ❧ CHURCH, STATE, AND SCHOOLS

ON November 17, 1964, a short, stoutish, balding bishop with pink cheeks and a rather frail, high-pitched voice stood up in the aula and opened the debate on Christian education. The place was hushed, for this was Francis Cardinal Spellman of New York, the head of the richest archdiocese in the world, which is said to contribute more money to the Vatican's charitable enterprises than the whole continent of Europe.

While Bishop Fulton J. Sheen is recognized in the Catholic world as Mr. Money Bags because his chief function (successfully exercised) is to raise money for Catholic missions, Cardinal Spellman is recognized as Mr. Money Power. His influence in Rome was particularly evident during the reign of Pius XII, and for many years, until the Council began, he was regarded as the unofficial American primate. Since the Vatican will not permit the elevation of any one Cardinal to that official role for fear of encouraging too much "Americanism," Spellman's primacy has always been unofficial. He is recognized in his own right as one of the most strenuous defenders of Catholic education in the world, including the claims of Catholic education for public tax funds. He had become world famous in 1949 by attacking Mrs. Roosevelt when she championed the traditional American gospel of public money for public schools only. At that time he had called Mrs. Roosevelt's pleas for preserving the American tradition on church and state "documents of discrimination unworthy of an American mother," and had been met with such a storm of adverse criticism that he had been forced by public opinion to make an apology, some said by the orders of the Pope himself.

Although Spellman was chastened by that experience, his new humility did not last long. He returned to the attack in 1952 by accusing the National Education Association of fostering a Jim Crow philosophy toward Catholic children because of the N.E.A.'s opposition to tax appropriations for Catholic schools. Three days before the inauguration of the first Catholic President, in January 1961, Spellman, acting against the advice of his most experienced political and clerical associates, issued a public demand for an equal share for Catholic schools in any federal educational appropriations. He implied that any rejection of his demand would amount to "economic compulsion" and a denial of "that freedom of religion guaranteed by our country's Constitution." The demand horrified President Kennedy whose opposition to such a program as unconstitutional had been frequently voiced. Spellman's public attacks on the Kennedy policy continued until the latter's death in 1963. In 1962, in criticizing Kennedy's program of aid to public schools only, the Cardinal called it "a terrible crime" to exclude Catholic children and parents from the benefits of a federal aid bill.[1]

Now, as he stood up in the aula to lead off the Council's debate on education, he was repeating the same theme with worldwide implications. But his words at the Council in 1964 were much bolder and more comprehensive than the language he had used in his attack on Mrs. Roosevelt in 1949. He asked that the Declaration on Education before the Council be strengthened to guarantee "distributive justice" to Catholic children and their parents. In making this demand he used the same denials of his larger purpose that he had used in 1949. At that time he had denied that he was asking for anything more than fringe benefits for American Catholic schools. This time he began by assuring the world that the intention of the schema was "not necessarily to seek money from the public treasury for religious schools." Thereafter he immediately proceeded to contradict this generalization by asking for an amendment that would make sure that Catholic schools wherever feasible secured tax dollars. His amendment read:

> Parents should be free to choose the schools they wish for their children. They should not in consequence of their choice be subject to unjust economic burdens which would infringe upon this freedom of choice. Since it is the function of the State to facilitate civil freedoms, justice and equity demand that a due measure of public aid be available to parents in support of the schools they select for their children. Moreover, if these schools serve the public service of popular education, the fact that they may be religious in their operation should not exclude them from a rightful measure of public support.[2]

For European Catholics there was nothing particularly novel in Cardinal Spellman's amendment. As we have already seen, the same principle was squeezed into a paragraph of the Council's Declaration on Religious Liberty. All recent popes have embodied such demands in their public and official utterances without even tipping their tiaras in the direction of the contrary precedents in the United States Constitution and American experience. In Europe the Church has continued through the centuries to demand, and often to secure, public revenues even for the strictly devotional portions of the Church enterprise, and sometimes such revenue has been secured even from Communist governments.

Why should not the same principle be applied to financial support for the educational portion of the Church structure in democratic countries? For most of Western Europe, for Protestant nations as well as for Catholic nations, "distributive justice" had come to include tax support for sectarian schools as a matter of course. The predominantly Catholic countries had come to the policy automatically in their natural historical growth. Often the practice of special tax grants had been embodied in Vatican concordats to make sure that no sudden surge of anti-clerical sentiment would upset the arrangement. Such predominantly non-Catholic countries as Germany and the Netherlands had come to adopt the policy after a struggle, the Netherlands as late as 1920. Britain had adopted it as part of the Anglican tradition. France after a long struggle against clerical power which began in the

1880's and culminated temporarily in the laws separating church and state in 1905, had swung back under Catholic pressure to a system that gave Catholic schools a considerable grant of public revenue indirectly.

Italy, with its powerful anti-clerical minority, had fought a long see-saw battle for genuinely public schools for a century, usually losing out to the Church, which continued to retain its monopoly on religious instruction in the national schools. Now the Church is trying to extend its educational domain in Italy at taxpayers' expense. Italy remains a living demonstration of the fact that any grant to Catholic education is a natural prelude to a larger demand. The battle between public and clerically controlled education is just as bitter there today as it is in non-Catholic countries, with the public features of education constantly enduring clerical sabotage. Twice, in 1964 and 1966, the Christian Democratic and Socialist coalition government headed by Premier Aldo Moro fell because of bitter disputes over clerical demands in the field of education.

When Spellman spoke for tax support for Catholic schools he was voicing not only traditional European political gospel but traditional papal gospel. In the bible of modern Catholic philosophy on education, the 1930 encyclical of Pius XI on Christian Education, it had been assumed without argument that Catholic education should be aided by public funds. The state, it was claimed, had only a secondary right in education to begin with, and "education belongs pre-eminently to the Church, by reason of a double title in the supernatural order." "The State," said Pius XI graciously, "may . . . reserve to itself the establishment and direction of schools intended to prepare for certain civic duties and especially for military service, provided it be careful not to injure the rights of the Church or of the family in what pertains to them."[3] Pius asserted that everything in education of a moral nature belonged to the Church.

Spokesmen for Catholic education in the United States have amplified that gospel at Congressional hearings by declaring flatly that "government itself has nothing to teach."[4] By this assertion they have meant to convey the notion that it is the Church which has primary responsibility for the ideological content of the education of Catholics, while the state has responsibility for special training for government services and military activity. The conflict here is particularly profound in the United States, since the public school system has been based upon the assumption that education, all education except religious education, is a primary government responsibility, as significant a democratic function as the maintenance of communications and national defense. Protestantism asserted considerable authority in the early years of American education, but that authority has now been virtually eliminated and the public school system has been accepted as a democratic and nonclerical phenomenon. Thus, the American experience is set off in sharp contrast to the European experience. The United States is the only Western democracy with a predominantly Christian population that has never had a Catholic background, and perhaps that is the basic reason why it has accepted with wholehearted zeal the gospel that a common school system should not be controlled by any church. Simultaneously the United States has helped to make it possible for the world's leading opponent of that gospel, the Roman Catholic Church, to develop in freedom the largest purely sectarian school system in the world, with approximately 5,700,000 students.

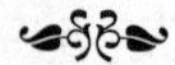

Although the exact wording of the Spellman amendment was never written into the final Declaration on Christian Education, its substance was accepted as the financial-educational gospel of Vatican II. The final draft adopted by the Council spoke almost as plainly as the Spellman amendment: "Parents, who have the first and inalienable duty and right to educate their children, should enjoy true freedom in their choice of schools. Consequently, public authority, which has the obligation to oversee and defend the liberties of citizens, ought to see to it, out of a concern for distributive justice, that public subsidies are allocated in such a way that, when selecting schools for their children, parents are genuinely free to follow their consciences."

The final Declaration on Christian Education was a strange blend of old and new ideas. It affirmed the proposition that "the office of educating belongs by a unique title to the Church," but it also affirmed that: "Since every man of whatever race, condition, and age is endowed with the dignity of a person, he has an inalienable right to an education corresponding to his proper destiny and suited to his native talents, his sex, his cultural background and his ancestral heritage." After much argument behind the scenes, a single sentence was included in favor of "a positive and prudent sexual education," whatever that means.

At no time in the discussions in St. Peter's was there any substantial ventilation of the question whether subsidies for Catholic schools might violate the principle of the separation of church and state. To all intents and purposes this principle was nonexistent in the debates on education. If the American bishops knew that it existed, they did not want to talk about it in the aula. They carefully avoided any suggestion that they were defying the United States Constitution and the decisions of their own Supreme Court. They went along, apparently in complete docility, with Cardinal Spellman's concept of a separate Catholic school system entitled by natural right to secure tax support. They gave the green light to every campaign for tax funds for Catholic schools throughout the world, being careful to reserve for the decision of a commission to be created later the practical question whether any particular campaign for funds was "prudent."

The American bishops at the Council did not even challenge in public the coercive principle of the most famous educational canon in Catholic canon law, Canon 1374, which nominally compels Catholic parents to send their children to Catholic schools unless they receive episcopal exemption. It reads:

> Catholic children may not attend non-Catholic, neutral, or mixed schools, that is, those which are open also to non-Catholics, and it pertains exclusively to the Ordinary [bishop] of the place to decide, in accordance with instructions of the

Holy See, under what circumstances and with what precautions against the danger of perversion, attendance at such schools may be tolerated.

There is an official Catholic Church ruling, dated 1867, which, in interpreting this Canon, declares: "It is almost if not quite impossible for those circumstances to exist which would render attendance at non-Catholic universities free from sin."

Many American Catholic leaders, including the American Jesuits, have recognized the inconsistency and uselessness of Canon 1374 in a nation which prides itself on liberty of choice in education. *America*, in an editorial published between the third and fourth sessions, declared that: "This law of the Church is not and cannot be rigorously enforced in the United States. There are not enough Catholic schools to accommodate all Catholic children. Even if there were, we doubt whether it would serve the cause of Catholic education in a free society to impose it as a law on the members of the Church."[5] The Jesuit editors argued that the properly instructed conscience of a Catholic parent would always choose the Catholic school wherever possible.

James O'Gara of *Commonweal* went a little further than the Jesuits and protested against the use of the coercive principle in campaigning against attendance at public schools. "In the parish in which I grew up," he said, "the pastor each September warned of the dark fate that awaited those Catholic children who went to the public school—and the even darker fate that awaited their parents." O'Gara contended that this kind of teaching was outdated, the product of an era when public schools were much more Protestant than they are today. Catholics in those days found themselves in schools which were like "islands in a hostile sea." In confronting the present situation of Catholic parents he asked: "Would we really like to see Catholics totally absent from the public school system? Are we to Christianize our environment by total withdrawal, by creating ethnic islands or isolated social pockets?"[6] Nevertheless the Council reaffirmed the coercion implicit in Canon 1374 by saying: "As for Catholic parents, the Council calls to mind their duty to entrust their children to Catholic schools, when and where this is possible." Cardinal Frings of Cologne was, in his own way, just as insistent as Cardinal Spellman in declaring in the debate on ecumenism in the second session: "We should insist on religious schools for the education of our children." (West Germany has no church-state financial problem in continuing such a policy since all sectarian schools may receive government tax support.)

Although the Council did not make any direct attack on public education as such, its insistence upon the necessity for Catholic training for Catholic pupils in *all* schools excluded the policy of religious neutrality as it had been developed in American public schools under Supreme Court decisions. The Council said: "The Church must be present with her own special affection and help for the great number who are being trained in schools that are not Catholic . . . especially by the ministry of priests and laymen who give them the doctrine of salvation in a way suited to their age and circumstances and provide spiritual aid in every way the times and conditions allow."

Inherent in this statement of Church educational policy by Vatican II is the second great conflict between the Catholic and the prevailing legal concept of education in the United States—the first is financial but this conflict is ideological. The Church insists not only on the theoretical primacy of the Church in the field of education but it also insists that it has the duty and responsibility to follow the Catholic child into any secular institution and give that child the full Catholic gospel either in the public classroom or in released-time classes. In prevailing Catholic dialectics this is not an illegal union of church and state but a sound form of "separation" in which the state gives secular learning to the Catholic child while the Church gives him religious and moral training. This is the policy in Catholic nations where Catholicism has the power to enforce it.

By a strange coincidence, while Vatican II was underscoring this Catholic policy on religion and education, the United States

Supreme Court was going farther in renouncing this policy than it had ever gone before. Its new position was announced in two decisions just before and just after the Council began.[7] In the Regents' Prayer decision of 1962 the Court outlawed from public classrooms a simple nondenominational prayer on the ground that its recitation by pupils was an illegal establishment of religion under the First Amendment—"Congress shall make no law respecting an establishment of religion, or prohibiting the free exercise thereof." In the following year the Court went even farther and outlawed, under the same constitutional principles, the reading of the Bible and the recitation of the Lord's Prayer as part of any religious exercise in any American public classroom.

American Catholics, whose forebears had been the original complainants against the reading of the King James version of the Bible in public schools, now saw those schools cleansed of all Catholic as well as all Protestant and Jewish features. They did not like the result. Their leaders were almost unanimous in denouncing the philosophy of the Supreme Court, although they were finally persuaded that a drive to amend the Constitution to reverse the Court's decision would not be prudent.

In financial matters the clash between Catholic policy and American constitutional policy in the field of education is even clearer than it is in matters of religious instruction. Although the United States Supreme Court has not yet written a comprehensive decision on all aspects of the financial issue, the Court's incidental references to the problem have clearly indicated that the Justices consider any across-the-board grants of tax funds to sectarian schools unconstitutional. In conceding the constitutionality of public grants for bus funds for parochial pupils under the Federal Constitution—by a vote of 5 to 4 in 1947—the court made it clear that such appropriations were legitimate only on the assumption that they could be considered grants to the child for personal safety, not grants to a sectarian school for its operations.[8] The Court denied general Catholic financial claims by saying: "No tax in any amount, large or small, can be levied to support any religious activities or institutions whatever they may be called, or whatever form they may adopt to teach or practice religion."

No one can deny that Catholic schools in the United States are primarily "religious institutions" or that they exist largely to "teach or practice religion." As Justice Jackson pointed out in his dissent in the above bus decision: "Catholic education is the rock on which the whole structure rests, and to render tax aid to its Church school is indistinguishable to me from rendering the same aid to the Church."

Justice Jackson's realistic interpretation of the place of the Catholic school in the Catholic power structure is supported by many papal documents on education, documents which make it quite impossible to argue that Catholic schools can be split into two segments, spiritual and secular, for the purpose of channeling tax funds into the secular portion only. In a strict sense, there is no secular portion of a Catholic school. Pius XI in his encyclical on Christian Education said that "it is necessary that all the teaching and the whole organization of the [Catholic] school and its teachers, syllabus and textbooks in every branch, be regulated by the Christian spirit, under the direction and maternal supervision of the Church." For good measure, Pius quoted Leo XIII: "It is necessary not only that religious instruction be given at certain fixed times, but also that every other subject taught be permeated with Christian [Catholic] piety."[9] Financially speaking, Catholic schools are built into the treasury of a parish, a diocese, or a religious order, and their government is subject to the Church itself.

This whole policy of rigid and complete clerical control of Catholic education was accepted at Vatican II without serious challenge, along with the traditional claim that the state owes the Catholic schools a living because they perform a public service. The American bishops, along with the other bishops, in confirming the Church's traditional claim to tax funds, rejected the reasoning of the United States Supreme Court on the subject, and also the reasoning of the first American Catholic President. President Kennedy had firmly declared that he considered across-the-board grants to sectarian schools unconstitutional, and he also accepted with apparent approval the two decisions of the Supreme Court in 1962 and 1963 outlawing prayer and Bible-reading from public schools as unconstitutional. Unfortunately, the rejection by Vatican II of Kennedy's views and the Supreme Court's views on school policy received almost no attention in the American press, although it was in many ways one of the most important events of the Council years. The shortage of discussion even in the press conferences was partly responsible for this strange omission. Education never became a great controversial issue in the aula, and controversy in St. Peter's had been accepted as the basic ingredient in legitimate headlines.

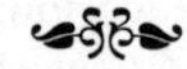

The thing that happened to the separation of church and state in the schools of the United States as a result of "the ecumenical spirit" of Vatican II might be described as How to Succeed in Wrecking the Constitution Without Really Trying, or The Special Uses of Religious Euphoria. In the new atmosphere of uncritical "brotherhood" Catholicism was able, with the help of pliant politicians and concessionist Protestants, to reach into the public treasury more successfully than it had ever done in the course of two decades of political lobbying in Washington. Three things happened in the United States which were just as important for the extension of Catholic power as anything which happened in St. Peter's. First, many Protestant organizations partially abandoned their long struggle against tax appropriations for parochial schools. Second, the Johnson administration, taking adroit advantage of the denominational euphoria, slipped through Congress several educational measures which chipped away the wall of separation between church and state in education very cleverly, granting millions of dollars in tangential aid to sectarian schools under the concepts of "welfare" and "poverty." Third, in partial negation of this drift, there was a surprising and important movement among Catholic liberals questioning the whole logic of the parochial school system itself. This third movement tended to slow up but not to halt the steady and persistent drive on the public treasury by the standard Catholic organizations throughout the country.

The partial surrender by certain elements of American Protestantism to Catholic demands for tax grants had been approaching for a number of years. Many Protestant colleges had begun to receive some federal appropriations long before the Johnson administration began. Self-interest had gradually altered traditional principles. Oddly enough, the leaders in the Protestant movement of concession came largely from the liberal seminaries of the East, such as Union Seminary in New York and Yale Divinity School, while the two largest Protestant denominations, Baptist and Methodist, tended to hold the financial line more firmly. America's largest single Protestant denominational group, the Southern Baptist Convention, spoke out most firmly against subsidies to sectarian elementary schools, while the Methodist bishops, late in 1965, issued a statement that could be construed as the definitive answer of moderate American Protestantism to the educational philosophy of Vatican II. Praising the new atmosphere of "harmony and friendship" in world Christianity, the bishops still resisted the use of such euphoria to gain access to the public treasury by saying:

> We recognize the right of churches to establish and conduct such [elementary and secondary] schools under their auspices if proper educational standards are maintained. We do not believe the right includes the obligation of government to support directly or indirectly such schools.
>
> We are concerned lest under the guise of "child benefits," increasing amounts of public funds be diverted to private education, until through the cumulative effect of piecemeal diversion of tax money the service rendered by the public schools be seriously impaired.
>
> We believe that public funds cannot be constitutionally, nor in the public interest, used to support non-public elementary and secondary schools which serve as channels for inculcating religious doctrine.
>
> We call upon our Methodist people to resist in every legitimate way the allocation of public funds to such agencies.[10]

This statement by orthodox Methodist bishops does not represent all American Protestantism, even liberal Protestantism. Several of the most liberal American Protestant leaders have turned out to be the most effective apologists for Catholic financial demands in education. Influential professors at Union Seminary in New York had taken the lead in attacking the Supreme Court's theories on the separation of church and state in education as early as 1948, using terms almost as severe as those employed by the Catholic bishops.[11] By 1962, Dr. John C. Bennett, the able progressive who was then dean and is now president of Union Seminary in New York, was declaring that somehow parochial school children "should be included within the educational purpose of the nation, [and] that their health and welfare can be aided without transgressing the principle of the separation of church and state." The concept of "health and welfare" was soon stretched to cover many parts of the Catholic educational enterprise. By 1965 Dr. Bennett was accepting with equanimity the thesis that "all forms of non-religious aid to pupils in parochial schools that are administratively feasible will come to be generally accepted."[12] In practice this policy, if pursued in the manner which is characteristic of Catholic policy throughout the world, could result in a tax contribution of 90 per cent of the operating costs of Catholic schools.

The chief American Protestant organization, the National Council of Churches, is not willing to accept the present drift toward public financial support for parochial schools, although it conditionally and mistakenly supported the Johnson educational program of 1965. Dean M. Kelley, one of its leading officials, pointed out before a Congressional hearing in May 1966 that the Johnson program had been accepted by many Protestants on the assumption that the child-benefit theory would not be stretched to cover such features as art, libraries, and music education in sectarian schools. He objected to a child-benefit concept which is "nothing but a ruse under which tax aid can go to church-related schools." He opposed an indefinite extension of the program until the government makes clear how the child-benefit theory is to be interpreted.

The drift toward public subsidies for Catholic schools in the United States is supported by two appealing theses, which were used persuasively at Vatican II's press conferences, that such subsidies are benefits for the child rather than the Church, and that "secular subjects" can be separated in the Catholic school system from pure religious instruction and legally endowed without injuring the principle of church-state separation. Both of these are fallacious.

Children, of course, receive benefit from a subsidy of Catholic schools, but so does the Church of which the school is a part. If the "child benefit" theory is subject to indefinite expansion it may easily be stretched to include the whole area of taxes for religion, and this is precisely what the Supreme Court attempted to prevent in a careful decision in 1947. Under the prevailing philosophy of American public education, every American child is entitled to the child benefit of a fully paid-up seat in an American public school, whose managers are forbidden to discriminate against any child on the basis of his faith or the lack of it. If the parents of any faith wish to decline the invitation to occupy the paid-up seats, their choice of alternative accommodations is their own, and likewise their financial responsibility is their own.

World Catholicism, as exemplified at Vatican II, rejects the philosophy behind this policy because it refuses to accept the prevailing American theory that education is primarily a government responsibility to be exercised through democratically owned and operated public schools. For more than a generation American Catholicism blocked general federal aid to public schools by demanding as a condition precedent to acceptance of federal aid that its own schools be given commensurate tax support. Its Washington blockade was finally victorious under President Johnson, a supremely practical politician.

When, in 1964 and 1965, President Johnson moved into the broken field of Protestant hesitations and Catholic pressure and put over two educational bills that siphoned off to Catholic schools many millions of "welfare" and "poverty" dollars, he was trading heavily on the new and uncritical ecumenical spirit produced by

Vatican II. In fact, it is probable that his maneuver would not have been successful without the new Protestant-Catholic concessionism that came from the Council. His two chief laws, the Economic Opportunity Act of 1964 and the Elementary and Secondary Education Act of 1965, gave many millions to sectarian schools without even providing for a court test of the delicate and vital constitutional issues involved. Most Protestant organizations put up only token resistance, and the bills went through Congress in a swift "ecumenical" triumph. Only a few militant organizations like the American Civil Liberties Union, the American Jewish Congress, and Protestants and Other Americans United for Separation of Church and State challenged the new sectarian concessions as unconstitutional. Their multiple suits, relying on the no-establishment clause of the First Amendment, are now on the way to final adjudication by the United States Supreme Court.

The leaders of the three militant defenders of church-state separation went back to the principles of Thomas Jefferson when he was fighting for religious freedom and the nonestablishment of religion in Virginia in 1786. They quoted the preamble of Jefferson's Act for Establishing Religious Freedom in Virginia, which said that "to compel a man to furnish contributions of money for the propagation of opinions which he disbelieves is sinful and tyrannical."[13] Appealing to these principles in *The New York Times*, Will Maslow, executive director of the American Jewish Congress, declared in 1965: "Neither the cause of the Catholic faith, nor of religion generally, nor of education, nor of democracy, nor of the American people is served by abandoning the great and immutable principles that have enabled church, state and freedom to flourish in America as nowhere else on earth."[14]

C. Stanley Lowell of P.O.A.U., testifying for militant Protestants before a Senate committee, pointed out that under the Johnson program

> . . . the libraries of church schools can be permanently stocked and subsidized and many kinds of teaching materials provided from Federal tax funds. This is direct and obvious aid to the budget of any school. . . . It makes a shambles of

the doctrine of separation of church and state. . . . Surely it is not necessary to help Methodist children via assistance to the Methodist Church, or Catholic children via assistance to Catholic parishes. . . . As a matter of fact, is it really a sound legislative concept at all to separate children by religious groups in order to cure their poverty? Is it, in short, any sounder procedure to subsidize religiously segregated schools than to subsidize racially segregated schools? If one is wrong, where is the virtue in the other?[15]

Perhaps the most powerful attack on the verbal artifices used in Catholic demands for school funds—both in America and elsewhere—was made before a Congressional committee in 1965 by Rabbi Richard G. Hirsch, representing the Committee on Social Action of Reform Judaism:

We deceive ourselves as a nation if we use semantics to conceal what has actually occurred. Both the language of the bill and the language of those who support it tend to create the illusion that it is the child, not the school, to which Federal aid is to be given. However, in the guise of aiding the child, this bill does aid the school. . . .

If the child benefit theory is to be used as the basis for providing private school children with textbooks, instructional materials and mobile services, then what cannot be given? . . . This bill does not, as some have maintained, avoid the church-state issue. It evades it. An end run around the principle can advance the ball of Federal assistance just as far as a direct plunge through the middle of the line. . . .

By tending to equate public and church schools in the eyes of the law as equally entitled to public support, this bill will greatly stimulate the creation of separate parochial school systems in every denomination. The temptation to sup at the trough is not one to which most religious denominations have shown any exceptional resistance. As a network of parochial schools mushrooms, support for public schools would constantly be diluted.[16]

In the discussions at Vatican II press conferences in the last session, after the adoption of the Johnson program of financial concessions to sectarian schools, the American bishops and *periti* were jubilant. They took it for granted that the no-establishment clause of the First Amendment had at last been successfully bypassed and that the Catholic view of government responsibility for the maintenance of sectarian schools had triumphed. They based their comments upon the standard Catholic claim that "distributive justice" calls for approximately equal contributions to Catholic school *children* as well as public school *children*, ignoring the fact that this artifice means support by general taxpayers of the most important segment of the Catholic Church. At home, in New York, *America* remarked joyfully: "The 'child benefit' principle is capable of being extended to every phase of education other than the directly religious."[17]

While American Catholicism was scoring this financial triumph in the European manner, there had begun to develop among American Catholic liberals a considerable flank movement against the Church's whole separatist policy in education. The movement produced many repercussions at the Council. Why was it necessary to have Catholic schools at all when the American Catholic community was no longer consigned to a cultural ghetto? Why indeed?

These questions burst into national headlines in 1963 when a book called *Are Parochial Schools the Answer?* by Mary Perkins Ryan reached the book stores.[18] Mrs. Ryan could not be dismissed as a "bad" Catholic or even, by ordinary standards, as a liberal Catholic. She had, four years earlier, published a book called *Christ and the Church* which was exceptionally devout. She now suggested the partial, not complete, abolition of parochial schools, not because she wanted less religion for Catholic children but because she wanted more religious faith and more scientifically cultivated instruction for these children. Why, she asked, should her church spend so much energy on "what is essentially an auxiliary service"? And she added that "in trying to provide a total Catholic education for as many of her young people as possible, we have been neglecting to provide anything like adequate religious formation for all those not in Catholic schools."

She pointed out that, in terms of manpower and time consumed, the Catholic schools are virtually overshadowing the Church itself. In 1961, out of 59,581 priests in the country, 12,840 devoted their time to education, 5,281 out of 11,502 Brothers were similarly engaged, and 103,141 Sisters out of 173,351. She argued that the Catholic school system grew out of a siege mentality that "also accounts for the authoritarian 'clericalized' structure of American Catholic life." She emphasized the prodigious expenditures required for a Catholic school system that was compelled to compete with the excellence of the publicly financed American schools.

Although Mrs. Ryan did not argue exclusively for any one solution of the Catholic educational problem, her analysis lent weight to a solution developed in Lexington, Massachusetts, by Monsignor George Casey, who had sent most of his Catholic students to public schools and given them religion after school hours in separate Catholic centers. Monsignor Casey had startled his people several years ago by suggesting in the Boston *Pilot* that parochial elementary schools "be phased out gradually and supplanted by a massive emphasis on regional high schools." The key reform in his plan, which had the backing of Cardinal Cushing, was a large Catholic center for the religious training of Catholic students enrolled in public schools for one hour each week, thirty weeks a year, staggered on a released-time basis. His parish recently opened the John F. Kennedy School of Religion for such Catholic public school pupils, with an enrollment of more than 2,000 and some 135 adult lay teachers. Similar plans have been developed recently in other centers in New England and the Middle West. The concept involved might ultimately prove to be the most practical solution of the issues raised in the present rivalry between the public and parochial school systems.[19]

The liberal Catholic movement in the United States, in its criticism of Catholic education, forced a considerable amount of rethinking of the whole problem at the very moment when the

Vatican Council was evading any thorough analysis. John Leo of *Commonweal* suggested that although present-day Catholic schools enroll slightly more than half of all American Catholic children, probably only one-third of tomorrow's Catholic children will attend such schools. The great American public school system, increasingly financed by federal funds, will soon become more than ever the natural place for American elementary education. Even the public universities will undoubtedly increase in importance and excellence, winning more and more Catholic students away from the clerically controlled institutions. Thomas J. Fleming, writing in the *Saturday Evening Post* on "The Crisis in Catholic Schools," declared: "The parochial school system is showing alarming symptoms of potential collapse."[20] He pointed out that there is an acute shortage of teaching recruits for religious orders and that in some parishes 50 to 75 per cent of the church offerings are necessary to subsidize the parochial schools. He raised the fundamental and all-important question whether in a democratic society that provides free education for all, "Catholic schools aren't an extravagant duplication."

In all of this discussion, however, very few Catholic voices in the United States were raised in support of the all-out Jeffersonian concept of church-state separation as distinct from the Catholic and European concept of partial church-state union. If Catholic demands for public revenues for Church schools were weakened by the new critical realism among Catholic liberals in the United States, the result was due to considerations of expediency rather than principle. Most of the Catholic liberals agree with most of the conservatives that sectarian schools have a moral claim to tax dollars. Jesuit leaders like John Courtney Murray go along with this view. So, if the Catholic hierarchy in the United States chooses to continue its present policy, it is difficult to avoid the conclusion that America is facing a hundred years' war over tax appropriations to Catholic schools. Americans are even more deeply divided on the subject than Europeans, and the Council only accentuated the division. For the time being at least, American law is on the side of those who are opposed to general support of sectarian education out of the public treasury, and the laws cannot be changed without a long and bitter struggle in which emotion will play a greater part than reason.

There is no doubt that the euphoria produced by the Council helped to advance Catholic financial aims in education by tending to equate good will with acquiescence in Catholic policy. The obvious truth that schools that are segregated by creed tend automatically to promote religious bigotry has been almost overlooked in the American press during the Council years. Yet it is this truth that is more important than all the other truths and half-truths in the discussion. As the *Manchester Guardian Weekly* said in an article shortly after the Council: "If the state finances schools that elaborate and confirm parental prejudice, it is using its resources to divide society along sectarian lines."[21]

CHAPTER SIXTEEN ❧ SWEETNESS AND LIGHT

All through the early sessions of the Council the schema that was finally called "The Church in the Modern World" served for the journalists as a kind of conditional, pluperfect Santa Claus who would come down the chimney to bring presents to those bored correspondents who had become weary of theological generalizations. Whenever these correspondents asked about what the Council intended to do in connection with the twentieth century, they were likely to hear the answer: "Wait until we get to Schema 17, or Schema 13"—the Schema was numbered 17 in the beginning and later shifted to 13 when surplus intervening material was eliminated.

The history of Schema 13 was checkered. The modern world as such had been so little in the minds of the original managers of the agenda, the gentlemen in the Roman Curia, that they did not even have a chapter on the subject. Then it became apparent, as acute correspondents and liberal bishops raised serious questions that were not confined to the realms of theology, that a kind of catch-all statement of some kind about the social ills of modern man was absolutely necessary. Cardinal Suenens of Belgium, in December 1962, was the chief initiator of the drive for such a statement.

The Curia officials were suspicious from the beginning because they felt such a chapter was bound to raise issues beyond their competence. But they finally acquiesced with the understanding that bothersome questions would be left to the end of the Council sessions, when they might very well be shunted off conveniently on the ground that time had run out. In spite of their hesitations and obstructions, it became more and more apparent as the Council proceeded that Schema 13 would be one of the most important items of the Council's history.

As it turned out, the Pope and the conservatives stripped the final form of the schema to the bone, omitting, as we have seen, any detailed treatment of birth control, priestly celibacy, mixed marriage, or divorce. The Fathers affirmed all the current policies on these subjects either by silence or by brief statements of confirmation, without even giving the liberal majority any real opportunity to debate them fully.

There were, however, so many things left to talk about that Schema 13 remained very important. The Church spoke out quite boldly on several great issues of modern life, and its statements were reasonably progressive. Oddly enough, the statements were largely confined to areas in which the bishops were not real experts. The less they knew the more they had to say. As one Polish bishop grumbled concerning the Schema: "It goes into too many detailed problems without proper competence." A Belgian bishop asked petulantly what in the world the text meant by the word "world," pointing out that a well-known book on biblical terminology gives six columns of meanings for that much-abused word, and that the proposed text of Schema 13 was not clear concerning any one of them.

A more common objection, which persisted to the end, was the criticism voiced by Bishop Elchinger of Strasbourg, that the schema was strong on the descriptions of the problems of the world and weak concerning the church's own program for reforming itself to meet these problems. The bishop said: "It says much about what the world is expected to do but not enough on what the Church should do. We should state clearly how the Church intends to realize the legitimate desires of mankind."

Schema 13 arrived on the Council floor in the third session, in October 1964, and was immediately subjected to two weeks of fire and crossfire. Then it was sent back to commission for very extensive revision, and it emerged in the form of a 30,000-word treatise in the fourth session, to be finally adopted after many revisions. It was an egregious piece of overwriting which could easily have been reduced to 10,000 words by a competent editor, and its Latin was so bad that several bishops publicly denounced it as almost incomprehensible. Even the benign Cardinal Bea said he had to resort to a French text to understand it. Cardinal Ruffini of Palermo remarked: "No one expected it to be Ciceronian, but in spots it is hardly Latin at all."

In spite of these defects, it was evident that the final text represented a real confrontation of real issues. Unfortunately, the bishops and theologians who drew up the final draft had never had any experience in writing a platform for the Republican or Democratic Parties of the U.S.A. They had not learned to say nothing briefly and make it sound like lofty wisdom. Although the language of many sections of the final draft resembled a hodge-podge of compromise about midway between the principles of Americans for Democratic Action and the Knights of Columbus, the compromise did not stop there. The old-guard theologians insisted on padding out the text with many pages of traditional dogmas in order to make sure that the Church in the modern world would be recognized as the same Church they had always served. Thus, in theological terms, the final document was a stand-pat document while in social philosophy it was the nearest thing to a revolutionary document produced by the Council.

It centered on four great issues of modern life that can be very inadequately summarized under the terms race, war, communist-atheism, and poverty. Under the umbrella of these words, the Fathers wandered all over the map of the current world, indulging in pages of tedious platitudes. But they also, for the first time in the history of Catholicism, faced some of the ugly facts of a non-Christian universe. The final schema was one of the few statements in the history of the Church to be addressed to non-Catholics.

For most of those non-Catholics it probably seemed very elementary, a mixture of devotional sentiment and trite moralism, but for many of the conservatives of the Church it must have seemed like a typhoon from Moscow. It took their beloved Church into perilous waters where all the winds of modern materialism were blowing. It offered drastic political solutions for many controversial issues. The conservatives were partially consoled by the fact that, although the exhortations were nominally addressed to the whole world, the writers of the text seemed to have forgotten themselves quite frequently and talked as if they were transmitting accepted Catholic dogmas to Christians only. Since this is what the Church had always done in the past, it came naturally.

In order to appease the conservatives, the text maintained the basic other-worldliness of the Church's theology. All suggestions for reform were made "under the light of Christ," whose name alone is adequate for salvation. The story of the world's creation in Genesis was blessed, along with the theory that man, made in holiness in Eden, has now fallen and "is engulfed by manifold ills which cannot come from his good Creator." These ills come, by inference, from a personal Devil. While recognizing earthly misery, the document contended that man has been created for a world of immortality beyond reach of such misery. The state as a cultural agency was subtly subordinated to the Church by the claim that: "As for public authority, it is not its function to determine the character of the civilization."

Having said this much to please the traditionalists, the schema then went on to say a great many practical things about the world's most controversial issues. Sweetness and light—Matthew Arnold's phrase—conquered dogma. The mixture of old theology and new sociology must have made some of the Fathers wince a little. They thought that they were getting beyond their depth and some of them said so. They quarreled with the description of the document as a "Constitution" on the theory that such a title presumed too much authority in strictly mundane matters. A compromise was finally adopted concerning the title of the document, and it was called a "Pastoral Constitution." The title was only moderately accurate. A more precise label would have been

Sociological and Political Constitution with Pastoral Accompaniments.

On the issue of racial justice the battle for a completely liberal commitment had been won long before Schema 13 reached a final vote. A few phrases on the subject were inserted in this last chapter to clinch the gospel. On this question the Church scarcely needed to say anything extensive or new because it had already acted in words and deeds throughout the world. In official doctrine the Church had become color-blind, and apparently no one at the Council even dreamed of challenging its gospel of racial decency.

The American bishops realized that in view of the constant race riots in the United States they had a special obligation to take the offensive against all racial intolerance. During the discussion of the schema on the Church, in the second session, Bishop Robert Tracy of Baton Rouge made the keynote speech on this subject and was backed by 147 American bishops. Bishop Tracy called on the Council to condemn all discrimination in the most specific language. "In the name of the bishops of the United States of North America," he proclaimed, "I want to suggest that in speaking of the People of God, we put clearer emphasis on the equality of everyone in the Church with no distinction on account of race."[1] He sat down amid thunderous applause.

It was appropriate that this concept should be expressed by a bishop of Louisiana, where racial violence had attracted worldwide attention. It was also appropriate that a little later one of the Louisiana advocates of racial justice, Archbishop Cody of New Orleans, should be elevated to the post of Archbishop of Chicago in succession to the late Cardinal Meyer. In 1965 the first American Negro bishop to be chosen since the Civil War was installed in Louisiana. American clerical leaders put the finishing touch upon their advanced gospel of racial justice in 1963 when the National Catholic Conference for Interracial Justice declared that: "The Catholic conscience condemns, abhors and rejects the underlying racist philosophy which speaks of racial intermarriage as depreciating a racial strain. Human persons are not cattle. The Catholic dogma, revealed by God, of the unity of the family cries out against this pagan ideology."[2] This was tantamount to saying that the Catholic Church in America would oppose all laws against miscegenation.

With such a record, the Church scarcely needed to include in the final draft of Schema 13 any more platitudes about racial justice. Its assurance was accepted by the whole world. The text said: "Therefore, this sacred Synod, proclaiming the noble destiny of man and championing the godlike seed which has been sown in him, offers to mankind the honest assistance of the Church in fostering that brotherhood of all men which corresponds to this destiny of theirs."

❧

When the fathers came to discuss war, peace, and international organization they found that the issues were more complex than the issue of race. Although Pope John in his *Pacem in Terris* had opened the door to new thinking about peace, his very general phrases had not done much to resolve specific issues. Both rightists and leftists within the Church attempted to appropriate his words. John deplored the arms race, but general deploring is rather simple when the deplorer does not have a large nation to defend against potential attack. John's demand for "progressive disarmament and an effective method of control" (see Chapter 2) was little more than a peace dove in a world of hawks.

Loopholes were obvious. What if one or more nations should refuse to reduce nuclear arms simultaneously? What if one or more nations should refuse to accept "effective controls"? Neither Pope John's idealistic encyclical nor Pope Paul's equally idealistic speech before the United Nations in October 1965 answered the hard contingent questions. Cardinal Alfrink of the Netherlands, debating the nuclear arms issue in the third session, insisted that the Council could not live up to the spirit of John's *Pacem in Terris* without banning both "clean bombs" and "dirty bombs."

Such peace sentiments were tremendously welcome to an American public that had become accustomed to the holy-war-against-Communism eloquence of Cardinal Spellman's recurring speeches at conventions of the American Legion. Until John and Paul had spoken, the Church had been rated, in spite of the peace appeals of several popes, as essentially a pro-war Church, always leaning toward any militant action against Communism. In the United States for many years before the advent of Pope John most of the Catholic journals could be counted upon to take the most aggressive conceivable line against any attempt to "appease" Communism. For many Catholic journals that meant a constant stream of disparaging comments against any public figure who attempted to advocate anything less than extreme, anti-Communist militancy. This was particularly true during the McCarthy era, when the diocesan press constituted an important reserve element of support for the junior senator from Wisconsin.

By the time the Council began, largely because of John's influence, the Vatican line on peace and war had shifted. The habitual scolding of Communism continued, but the suggestions for annihilating Communism by superior military power were no longer in evidence. The Vatican was groping for a middle position between the two great nuclear powers of East and West.

Living politically with one of the strongest Communist parties outside the Iron Curtain, the Church in Italy realized the necessity for a careful policy. It was geographically within easy striking distance of Soviet missiles, and within easier striking distance of its Italian Communist enemies. Both John and Paul recognized that neither Christianity nor civilization itself had any real chance of survival if full-blown atomic war between the United States and the Soviet Union should begin. Rome might be among the first casualties—including St. Peter's itself. Also, with great blocs of Catholic people living in European countries under apparently permanent Communist control, the Vatican had decided that it must continue the search for a *modus vivendi* with Communism in spite of abhorrence of Marxist teachings.

So, when the final utterances of Schema 13 on war, peace, and internationalism appeared, they seemed much too neutral for many Catholics who had been nurtured on traditional anti-Communism. Some American bishops considered them positively, even treasonably, soft.

On the whole, the incursions of the Council into this difficult territory of war and peace seemed very goodhearted but rather amateurish. The United Nations and the foreign offices of many Western powers had lived with these issues for years and learned to speak on them with great wisdom. Every noble thought on the subject expressed by the Fathers at the Council had been repeated at least a dozen times at the United Nations, usually with more knowledge and eloquence. Nevertheless, the Council's thoughts were distinctly worth expressing. In a sense they were startling in their liberal line. As one observer remarked, they "practically took the Vatican out of the cold war." This was a slight exaggeration, but there was enough truth in the statement to cause considerable rejoicing among peace advocates throughout the world —and considerable consternation among traditional Catholics.

If the Church had been a pro-war Church in the 1940's, it now suddenly emerged from the Council in 1965 as one of the most important and influential pro-peace forces in the world. Its loss of the Papal States seemed actually to have increased its political usefulness in this field by freeing it from the charge of national selfishness. Its above-the-nations status gave it a welcome coloration as an ally of internationalism. In endorsing the idea of an international community based on law, the Church came nearer to an endorsement of democracy than it had ever come before, denouncing tyranny and "totalitarian methods which violate the rights of the person or social groups."

When the problem of nuclear arms was first presented in the third session, the proposed phraseology of Schema 13 on the subject looked like a flat condemnation of the possession of such arms. Certainly it was a condemnation of any stockpiling of such arms. The statement declared that "every honest effort" should be made to proscribe nuclear war and to destroy and ban nuclear weapons.

Some of the American bishops were aghast. They had been

consistent advocates of America's build-up of nuclear power as a defensive measure to prevent conquest by the Soviet Union. Were they to be classed as immoral? Philip Hannan, then auxiliary bishop of Washington and now Archbishop of New Orleans, protested that "we must state with precision what is prohibited in waging war to those who justly and laudably defend liberty."[3] He did not mention the United States, the Soviet Union, or China, but it was obvious what he had in mind. And he added: "We must have complete and actual liberty to carry on a dialogue with militant atheists. No dialogue is possible if we fall into slavery." He called for a complete rewriting of the passage on nuclear arms to meet "the requirements of moral theology of the Church on conducting a just war." He returned to the attack in the fourth session, declaring that a proposed Council statement on nuclear arms was "unrealistic" and "a slur on United States policy." Although the American bishops did not officially go along with Hannan's proposals, they were obviously sympathetic. The main objection to this line of reasoning had already been stated by one of Britain's most influential churchmen, a Catholic convert, Abbot Christopher Butler, Superior General of the Benedictine Order in England. "All these arms," he remarked sourly, "are possessed with an eye to future use. If we think such preparation is legitimate, we had better say so openly and not hide behind a reference to the mere possession of the arms." Butler denounced the very "conditional intention" to use nuclear arms as "gravely immoral."

The Council produced many powerful speeches in defense of this rigorous peace position. One of the most moving utterances came in the fourth session from Bishop Pierre Voillon of Verdun, who reminded his hearers that in his single diocese 1,300,000 human beings had lost their lives as a result of war fought with "conventional" weapons. Of what use was it to distinguish between legitimate and illegitimate weapons? The opposition to war must be absolute. As Cardinal Martin of Rouen remarked: "The old distinction between offensive and defensive warfare is the next thing to useless . . . the world is on a volcano which can erupt at any time."

Bishop Hannan got some support from the British in the final debate on nuclear arms in the fourth session, but, when the final vote was taken his position was, in effect, defeated 1,710, to 483. The wording adopted was a compromise between the European and the Hannan positions. While it gave some solace to those who favored nuclear defense, the total result was very close to the gospel of Christian pacifism. Admitting that even the most horrible arms might serve a useful purpose as a deterrent to possible enemy attack, the text declared that "the arms race is an utterly treacherous trap for humanity" that may "spawn all the lethal ruin whose path it is now making ready." "Any act of war," said the Fathers, "aimed indiscriminately at the destruction of entire cities or extensive areas along with their population is a crime against God and man himself. It merits unequivocal and unhesitating condemnation." So, while the Council did not unconditionally and specifically condemn all possession of nuclear arms for defense, it condemned their use for any aim which could be called aggression. The final statement on war and peace was a modified triumph for neutralism and pacifism.

A similar triumph for the non-militants occurred when the question arose whether the Council should condemn Communism by name. Fifteen years before it would have been unthinkable that a Vatican Council could hesitate about the wisdom of such a condemnation. Communism was the Atheist Devil Incarnate. In July 1949 Pius XII had issued through the Holy Office a sweeping decree to the effect that anyone voting for the Communist ticket or even reading Communist literature would be subject to excommunication. Although Pius XII never officially withdrew the threat, he never dared to enforce it. At least 8,000,000 Italian Catholics defied him, and the Communist party continued blandly to grow and prosper.

By the time Vatican II arrived, there were many practical reasons why the Church should refrain from repeating such a blunder. It needed to avoid any exacerbation of old animosities. Also, it wanted to cultivate the Russian branch of the Orthodox Church, several of whose representatives had come to the Council as official observers. It wanted to save the Christian Democratic Party of Italy which, although it had supplied all the premiers of Italy since World War II, was barely surviving in a coalition government with Nenni Socialists who were both anticlerical and, to some extent, willing collaborators with Communism in Italy's chief labor organization.

The Christian Democratic Party itself was badly split, with a strong segment favoring a more neutral position between East and West. The Vatican, living in a nation where at least 25 per cent of the alleged Catholic population voted the Communist ticket, hesitated about alienating any more people than was absolutely necessary. In December 1964 it had swallowed as gracefully as possible the election of the right-wing Socialist, Giuseppe Saragat, as Italy's President after ten days of balloting in which the Communists finally broke the deadlock by supporting the victor. Although Saragat is a very polished and amiable gentleman and a sincere enemy of Communism, he is not a practising Catholic and his history is distinctly anti-clerical. There was irony in the fact that the Vatican was compelled by circumstances to accept a de facto non-Catholic President in its home country shortly after a predominantly Protestant United States had accepted a Catholic President.

The hesitation of the Council in condemning atheist Communism annoyed the conservatives among the Italian bishops very much. These bishops had already issued a strong independent condemnation of Communism and all it stood for. In the third session some two hundred bishops circulated a petition in favor of a separate schema, condemning Communism and Marxism. When, during the final session, it seemed that Schema 13 might go to press without condemning Communism by name, the rightists among the Italian bishops, headed by Bishop Luigi Carli of Segni, mailed to all the Council fathers a plea for stronger anti-Communist language, declaring that "Vatican II will be cowardly if it does not condemn Communism." It was said that Carli had secured the signatures of over 450 Council fathers on a petition calling for such a denunciation of Communism by name. He declared that "Eventual silence by the Council, after the latest Popes and the Holy Office have said so much about Communism, would be equivalent to disavowing all that has been said and done up until now, and would signify minimizing the danger and intrinsic gravity of Communism."[4] His group proposed an amendment to the statement on atheism, saying that since Communism denies "the existence of God and of all religious values, especially supernatural ones" and since "it violates in many ways the genuine dignity of the person, the family and married life," it "must be rejected."

Somewhat to the world's surprise, the governing commissions of the Council, in spite of 209 requests from individual bishops to the contrary, dismissed the request for a condemnation of Communism by name in a footnote. The Council finally approved a statement about atheism over which *The New York Times* put the historic headline: "Catholics Urged to Love Atheists." The new Vatican soft line on atheism followed the appointment of a special Secretariat for Non-Believers, headed by Cardinal Koenig of Vienna.

Of course, there was nothing in the new policy to suggest that the Church condones the "poisonous doctrines" of atheism or Marxist Communism. But, as the text of the final statement on atheism reads: "While rejecting atheism, root and branch, the Church sincerely professes that all men, believers and non-believers alike, ought to work for the rightful betterment of this world in which all alike live; such an ideal cannot be realized, however, apart from sincere and prudent dialogue. . . . She [the Church] courteously invites atheists to examine the Gospel of Christ with an open mind." The new policy was, in effect, an olive branch held out to the Iron Curtain countries with a view to making the fate of Catholics in those countries more bearable.

There was no indication that the Communist countries accepted the olive branch. Their "dialogue," particularly with the Catholics of Poland, where Church-State differences have been most acute, showed no signs of greater dialectical decency after the Council had ended. In Italy, however, the new and somewhat more gentle attitude of the Vatican toward Communism bore fruit. The Communists, always hostile to the Christian Democrats, still admitted that the Church might have some virtues. Luigi Longo, the new leader of Italy's Communist Party, admitted early in 1966 that, in spite of Karl Marx, Catholic teaching might not always be considered the opiate of the people.

Perhaps the most important immediate gain that came out of the whole debate on war and peace was a new official attitude toward conscientious objectors. For American Catholics a lenient policy toward conscientious objectors by our Federal Government has been an accepted procedure for a long time. Any young man in the American draft who can prove that his conscientious objection to service has some connection with a past religious opposition to war can ordinarily secure special classification for noncombatant service. Although there is no Constitutional right for such exemption in the United States—the Government could if it wished constitutionally draft clergymen—a long legislative tradition has been built up in favor of the exemption of authentic conscientious objectors. Recent court decisions have even extended the exemption to nontheists.

Some of the American bishops must have been surprised when they arrived in Italy for the Council and discovered not only that Italy had no legal provisions for the exemption of conscientious objectors but that even Pope John had not publicly favored such laws. Sparked by the redoubtable Thomas D. Roberts, formerly Archbishop of Bombay, the Council's most courageous rebel, the advocates of the rights of conscientious objectors finally succeeded in getting into Schema 13 a clear endorsement of such rights, declaring that "it seems right that laws make humane provisions for the case of those who for reasons of conscience refuse to bear arms, provided however, that they agree to serve the human community in some other way."

❧

When the Fathers came to discuss poverty and economic organization, they sounded like a Social Democratic convention representing a party out of power. "Never," they proclaimed, "has the human race enjoyed such an abundance of wealth, resources and economic power, and yet a huge proportion of the world's citizens are still tormented by hunger and poverty, while countless numbers suffer from total illiteracy." In advocating a new Secretariat Against Poverty and Hunger—not yet established—Cardinal McCann of Capetown declared: "There are two worlds, those who have, and those who have not. But the goods and the fruits of the world are intended for all men."

If these discoveries were not new, it was at least a novelty to have one of the great conservative ecclesiastical bodies of the world facing facts so frankly. The Fathers eloquently deplored everything that was evil in the social system and said over and over again that certain things ought to be done. They were obvious amateurs when it came to telling the world exactly how their ideals should be realized, but they demonstrated an almost revolutionary concern. Their pronouncements on poverty and wealth were distinctly pro-labor, and no capitalist could have gained much satisfaction from them except a very, very good capitalist. Industrial disputes should be settled amicably but "a strike, nevertheless, can remain even in present-day circumstances a necessary, though ultimate, aid for the defense of the workers' own rights." Workers have a right to form labor unions and to share in determining working conditions. Support must be guaranteed for the ill and the old by somebody, and suitable work must be provided for the able-bodied. Rich nations must help poor nations, and rich people must help poor people. "The contrast between the economically more advanced countries and other countries is becoming more serious day by day, and the very peace of the world can be jeopardized thereby." The youth of all classes must be educated. A certain amount of "socialization" may be advisable but caution must be exercised at this point since the political community alone should not have too much power. All economic activity is to be carried on "within the limits of the moral order so that God's plan for mankind may be realized."

This last sentence was a sop to the conservatives, who, by this time, were wondering whether their Church was headed straight for socialism. It wasn't, but the statements of the Council on poverty served to remind the Americans that the headquarters of the Roman Catholic Church are located in a continent where the word "socialism" is almost as blandly virtuous as the word "democracy" is in the United States.

On the whole, conservatives could get little satisfaction from the Council's pronouncements on poverty. The paternalism of Leo XIII had been superseded by something much more modern and realistic. Only on the subject of birth control and overpopulation did the Council still speak with the cautious voice of the nineteenth century. The fathers conceded that the decision about the number of children in a family should be left to "the right judgment of the parents," but they hastened to add that this right judgment "presupposes a rightly formed conscience in harmony with the moral order" (see Chapter 13).

There were some among the fathers who were not content with treating poverty in the external world; they wanted a complete revolution in the practice of poverty within the Church itself. They realized that while they were functioning within the richest private corporation in the world, possessing a greater gap between cardinals and parish priests than most commercial corporations demonstrate in their economic stratification, they were living in glass houses when they talked about poverty, riches, and social justice. The Dutch Documentation Center at the Council put out during the second session a most provocative summary challenging the Church's complacency concerning the internal practices of poverty and pomp in the Church. It said: "There generally is, in the hierarchical set-up of the Church, especially at the Vatican, too great a semblance of riches, ostentation, affectation of exalted wisdom—such attitudes are remnants of the past and in no way conducive to the poverty of Jesus."[5]

The needling Dutch document suggested (1) simplification of the habits of bishops and prelates, with the removal of excessive ornamentation on the bishops themselves and within the churches; (2) the elimination of ecclesiastical titles and elaborate receptions given to Church dignitaries; (3) equalization of the stipends paid to priests; (4) the redistribution of vast rural lands now held by the Church, and (5) reduction in the ornate treasures in certain churches.

But no one in high places at Vatican II suggested the one obviously necessary preliminary step required for a confrontation on the problem of Church poverty, that a responsible Church should let its own people know the facts concerning its own wealth. The control of the Church's wealth is still monolithic, and the facts about that wealth are utterly secret. The Catholic Church is probably the only great corporation in the modern world that never attempts to give its stockholders a picture of their holdings. The reason, of course, is that the Catholic people are not financial citizens or stockholders in "their own" Church. Property, from the Dome of St. Peter's to the smallest mission school in Africa, is so owned and controlled from the Vatican that the power of ownership always lies in Rome, and the statistics of ownership are buried in impenetrable secrecy.[6] There was no move at the Council, either verbal or otherwise, to disturb this essentially monolithic feature of Catholic power.

CHAPTER SEVENTEEN ❧ BALANCE SHEET

Having spoken somewhat critically of the too, too balanced judgments of Pope Paul, I come now with trepidation to the task of striking a balance sheet for this whole complex phenomenon known as Vatican II. Here I abandon all pretense of impersonal judgments and launch out into a mixture of appraisal and prophecy, convinced that an author has responsibility to speak his own mind not only on passing events but also on their implications and potential results. In this enterprise I have one great advantage over Pope Paul. I am laboring under no necessity to please anybody, nor do I have any tradition of infallibility to maintain or any phalanx of Curial bureaucrats to appease.

According to the dictionaries, a balance sheet is a statement in tabular form designed to show assets and liabilities, profit and loss, as of a specific date. Although I shall attempt to summarize certain major items in profit and loss, any genuine appraisal of Vatican II must go far beyond static notions and attempt to catch the meaning of two great forces in motion, the force of world Catholicism and the force of Western culture.

The analogy often used to simplify Einstein's theory of relativity is appropriate here. Two trains on separate, parallel tracks are moving in the same direction. The passenger in Train A, which is moving slightly faster than Train B, looks out of the window casually and thinks that his train is moving very slowly past Train B, which seems to him to be standing still. Actually, both trains are moving quite rapidly. The passengers in both trains tend to judge their motion in terms of relative velocity.

The appraisal of Vatican II should be built around that analogy. The yardstick of measurement must be one of relative velocity in moving from a point in history.

In terms of its own history, the Roman Catholic Church moved rapidly and accomplished much during Vatican II. Hence the Council can be called a gigantic success. In terms of the movement of Western culture, however, the Council moved so slowly that it almost stood still. In an age when culture and science had moved farther in two centuries than the whole world had progressed up to that point in time, Vatican II chose to cling to dogmas and policies that were centuries out of date, dogmas and policies that could have been abandoned without any surrender of spiritual ideals. In terms of twentieth-century velocity, the Council brought Catholicism from the thirteenth to the seventeenth century, no mean achievement, but it still left this largest segment of world Christianity three hundred years behind the times. The non-Catholic world was happy about the result, and justly so. At last Catholicism was moving in the right direction, toward the reality of modern life. But Vatican II also revealed that the Church, with all its progress, was still pre-American both in the rigidity of its dogma and the autocracy of its power structure.

If a balance sheet of the Council is to be based on sound comparisons, it must take into account the actual position of the Church at its beginning. In those terms the Church scored a substantial gain through the Council, partly because at the beginning the Church was on the defensive in a hostile world, in a condition of deep depression far worse than the official statistics indicated. When Pope John ascended the papal throne in 1958, the power of the Church was receding in every continent except North America and in almost every nation except the United States, West Germany, the Netherlands, and the Irish Republic.[1] In summoning the Council Pope John was not leading from strength but from weakness. He spoke as the head of a beleaguered church, beleaguered by the greatest surge of nonfaith in all history and by the rise of nations in Europe, Asia, and Africa that were militantly anti-Christian as well as anti-Catholic.

The Church claims 590,000,000 members, nearly one-fifth of

the world's total population, but anyone familiar with Catholic developments knows that these figures are wildly exaggerated. The annual estimates of an increase in world Catholic figures are based largely on hope rather than reality, since fallen-away membership is not properly recorded. An estimate of 400,000,000 is probably optimistic for the world's practising Catholics. The new Superior General of the Jesuits, Father Peter Arrupe, speaking presumably of baptismal totals, said in 1965 at the fourth session of the Council: "In 1961 Catholics formed 18 per cent of the [world's] population; today they form 16 per cent." His estimate would put the baptized Catholics at about 480,000,000, and this figure undoubtedly includes many millions who never go near the Church in their adult life.

The London *Tablet*, using optimistic baptismal statistics in an article in 1965, said that "in all categories [of Christianity] the nominal adherents heavily outweigh the real and committed believers, and in almost every country, save a few like Ireland and the Netherlands, the Christians find themselves members of largely de-Christianized societies, in which the majority of their neighbors, colleagues in work and contemporaries engaged in constant interaction with them, do not share their beliefs."[2] In this rear-guard position, Catholicism has suffered relatively more than Protestantism since World War II because the Church has had more to lose through the upsurge of atheist Communism, particularly in such former Catholic strongholds as Hungary and Poland. Although the Catholic statisticians still valiantly count 72,000,000 members behind the Iron Curtain, including 3,000,000 in Communist China, they know that these figures are largely hypothetical. They know, for example, that Chinese Catholic schools and welfare institutions have been closed for years and that Catholic missionaries have been forced to flee for their lives.

The epic of decline and decay is just as significant in some regions claiming to be almost wholly Catholic. Latin America, claiming about one-third of the world's Catholic population, is actually about 10 to 15 per cent Catholic, with one priest for each 5,000 members and a family structure that is 60 per cent illegitimate.[3] After centuries of Church guardianship over education, some 7,000,000 children in Latin America never go to school at all, and only two in ten complete their primary education. Latin America is supposed to be the fastest growing section in the world, with India and China competing for that dubious distinction, but in all three of these regions the growth is not favorable to Catholicism. After 1,500 years of missionary effort in India, even during the centuries under "Christian" rulers, the Church never captured 2 per cent of the people. Catholicism in India is now losing ground as a non-Asiatic faith. In Africa, Mohammedanism is said to be gaining ten times as many converts as Catholicism, largely because Catholicism—like Christianity itself—is a "white man's religion."[4] Latin American bishops, traditionally the allies of a corrupt landholding aristocracy, are now desperately trying to change the social image of their Church but it is probable that their worthy efforts have come too late.

The conditions and prospects of the Church are almost as depressed in several of its official strongholds in Europe. Spanish and Portuguese Catholicism, tied to the dictatorships of Franco and Salazar, provokes the hostility of most European workers and risks ruin when these pro-Catholic dictatorships fall. The situation is only a little better in France. Although 83 per cent of the French people are baptized Catholics, scarcely a quarter even take Easter communion. The great majority live in what one French priest has described as "practical paganism." Vocations of young Frenchmen to the priesthood dropped more than one-half in the decade preceding Vatican II.[5]

In Italy, where the Church claims 99.4 per cent of the population, Catholicism is a little stronger because of national loyalties and because the power structure of the Church is essentially Italian. Under these circumstances it is relatively easy to produce a crowd of 50,000 in St. Peter's Square for any papal show. But how much does such an exhibition mean? By a generous estimate, Italy is one-third Catholic.[6] The number of priests in Italy declined about 70 per cent between Vatican I and Vatican II while the population was almost doubled. In Italy the practice of Catholicism is, for the most part, a matter for women. There is no reason to believe that Italian male devotion has increased since 1940 when Cardinal Lavitrano estimated that only 12 per cent of Italian men received communion at Easter, the most obligatory of all attendance commitments of the Church. One Jesuit writer estimated during the Council that at least 90 of the 310 dioceses in Italy were not solvent and had to be kept alive by cash contributions from the Vatican.

These pessimistic facts about the actual condition of world Catholicism at the time of the beginning of the Council point up two conclusions that are pertinent to an appraisal. First, Pope John's *aggiornamento* was not a matter of personal taste or personal choice; it was sound strategy dictated by the pressure of the forces of decline and decay, an institutional necessity at a moment of crisis.

Second, Vatican II's accomplishment in transforming the world Catholic image from an image of defeat to an image of victory and progress was a spectacular triumph. It was made possible, of course, by the willingness of the world's news media to give the Church something better than an even break, but the forces of liberalism at the Council made possible the relative kindness of the public opinion media. The purveyors of a glossy picture of moral triumph had something to latch on to. Through the fortunate—fortunate for the Church—combination of internal upheaval and journalistic appreciation, the decay and mismanagement within the institution were almost overlooked. Its autocracy was accepted as benevolent if not inevitable. The world was given the impression, through papal pageantry and its accompanying inflation in press and television, that the Church was in a position of regal leadership in the moral life of the West. The Pope suddenly became for many the most prestigious individual alive. In terms of institutional accomplishment the Council thus achieved more than a hundred thousand missionaries could have effected in a hundred thousand years. Hence, for the Catholic Church as an institution that courts fame and power, the balance sheet of Vatican II will always show an immense surplus on the credit side.

The publicity gains of Vatican II can best be appreciated by looking back at the treatment accorded to the Church by the American press during Vatican I in 1870, and comparing it with the 1962–1965 coverage. Father J. Ryan Beiser has written for the Catholic University of America a study of the reception given to Vatican I by American secular newspapers.[7] "In general," he reports, "the New York press was opposed to everything Catholic. . . . The press wanted Roman control to be discredited and broken." The critical language used by editors in 1870 would be quite inconceivable in today's journals. "The Council," said the *New York Herald* in 1870, "is a big farce, a grand archeological show, a revival of Middle-age sentiment; but who can say it is more? If it is more, what is it? This perhaps—for the world there is no falling back. We cannot again become children. No more can the world."

The famous cartoonist Thomas Nast regularly produced for *Harper's Weekly* during the sessions of Vatican I cartoons that were bitterly scornful of the Pope. "I Am Now Infallible" was the caption of one showing Pius IX, with his tiara tipped at a rakish angle, sitting far out on the limb of a tree called the nineteenth century, calmly sawing off the limb, destined to fall with the "Jesuits" into a pit called "Dark Ages."

The *Nation* of those days, describing Pius IX as "a very simple-minded and somewhat fanatical old monk, in the hands of very bad advisors," said: "We do not believe that a true and satisfactory reconciliation of the Catholic Church, as its Doctors define it, with modern society will ever be affected [sic]." *The Times*, according to Father Beiser, was "vigorously hostile," supporting the No-Popery campaign. "Nativistic Protestantism was the chief basis for its attitude." The *New York Tribune*, ridiculing some of the alleged relics displayed in Roman Churches—the wing of the Angel Gabriel, the rope used by Judas, the beard of Noah, etc.—published an ugly gibe at the Council in the form of a prayer, handed about by the Americans at Rome. It read:

> Our Father who art in the Vatican: Infallible be thy name: Thy Temporal Sovereignty come: Thy will be done in

Europe and in America as it is in Ireland. Give us this day our tithes and titles, and forgive us our trespasses as we give plenary indulgences to those who pay penitently unto us: lead us not into Oecumenical Councils, but deliver us from thinking: for thine is the Crozier, the key, and the tiara, Rome without end Amen.

Can anyone imagine such overt anti-Catholic ridicule in an American newspaper today? Or can anyone imagine an American broadcasting company in this century showing fundamental disrespect for a pope, either pictorially or in words? The distance between the broad and malicious journalistic anti-Catholicism of 1870 and the respectful, almost reverent approach to papal personalities during Vatican II is a yardstick for the measurement of Catholic triumphs in American public opinion.

And yet, on particular issues, the American press and television networks were quite frank and revealing in exposing Catholic deficiencies, and the journalists of both the secular press and the liberal Catholic press were courageous and accurate in delineating this exposure. *The New York Times*, *Time*, and *Newsweek* were notable in the volume and accuracy of their coverage. While the Pope as an individual monarch gained in stature by public exhibition, some of his ideas were exposed as absurd, and the exposure made a profound impression on the Catholic community as well as the non-Catholic community. Millions of Catholics for the first time read descriptions of standard Catholic policies in which those policies were made to appear archaic or absurd or both. This was particularly true of the Church's doctrine on sex as advocated by celibate prelates. It was true to a lesser extent of the exposure of the Church's autocratic power structure. When the great news media began to quote severe criticisms of some aspects of Catholic policy, even by Catholic cardinals and bishops, Catholic liberals throughout the world took courage. In the end their chorus of criticism went far beyond the published flood of non-Catholic criticism. In fact, it was the criticism of Catholicism by Catholics that stole the headlines in the United States. American editors, fearful of any possible allegation that their journals might be anti-

Catholic, fell back with a sense of security on Catholic muckrakers who performed the task of exposure with great gusto.

In many ways this wave of published criticism of specific clerical shortcomings, and the resultant clamor of public discussion of the issues involved, was the greatest single intellectual gain from the Council. Criticisms became permissible within Catholicism partly because of the volume of criticism in the secular press, where the Catholic hero was the liberal reformer, not the conventional defender of the faith. The great waves of critical comment came back to the Fathers at the Council and undoubtedly influenced their speeches and their votes. The total effect was to downgrade the Ottavianis and their allies and to upgrade the anti-Curial forces.

No one knows how much this new liberalism of the Council period will mean in the future. Can the Catholic reformers stand up to the entrenched leaders of their Church when the excitement of the Council period has evaporated? The conservatives still have the key positions from which to strike back at all rebellion against their authority, and Pope Paul appears to be much closer to their traditional authoritarianism than he is to the outlook of the would-be reformers. But meanwhile, in the United States at least, the entrenched conservatives are on the defensive. It is no longer popular to stand pat on old programs. Since no bishop relishes unpopularity, there are few prelates who care to follow Cardinal McIntyre, for example, and issue statements that approach the spirit of the John Birch Society.

In terms of rhetorical accomplishment the Council could not be called successful. Its sixteen promulgated texts, running to more than 100,000 words, were often tedious and trite. Their findings, even in an age when science had far outstripped religion in the vigor of its explorations of the problems of life, were based on the fantastic assumption that the Ruler of the Universe had chosen one group of narrowly educated prelates in one Church to be the prime ducts for the transmission of all divine truth to an unenlightened humanity.

The Fathers, if they had taken the advice of some good secular editors, could easily have said in five words what they said in ten. Many of the theological things they had to say were half-truths or fantasies based on self-interest. In various texts scholarship was honored more in the breach than the observance, since all concessions to new thought had to be balanced with reassertions of old dogmas. Up to the very end of the Council, the fiction had to be maintained that no fundamental dogma of the Church ever changes; it only "develops." The Fathers could not flatly admit doctrinal error in the past, since the rules of their Church forbade such an admission and they knew that their own authority in a tightly controlled system of thought would be weakened by such a concession.

In homiletic terms, the sixteen promulgated texts were very earnest and pious, laying down sweeping moral generalizations with great assurance, but often bypassing the most pertinent facts in the modern world. It was obvious that various cliques of prelates and *periti* had been allowed to express their pent-up penchant for preaching without benefit of editorial scissors. Almost every schema contained needless repetitions of Catholic claims to supreme, if not quite exclusive, possession of the truth. But in spite of this rhetorical padding, the final product was a gain for realism. The Church came out of the Middle Ages like Rip van Winkle, rubbing the sleep out of its eyes and seeming to gaze with wonder for the first time on a world it had never before examined.

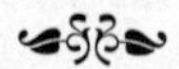

Aside from the very valuable ventilation of critical issues generated by the Council there are at least four other specific gains that deserve to be described as credits on any balance sheet.

1. *Liturgy reform.* The partial shift from the gobbledegook of Latin ritual to a language understood by common Catholic communicants is a shift toward realism and away from obscurant-

ism. The new vernacular may be less elegant and less poetic than the language of tradition, but the change helps to bring men closer to life by substituting understanding for magic. The new realism of language has been accompanied by an improvement in manners and communications. Some priests in some rituals may now face their congregations instead of turning their backs.

2. *Admission of possible mistakes in the past.* When both Pope John and Pope Paul admitted almost tearfully that somebody on the Catholic side might possibly have been in error in some activities during the sixteenth-century Reformation and the eleventh-century Great Schism, this was a great emotional gain for honesty in Christian interrelationships. The admissions were vague and general, but no one doubts their genuineness. Perhaps, in the twenty-first century, some pope will go farther and actually concede that his Church may have been doctrinally mistaken.

3. *Limited religious liberty, in principle.* This has already been discussed in Chapter 6. While the product failed to live up to its advertising, it marked a great advance in Catholic policy, perhaps the greatest single advance in principle during all four sessions of the Council.

4. *The commitment to social reform.* This was probably the greatest practical advance of Vatican II. It brought the Church down from pie in the sky to the great human movements for peace, racial justice, and plenty. In many cases the priests had not only stayed too long in heaven or purgatory, thus ignoring the world that really mattered to their constituents, but they had allied themselves with the forces of political and economic reaction, shirking responsibility for worldly suffering. When the schema on the Church in the Modern World finally committed them to earthly goals, they began a process of escape from escapism that can never be reversed. The aloof Perfect Society of another world is now being replaced by the struggle for a more perfect society among men. Men are not always moved most effectively by the most sophisticated thought. The rather naive idealism of the Council Fathers in dealing with war and peace may

actually tip the delicately balanced scales against a third World War. The Fathers wrote a freshman textbook in Catholic social science, which was all to the good because, in this case, their Church was not ready for a graduate textbook.

❧

Balancing these four substantial credits are four equally substantial debits:

1. *Continued opposition to birth control.* This was the greatest single defeat for intelligence at the Council sessions. If Pope Paul finally makes some slight alteration in the old rule, it will be too late to redeem his reputation or that of the Council in this area. Nothing less than complete abrogation of the old rule will satisfy the modern world. If, on the contrary, the Church should succeed in imposing its restrictive rules against contraception on all its members, that single mistaken policy would more than cancel out all the accomplishments of Catholicism in two thousand years. For overpopulation is not an isolated evil; it is an evil from which nearly all other evils are bound to flow. An overcrowded world is sure to become an unmanageable world. Fortunately, some Catholics are practicing effective birth control, despite the veto power of their celibate priests. Whatever the Vatican now says on the subject, the priestly prohibitions will probably be observed in the future to the Church's discredit only by the poor and the ignorant.

2. *The reassertion of Catholic claims on the public treasury.* Vatican II, either expressly or by implication, confirmed all existing arrangements, either by concordat or independent legislation, that give tax funds to priests and/or Catholic schools. The Fathers issued unequivocal statements asserting that such financial claims are a matter of justice, and they did not even make a courtesy bow in the direction of the contrary principles of the Constitution of the United States. This debit is particularly important for the American future because, under the influence of that ecumenical amiability which has flowed from the Council, our politicians,

with ecclesiastical encouragement, are substituting a be-kind-to-all religions policy for the Constitutional policy of the separation of church and state. As we saw in Chapter 16, the financial wall of separation between church and state in the schools is being nibbled away bite by bite, and the nibbling has become both a Protestant as well as a Catholic phenomenon. The support of this acquisitive tendency by Vatican II should remind Americans that throughout all history prelates of all faiths have been just as ready as secular leaders to feed fully at the public trough. Americans who still believe in the Jeffersonian principle of separation of church and state should beware of an appeaser's role in defending the wall of separation. It was Winston Churchill who said once that an "appeaser is one who feeds a crocodile hoping it will eat him last."

3. *The continuation of papal autocracy*. Although Vatican II was not as much of a papal rubber stamp as Vatican I in 1870, there was only a slight difference in papal arrogance between the two, since Vatican II confirmed the whole machinery of papal absolutism inaugurated in 1870. Both Pope John and Pope Paul on occasion broke into Council proceedings with arbitrary decisions that were contrary to Council opinion, without so much as addressing a by-your-leave in the direction of obedient bishops. Thus the Council became a spectacle in servility as well as a spectacle in progress.

4. *Discrimination in mixed marriage*. This continues to be the ugliest and most bigoted manifestation of Catholic policy. The policy was so slightly altered by the Pope's pronouncement of reform in March 1966 that the reorganized procedure will only add insult to injury. When, after four years of behind-the-scenes debates, only two minor changes came forth, it furnished unpleasant evidence that clerical intolerance still exists in the highest places. No alteration in present usage can be considered worthwhile by non-Catholics until pledges concerning the religion of the children of mixed marriages are completely eliminated and the choice is left to the parents without any priestly interference.

There are three rather striking omissions from this brief and preliminary balance sheet of four credits and four debits. The collegiality of bishops is not listed as a definite credit, nor is the movement toward Christian unity, or the statement on the Jews. All three of these phenomena, it seems to me, are of uncertain value. They fall between credit and debit status. It is still not clear whether they should be recorded as substantial achievements or relative defeats.

The collegiality of bishops is omitted because it is still too early to determine whether the new mechanism for its realization, the Episcopal Synod, will amount to anything more than window-dressing. A first session of the new Synod has been called by Pope Paul for 1967. It will undoubtedly attract world-wide attention, and the Vatican news releases will stress the decentralizing features of the new mechanism. Bishops will come to Rome from all parts of the world, and the majority of them will be chosen by national bishops' conferences, presumably without conspicuous pressure from Rome. All this will be an excellent public relations gesture, and it will also be very healthful for a Church that has been for so long controlled exclusively from the top.

But it must be remembered that the new mechanism will still provide no representation for priests or people, and the agenda for its deliberations will still be controlled by one Supreme Pontiff who will have the continuing power to appoint all bishops and to confirm or veto every conclusion reached by an Episcopal Synod. Undoubtedly all modern pontiffs—Pope Paul and his potential successors—will give great weight to advice coming from such a source. But will the advice given keep pace with twentieth-century needs? The bishops engaged in the enterprise will have a tremendous vested interest in the maintenance of their own status. They will be the representatives of the pope, not of the Catholic people. It is conceivable that in the long run their new institution will settle back into the grooves of clerical tradition and actually postpone the arrival of the day when the Catholic people gain participating rights in the government of their own Church.

Paternalistic colonial mechanisms have a way of blocking the coming of genuine democracy, both in politics and in religion.

The omission of the subject of Christian unity from any current balance sheet is understandable because the Council did not settle any of the basic issues now separating Catholicism, Protestantism, and Orthodoxy. The Church did not choose to renounce a single one of the doctrinal positions on which it bases its claim to Christian pre-eminence. Although ecumenical manners greatly improved, the nonecumenical dogmas remained in status quo.

The uncertainty of all future moves toward Christian unity is best revealed by running through a brief checklist of the elementary questions that non-Catholics are asking about possible reunion. Would a united church of Christ—it might actually be called that—come under the executive direction of a pope? If so, what would he be called and how would he be chosen? What power would he have to appoint, remove, or transfer bishops and clergymen? In the preliminary discussions looking toward the creation of such a united church, how would the negotiations be conducted? Would all roads for negotiation lead to Rome? Would representatives of all interested churches meet on a plane of dialectical and hortatory equality? If a united church should be formed, would its clergymen be allowed to marry? What of ritual, creeds, religious orders, and clerical dress? What of indulgences, purgatory, relics, new saints, and modern miracles?

If these questions seem premature, farfetched and impolite, they are not nearly as impolite as the questions that are being asked in the field of family life and the relations between church and state. And all of these questions must be faced honestly if the ecumenical movement is to be honestly pursued. Would a more ecumenical Catholicism still insist on a separate school system financed by all taxpayers? Would a Catholicism serving as part of a united Christendom continue its opposition to birth control? To divorce? To equality between sects, Christian and otherwise, in mixed marriage? (It must be assumed that, regardless of church union between Rome and the main segments of Orthodoxy and

Protestantism, there would still be many large segments left outside, such as the Baptists and the much-fragmented evangelicals of the United States. The relationships between the absorbed denominations and the nonabsorbed would still require delicate adjustments.)

American Protestants, wishing devoutly to move toward Christian reunion, are bound to feel somewhat appalled by the prospect of negotiating with representatives of a wholly authoritarian power, capable of reversing the judgment of the masses of its own people and even of its own negotiators. In such negotiations—assuming that they are started in good faith—could any tentative concession be made with a sense of security? Some potential Protestant negotiators might think of the sad analogy of the Popular Front Movement in American politics in the 1930's when relatively innocent liberals sat down to bargain with the representatives of Stalin and found themselves completely outmaneuvered by a Machiavellian strategy designed for the benefit of the Big Brother in Moscow. The day has gone by when any responsible Protestant leader would accuse the Vatican of harboring any of the conspiratorial aims of the Kremlin, but the truth can scarcely be avoided that both institutions are so topheavy with imperial power, political and clerical, that democracies will always find it difficult to deal with them.

In appraising Vatican II's handling of the Jewish issue it is impossible to give the Church a credit on the balance sheet in spite of the many personal manifestations of good will toward the Jewish people by the Fathers. While the Council officially repudiated anti-Semitism, its repudiation was too hesitant and ambiguous to be convincing to those who cared to remember Auschwitz and the silence of Pius XII at the worst moment in all history for a Christian leader to maintain silence. Here the burden of responsibility must rest squarely on the shoulders of Pope Paul himself. He may not be personally anti-Semitic but his institutional loyalties, at a crucial moment, seemed to take precedence over his humanity. It never seems to have occurred to him that there might be occasions in history when a church has the duty to die rather than compromise on a supreme moral issue. In defending Pius XII and the German policy of his Church during World War II, he went far beyond the limits of filial duty and demonstrated a kind of institutional narcissism, protecting his Church against criticism that was so valid it should have led to unqualified public penance rather than evasive apologias. His own apologia for Pius XII was not sweetened by a post-Council statement from Italy's right-wing leader, Bishop Luigi Carli of Segni, that Judaism "carries in fact always with it, one would say by its very nature, the judgment of condemnation by God."

The ultimate appraisal of Vatican II must go beyond purely Christian values and ask what the Council can mean to the secular world. That world—the unbelieving world and the indifferent world—quite possibly embraces the actual majority of the people of Europe and the Americas, and their interests cannot be ignored.

On the whole, the secularists should give Vatican II a B-plus for effort. Regardless of some reactionary commitments, the Council opened the doors of an ancient institution to the wholesome ventilation of modern thought. The institution can never again be quite as obnoxious an obstacle to cultural and scientific progress as it has so often been in the past. The present trend is irreversible.

In spite of this assured, temporary gain, however, the appraisal of the Council by the secular world must be more severe than the sectarian appraisal. The secular world cannot assume willy-nilly that Christian unity could ever be a good thing in itself simply because it might eliminate some waste, duplication, and bickering. Secularists with a broad moral outlook are also bound to ask whether a gigantic world Christian federation or super-church might not also eliminate some personal liberty, impose unwelcome pressures for conformity, and ultimately reduce the unbeliever and the Jew to a lower status. They must view with some apprehension any possible centralization of nearly all the clerical power in Christendom under one system of nondemocratic controls. Certainly the secular world cannot, without reservations, accept the moral authority of a dictatorial power structure if this leads in the direction of reactionary family policies and those creeping encroachments on the public treasury that have become so characteristic of European Catholicism. From the secular point of view a Christian unity that included among its ingredients clerical reaction, anti-science, sexual fanaticism and the exploitation of non-Christian taxpayers for the benefit of the Christian Establishment might be far worse than the reasonably temperate religious pluralism we now possess.

In the secular appraisal, Vatican II must bear full responsibility for the questions that it did not answer as well as the questions to which it gave totally unrealistic answers–if Catholicism or its ecumenical successor is to qualify for the moral leadership of the West. As of the date of the termination of the Council, Catholicism had not qualified. It had changed, but not enough for the acceptance of reasonable men. It had retained insufferable barnacles of superstition. It had not given reasonable answers on birth control, divorce, mixed marriage, public education, internal Church censorship, papal dictatorship, and the separation of church and state. These areas are particularly critical for Americans because they are the areas in which Catholic policy differs most sharply from prevailing American policy.

What the Council finally means to Western culture will depend on Rome's follow-up. Probably the follow-up–the revision of canon law and the world-wide implementation of the Council decrees–will be of great advantage to democracy and to interreligious peace. But no one can tell. It is more than a cliché to say that from the point of view of the American way of life Vatican II is still on trial. (The American way of life is also on trial in the light of the Council's philosophy, but the elaboration of that thought is beyond the scope of this book.) As of the day when the Council ended in 1965, the Church had not yet resolved the most critical issues that lie between an American freedom based on the separation of church and state and a European style of clerical power based on the partial union of church and state. Hence the new euphoria that came out of Vatican II like a perfumed mist must not be welcomed unconditionally. A nation that has inherited its concepts of church and state largely from Thomas Jefferson must carefully weigh the philosophy of Rome and balance it realistically against the philosophy of Monticello.

Meanwhile, having expressed so many doubts and reservations about the Council, it is well to add that in terms of human welfare Vatican II made a great contribution to the future precisely because it was not confined to the areas of ecclesiastical dispute. Almost unwillingly, the reach of the bishops exceeded their grasp. They became, through the Council with its open-window policy, catalytic agents in a world they had previously shunned. Old, festering sores of prejudice were healed by exposure to the ecumenical air. In spite of Curial narrowmindedness, Catholics, Protestants, and Jews throughout the world began to engage in new grass-roots, practical cooperation without benefit of theology. Sound institutional forms of welfare cooperation among all faiths are today springing up everywhere, partly as a result of the Council's pronouncements on the Church in the Modern World.

This new cooperation at the level of social reform will not lead to Christian reunion in our time. Perhaps it will never lead to Christian reunion at all. Certainly it should never, never lead to reunion unless the amalgamation is predicated on a reasonable amount of ecclesiastical self-government and the separation of church and state. But reunion never was the primary aim of Vatican II. Its final balance sheet should be viewed in the light of Pope John's original desire for *aggiornamento*, an updating, a renewal. John willed it for his own Church but history went beyond the limits of his dream.

NOTES

A COMMENT ON SOURCES

The literature on Vatican II is already so voluminous that it would require a whole volume simply to list the important books and magazine articles on the subject. Although I shall refer in these notes to a number of valuable works, there is no pretense that they cover the whole field. I have limited the references almost entirely to books and periodicals readily available in the English language, and when Catholic statements are quoted I have favored Catholic books or journals published under episcopal auspices. Of course the only strictly official summaries of Catholic doctrine are in Latin, and the two most widely cited Latin sources are the *Acta Apostolicae Sedis*, the periodical published by the Holy See, and abbreviated by the letters AAS; and *Enchiridon Symbolorum, Definitionum et Declarationum de Revus Fidei et Morum* (Manual of Creeds, Definitions and Declarations on Matters of Faith and Morals) compiled by H. Denzinger, abbreviated to Denz. In nearly all cases I have chosen to cite versions of Catholic teaching in the English language published in the United States. My major sources have been abbreviated as follows:

Vatican II Speeches. Although nearly all the speeches in St. Peter's were in Latin, excellent translations and summaries in English were supplied orally and in writing to correspondents daily after the first session. I have relied occasionally on the oral translations of Monsignor Edward Heston and associates at the English language press conferences, but in most cases I have relied on two written sources: (1) the *Concilio Ecumenico Vatican II* (hereinafter called CEV), the mimeographed daily summaries of speeches given to the press at the Council, and (2) the English translations of important speeches both at St. Peter's and elsewhere issued by the Divine Word News Service (hereinafter called DWNS), edited under the direction of Father Ralph M. Wiltgen and distributed to subscribers at the Vatican. Occasionally I have taken phrases from *Council Speeches of Vatican II* edited by Father Yves Congar and others, published by Sheed and Ward, hereinafter called *Speeches*. I have found most useful the chronologies and calendars of the Council contained in the books of Xavier Rynne, published by Farrar, Straus and Giroux, Inc.

Texts of Council Decrees. For English translations of all texts I have relied chiefly on the mimeographed texts approved by the National Catholic

Welfare Conference of the United States and handed out at the Vatican Press Office, but occasionally I have relied on the improved English translations in *The Documents of Vatican II* (hereinafter called *Documents*) edited by Walter M. Abbott, S.J., and published by the Guild Press of New York. This complete rendition in English of all sixteen texts promulgated by Vatican II can be purchased in paperback for only $.95. In view of the availability of this work, I have not included in this book the page numbers of quotations from the promulgated documents, since it will usually be quite clear from my text which sections are quoted.

Canon Law Sources. I have relied on the 1948 edition of a standard American work, *Canon Law: A Text and Commentary* by T. Lincoln Bouscaren, S.J., and Adam C. Ellis, S.J., published by Bruce Publishing Co., hereinafter called *Canon Law.* Since canons are numbered and printed in order in this work, it has not been necessary to refer to page numbers. For legal cases under canon law I have relied on *The Canon Law Digest,* by T. Lincoln Bouscaren, S.J., published in various years by the Bruce Publishing Co., hereinafter called *Canon Law Digest.*

Statistical and Doctrinal Information. For statistical and general facts I have relied chiefly on the *National Catholic Almanac* of the United States, prepared annually by St. Anthony's Guild and distributed by Doubleday, hereinafter called *Catholic Almanac.* Among doctrinal summaries I have relied in part on *The Church Teaches,* edited by John F. Clarkson, S.J., and others (Herder, 1962), hereinafter called *Teaches;* and *Fundamentals of Catholic Dogma,* by Ludwig Ott (Herder, 1958). For standard American Catholic attitudes I have relied for quotations chiefly upon the leading chain diocesan weekly of the United States, the *Register;* for the position of American Catholic liberals the obvious choices are *Commonweal* and the *National Catholic Reporter.*

The Periodical Press. Any author of a book on Vatican II must be deeply indebted to the enterprise of the journalists who covered the daily events so faithfully and who frequently unearthed hidden facts with remarkable skill. I came to admire their professional competence and, in many cases, to enjoy their friendship. They wrote the most important histories of Vatican II, the day-by-day contemporary accounts that helped to change the Council's course of conduct. The coverage of *The New York Times,* with Robert C. Doty; of *Time,* with Robert Blair Kaiser and Israel Shenker; of *Newsweek,* the United Press International, the Associated Press, the Baltimore *Sun,* and the *New York Herald Tribune* were all notable, as were the denominational summaries in the *National Catholic Reporter, America, Commonweal,* and *The Christian Century.* In the United States the *Saturday Evening Post, Look,* and *Harper's Magazine* followed up the Council reports with revealing special articles. All writers in the field should be grateful to *The New Yorker* for cracking the Council's barrier of secrecy in the first session by publishing Xavier Rynne's *Letters from Vatican City.*

I owe a debt to Florence Miller of Vermont for superlative secretarial aid.

CHAPTER ONE
WHAT WAS THIS COUNCIL?

1. A quick chronological summary of previous Councils is given by Father Hans Kung in *The Council, Reform, and Reunion*, Sheed and Ward, 1961. For background information about the Vatican, Robert Neville's *The World of the Vatican*, Harper and Row, 1962, is exceptionally useful. For colorful illustrated descriptions see *Outsider in the Vatican*, by Frederick Franck, Macmillan, 1965.

2. A description of the method of appointing bishops in the United States is in *Canon Law Digest*, I, pp. 194ff.

3. *The Second Vatican Council*, Hawthorn, 1962, p. 4.

4. Cogley, *America*, March 27, 1965; Baum, *Commonweal*, December 11, 1964.

5. *Catholic Almanac*, 1966, estimated the world Catholic population at 590,040,168, basing its statistics on the *Annuario Pontificio* of 1965 and the figures of the Catholic Students' Mission Crusade. The Catholic population of the United States was reported at 45,640,619, or 23.4 per cent of a total of 194,631,000. Such statistics are notoriously unreliable since (1) dropouts are not systematically recorded, and (2) Catholic figures cover baptized individuals, not practising Catholics.

6. *National Catholic Reporter*, July 14, 1965. The American Institute of Management has made several "audits" of the Vatican and found it quite "efficient." The appraisals were absurd because they did not face squarely the issues of dictatorship and government by the aged.

7. Brazil's Catholic population is reckoned at 71,060,370 in a total of 76,409,000; Italy's at 50,992,200 in a total of 51,300,000; that of the United States is listed above. The estimate concerning American seminary students was published in the *Register*, August 25, 1963. According to figures "compiled by Bishop Fulton Sheen" and published in the *Register*, October 13, 1951, "Only four per cent of the total number of Catholic missionaries are from America but world missions rely upon the United States for more than 50 per cent of their financial support." Many Catholic writers have confirmed the estimate that American Catholics contribute more than half of the contributed revenue of the Vatican. (This does not include the very large income from investments.) Camille Cianfarra, Vatican correspondent of *The New York Times* said in 1944 (*The Vatican and the War*, p. 30) that the material contribution of the American church "not only easily exceeded that of any other nation, but was probably greater than that of all the rest of the world put together." The American proportion has almost certainly increased since then, although no financial estimates concerning the Vatican can be proved statistically because the Church insists on complete financial secrecy. Carlo Falconi in his *Pope John and the Ecumenical Council* (p. 342) published by World Publishing Co., estimated that the United States provides "almost all," about nine-tenths, of the finances of Propaganda Fide (the Church's missionary agency), the central Curia of the Church, and the Church in Latin America.

8. *Letters to Mary Gladstone*, p. 142.

9. Brooklyn *Tablet*, November 4, 1965, from *Ya;* London *Tablet* on Arrupe speech, October 2, 1965.

CHAPTER TWO
JOHN AND THE BEGINNING

1. Many good sidelights on Pope John are in Neville and Falconi *supra;* and, in addition to the many biographies, there is Pope John's *Journal of a Soul*, McGraw-Hill, 1965.
2. Text in *Catholic Almanac*, 1959, p. 53.
3. *Catholic Almanac*, 1959, p. 95. John's letter to women religious, *ibid.*, 1963, p. 194.
4. Text of *Aeterna dei Sapientia* in *Catholic Almanac*, 1963, p. 182.
5. Text of *Mater et Magistra*, *The New York Times*, July 15, 1961; *Catholic Almanac*, 1962, p. 170; and *Congressional Record*, July 28, 1961.
6. *America*, November 4, 1961.
7. Text of *Pacem in Terris*, *The New York Times*, April 11, 1963; *Catholic Almanac*, 1964, p. 186.
8. *America*, July 13, 1963.
9. *La Nazione*, April 14, 1963.
10. Text of this address, *Catholic Almanac*, 1961, p. 168.

CHAPTER THREE
PAUL, THE INSTITUTIONAL MAN

1. Many interesting details about Paul were contained in an article by his nephew in *Look*, February 25, 1964.
2. *The Christian Century*, August 26, 1964. The text of *Ecclesiam Suam* is in *Catholic Almanac*, 1965, p. 180.
3. *Time*, September 24, 1964.
4. *Commonweal*, April 24, 1964.
5. Letter in *Time*, September 18, 1964.
6. Quotes from Pope Paul, in *The Mind of Paul* by James Walsh, S.J., Bruce Publishing Co., 1964.
7. London *Tablet*, November 30, 1963.
8. A favorable estimate of Paul was in the Newsletter of the Federal Council of Protestant Churches in Italy, No. 11 (mimeographed), 1963.
9. *New Republic*, July 6, 1963.
10. *Catholic Almanac*, 1964, p. 212.

CHAPTER FOUR
COLLEGIALITY TO INFALLIBILITY

1. The doctrine, based on Matthew 16:16–19, is summarized in the *Catholic Almanac*, 1966, pp. 174–6; and in *Teaches*, pp. 86–102. On July 18, 1870, the First Vatican Council defined the primacy and infallible authority of the Roman Pontiff and anathematized all those who question the descent of papal authority from Peter as follows:

In open opposition to this very clear teaching of the Holy Scriptures, as it has always been understood by the Catholic Church, are the perverse opinions of those who wrongly explain the form of government established by Christ in his Church; either by denying that Peter alone in preference to the other apostles, either singly or as a group, was endowed by Christ with the true and proper primacy of jurisdiction; or by claiming that this same primacy was not given immediately and directly to St. Peter, but to the Church and through the Church to Peter as to an agent of the Church.

Therefore, if anyone says that the blessed Apostle Peter was not constituted by Christ the Lord as the Prince of all the Apostles and the visible head of the whole Church militant, or that he received immediately and directly from Jesus Christ our Lord only a primacy of honor and not a true and proper primacy of jurisdiction: let him be anathema . . . if anyone says that it is not according to the institution of Christ our Lord himself, that is, by divine law, that St. Peter has perpetual successors in the primacy over the whole Church; or if anyone says that the Roman Pontiff is not the successor of St. Peter in the same primacy: let him be anathema. (*Teaches* pp. 96–7.)

The Church's canons concerning the popes and the hierarchical structure are Canons 218–328.

2. Whole libraries have been written on Peter, primacy, infallibility and the associated problems. Valuable works include: James T. Shotwell and Louise R. Loomis, *The See of Peter*, Columbia University Press, 1927; Frederick C. Grant, *Rome and Reunion*, Oxford University Press, 1965; J. B. Bury, *History of the Papacy in the 19th Century* (Introduction by Frederick C. Grant), Schocken Books, New York, 1964; George Salmon, *The Infallibility of the Church*, Searcy, Kansas, 1948; Abbot Basil Christopher Butler, *The Church and Infallibility*, Sheed and Ward, 1954; Monsignor Charles Journet, *The Primacy of Peter from the Protestant and from the Catholic Point of View*, Newman Press, Westminster, Md., 1954; Oscar Cullmann, *Peter, Disciple, Apostle, Martyr*, S.C.M. Press, London, 1962; Geddes MacGregor, *The Vatican Revolution*, Beacon Press, 1957; C. J. Cadoux, *Catholicism and Christianity*, Allen and Unwin, 1928; Kirsopp Lake, *An Introduction to the New Testament*, Christophers, London, 1938; Vittorio Subilia, *The Problem of Catholicism*, Westminster Press, 1964; Lord Acton, *Essays on Freedom and Power*, Beacon Press, 1948. MacGregor, in Appendix I, has the texts of Vatican I's decrees in both Latin and English.

3. The claim was quite true. The Italian victory is described in Bury, *supra*, Chapter VII.

4. CEV, October 10, 1963.

5. Pope Paul's address was analyzed temperately by Michael Novak in *Commonweal*, October 18, 1963.

6. Karl Rahner and Joseph Ratzinger, *The Episcopate and the Primacy*, Herder, 1962, p. 41.

7. See Note 1 above.

8. Rahner and Ratzinger, *supra*, p. 67.

9. *The New York Times*, September 27, 1965.
10. *The Open Church*, Macmillan, 1964, p. 130.
11. DWNS, October 28, 1963.
12. *Ibid.*, October 25, 1963.
13. Later published in *National Catholic Reporter*, October 25, 1963.
14. *Ibid.*, November 4, 1963.
15. *Commonweal*, January 15, 1965.
16. *American Ecclesiastical Review*, August 1962.
17. *National Catholic Reporter*, May 5, 1965.
18. London *Tablet*, December 11, 1965.

CHAPTER FIVE
RELIGIOUS LIBERTY, EXTERNAL

1. Bishop DeSmedt's *relatio* issued November 19, 1963; Protestant comment in release by Protestant Federation of Italy, November 26, 1963.

2. Murray's first book was *We Hold These Truths*, Sheed and Ward, 1960. A recent analysis of his theories is *John Courtney Murray: Contemporary Church-State Theory* by Thomas T. Love, Doubleday, 1965. Murray's own interpretation of the Declaration on Religious Freedom is in *Documents*, p. 672, and in *America*, April 23, 1966. A criticism of Murray by S. F. Carrillo de Abornoz is in *The Christian Century*, September 15, 1965.

3. *The New York Times*, December 2, 1963.

4. DWNS, September 23, 1963.

5. DWNS, September 15, 1965.

6. An analysis of the restrictions on religious liberty in Spain, together with the key provisions of the 1953 Concordat between Spain and the Vatican, are in my *Freedom and Catholic Power in Spain and Portugal*, Beacon Press, 1962.

7. Dr. S. F. Carrillo de Abornoz of the Secretariat for Religious Liberty, World Council of Churches, declares in his 1964 pamphlet *Religious Liberty*, issued by the World Council, that in Colombia "there are decrees of the Ministry of Education which require all students in all public schools (even in those created or supported by the U.S. Alliance for Progress) to receive classes in the Roman Catholic religion and to attend mass on Sundays and feast days." Other important writings of this author in this field are: *The Ecumenical Review*, January 1966; and booklets published by the World Council of Churches on *Roman Catholicism and Religious Liberty* (1959); and *The Basis of Religious Liberty* (1963).

8. Brooklyn *Tablet*, July 22, 1965.

9. *The New York Times*, October 14, 1964.

10. DWNS, September 23, 1964.

11. *Ibid.*

12. *The New York Times*, November 20, 1964.

13. Brief quoted portions of *Quanta Cura* and *The Syllabus of Errors*, both issued on December 8, 1964, are in *Teaches*, pp. 85–6; and more complete documentation is in Henry Bettenson, *Documents of the Christian Church*, Oxford, 1963.

14. In his *History of Christianity*, Ronald Press, 1956, p. 235.

15. Published by Paulist Press, 401 West 59th St., New York 10019.

16. This chief debate on religious liberty was partially recorded in CEV, September 17, 1965.

17. *America*, April 16, 1966.

18. The World Council points were published in *Ecumenical Review*, October 1965.

19. NCWC Release, December 10, 1965.

20. *Register*, October 3, 1965.

21. *Christian Science Monitor*, September 24, 1965.

CHAPTER SIX
RELIGIOUS LIBERTY, INTERNAL

1. *America*, January 23, 1965.

2. DWNS, November 22, 1963.

3. *Commonweal*, December 6, 1963.

4. *America*, September 14, 1963.

5. *Rome and Reunion*, p. 185.

6. The basic canons on literary censorship are 1384–1405. The penalty for violation is outlined in Canon 2318.

7. *Harper's Magazine*, December 1963.

8. *Register*, February 6, 1966.

9. *Commonweal*, February 26, 1965.

10. *Newsweek*, November 21, 1964.

11. Quoted by Adamo, *America*, August 14, 1965.

12. *Commonweal*, February 19, 1965.

13. *Saturday Evening Post*, November 28, 1964. Archbishop Roberts, a Jesuit, had contributed a notable chapter on "Contraception and War" to *Objections to Roman Catholicism*, edited by Michael de la Bedoyere, Lippincott, 1965; and earlier he had written *Black Popes*, Sheed and Ward, 1954, in which he entitled Part One "Obedience: Jewel and Fake."

14. *The Human Church*, Doubleday, 1966.

15. *Commonweal*, December 10, 1965. *Ave Maria* of January 8, 1966, made public the case histories of thirteen "silenced" priests, silenced by episcopal power, in many cases without proper hearings.

CHAPTER SEVEN
THE JEWS

1. The text of *Redemptoris Nostri*, issued October 23, 1949, is in *Catholic Almanac*, 1950, p. 59.

2. For the statements of Chrysostom and others, see *Europe and the Jews*, by Malcolm Hay, Beacon Press, 1960, pp. 27ff.

3. *Saturday Review*, June 19, 1965.

4. Published by Macmillan, 1964.

5. Published by Bloch, p. 103.

6. *Speeches*, p. 169.

7. Report by the Federal Council of Protestant Churches in Italy, October 30, 1965.

8. *Commonweal,* October 2, 1964.

9. *The Christian Century,* May 5, 1965, and *National Catholic Reporter,* April 14, 1965; with a slightly different translation in *The New York Times,* April 8, 1965.

10. May 10, 1965.

11. *Look,* June 2, 1964.

12. *Register,* December 12, 1965. Spanish textbooks are discussed in my *Freedom and Catholic Power in Spain and Portugal.*

13. Published by Holt, Rinehart and Winston, 1964. See also Malcolm Hay *supra;* Paul Winter, *On the Trial of Jesus,* Exposition Press, 1948; and Max Dimont, *Jews, God and History,* New American Library, 1962.

14. A careful account of the Hitler-Vatican Concordat of July 9, 1933, plus extensive bibliography in German and English, are given in Chapter 3 of Guenter Lewy's *The Catholic Church and Nazi Germany,* McGraw-Hill, 1964.

15. The Pius XII documents were published by Great Britain and summarized in *The New York Times,* November 19, 1964.

16. Text in *Five Encyclicals,* Paulist Press, p. 125. For background study of Sturzo and period, see Richard A. Webster, *The Cross and the Fasces,* Stanford University Press, 1960.

CHAPTER EIGHT
HOW MUCH CHRISTIAN UNITY?

1. *Direction Unity,* Vol. I, No. 1, 1965, published by National Catholic Welfare Conference.

2. *Vatican II, the Theological Dimension,* edited by Anthony D. Lee, Thomist Press, 1963, pp. 552–3.

3. *The Christian Century,* September 9, 1964.

4. London *Tablet,* September 7, 1963.

5. *Canon Law Digest,* II, p. 183. When a Catholic is converted to Protestantism, the Church is very severe in punishing him, even denying the validity of his marriage in his new faith. The following question and answer were published not in Spain but in the chief diocesan journal of the United States, *The Register,* June 26, 1966, more than six months after the end of Vatican II, in the journal's theological "Ask and Learn" column: QUESTION: *What happens when a Catholic says she is no longer a Catholic but has joined another religion? Doesn't she always remain a Catholic? What if she marries in her new religion?* ANSWER: Her act of joining another religion automatically excommunicates her, but she is not in the same class with those born and reared outside the Church. The penalty of excommunication does not erase her guilt in deserting her religion or cancel her obligation to return to the Church.

The excommunication carries with it several penalties, such as the deprivation of the sacraments, of the public prayers, indulgences, and suffrages of the Church, and of ecclesiastical burial.

On the other hand, she is obliged to marry in the Church, so that if she attempts marriage outside it, the marriage is invalid.

6. *Ecumenical Dialogue at Harvard*, edited by Samuel H. Miller *et al.*, Harvard University Press, 1964, p. 63.

7. The long and dismal story of Catholic rejection of unity efforts in the past is documented in *Canon Law Digest*, I, pp. 619–22. There is a summary of some features in my *American Freedom and Catholic Power*, pp. 326–330. See also Canon 1325, prohibiting most discussions on faith with non-Catholics.

8. London *Tablet*, November 21, 1964.

9. Text in *Teaches*, pp. 36–9.

10. *American Ecclesiastical Review*, Vol. CXXXIV, 1956.

11. *Look*, October 6, 1964; *Observer in Rome*, Doubleday, 1964.

12. *Manchester Guardian Weekly*, January 7, 1966.

13. Although the Church of England still nominally includes 27 million baptized Englishmen, a Gallup poll, as reported in the *Guardian*, September 23, 1965, indicated that baptisms have slumped sharply in the last decade and that 45 per cent of the population regard religion as "largely old-fashioned and out of date." A 1957 Gallup poll had indicated that only 9 per cent of the alleged members in churches presided over by the Archbishop of Canterbury attended church on a particular Sunday. The decay has affected the Catholic Church also, although Catholicism appears to be gaining on Protestantism in Britain. As early as 1955 (*Register*, April 24, 1955), Paul H. Hallett claimed that "every denomination save the Catholic has been declining year by year. . . . Assuming Protestant decrease and Catholic increase at the present rates, Catholics in Britain will outnumber all the other Christian bodies together within the next five years." There is some drift toward Rome among the Anglican clergy, but only about one-fourth of such clergy wear distinctive Roman vestments.

14. Clement Englert, *Catholics and Orthodox*, Paulist Press, 1960, p. 6.

15. But this mutual revocation was not favorably received by the Orthodox churches of Russia and Greece, apparently because Russian and Greek leaders thought Athenagoras had exceeded his authority. For informed discussions see London *Tablet*, February 5, 1965, October 13, 1962, and November 21, 1964.

16. *Register*, September 1, 1963.

17. Text in *Catholic Almanac*, 1963, p. 184.

18. London *Tablet*, June 19, 1965, and *National Catholic Reporter*, May 12, 1965.

19. Quoted by an authority in this field, Hubert Butler, *Irish Times*, April 15, 1964.

CHAPTER NINE

MARY, SCRIPTURE AND TRADITION

1. *New York Herald Tribune*, October 30, 1963.

2. The Koenig-Santos debate was summarized in a special CEV document of October 29, 1963.

3. *Atlantic Monthly*, August 1962.

4. The literature of Mariology is immense. At the Council the Dutch Documentation Center put out a special summary, "Some Ideas on the Mariology of Today," No. 56. Abbot Butler's speech on the subject was released October 25, 1963. *The American Ecclesiastical Review*, July 1962, summarized "The Marian Cult and Canon Law," citing Canon 1276 which directs that "all the faithful should with filial devotion honor above others the Blessed Virgin." A recent Catholic work is that of Edward Schillebeeckx, *Mary, Mother of the Redemption*, Sheed, 1964. Cardinal Suenen's work is called *Mary, the Mother of God*, Hawthorn Books, 1959. The Italian Protestant criticism of Pope Paul and Mariology at the Council was in the newsletter of the Protestant Federation of Italy, November 8, 1963, concluding with the statement: "It is extremely difficult to understand, from an ecumenical point of view, how Christian unity can be placed beneath the tutelage of Mary and how it can be possible to assign her any kind of ecumenical function." A valuable analysis by a Dutch Protestant scholar is contained in G. C. Berkouwer, *The Second Vatican Council and the New Catholicism*, W. B. Erdmans, Grand Rapids, Michigan, 1965. Earlier non-Catholic analyses of Mariology are contained in C. Anderson Scott, *Romanism and the Gospel*, Westminster, 1946; Frederick C. Grant, *Rome and Reunion*, Oxford University Press, 1965; and A. D. Howell-Smith, *Thou Art Peter*, Watts, London, 1950.

5. The nine passages are: John 2:12; Matt. 12:46; Mark 3:31; Luke 8:19; Matt. 13:55; Mark 6:3; John 7:3–5; Acts 1:14; and I Cor. 9:5.

6. Text of the Assumption encyclical, *Catholic Almanac*, 1951, p. 69.

7. François Mauriac, *The Stumbling Block*, Philosophical Library, 1952, p. 22.

8. *Commonweal*, November 15, 1963.

9. *America*, February 22, 1964.

10. The literature of biblical origins lies beyond the scope of this study, but a beginning can be made through the *Encyclopaedia Britannica* and its bibliographies, particularly the articles "Gospels" and "Matthew" by the Harvard scholar, H. H. Koester; and the works of Frederick C. Grant are notable.

11. Text in *Catholic Almanac*, 1966, p. 194.

CHAPTER TEN
SEX, CELIBACY AND WOMEN

1. DWNS, October 16, 1963.

2. CEV, October 29, 1964.

3. Text in *Five Encyclicals*, p. 117.

4. The sexual attitudes of Catholicism, including those of St. Augustine, are discussed in detail by a Catholic scholar, John T. Noonan, in *Contraception*, Harvard University Press, 1965. The classic non-Catholic work on celibacy is H. C. Lea's *History of Sacerdotal Celibacy in the Christian Church*, Ballantine, London, 1907.

5. In Pierre Veuillot, *The Catholic Priesthood*, Newman, 1958, p. 146.

Preface by Montini, now Paul VI. Pius XII's statements on virginity in same work, pp. 291 and 317.

6. *Commonweal*, May 15, 1964.

7. June 16, 1965. *Occidentalis* appeared in the issue of June 9, 1965.

8. *Saturday Evening Post*, March 12, 1966.

9. *Register*, June 21, 1964.

10. CEV, October 11, 1965.

11. *The New York Times*, October 20, 1965. The celibacy rule is undoubtedly the chief cause of seminary dropouts in the United States. One study of such dropouts, cited in the *National Catholic Reporter*, of June 30, 1965, and the *Register* of July 4, 1965, showed that in one period studied more than 83 per cent of the students entering minor seminaries to start study for the priesthood were never actually ordained as priests. Father Benedict McCormick in *Commonweal*, November 29, 1963, estimated that nine out of ten American young men who begin study for the priesthood do not persevere.

12. *Commonweal*, November 29, 1963.

13. *Ibid.*, April 16, 1965.

14. *Convent Life*, edited by Joan M. Lexau, Dial, 1964, p. 80.

15. *Harper's Magazine*, August 1965. This material was later incorporated in the book, *The De-Romanization of the American Catholic Church* by Edward Wakin and Father Joseph F. Scheuer, Macmillan, 1966.

16. *National Catholic Reporter*, March 23, 1966.

CHAPTER ELEVEN
MARRIAGE AND DIVORCE

1. Actually the debate was not entirely cut off for certain leaders. Cardinals Ottaviani, Browne, and Alfrink indulged in comments on October 30; and Cardinals Ruffini and Conway as well as Archbishop Krol and Bishop Fearns (for Cardinal Spellman) discussed chiefly mixed marriage on November 20.

2. The primary canon laws of the Church on marriage and sexual issues, numbering 131, occupy nearly 200 pages in the standard works. Canon 1012 describes marriage as a sacrament and Canon 1013 says that its primary end is the "procreation and education of children." Canon 1143 declares that a woman to whom the solemn nuptial blessing has once been given cannot receive it again in a subsequent marriage. Canon 1142 says specifically that "chaste widowhood" is "more honorable" than a second or subsequent marriage.

3. *Canon Law Digest*, V, p. 515.

4. See John T. Creagh, *A Commentary on the Decree Ne Temere*, Catholic University Press, 1908.

5. Vol. II, pp. 168ff.

6. The Prato story was told in part in *The New York Times*, March 9, 1958; *Time*, March 10, 1958; and the Brooklyn *Tablet*, January 3, 1959.

7. *The New York Times*, June 7, 1962; Brooklyn *Tablet*, July 7, 1962.

8. *America*, September 28, 1963.

9. But no new studies on a comprehensive scale have been made in recent years to prove this. A study summarized in *Ave Maria* in 1956 estimated that the pledges in mixed marriages to rear children as Catholics are kept in only about 30 per cent of the cases, but, of course, it is likely that the proportion is even lower in the case of mixed marriages not recognized as marriages, *i.e.*, those performed by public officials and non-Catholic clergymen, and these "invalid" marriages may number half of the "valid" type. See pp. 195 and 384 of my *American Freedom and Catholic Power;* John L. Thomas, S.J., *The American Catholic Family*, Prentice-Hall, 1956; and C. Stanley Lowell, *Protestant-Catholic Marriage*, Broadman Press, 1962.

10. *Marriage*, April 1963.

11. *America*, June 15, 1963.

12. Debate on draft statement, DWNS, November 19, 1964; *The New York Times*, November 21, 1964.

13. Marriage with non-Christians is covered primarily by Canons 1070–1.

14. *Speeches*, p. 150.

15. CEV, November 27, 1963.

16. English text in London *Tablet*, March 26, 1966.

17. *The Christian Century*, April 6, 1966.

18. The British estimate is that of Cecil Northcott, *The Christian Century*, April 6, 1966.

19. CEV and DWNS, September 29, 1965.

20. Brooklyn *Tablet*, September 23, 1965.

21. Prostitution in Italy was discussed in two articles in the Rome *American*, October 20 and November 13, 1965.

22. October 7, 1965.

23. *The New York Times*, February 4, 1966, and *National Catholic Reporter*, February 16, 1966.

24. The Radziwill story was summarized in the Brooklyn *Tablet*, February 20, 1964, in a dispatch from the News Service of the National Catholic Welfare Conference.

25. *Register*, March 8, 1964.

CHAPTER TWELVE
BIRTH CONTROL AND SO FORTH

1. Full text of Pope Paul's speech in *The New York Times*, October 5, 1965.

2. *The New York Times*, October 6, 1965.

3. The F.A.O. facts were in its document, *The Basic Freedom: Freedom from Hunger*, 1965.

4. *Congressional Record*, May 3, 1966, p. 9128.

5. Genesis 38:6–10.

6. *American Ecclesiastical Review*, December 1962.

7. *The New York Times*, September 28, 1965.

8. *Register*, November 21, 1965.

9. *Estelle T. Griswold v. Connecticut*, 381 U.S. 479, summarized in *The New York Times*, June 8, 1965.

10. *Wall Street Journal*, February 3, 1965.

11. *Population Crisis*, the Hearings of the Subcommittee on Foreign Expenditures of the Committee on Government Operations, U.S. Senate, 89th Congress, First Session, on S. 1676, beginning June 22, 1965.

12. *Saturday Evening Post*, April 4, 1964.

13. *Commonweal*, June 5, 1964.

14. *Ibid.*

15. *The New York Times*, March 3, 1966; see also *ibid.*, April 10, 1966, and January 9, 1965.

16. Gruening hearings, March 3, 1966.

17. *The New York Times*, November 29, 1965.

18. *Commonweal*, December 24, 1965. See also an article by Lois R. Chevalier, "The Secret Drama Behind the Pope's Momentous Decision on Birth Control," *Ladies Home Journal*, March 1966.

19. In *The New York Times*, April 25, 1965, and in his later book *Abortion*, Bobbs-Merrill, 1966. An informative article on "Criminal Abortion: Human Hardship and Unyielding Laws" by Zad Leavy and Jerome M. Kummer was published in the *Southern California Law Review*, Winter, 1962.

20. *Look*, October 19, 1965.

21. The California battle was described in *The Christian Century*, May 13, 1964.

22. According to the Catholic doctrine on sterilization, summarized in *Catholic Almanac*, 1964, p. 129, "sterilization for directly contraceptive purposes constitutes a violation of bodily integrity and hence is a grave offense against the Fifth Commandment."

CHAPTER THIRTEEN
THE MIRACULOUS UNDERWORLD

1. Canons 911–924 cover indulgences. According to Canon 930 an indulgence for the living cannot be applied to any other living person than the one who gains it, but there is an exception for dying persons who may benefit by way of absolution effective at the moment of death. Under Canon 912 the pope has supreme power over all indulgences. The classic background work in this field is H. C. Lea, *History of Auricular Confession and Indulgences in the Latin Church*, Philadelphia, 1896. The article on Indulgences in *Hastings Encyclopedia of Religion and Ethics* is also valuable.

2. My notes, and *Commonweal*, November 26, 1965. See also articles by Dean Peerman, *The Christian Century*, December 8, 1965, and by John Cogley, *The New York Times*, November 11, 1965.

3. DWNS, November 29, 1963.

4. *Figaro*, November 8, 1965.

5. The Luther story is told in part in *Encyclopaedia Britannica*, under "Luther," "Reformation," and "Indulgences." For condemnation of Luther and action of Council of Trent, see *Teaches*, pp. 320–1.

6. *Observer,* November 14, 1965.

7. Published by Benziger. See also the schedule of plenary indulgences in *Canon Law,* pp. 354ff.

8. *Teaches,* pp. 214–6.

9. *Catholic Almanac,* 1965, p. 300.

10. Frutaz facts summarized in *Register,* October 31, 1965.

11. *Commonweal,* November 19, 1965.

CHAPTER FOURTEEN
CHURCH, STATE AND DIPLOMACY

1. Text in *Social Wellsprings,* edited by Joseph Husslein, Bruce Publishing Co., 1940.

2. *Canon Law Digest,* IV, p. 8.

3. Major provisions in the Vatican-Mussolini agreements are in Appendix I of my *Communism, Democracy and Catholic Power,* Beacon Press, 1951. Current lists of Vatican diplomats are in annual *Catholic Almanac.*

4. *America,* July 13, 1963.

5. The Weigel quote is from Robert W. Gleason, S.J., *In the Eyes of Others,* Macmillan, 1962, p. 43.

6. Rome *American* and *The New York Times,* October 17, 1963.

7. Published by Princeton University Press, 1959.

8. *Register,* June 16, 1963.

9. *The New York Times,* November 1, 1951.

10. *Ibid.,* July, 18, 1963.

11. *Ibid.,* June 3, 1963.

12. For some of the Vietnam background see a 1965 publication of the Center for the Study of Democratic Institutions, *How the United States Got Involved in Vietnam,* by Robert Scheer; and an article, "Buddhists in Saigon" by Kenneth W. Morgan, *The Christian Century,* January 26, 1966.

13. Important aspects of the Puerto Rican story were covered in *The New York Times,* October 28 and 29, 1960; and in Brooklyn *Tablet,* October 29, 1960.

14. *Register,* May 22, 1957.

CHAPTER FIFTEEN
CHURCH, STATE AND SCHOOLS

1. NCWC dispatch, February 16, 1962. See section "Spellman v. Kennedy," in my *Religion and the Schools,* Beacon Press, 1963, pp. 122ff.

2. CEV, November 7, 1964.

3. *Five Encyclicals,* p. 40.

4. The phrase is taken from a revealing document by Monsignor William E. McManus, now head of Chicago's Catholic schools, summarizing official Church policy, in Senate Hearings on Federal Aid to Education, 80th Congress, First Session, April 25, 1947, pp. 242ff. Monsignor (then Father) McManus declared: "In the field of education separation of church and state bars

the Government from inquiring into the religious or nonreligious character of any school receiving its aid. Government may only ask: 'Is this school an institution to which parents may send their children in compliance with the compulsory education laws of the State?' If the answer is in the affirmative, the school is entitled to public support."

5. *America*, January 23, 1965.

6. *Commonweal*, April 23 and 30, 1965.

7. *Engel v. Vitale*, 370 U.S. 421 (1962); *Abington v. Schempp*, 374 U.S. 203 (1963).

8. *Everson v. Board of Education*, 330 U.S. 1 (1947).

9. *Five Encyclicals*, p. 60.

10. *Michigan Christian Advocate*, December 2, 1965.

11. *Christianity and Crisis*, July 5, 1948.

12. Dr. Bennett's 1962 statement was in *Christianity and Crisis*, May 28, 1962; his 1965 statement in *Catholic World*, September 1965. But some important Protestant leaders take a contrary view and the National Council of Churches is still firm in its official utterances in opposition to across-the-board financial grants to parochial schools. See chapter on "Protestants and Parochial Schools" by Dean M. Kelley, executive director of the Council's Department of Religious Liberty, in *Federal Aid and Catholic Schools*, edited by Daniel Callahan, Helicon, 1964; and *Public Funds for Parochial Schools* by George R. LaNoue, National Council of Churches, 1963. Kelley's 1966 testimony was summarized in *The Christian Century*, May 11, 1966.

13. The story of the act is told by Leo Pfeffer in *Church, State, and Freedom*, Beacon Press, 1953 (Revised, 1966), Chapter 4.

14. In letter to *The New York Times*, February 14, 1965.

15. Published by P.O.A.U., 1633 Massachusetts Ave. N.W., Washington, D.C.

16. *Congressional Record*, February 17, 1965, p. A 686. Of the church-state cases now in the courts directly affecting tax appropriations to sectarian schools, the most important is the Maryland case of *The Horace Mann League v. Board of Public Works of Maryland* in which the highest court of Maryland decided in June 1966 that tax appropriations to one Methodist and two Catholic colleges were unconstitutional–see *Congressional Record*, June 9, 1966, for text.

17. *America*, April 24, 1965.

18. Published by Holt, Rinehart and Winston, 1963.

19. The Casey plan as developed in Lexington, Mass., is described in a booklet, "Modern Schools of Religion" issued by the National Catholic Welfare Conference.

20. *Saturday Evening Post*, October 26, 1963.

21. *Manchester Guardian Weekly*, February 24, 1966.

CHAPTER SIXTEEN
SWEETNESS AND LIGHT

1. *Speeches*, p. 175.

2. *The New York Times*, November 18, 1963.

3. DWNS, November 10, 1964.

4. *Ibid.*, November 15, 1965.

5. Dutch Documentation Center, No. 77, 1963.

6. Because of this secrecy it is impossible to make any entirely accurate estimate of total Vatican wealth, but there is little doubt that the Roman Catholic Church is the wealthiest nongovernment organization in the world. *The Economist* of London in its issue of March 27, 1965, using "the most conservative estimate that it is reasonable to make," estimated that the pope is "far and away the world's largest shareholder, with a portfolio of quoted securities the world over totalling the equivalent of over $5,600,000,000. Of this, only about a tenth is held in Italy." This estimate did not include land and art treasures. *The Economist* estimated the Church's total wealth at far beyond $5,600,000,000. Various denials were made by Catholic individuals, but no official disclosures have been made to inform the public. *Time*'s reliable Rome bureau was evidently the source of that magazine's estimate, published in the issue of February 26, 1965: "Bankers' best guesses about the Vatican's wealth put it at $10 billion to $15 billion. Of this wealth, Italian stockholdings alone run to $1.6 billion, 15 per cent of the value of listed shares on the Italian market." The only sure financial figure in the whole mystery is that in the 1929 settlement with Mussolini the pope received about $39 million in cash and $52 million in government bonds—and this amount, as *Time* puts it, "shrewdly invested in stocks and real estate" has multiplied many times. A Catholic publication, *Herder Correspondence*, March 1965, summarizes the various estimates and concludes that no authoritative facts are available except the 1929 figures.

CHAPTER SEVENTEEN
BALANCE SHEET

1. See "Vocations in Western Europe," an article by John J. Micheli Navone, S.J., in *American Ecclesiastical Review*, November 1962. There has been a general decline of vocations to the priesthood in Western Europe for many years. Although the Netherlands, Belgium, and Ireland have a comparative wealth of priests, even West Germany has a priest shortage, while Austria, once the great bastion of Catholic power in Europe, now has the lowest ratio of theological students to the Catholic population of all European Catholic countries. Cardinal Alfrink of the Netherlands admitted in September 1965 in Rome that although his country is supplying 5,000 priests and 70 missionary bishops to other countries, the nation has been losing in the number of Catholic priestly vocations. The estimate of 400,000,000 actual Catholics in the world has been used in Catholic publications, but it cannot be anything more than a guess in view of present statistical methods used in totaling religious "members." The Arrupe estimate was in CEV, September 27, 1965. See London *Tablet* June 26 and July 2, 1965, for articles on Catholicism in West Germany; and *Catholic Almanac*, 1965, p. 402 for description of anti-Church measures in East Germany. The Catholic gain in Australia and New Zealand is admittedly due almost entirely to immigra-

tion. Bishop Lancelot Goody of Western Australia declared at a Council press panel in 1963 that "The great majority of the people of Australia and New Zealand today practice no religion." See three articles on "Catholicism: Prospects and Problems" in *The Christian Century*, July 10, 17, and 24, 1963.

2. London *Tablet*, April 24, 1965.

3. See various summaries of "The Church in Latin America" in *Catholic Almanac*, 1964 and 1966; *America*, February 16, 1963 and May 30, 1964; *Time*, August 16, 1963; *Commonweal*, March 12, 1965.

4. *The Christian Century*, March 4, 1964.

5. *Register*, July 27, 1962; Brooklyn *Tablet*, June 18, 1964.

6. *Herder Correspondence*, December 1965, describes the bad distribution of dioceses in Italy and complains that there is a "serious lack of priests" in Rome itself. James Johnson wrote a valuable series of articles on the Church in Italy in the *National Catholic Reporter*, in January 1965. The Lavitrano estimate was described in *The New York Times*, February 7, 1940.

7. J. Ryan Beiser, *The Vatican Council and the American Secular Newspapers, 1869–70*, Catholic University of America Press, 1941. See also, for colorful description of American reactions, Anson Phelps Stokes, *Church and State in the United States*, Vol. I, Harper, 1950.

INDEX